D1266777

THE WORKS OF JAMES BUCHANAN

*This letterpress edition is limited to
750 copies, of which this is*

No. 455......

THE WORKS

OF

JAMES BUCHANAN

Comprising his Speeches, State Papers,
and Private Correspondence

Collected and Edited

By

JOHN BASSETT MOORE

VOLUME IX
1853-1855

DISCARD

Philadelphia & London

J. B. Lippincott Company

1909

J 108
9

Copyright, 1909
By
J. B. Lippincott Company

276486
SEP 1 1909

THE
CHICAGO
PUBLIC LIBRARY

Printed by J. B. Lippincott Company
The Washington Square Press, Philadelphia, U. S. A.

CONTENTS *of* VOLUME IX

1853.

CONTENTS OF VOLUME IX

1855.

CONTENTS OF VOLUME IX

The Works

OF

James Buchanan

TO PRESIDENT PIERCE.[1]

WHEATLAND, near LANCASTER, 11 June 1853.

MY DEAR SIR/

I learn by your letter of the 2d Instant that the final execution of the Fishery & Reciprocity Treaty cannot await the settlement of the Central American questions, without serious & imminent danger of actual collision between the two Countries, upon the Fishing grounds.

Under this statement of facts, Heaven forbid! I should entertain the most remote idea that the negotiations between Governor Marcy & Mr. Crampton ought to be delayed for a single moment, on account of my suggestion! On the contrary, it affords me very great satisfaction to learn that a fair prospect exists of the speedy conclusion of the Treaty, though I shall ever deem it unfortunate that the Central American questions could not have been definitively settled in the same negotiation. The absurd construction imposed by the British Government upon our Fishing Convention, (if I may be permitted to employ such an epithet upon so grave a subject,) enforced as it has been by suddenly sending a large fleet to the Fishing grounds, & this too without previous notice, had its far reaching design. This was to obtain from us the Reciprocity Treaty. Under such circumstances, I should have said to Great Britain, in the beginning, you shall have the Treaty; but to obtain it, you must, at the same time, consent to withdraw your protectorate from the Mosquito coast & restore the Colony of the Bay of Islands to the Republic of Honduras. By not pursuing this course, I fear we have lost

---

[1] Buchanan Papers, Historical Society of Pennsylvania.

the golden opportunity, for years to come, of settling the Central American questions in an honorable & satisfactory manner. Still, it is vain to indulge in useless regrets.

Then to the point. I have reconsidered the question of the mission to London, according to promise, & have determined to accept it; but this solely & exclusively to gratify your wishes & to prevent the embarrassment which you think my declination of it would occasion to your administration. In the success of that administration I consider that the interests of the Country & the continued ascendancy of the Democratic party are deeply involved. From the beginning I determined to give it my earnest, active, & ardent support, & neither the strength of this resolution nor my warm personal regard & esteem for yourself has been in the slightest degree impaired by my peculiarly unfortunate efforts to obtain office for friends whom I deemed the most deserving & popular.

Having made up my mind, I shall go to London cheerfully & do my best, relying always upon your own confidence, friendship, & support, which will be indispensable to the success of my mission.

From your friend very respectfully

JAMES BUCHANAN.

HIS EXCELLENCY FRANKLIN PIERCE.

TO PRESIDENT PIERCE.[1]

WHEATLAND, near LANCASTER, 14 June 1853.

MY DEAR SIR/

I have this moment received yours of the 11th Instant & now enclose you Mr. Appleton's resignation. I cannot imagine how I neglected to do this before. It will be very difficult to supply his place.

If you have changed your mind in regard to the place where our important negotiations with England shall be conducted, you would confer a great favor upon me by informing me of this immediately. I stated to you in our first conversation on the subject that Mr. Polk, after due deliberation, had determined that such negotiations should be conducted under his own eye at

---

[1] Buchanan Papers, Historical Society of Pennsylvania.

Washington; & it would not give me the slightest uneasiness to learn that, upon reconsideration, such had become your determination. I should, however, consider it a fatal policy to divide the questions. After a careful examination & study of all these questions & their mutual bearings upon each other & upon the interests of the two Countries, I am fully convinced that they can only be satisfactorily adjusted all together. Indeed, from what you said to me of your conversation with a Senator & from what I have since learned, I believe it would be difficult to obtain the consent of two thirds of the Senate to any partial Treaty. The South, whether correctly or not, will probably be averse to a reciprocity Treaty confined to the British North American Provinces; & it would be easy for hostile demagogues to proclaim, however unjustly, that the interests of the South had been bartered away for the Fisheries. But the South might & probably would be reconciled to such a Treaty, if it embraced a final & satisfactory adjustment of the questions in Central America.

If you have changed your mind, & I can imagine many reasons for this, independently of the pressure of the British minister to secure that which is so highly prized by his Government,—then I would respectfully suggest that you might inform Mr. Crampton you are ready & willing to negotiate upon the subject of the fisheries & reciprocal trade; *but this in connection with our Central American difficulties;* that you desire to put an end to all the embarrassing & dangerous questions between the two Governments, & thus best promote the most friendly relations hereafter; & that you will proceed immediately with the negotiation & bring it to as speedy a conclusion as possible, whenever he shall have received the necessary instructions. Indeed, the Treaty in regard to reciprocal trade & the fisheries might, in the mean time, be perfected, with a distinct understanding, however, that its final execution should be postponed until the Central American questions had been adjusted. In that event, as I informed you, when at Washington, if you should so desire, I shall be most cordially willing to go there as a private individual & render you all the assistance in my power. I know, as well as I live, that it would be vain for me to go to London to settle a question peculiarly distasteful to the British Government, after they had obtained at Washington that which they so ardently desire.

I write this, actuated solely by a desire to serve your administration & the Country. I shall not be mortified, in the slightest degree, should you determine to settle *all* the questions in Washington.   Whether or not, your administration shall not have a better friend in the Country than myself, nor one more ardently desirous of its success; & I can render it far more essential service as a private citizen at home than as a minister in London.

With my very kindest regards for Mrs. Pierce & Mrs. Means, I remain, very respectfully your friend

JAMES BUCHANAN.

HIS EXCELLENCY FRANKLIN PIERCE &c. &c.

P. S.   I should esteem it a personal favor to hear from you as soon as may be convenient.

TO PRESIDENT PIERCE.[1]

WHEATLAND, near LANCASTER, 23 June 1853.

MY DEAR SIR/

Not having yet been honored with an answer to my letter of the 14th Instant, I infer from your silence, as well as from what I observe in the Public Journals, that you have finally changed your original purpose & determined that our important negotiations with England shall be conducted under your own eye at Washington, & not in London.   Anxious to relieve you from all embarrassment upon the subject, I desire to express my cordial concurrence in such an arrangement, if it has been made: & I do this without waiting longer for your answer, as the day is now near at hand which was named for my departure from the Country.[2]   Many strong reasons, I have no doubt, exist, to render this change of purpose entirely proper & most beneficial for the public interest.   I am not at all surprised at it, having suggested to you, when we conversed upon the subject, that Mr. Polk, who was an able & a wise man, had determined that our important negotiations with foreign powers, so far as this was possible, should be conducted at Washington, by the Secretary of State, under his own immediate supervision.   With such a change I shall be altogether satisfied, nay personally gratified, because it will produce a corresponding change in my determination to accept the English mission.

---

[1] Buchanan Papers, Historical Society of Pennsylvania.

[2] July 9.

I never had the vanity to imagine that there were not many Democratic Statesmen in the Country who could settle our pending questions with England quite as ably & successfully as myself; & it was, therefore, solely your own voluntary & powerful personal appeal to me to undertake the task which could have overcome my strong repugnance to go abroad. Indeed, when I stated to you how irksome it would be for me, at my period of life & with my taste for retirement, again for the second time to pass through the routine & submit to the etiquette necessary in representing my country at a foreign court, you kindly remarked, you were so well convinced of this, that you would have never offered me the mission, had it not been for your deliberate determination that the negotiations on the grave & important questions between the two Countries should be conducted by myself at London, under your instructions; observing that, in your opinion, better terms could be obtained for our Country at the fountain of power, than through the intermediate channel of the British minister at Washington.

At any time, a foreign mission would be distasteful to me; but peculiar reasons of a private & domestic character existed at the time I agreed to accept the British mission, & still exist, which could only have yielded to the striking view you presented of the high public duty which required me to undertake the settlement of these important questions.

You will, therefore, be kind enough to permit me, in case your enlightened judgment has arrived at the conclusion that Washington & not London ought to be the seat of the negotiations, most respectfully to decline the mission. For this, you have doubtless been prepared by my letter of the 14th Instant.

With my deep & grateful acknowledgments for the high honor you intended for me, & my ardent & sincere wishes for the success & glory of your administration, & for your own individual health, prosperity, & happiness, I remain
Very respectfully, yr. friend
JAMES BUCHANAN.

HIS EXCELLENCY FRANKLIN PIERCE &c. &c. &c.

FROM PRESIDENT PIERCE.[1]

WASHINGTON, D. C. June 26, 1853.

MY DEAR SIR

I was much surprised by the perusal of your letter of the 23d inst., received this morning.

I had seen no letter from you since that to which I replied on the 11th inst., and was mortified that thro' a mistake of my own, and from no neglect of my private secy., it had been misplaced from a large mail of the 17th with one or two other letters and had thus entirely escaped my notice. The motives which led me to desire your acceptance of the mission to England were fully stated, first, I think, in my note addressed to you at Wheatland, and subsequently in our personal interview.

The general views which were expressed by me at that interview as to the relative advantages of conducting the negotiations here or at London have undergone no change. Still, the present condition of affairs with respect to the fisheries, and the various questions connected therewith, have seemed to demand that they be taken up at once, where Mr. Crampton & Mr. Everett left them. Recent developments have inspired the belief that the fisheries, the reciprocity question &c., will leave no ground of concession which could be available in the settlement of the questions in Central America. The threatening aspect of affairs on the coast, in the provinces, has of necessity called for several conversations between Mr. Crampton & the Secretary of State with a view to keep things quiet there, and if practicable to agree upon terms of a satisfactory adjustment. To suspend these negotiations at this moment, in the critical condition of our interests in that quarter, might I fear prove embarrassing if not hazardous. That a treaty can be or had better be concluded here I am not prepared to say. I have no wish upon the subject except that the negotiations be conducted wherever they can be brought to the most speedy and advantageous termination. The great respect for your judgment, experience, high attainments and eminent abilities which led me to tender to you the mission to England, will induce me to commit to your hands all the pending questions between the two Countries unless the reasons for proceeding here with those to which I have referred shall appear quite obvious. I need not say that your declination at this time would be embarrassing to me and for many reasons a matter to be deeply regretted.

I thank you for your generous expressions and assure you that your heart acknowledges no feelings of personal kindness to which mine does not respond.

If the tax be not too great, will you oblige me by visiting Washington again? I trust a comparison of conclusions with the facts before us may conduct to a result mutually satisfactory.

With the highest [respect] yr. friend

FRANK. PIERCE.

HON. JAMES BUCHANAN
    Wheatland, Pa.

------

[1] Buchanan Papers, Historical Society of Pennsylvania.

TO PRESIDENT PIERCE.[1]

WHEATLAND, near LANCASTER, June 29th, 1853.
MY DEAR SIR:—

Your favor of the 26th inst. did not reach Lancaster until yesterday afternoon. I had thought it strange that you did not answer my letter of the 14th instant; but this accidental omission has been kindly and satisfactorily explained by your favor of the 26th.

It is, perhaps, scarcely necessary for me to repeat my unchanged purpose to accept the English mission and go to London without delay, if it be still your determination to intrust me with the settlement of the reciprocity, the fishery and the Central American questions. I confess, however, that I do not perceive how it is now possible, employing your own language, " to suspend negotiations (in Washington) at this moment " on the reciprocity and fishery questions. I agree with you that it was quite natural that the negotiations " should be taken up at once, where Mr. Crampton and Mr. Everett left them." This could only have been prevented by an official communication to Mr. Crampton, upon offering to renew the negotiation, informing him of the fact that you had appointed me minister to London for the very purpose of settling these, as well as the Central American, questions.

In regard to our Central American difficulties, I still entertain, after more mature reflection, the most decided opinions—I might even say convictions. Whilst these difficulties are all embarrassing, one of them is attended with extreme danger. I refer to the establishment by Great Britain of the Colony of the Bay of Islands. This wrong has been perpetrated, if I understand the question, in direct violation of the Clayton and Bulwer treaty. Our national honor imperatively requires the removal of this colony. Its withdrawal ought to be a sine qua non in any negotiation on any subject with the British government. With what face could we ever hereafter present this question of violated faith and outraged national honor to the world against the British government, if whilst, flagrante delicto, the wrong unexplained and unredressed, we should incorporate the British North American provinces, by treaty, into the American Union, so far as reciprocal free trade is concerned? How could we, then,

---

[1] Curtis's Buchanan, II. 87.

under any circumstances, make this a casus belli? If a man has wronged and insulted me, and I take him into my family and bestow upon him the privileges of one of its members, without previous redress or explanation, it is then too late to turn round and make the original offence a serious cause for personal hostilities. It is the first step which costs; and this ought to be taken with a clear view of all the consequences. If I were placed in your exalted and well merited station, my motto should be, " all the questions or none." This is the best, nay, perhaps the only mode of satisfactorily adjusting our difficulties with that haughty, overreaching and imperious government. My sole object in agreeing to accept a mission, so distasteful to me in all other respects, was to try the experiment, under your instructions, well knowing that I should receive from you a firm and enlightened support. I still cherish the confident belief we should have proved successful. It would now seem to be too late to transfer the negotiation to London; but you may still insist that *all* the questions shall be settled together in Washington. They still remain there just as they were in Mr. Fillmore's time. Why, then, should Mr. Crampton have received instructions in two of them, and not in the third?

But I have said and written so much to yourself and Governor Marcy upon the danger of dividing these questions, that I shall only add that, were I a Senator, I could not in conscience vote for the ratification of any partial treaty in the present condition of our relations with Great Britain. And here I would beg respectfully to make a suggestion which, if approved by you, might remove all difficulties. Let Governor Marcy and Mr. Crampton arrange the reciprocity and fishery questions as speedily as possible; and then let me carry the perfected projet with me to London, to be executed there, provided I shall succeed in adjusting the Central American questions according to your instructions; but in no other event. In this manner the reciprocity question, as arranged by the Secretary of State, might still be used as the powerful lever to force a just settlement of the Central American questions. Indeed, in communicating your purpose in this respect to Mr. Crampton, Governor Marcy might address him a note which would essentially assist me in the Central American negotiation. As the reciprocity and fishery treaty would not be submitted to the Senate until December, this arrangement would be productive of no delay.

I should cheerfully visit Washington, or go a thousand miles to serve you in any manner, but I doubt whether this would be good policy under existing circumstances. The public journals would at once announce that I had arrived in Washington to receive my commission and instructions, and depart for Europe. Finding this not to be the case, they would presume that some misunderstanding had occurred between you and myself, which prevented me from going abroad. Is it not better to avoid such suspicions? If I should not go to England, a brief explanation can be made in the *Union* which will put all right, and the whole matter will be forgotten in a week. After all, however, should you still wish me to go to Washington, please to have me telegraphed, because the mail is almost always two, and sometimes three days in reaching me.

In regard to myself personally, if the expedient which I have suggested should not be adopted, or something similar to it, then I should have no business of importance to transact in London, and should, against all my tastes and inclinations, again subject myself to the ceremonies, etiquette and round of gaiety required from a minister at a foreign court. But this is not all. I should violate my private and social duties towards an only brother, in very delicate health, and numerous young relatives, some of whom are entirely dependent upon me and now at a critical period of life, without the self-justification of having any important public duties to perform. So reluctant was I, at the first, to undertake the task which, in your kindness, you had prescribed for me, that my mind was not finally made up, until a distinguished Senator bluntly informed me, that if I shrank from it, this would be attributed to a fear of grappling with the important and dangerous questions with England which had been assigned to me, both by the voice of the President and the country.

I regret that I have not time, before the closing of the mail, to reduce my letter to any reasonable dimensions.

From your friend, very respectfully,

JAMES BUCHANAN.

FROM PRESIDENT PIERCE.[1]

WASHINGTON, D. C. July 2, 1853.

MY DEAR SIR

Your letter of the 29th was received this morning and I have carefully considered its suggestions. The state of the questions now under discussion between Mr. Crampton and Gov. Marcy cannot with a proper regard for the public interests be suspended. It is not to be disguised that the condition of things on the coast is extremely embarrassing, so much so as to be the source of daily solicitude. Nothing, it is to be feared, but the prospect of a speedy adjustment will prevent actual collision. Mr. Crampton had become so deeply impressed with the hazards of any ill-advised step on either side that he left this morning with the view of having a personal interview with Sir George Seymour. Thus, while I am not prepared to say that a treaty can be concluded here or that it will prove desirable on the whole that it should be, it is quite clear to my mind that the negotiations ought not to be broken off, and that, with a proper regard to our interests, the announcement cannot be made to Mr. Crampton that the final adjustment of the fishery question must await the settlement of the Central American questions. Believing that the instructions now prepared would present my views in relation to the mission in the most satisfactory manner, they will be forwarded to you tomorrow.

I need not repeat the deep regret your declination would occasion on my part. What explanation could be given for it I am unable to perceive.

I am with the highest respect

Truly yr. friend

FRANK. PIERCE.

HON. JAMES BUCHANAN,
Wheatland, Pa.

FROM MR. MARCY.[1]

Private.

STATE DEPARTMENT,
WASHINGTON, July 5th '53.

MY DEAR SIR:—

I expected you would be again in Washington before you left for England, but as this is uncertain I have concluded to send by the bearer, Mr. W. G. C. Mann, the instructions which have been prepared for you. I have preferred to send them in this way, lest they should not reach you in season if entrusted to the mail.

I should have been pleased with an opportunity of submitting them to you, and having the benefit of any suggestions you might make thereon; but I shall not have it, as you will not probably be here before your departure on your mission. The instructions have been carefully examined by the President, and made conformable to his views. Should there be other docu-

---

[1] Buchanan Papers, Historical Society of Pennsylvania.

ments than those now sent which it would be proper for you to take out, they will be forwarded to our Despatch agent at N. York and by him handed to you.

Very respectfully your obt. Servt.

W. L. MARCY.

HON. JAS. BUCHANAN.

TO PRESIDENT PIERCE.[1]

WHEATLAND, near LANCASTER, July 7, 1853.

MY DEAR SIR:—

Yours of the 2d inst., postmarked on the 4th, did not reach me until this morning at too late an hour to prepare and send an answer to Lancaster in time for the southern mail. Young Mr. Mann arrived and left last evening, a *most decided contre-temps.* Had your letter preceded him, this would have saved me some labor, and, although a very placid man, some irritation.

Although the opinions and purposes expressed in my letters of the 14th, 23d and 29th ultimo remain unchanged, yet so great is my personal desire to gratify your wishes that I shall take the question under reconsideration for a brief period. I observe from the papers that you will be in Philadelphia, where I anticipate the pleasure of paying you my respects. Then, if not sooner, I shall give your letter a definite answer.

I hope that in the meantime you may look out for some better man to take my place. You may rest assured I can manifest my warm friendship for your administration and for yourself far more effectively as a private citizen of Pennsylvania than as a public minister in London.

From your friend,
Very respectfully,

JAMES BUCHANAN.

---

[1] Curtis's Buchanan, II. 90.

MEMORANDUM BY BUCHANAN

ON HIS APPOINTMENT AS MINISTER TO ENGLAND.[1]

[July 12, 1853.]

Although gratified with this offer,[2] I felt great reluctance in accepting it. Having consulted several friends, in whose judgment I have confidence, they all advised me to accept it, with a single exception (James L. Reynolds). I left Lancaster for Washington on Thursday, 7th April, wholly undecided as to my course. On Friday morning (8th April) I called upon the President, who invited me to dine with him " *en famille* " that day. The only strangers at the table were Mr. John Slidell and Mr. O'Conor. After the dinner was over the President invited me up to the library, where we held the following conversation:

I commenced by expressing to him my warm and grateful acknowledgments for the offer of this most important mission, and said I should feel myself under the same obligations to him whether it was accepted or declined; that at my age, and contented and happy as I was at home, I felt no disposition to change my position, and again to subject myself to the ceremonious etiquette and round of gaiety required from a minister at a foreign court.

Here the President interrupted me and said: " If this had been my only purpose in sending you abroad, I should never have offered you the mission. You know very well that we have several important questions to settle with England, and it is my intention that you shall settle them all in London. The country expects and requires your services as minister to London. You have had no competitor for this place, and when I presented your name to the cabinet they were unanimous. I think that under these circumstances I have a right to ask you to accept the mission."

To this I replied that Mr. Polk was a wise man, and after deliberation he had determined that all important questions with foreign nations should be settled in Washington, under his own

---

[1] Curtis's Buchanan, II. 76. The date given to this memorandum by the editor is to a certain extent conjectural, but, as the paper evidently was completed soon after the events which it so minutely describes, the date assigned is that of the day after Mr. Buchanan announced his final decision to President Pierce.

[2] See President Pierce to Mr. Buchanan, March 30, 1853, and Mr. Buchanan to President Pierce, April 2, 1853, supra.

immediate supervision; that he (President Pierce) had not, perhaps, seriously considered the question.

He promptly replied that he had seriously considered the question, and had arrived at the conclusion that better terms could be obtained in London at the seat of power than through an intermediate agent in this country; and instanced the Oregon negotiation as an example.

From this opinion I did not dissent, but asked: "What will Governor Marcy say to your determination? You have appointed him Secretary of State with my entire approbation; and I do not think he would be willing to surrender to your minister at London the settlement of these important questions, which might reflect so much honor upon himself."

He replied, with some apparent feeling, that he himself would control this matter.

I interposed and said: "I know that you do; but I would not become the instrument of creating any unpleasant feelings between yourself and your Secretary of State by accepting the mission, even if I desired it, which is not the case."

He replied that he did not believe this would be the case. When he had mentioned my name to the cabinet, although he did not say in express terms I should be entrusted with the settlement of these questions, yet from the general tone of his remarks they must have inferred that such was his intention. He added, that after our interview he would address a note to Governor Marcy to call and see him, and after conversing with him on the subject he would send for me.

I then mentioned to him that there appeared to me to be another insurmountable obstacle to my acceptance of the mission. I said: "In all your appointments for Pennsylvania, you have not yet selected a single individual for any office for which I recommended him. I have numerous other friends still behind who are applicants for foreign appointments; and if I were now to accept the mission to London, they might with justice say that I had appropriated the lion's share to myself, and selfishly received it as an equivalent for their disappointment. I could not and would not place myself in this position."

His answer was emphatic. He said: "I can assure you, if you accept the mission, Pennsylvania shall not receive one appointment more or less on that account. I shall consider yours as an appointment for the whole country; and I will not say that Pennsylvania shall not have more in case of your acceptance than if you should decline the mission." I asked him if he was willing I should mention this conversation publicly. He said he would rather not; but that I might give the strongest assurances to my friends that such would be his course in regard to Pennsylvania appointments.

We then had a conversation respecting the individual appointments already made in Pennsylvania, which I shall not write. He told me emphatically, that when he appointed Mr. Brown collector, he believed him to be my friend, and had received assurances to that effect; although he knew that I greatly preferred Governor Porter. He also had been assured that Wynkoop was my friend, and asked if I had not recommended him; and seemed much surprised when I informed him of the course he had pursued.

I then stated, that if I should accept the mission, I could not consent to banish myself from my country for more than two years. He replied, that at the end of two years I might write to him for leave to return home, and it should be granted; adding, that if I should settle our important questions with England at an earlier period, I might return at the end of eighteen months, should I desire it.

The interview ended, and I heard nothing from the President on Friday evening, Saturday or Sunday, or until Monday morning. In the mean time, I had several conversations with particular friends, and especially with Mr. Walker (at whose house I stayed,) Judge Campbell and Senator Bright, all of whom urged me to accept the mission. The latter informed me that if I did not accept it, many would attribute my refusal to a fear or an unwillingness to grapple with the important and dangerous questions pending between the United States and Great Britain.

On Sunday morning, April 10th, the *Washington Union* was brought to Mr. Walker's, from which it appeared that the session of the Senate would terminate on the next day at one o'clock, the President having informed the Committee to wait upon him, that he had no further communications to make to the body. At this I was gratified. I presumed that the President, after having consulted Governor Marcy, had concluded not to transfer the negotiations to London; because it had never occurred to me that I was to go abroad on such an important mission without the confirmation of the Senate. Mr. Walker and myself had some conversation on the subject, and we agreed that it was strange the Senate had been kept so long together without submitting to them the important foreign appointments; as we both knew that in Europe, and especially in England, since the rejection of Mr. Van Buren's appointment, a minister had not the proper prestige without the approbation of the co-ordinate branch of the Executive power.

On Sunday morning, before dinner-time, I called to see Jefferson Davis.[1]   We had much conversation on many subjects. Among other things, I told him it was strange that the foreign appointments had not been agreed upon and submitted to the Senate before their adjournment.   He replied that he did not see that this could make any difference; they might be made with more deliberation during the recess.   I said a man was considered but half a minister, who went abroad upon the President's appointment alone, without the consent of the Senate, ever since the rejection of Mr. Van Buren.   He said he now saw this plainly; and asked why Marcy had not informed them of it,— they trusted to him in all such matters.   The conversation then turned upon other subjects; but this interview with Mr. Davis, sought for the purpose of benefiting my friend, John Slidell, who was then a candidate for the Senate, has doubtless been the cause why I was nominated and confirmed as minister to England on the next day.

On Sunday evening a friend informed Mr. Walker and myself that a private message had been sent to the Senators still in town, requesting them not to leave by the cars on Monday morning, as the President had important business to submit to them.   This was undoubtedly the origin of the rumor which at the time so extensively prevailed, that the cabinet was about to be dissolved and another appointed.

On Monday morning, at ten o'clock, I received a note from Mr. Cushing,[2] informing me that " the President would be glad to see me at once."   I immediately repaired to the White House; and the President and myself agreed, referring to our former conversation, though not repeating it in detail, that he should send my name to the Senate.   If a quorum were present, and I should be confirmed, I would go to England; if not, the matter was to be considered as ended.   Thirty-three members were present, and I was confirmed.   On this second occasion, our brief

---

[1] Mr. Davis was Secretary of War.
[2] Attorney General.

conversation was of the same character, so far as it proceeded, with that at our first interview. He kindly consented that I should select my own Secretary of Legation; and without a moment's hesitation, I chose John Appleton, of Maine, who accepted the offer which I was authorized to make, and was appointed. I left Washington on Tuesday morning, April 12th.

At our last interview, I informed the President that I would soon again return to Washington to prepare myself for the performance of my important duties, because this could only be satisfactorily done in the State Department. He said he wished to be more at leisure on my return, that he might converse with me freely on the questions involved in my mission; he thought that in about ten days the great pressure for office would relax, and he would address me a note inviting me to come.

I left Washington perfectly satisfied, and resolved to use my best efforts to accomplish the objects of my mission. The time fixed upon for leaving the country was the 20th of June, so that I might relieve Mr. Ingersoll on the 1st of July.

I had given James Keenan of Greensburg a strong recommendation for appointment as consul to Glasgow. As soon as he learned my appointment as minister to England, he wrote to me on the 14th of April, stating that the annunciation of my acceptance of this mission had created a belief among my friends there that no Pennsylvanian could now be appointed to any consulship.

On the 16th of April, I wrote to him and assured him, in the language of the President, that my appointment to the English mission would not cause one appointment more or one appointment less to be given to Pennsylvania than if I had declined the mission.

In answer, I received a letter from him, dated April 21st, in which he extracts from a letter from Mr. Drum, then in Washington, to him, the following: " I have talked to the President earnestly on the subject (of his appointment to Glasgow), but evidently without making much impression. He says that it will be impossible for him to bestow important consulships on Pennsylvania who has a cabinet officer and *the first and highest mission.* Campbell talks in the same strain; but says he will make it his business to get something worthy of your acceptance."

For some days before and after the receipt of this letter, I learned that different members of the cabinet, when urged for consulates for Pennsylvanians, had declared to the applicants and their friends that they could not be appointed *on account of my appointment to London,* and what the President had already done for the State.[1]   One notable instance of this kind occurred between Colonel Forney and Mr. Cushing.   Not having heard from the President, according to his promise, I determined to go to Washington for the purpose of having an explanation with him and preparing myself for my mission.   Accordingly, I left home on Tuesday, May 17th, and arrived in Washington on Wednesday morning, May 18th, remaining there until Tuesday morning, May 31st, on which day I returned home.

On Thursday morning, May 19th, I met the President, by appointment, at 9½ o'clock.   Although he did not make a very clear explanation of his conversation with Mr. Drum, yet I left him satisfied that he would perform his promise in regard to Pennsylvania appointments.   I had not been in Washington many days before I clearly discovered that the President and cabinet were intent upon his renomination and re-election.   This I concluded from the general tendency of affairs, as well as from special communications to that effect from friends whom I shall not name.   It was easy to perceive that the object in appointments was to raise up a Pierce party, wholly distinct from the former Buchanan, Cass, and Douglas parties; and I readily perceived, what I had before conjectured, the reason why my recommendations had proved of so little avail.   I thought I also discovered considerable jealousy of Governor Marcy, who will probably cherish until the day of his death the anxious desire to become President.   I was convinced of this jealousy at a dinner given Mr. Holmes, formerly of South Carolina, now of California, at Brown's Hotel on Saturday, May 21st.   Among the guests were Governor Marcy, Jefferson Davis, Mr. Dobbin, and Mr. Cushing.   The company soon got into high good humor. In the course of the evening Mr. Davis began to jest with Governor Marcy and myself on the subject of the next Presidency, and the Governor appeared to relish the subject.   After considerable *bagatelle,* I said I would make a speech.   All wanted to hear my speech.   I addressed Governor Marcy and said: " You and I ought to consider ourselves out of the list of candidates.   We are both growing old, and it is a melancholy spectacle to see old men struggling in the political arena for the honors and offices of this world, as though it were to be their everlasting

---

[1] See Mr. Buchanan to President Pierce, April 27, 1853, Mr. Buchanan to Mr. Johnson, May 3, 1853, and Mr. Buchanan to Mr. Marcy, May 12, 1853, supra.

abode.   Should you perform your duties as Secretary of State to the satisfaction of the country during the present Presidential term, and should I perform my duties in the same manner as minister to England, we ought both to be content to retire and leave the field to younger men.   President Pierce is a young man, and should his administration prove to be advantageous to the country and honorable to himself, as I trust it will, there is no good reason why he should not be renominated and re-elected for a second term."   The Governor, to do him justice, appeared to take these remarks kindly and in good part, and said he was agreed.   They were evidently very gratifying to Messrs. Davis, Dobbin, and Cushing.   Besides, they expressed the real sentiments of my heart.   When the dinner was ended, Messrs. Davis and Dobbin took my right and left arm and conducted me to my lodgings, expressing warm approbation of what I had said to Governor Marcy.   I heard of this speech several times whilst I remained at Washington; and the President once alluded to it with evident satisfaction.   It is certain that Governor Marcy is no favorite.

I found the State Department in a wretched condition. Everything had been left by Mr. Webster topsy turvy; and Mr. Everett was not Secretary long enough to have it put in proper order; and whilst in that position he was constantly occupied with pressing and important business.   Governor Marcy told me that he had not been able, since his appointment, to devote one single hour together to his proper official duties.   His time had been constantly taken up with office-seekers and cabinet councils. It is certain that during Mr. Polk's administration he had paid but little attention to our foreign affairs; and it is equally certain that he went into the Department without much knowledge of its appropriate duties.   But he is a strong-minded and clear-headed man; and, although slow in his perceptions, is sound in his judgment.   He may, and I trust will, succeed; but yet he has much to learn.

Soon after I arrived in Washington on this visit, I began seriously to doubt whether the President would eventually entrust to me the settlement of the important questions at London, according to his promise, without which I should not have consented to go abroad.   I discovered that the customary and necessary notice in such cases had not been given to the British government, of the President's intention and desire to transfer the negotiations to London, and that I would go there with instructions

and authority to settle all the questions between the two governments, and thus prepare them for the opening of these negotiations upon my arrival.

After I had been in Washington some days, busily engaged
in the State Department in preparing myself for the duties of my
mission, Mr. Marcy showed me the projet of a treaty which had
nearly been completed by Mr. Everett and Mr. Crampton, the
British minister, before Mr. Fillmore's term had expired, creating
reciprocal free trade in certain enumerated articles, between the
United States and the British North American provinces, with
the exception of Newfoundland, and regulating the fisheries.
Mr. Marcy appeared anxious to conclude this treaty, though he
did not say so in terms. He said that Mr. Crampton urged its
conclusion; and he himself apprehended that if it were not concluded speedily, there would be great danger of collision between
the two countries on the fishing grounds. I might have answered, but did not, that the treaty could not be ratified until
after the meeting of the Senate in December; and that in the
mean time it might be concluded at London in connection with
the Central American questions. I did say that the great lever
which would force the British government to do us justice in
Central America was their anxious desire to obtain reciprocal
free trade for their North American possessions, and thus preserve their allegiance and ward off the danger of their annexation to the United States. My communications on the extent
and character of my mission were with the President himself,
and not with Governor Marcy; and I was determined they should
so remain. The President had informed me that he had, as he
promised, conversed with the Governor, and found him entirely
willing that I should have the settlement of the important questions at London.

The circumstances to which I have referred appeared to me
to be significant. I conversed with the President fully and freely
on each of the three questions, viz: The reciprocal trade, the
fisheries, and that of Central America; and endeavored to convince him of the necessity of settling them all together. He
seemed to be strongly impressed with my remarks, and said
that he had conversed with a Senator then in Washington, (I
presume Mr. Toucey, though he did not mention the name,) who
had informed him that he thought that the Senate would have
great difficulty in ratifying any treaty which did not embrace
all the subjects pending between us and England; and that for

this very reason there had been considerable opposition in the body to the ratification of the Claims Convention, though in itself unexceptionable.

The President said nothing from which an inference could be fairly drawn that he had changed his mind as to the place where the negotiation should be conducted; and yet he did not speak in as strong and unequivocal terms on the subject as I could have desired.

Under all the circumstances, I left Washington, on the 31st of May, without accepting my commission, which had been prepared for me and was in the State Department. On the 5th of June I received a letter from Governor Marcy, dated on the first, requesting me to put on paper my exposition of the Clayton and Bulwer treaty. In this he says nothing about my instructions on any of the questions between this country and England, nor does he intimate that he desires my opinion for any particular purpose. On the 7th of June I answered his letter. In the concluding portion of my letter, I took the occasion to say: " The truth is that our relations with England are in a critical condition. Throw all the questions together into hotchpot, and I think they can all be settled amicably and honorably. The desire of Great Britain to establish free trade between the United States and her North American possessions, and by this means retain these possessions in their allegiance, may be used as the powerful lever to force her to abandon her pretensions in Central America; and yet it must be admitted that, in her history, she has never voluntarily abandoned any important commercial position on which she has once planted her foot. It cannot be her interest to go to war with us, and she must know that it is clearly her interest to settle all the questions between us, and have a smooth sea hereafter. If the Central American question, which is the dangerous question, should not be settled, we shall probably have war with England before the close of the present administration. Should she persist in her unjust and grasping policy on the North American continent and the adjacent islands, this will be inevitable at some future day; and although we are not very well prepared for it at the present moment, it is not probable that we shall for many years be in a better condition."

I also say in this letter to Governor Marcy, that " bad as the treaty (the Clayton and Bulwer treaty) is, the President cannot annul it. This would be beyond his power, and the attempt would startle the whole world. In one respect it may be employed to great advantage. The question of the Colony of the Bay of Islands is the dangerous question. It affects the national honor. From all the consideration I can give the subject, the establishment of this Colony is a clear violation of the Clayton and Bulwer treaty. Under it we can insist upon the withdrawal of Great Britain from the Bay of Islands. Without it we could only interpose the Monroe doctrine against this colony, which has never yet been sanctioned by Congress, though as an individual citizen of the United States, I would fight for it to-morrow so far as all North America is concerned, and would do my best to maintain it throughout South America."

This letter of mine to Governor Marcy, up till the present moment, June 25, has elicited no response. . . .

Having at length determined to ascertain what were the President's present intentions in regard to the character of my mission, I addressed him a letter, of which the following is a copy, on the 14th June. . . .[1]

From the important character of this letter and the earnest and reiterated request which I made for an early answer, I did not doubt but that I should receive one, giving me definite information, with as little delay as possible. I waited in vain until the 23d June; and having previously ascertained, through a friend, that my letter had been received by the President, I wrote him a second letter on that day, of which the following is a copy. . . .[2]

To this letter I received an answer on Tuesday evening, June 28th, of which the following is a copy. . . .[3]

Wednesday, July 6th, at about 6 o'clock in the afternoon, Mr. Mann, son of the Assistant Secretary of State, arrives and presents me with a private letter from Governor Marcy dated on the day previous, and a sealed package which, upon opening, I found contained my commission and instructions as minister to Great Britain, without the slightest reference to the previous correspondence on the subject between the President and myself, and just as though I had accepted, instead of having declined the mission, and was now on the wing for London. He was to

---

[1] Here follows, in the memorandum, Mr. Buchanan's letter to President Pierce of June 14, 1853, which is given in its proper order, supra.

[2] For this letter, see Mr. Buchanan to President Pierce, June 23, 1853, supra.

[3] See President Pierce to Mr. Buchanan, June 26, 1853, supra. For Mr. Buchanan's reply, see Mr. Buchanan to President Pierce, June 29, 1853, supra.

find me wherever I might be.   He left about sunset or between that and dark. .*Vide* Governor Marcy's letter.[1]

Thursday morning, July 7, the following letter from the President came to hand, postmarked Washington, July 4th. . . .[2]

On Monday evening, July 11, 1853, I went to Philadelphia to meet the President, according to my appointment.[3]   I saw him on Tuesday afternoon at the head of the military procession, as it marched from Market Street down Sixth to Independence Hall. He was on the right of General Patterson, and being a good horseman, he appeared to much advantage on horseback.   He recognized me, as he rode along, at the window of the second story of Lebo's Commercial Hotel.

The reception of the President in Philadelphia was all that his best friends could have desired.   Indeed, the Whigs seemed to vie with the Democrats in doing honor to the Chief Magistrate. Price Wetherell, the President of the Select Council, did his whole duty, though in a fussy manner, and was much gratified with the well-deserved compliments which he received.   The dinner at McKibbins' was excellent and well conducted.   We did not sit down to table until nearly nine o'clock.   The mayor, Mr. Gilpin, presided.   The President sat on his right, and myself on his left.   In the course of the entertainment he spoke to me, behind Mr. Gilpin, and strongly expressed the hope that I would accept the mission, to which I made a friendly, but indefinite answer.   He then expressed a desire to see me when the dinner should be ended; but it was kept up until nearly midnight, the President cordially participating in the hilarity of the scene.   We then agreed to meet the next morning.

After mature reflection, I had determined to reject the mission, if I found this could be done without danger of an open breach with the administration; but if this could not be done, I was resolved to accept it, however disagreeable.   The advice of Governor Porter, then at McKibbins', gave me confidence in the correctness of my own judgment.   My position was awkward and embarrassing.   There was danger that it might be said (indeed it had already been insinuated in several public journals), that I had selfishly thrown up the mission, because the fishery question had not been entrusted to me, although I knew that

---

[1] See Mr. Marcy to Mr. Buchanan, July 5, 1853, supra.

[2] See President Pierce to Mr. Buchanan, July 2, 1853, supra.

[3] See Mr. Buchanan to President Pierce, July 7, 1853, supra.

actual collision between the two countries on the fishery grounds might be the consequence of the transfer of the negotiation to London.   Such a statement could only be rebutted by the publication of the correspondence between the President and myself; but as this was altogether private such a publication could only be justified in a case of extreme necessity.

Besides, I had no reason to believe that the President had taken from me the reciprocity and fishery questions with any deliberate purpose of doing me injury.   On the contrary, I have but little doubt that this proceeded from his apprehension that the suspension of the negotiation might produce dangerous consequences on the fishing grounds.   I might add that his instructions to me on the Central American questions were as full and ample as I could desire.   Many friends believed, *not without reason,* that if I should decline the mission, Mr. Dallas would be appointed; and this idea was very distasteful to them, though not to myself.

The following is the substance of the conversation between the President and myself on Wednesday morning, the 13th of July, partly at McKibbins', and the remainder on board the steamer which took us across to Camden.   It was interrupted by the proceedings at Independence Hall on Wednesday morning.

The President commenced the conversation by the expression of his strong wish that I would not decline the mission.   I observed that the British government had imposed an absurd construction on the fishery question, and without notice had suddenly sent a fleet there to enforce it, for the purpose, as I believed, of obtaining from us the reciprocity treaty.   Under these circumstances I should have said to Great Britain: You shall have the treaty, but you must consent at the same time to withdraw your protectorate from the Mosquito Coast, and restore to Honduras the colony of the Bay of Islands.   That this course might still be adopted at Washington, and that in this view all the negotiations had better be conducted there.   Without answering these remarks specifically, the President, reiterating his request that I should accept the mission, spoke strongly of the danger of any delay, on our part, in the adjustment of the fishery question, and said that Mr. Crampton, deeply impressed with this danger, had gone all the way to Halifax to see Admiral Seymour, for the purpose of averting this danger.   I observed that it was far, very far from my desire, in the present state of the negotiation, to have charge of the fishery negotiation at London; but still insisted that it was best that the Central American questions should also be settled at Washington.   To this he expressed a decided aversion. He said that serious difficulties had arisen, in the progress of the negotiations, on the reciprocity question, particularly in regard to the reciprocal registry of the vessels of the two parties; and it was probable that within a short time the negotiation on all the questions would be transferred to me at London, and that my declining the mission at this time would be very embarrassing to his administration, and could not be satisfactorily explained.   I replied that I thought it could.   It might be stated in the *Union* that after my agreement to accept the mission, circumstances had arisen rendering it necessary that the negotiations with which I was to be entrusted at London, should be conducted at Washington; that I myself was fully convinced of this necessity; but that this change had produced a corresponding change in my determination to accept a mission which I had always been reluctant to accept, and we had parted on the best and most friendly terms. Something like this, I thought, would be satisfactory.

He answered that after such an explanation it would be difficult, if not impossible, to get a suitable person to undertake the mission.   He had felt it to be his duty to offer me this important mission, and he thought it was my duty to accept it.   He said that if the Central American questions should go wrong in London, entrusted to other hands than my own, both he and I would be seriously blamed.   He said, with much apparent feeling, that he felt reluctant to insist thus upon my acceptance of a mission so distasteful to me.

Having fully ascertained, as I believed, that I could not decline the mission without giving him serious offence, and without danger of an open rupture with the administration, I said: " Reluctant as I am to accept the mission, if you think that my refusal to accept it would cause serious embarrassment to your administration, which I am anxious to support, I will waive my objections and go to London."   He instantly replied that he was rejoiced that I had come to this conclusion, and that we should both feel greatly the better for having done our respective duties. He added that I need not hurry my departure.   I told him that although my instructions gave me all the powers I could desire on the Central American questions, yet they had not been accompanied by any of the papers and documents in the Department relating to these questions; that these were indispensable, and without them I could not proceed.   He expressed some surprise at this, and said he would write to Governor Marcy that very evening. I told him he need not trouble himself to do this, as I should write to him myself immediately after my return home.

This was on the river. I accompanied him to the cars, where I took leave of him, Mr. Guthrie, Mr. Davis and Mr. Cushing, who all pressed me very much to go on with them to New York.

TO MR. MARCY.[1]

(No. 1.)   WHEATLAND, near LANCASTER, 14 July 1853.
SIR/

I received on Wednesday evening the 6th Instant, by the hands of W. G. C. Mann, Esquire, a sealed package containing my commission as " Envoy Extraordinary & Minister Plenipotentiary of the United States of America at the Court of the United Kingdom of Great Britain & Ireland," together with your General Instructions (No. 1) dated on the 1st Instant & the different documents therein mentioned. Also, your Special Instructions (No. 2) dated on the 2d Instant.

As by the latter, " the whole Central American question, so far as Great Britain has seen fit to connect herself with it, is entirely confided to your [my] management, under such instructions as you [I] may from time to time desire, or such as the President may consider himself called upon to furnish, in the progress of the discussions which may arise thereon; " it has become indispensable that I should receive, before my departure from the Country, copies of every document in the Department of State having any material bearing upon this question, except such as may be found in the Archives of the Legation at London. The transfer of the negotiation from Washington to that City renders this all important. Before my first introduction of the subject to the British Minister for Foreign Affairs, it is necessary that I should understand the question in all its relations. For this purpose, it is essential that I should be fully informed of the nature & extent of the pretensions of the British Government to interfere in Central America & the reasons on which they are founded. You will, therefore, be kind enough to cause copies of all such documents to be transmitted to me, at your earliest

----

[1] MSS. Department of State, 65 Despatches from England.

convenience; as I am anxious to proceed on my mission, with as little delay as possible. Among these, I might mention two letters to the Department which I perused when last at Washington; one from W. S. Murphy, Special Agent &c., dated, according to my recollection, in January, 1842, & the other from Mr. Harrison, our Consul at Jamaica, dated in March of the present year. When there, you read to me a paper containing the opinion of certain British law officers on the construction of the Clayton & Bulwer Treaty; which would, also, be important.

Your instructions do not seem to contemplate, at least for the present, any attempt to acquire the Island of Cuba from Spain, by purchase. I should be glad to know the policy of the President in regard to the acquisition of this Island, as soon as it shall be definitively determined; &, under your instructions, to render any such incidental services in the accomplishment of this important object, as may be deemed compatible with my position & duties as Minister of the United States at London.

I shall, most cheerfully, execute your instructions in regard to Cuba, according to my best ability; but in order to do this effectually, ought I not to possess all the information in the Department, directly bearing on the objects of these instructions?

Yours very respectfully

JAMES BUCHANAN.

HON: WILLIAM L. MARCY.
    Secretary of State.

P. S. Copies of all the papers relating to San Juan de Nicaragua will be highly important, & may be wanted the first of all.

TO CITIZENS OF LANCASTER.[1]

WHEATLAND, near LANCASTER, 23 July 1853.

GENTLEMEN/

I have received your very kind invitation, in behalf of my friends and neighbours, to partake of a public dinner before my departure for England.

No event of my past life has afforded me greater satisfaction than this invitation;—proceeding as it does, without distinc-

---

[1] Buchanan Papers, Historical Society of Pennsylvania; Curtis's Buchanan, II. 93.

tion of party, from those who have known me the longest & known me the best. Born in a neighbouring County, I cast my lot among you when little more than eighteen years of age, & have now enjoyed a happy home with you for more than forty three years, except the intervals which I have passed in the public service. During this long period, I have experienced more personal kindness both from yourselves & from your fathers than has, perhaps, ever been extended to any other man in Pennsylvania who has taken so active a part, as I have done, in the exciting political struggles which have so peculiarly marked this portion of our history.

It was both my purpose & desire to pass the remainder of my days in kind & friendly social intercourse with the friends of my youth & of my riper years, when invited by the President of my choice, under circumstances which a sense of duty rendered irresistible, to accept the mission to London. This purpose is now postponed,—not changed. It is my intention to carry it into execution, should a kind Providence prolong my days & restore me to my native land.

I am truly sorry not to be able to accept your invitation. Such are my engagements, that I can appoint no day for the dinner when I could, with certainty, promise to attend. Besides, a farewell dinner is at best but a melancholy affair. Should I live to return, we shall then meet with joy; & should it then be your pleasure to offer me a welcome home dinner, I shall accept it, with all my heart.

I cherish the confident hope that, during my absence, I shall live in your kindly recollection; as my friends in Lancaster County shall ever live in my grateful memory.

Cordially wishing you & yours, under the blessing of Heaven, health, prosperity, & happiness, I remain,

Your friend & fellow-citizen

JAMES BUCHANAN.

C. HAGER, WILLIAM B. FORDNEY, E. C. REIGART, B. C. BACHMAN, WM. MATHIOT, GEORGE H. KRUG, & N. ELLMAKER, ESQUIRES, & others.

TO MR. JOHNSON.[1]

WHEATLAND, near LANCASTER, 26 July 1853.
MY DEAR SIR/

In the hurry & bustle of preparation to leave my native land I have time to say scarcely any thing more to you than Farewell! May God bless you! And may you & yours live long & live happy! I hope you will let me hear from you in London, as you shall certainly hear from me.

I very much desired to write you a long letter; but engagements of a pressing nature & company have prevented. The mission has been changed into one which I should never have originally accepted. I did my best to get clear of it, at the last moment; but I discovered this would produce an open rupture with the administration. The happiest day I shall pass during my absence will be the day on which I shall discover the shores of my native land rising from the ocean on my return, should Heaven bless me & prolong my days until that happy event. Still I do not expect to be miserable.

Miss Harriet & Miss Hetty desire to be most kindly remembered to you. In haste, I remain as ever, very respectfully

Your grateful friend

JAMES BUCHANAN.

HON: CAVE JOHNSON.

TO MR. MARCY.[2]

(No. 3.)   WHEATLAND, near LANCASTER, 27 July 1853.
SIR/

Among the papers which you have furnished me, I find a copy of a communication from Lord Clarendon to Mr. Crampton dated on 27 May, 1853, in which he states, that " Her Majesty's Government have already, on many occasions, within the last twelve months, made overtures of the fairest & most liberal & practical character to the United States Government, inviting that Government to go hand in hand with the Government of Great Britain in devising & establishing a scheme of adjustment by which the affairs of Central America, Mosquito included, shall

---

[1] Buchanan Papers, Historical Society of Pennsylvania.
[2] MSS. Department of State, 65 Despatches from England.

be satisfactorily & permanently settled, and the honor of Great Britain, as ancient protector of Mosquito shall be preserved intact."

I do not find among the papers transmitted to me copies of the " overtures," to which his Lordship refers. Before I can answer this communication satisfactorily, it is indispensable that I should be apprised of the nature & extent of these " overtures." I would thank you, therefore, to furnish me all the necessary information on this subject, before my departure from New York.

I do not discover, among the papers which you have communicated, the President's full power to conclude a Treaty with Great Britain on the Central American questions. This, I presume, is a mere oversight.

It is of great importance that I should understand precisely what are the terms & conditions which the President would require in such a Treaty. Although I feel greatly honored by the high confidence reposed in me by the President, yet I should be unwilling to conclude a Treaty with the British Government upon these complicated, embarrassing, & dangerous questions, without instructions as to the particular stipulations which would be satisfactory to my own Government; & especially as to the terms which would be required as a sine qua non. Such instructions will present definite objects, to the accomplishment of which all my efforts shall be concentrated & directed. I respectfully request, therefore, that you will devote your attention to this subject, at your earliest convenience.

I have another suggestion to make;—and this in regard to the Colony of the Bay of Islands. I am happy to know we agree in opinion, that this Colony has been established by the British Government in direct violation of the Clayton & Bulwer Treaty. Such is, also, the opinion of the Committee on Foreign Relations of the Senate, which is entitled to great respect. The establishment of this Colony, then, stands out in bold relief from the other aggressions of the British Government in Central America. Ought there not to be a solemn & formal protest made to that Government, in the name of the President, against this establishment, accompanied by a demand that it shall be withdrawn? Perhaps this may have already been done; & in that case, my suggestion will go for nothing. If not, I shall be happy to receive the President's authority to make such a Protest.

I have never yet seen a copy of the Convention with Great Britain of the 8th February last, referred to in your instructions,

No. 2; but it has doubtless been communicated to the Legation at London.

I am anxious, if possible, to take out with me to London the Congressional Globe & Appendix for the last session of Congress, on account of the Debates which they contain on the Monroe Doctrine & the Clayton & Bulwer Treaty.   Might they not be transmitted in the Despatch Bag?

It is my purpose to leave this place for Philadelphia on Monday morning next & to arrive in New York on Wednesday, where I shall remain until the departure of the Atlantic on Saturday the 6th proximo.

Yours very respectfully

JAMES BUCHANAN.

HON: WILLIAM L. MARCY,
　　Secretary of State.

FROM PRESIDENT PIERCE.[1]

WASHINGTON, D. C. July 27, 1853.

MY DEAR SIR

Have you come to a conclusion as to the person whom you would desire to have designated to fill the place of Mr. Appleton as Secy. of Legation at London?

I have seen no Gentleman, since I came to Washington, who, in my judgment, possesses to a great extent the qualifications and accomplishments you would wish to secure than Hon. Donn Piatt of Cincinnati, Ohio.

Judge Piatt is about 30 years old—a Gentleman of high intelligence—possesses great advantages of person & address—and is withal modest and unobtrusive.   He is to sail for Europe with his wife next Saturday, but would accept the position referred to and join you whenever notified.

I write, not with a desire to control your judgment, but barely to make a suggestion.

In haste,

Very truly yr. friend,

FRANKLIN PIERCE.

HON. JAMES BUCHANAN
　　Wheatland, near Lancaster, Pa.

---

[1] Buchanan Papers, Historical Society of Pennsylvania.

TO PRESIDENT PIERCE.[1]

WHEATLAND, near LANCASTER, 29 July 1853.
MY DEAR SIR/
I have just received your favor of the 27th Instant strongly suggesting the appointment of Judge Piatt of Cincinnati as Secretary of Legation to the British mission. Mr. Sickles left here this afternoon, & I was very much pleased with him. There is some strange mistake in this matter. I had been induced to believe that you favored the appointment of Mr. Sickles; & indeed, he was under this impression himself. He had been highly & warmly recommended to me; but as I would not favor the appointment of any man who was to become a member of my family, without a personal acquaintance, I used some management to obtain a personal interview with him without any committal; & I confess I think that his manners, appearance, & intelligence are all that could be desired. I hope, as the matter has gone so far, you will be kind enough to confer the appointment upon him.

Yours very respectfully

JAMES BUCHANAN.

HIS EXCELLENCY FRANKLIN PIERCE &c. &c. &c.

FROM PRESIDENT PIERCE.[1]

WASHINGTON
July 31, 1853.
MY DEAR SIR—
I concur with you entirely with regard to the qualifications of Mr. Sickles, and his commission was made out immediately upon the presentation of your letter yesterday. Mr. S. will leave for New York this evening.

My letter in relation to Judge Piatt was written with his knowledge before I knew that you desired the appt. of Mr. S. or that he would accept it.—With the best wishes for your health & happiness

Yr. friend

FR. PIERCE.

HON. J. BUCHANAN.

---

[1] Buchanan Papers, Historical Society of Pennsylvania.

TO MISS LANE.[1]

ASTOR HOUSE, NEW YORK, 4 August 1853.
MY DEAR HARRIET/

John Van Buren called to see me this morning & was particularly amiable. He talked much of what his father had written & said to him respecting yourself, expressed a great desire to see you, & we talked much bagatelle about you. He intimated that his father had advised him to address you. I told him he would make a very rebellious nephew & would be hard to manage. . . .[2] He asked where you would be this winter & I told him that you would visit your relatives in Virginia in the course of a month & might probably come to London next spring or summer. He said he would certainly see you: & asked me for a letter of introduction to you, which I promised to give him. As he was leaving, he told me not to forget it but give it to the proprietors of Astor House before I left, & I promised to do so. I told him that you had appreciated his father's kindness to you, felt honored & grateful for his attentions, & admired him very much. He knew all about your pleasant intercourse with his father in Philadelphia. There was much other talk which I considered & still consider to be bagatelle; yet the subject was pursued by him. As I have a leisure moment, I thought I would prepare you for an interview with him in case you should meet.

John Van Buren is a man of rare abilities & great wit, & is quite eminent in his profession. His political course has been eccentric, but he still maintains his influence. I never saw him look so well as he did to-day. I repeat that I believe all this to be bagatelle; & yet it seemed to be mingled with a strong desire to see you.

Saturday Morning, 6 Aug:—I passed an hour last evening with Mrs. Sickles. She is both handsome & agreeable. And now, my dear Harriet, with the blessing of God, I shall go aboard the Atlantic this morning with a firm determination to do my duty & without any unpleasant apprehensions of the result. Relying upon that gracious being who has protected me all my life until the present moment & has strewed my path with blessings, I go abroad once more in the service of my country, with

---

[1] Buchanan Papers, private collection.
[2] The passage here omitted is now illegible.

fair hopes of success. I shall drop you a line from Liverpool, immediately upon my arrival.

    With my kindest regards for Miss Hetty, I remain

Yours affectionately

JAMES BUCHANAN.

MISS HARRIET LANE.

TO MISS LANE.[1]

ADELPHI HOTEL, LIVERPOOL 17 August 1853.

MY DEAR HARRIET/

    I arrived in Liverpool this morning after a passage of about ten days & sixteen hours. I was sea sick the whole voyage, but not near so bad as I had anticipated or as I was in going to & returning from Russia. Captain James West of Philadelphia, the commander of the Atlantic, is one of the most accomplished & vigilant officers & one of the most kind & amiable men I have ever known. I never wish to cross the Atlantic in any but a vessel commanded by him. We did not see the sun rise or set during the whole voyage. The weather was either rainy or cloudy throughout but many of the passengers were agreeable. Upon arriving here I found Mr. Lawrence who came from London to receive me. It is my purpose to accompany him to London tomorrow where I shall at the first stop at the Clarendon House. I do not yet know whether I shall take or rather whether I can obtain Mr. Ingersoll's house or not. I thought I would have to remain here some days to recruit; but I had scarcely got upon land before I felt perfectly well & have enjoyed my dinner very much,—the first meal for which I felt any appetite since I left New York. I shall write to you again as soon as I am settled at London;—or probably sooner.

    Although I left Wheatland with regret & a heavy heart, yet I am resigned to my destiny, & shall enter upon the performance of my duties, with God's blessing, in a determined & cheerful spirit.

    I received your letter in New York. I had not supposed there was any thing serious in Lily's apprehensions.

    In the midst of calls & engagements, I have not time to write

---

[1] Buchanan Papers, private collection. Imperfectly printed in Curtis's Buchanan, II. 99.

you a longer letter.   Please to keep an eye on Eskridge & James
Reynolds, as you promised.

Give my affectionate regards to Miss Hetty & Eskridge &
remember me to all my friends.   In haste, I remain your affectionate uncle,

JAMES BUCHANAN.

MISS HARRIET LANE.

P. S.   I shall direct this letter to Eskridge, supposing that
you may have left Wheatland before its arrival.   Remember me
very kindly to Mr. Reynolds, Miss Kate, & all the Reynolds.
Remember me affectionately to brother Edward & his family.
Take good care of yourself.   I shall buy a new hat when I reach
London, & do not think my fortune has been spoiled by wearing
the old one hitherto.

TO MR. MARCY.[1]

(No. 4.)   U. STATES LEGATION, LONDON 24 August 1853.
SIR/

I arrived in Liverpool on Wednesday the 17th Instant, & in
this City on the day following.

All the necessary preliminaries having been arranged according to your instructions I was yesterday presented to the
Queen, at her summer residence at Osborne, in the Isle of Wight,
by the Earl of Clarendon, her Majesty's Secretary of State for
Foreign Affairs.   In delivering my letter of credence, I expressed
the desire of the President & people of the United States to promote the most friendly relations with her Majesty's Government;
& said I should be most happy, if, during my mission, I might
prove in any degree instrumental in strengthening & consolidating these relations, so desirable for both nations.   She received
these expressions in a kind & courteous manner, without making
any formal reply.   She, then, inquired for the health of the
President; & asked me if I had ever been in England before.
After I had given appropriate answers to these questions in their
order, the interview terminated.

Mr. Ingersoll & myself went together to Osborne; he to have
his audience of leave, & I to be presented.

My presentation was accompanied with but little formality;

---

[1] MSS. Department of State, 65 Despatches from England.

& was such as is usual when Ministers are presented to the Queen at the summer residence. Indeed, there seemed to be but few persons about the palace; though we were hospitably received & entertained during our brief visit. Had this been postponed until after Friday, it must have been deferred until her Majesty's return from Scotland in November, which would have been a source of much inconvenience.

Although I had considerable conversation with Lord Clarendon, yet no part of it related to political affairs.

It affords me great pleasure to state that Mr. Ingersoll's kindness & attentions towards myself have been all I could have desired. He has conducted himself throughout his Mission in such an acceptable manner as to leave a very favorable impression behind.

I had the honor of receiving your Number 7, of the 30th ultimo, at New York previous to my departure for Liverpool; & I shall look with some degree of anxiety for " the views of the President " in regard to the terms & conditions which he would require in a Treaty with Great Britain for the settlement of the Central American questions; & also, for his authority to present a protest to this Government against their establishment of the Colony of the Bay of Islands.

August 26. The commissions of James M'Dowell, John L. Nelson, & Philip J. Heartt, Esquires, have just been returned to the Legation, together with the Queen's Exequaturs for them to act as Consuls of the United States, respectively, at Leith, Turk's Island, & Glasgow.

Yours very respectfully

JAMES BUCHANAN.

HON: WILLIAM L. MARCY
    Secretary of State.

FROM NATHANIEL HAWTHORNE.

(Enclosure A. 1. in No. 14.[1])

CONSULATE UNITED STATES, LIVERPOOL, 24 Aug. 1853.

SIR,
    I have to request your opinion and advice under the following circumstances.
    The American clipper ship " Sovereign of the Seas " is now loading at this Port for Melbourne, Australia, and with the probability of making a

---

[1] See despatch to Mr. Marcy, No. 14, Nov. 1, 1853, infra.

remarkably quick passage, her commander submitted a proposal to the Post Office authorities to carry out the Mails—the proposal, as I understand, being to take them for £500, guaranteeing to deliver them in Melbourne in 70 days or forfeit £20 for each day beyond that time. This proposal however was rejected, and the Captain stated he should refuse to take them, and was answered that he would be compelled. To-day the enclosed paper, containing extracts of Acts of Parliament relating to the carriage of letters by ship, is sent to the Captain through his agent, and his attention called to the last paragraph, in which is contained the substance of Section 6 of the Act 1 Vict. Cap. 36, as extended by 3 & 4 Vict. Cap. 96, Sect. 37, " and for compelling the observance of the Provisions of the Post Office Laws relating to the conveyance of ship letters, be it enacted that every master of a vessel outward bound who shall refuse to take a Port letter Bag delivered or tendered to him by an Officer of the Post Office for conveyance shall forfeit two hundred pounds; " and he appeals to me to be advised whether he being an American vessel can be compelled to carry the British Mail, whether the Act in question extends to American vessels.

As it is a new question involving points of considerable doubt and delicacy, and it may be of some importance to American commerce, I have to submit it to you and request your opinion and advice.

On first view it does seem to me to be a hardship, and withal an injustice, that the English Government should compel an American vessel to carry mails on such terms as it shall deem fitting to prescribe, yet if such be the law—if the Act really does extend to American vessels as well as British, it will be for me to advise a strict compliance, until mutual negotiation shall provide a remedy.

The ship sails on the 3 of September, so that I will thank you for a reply accordingly.

With high respect I have the honor to be
Your obd. Servt.
(sd.)   N. HAWTHORNE.

TO LORD CLARENDON.

(Enclosure B. 2. in No. 14.[1])
UNITED STATES LEGATION, 25th August, 1853.
MY LORD,

I have the honor to inform you that Mr. Ingersoll has just delivered to me a communication from the Consul of the United States at Liverpool, dated on the 24th Inst., from which it appears that the Post Office Authorities at that place have claimed the right to compel the Captain of the American Clipper Ship the " Sovereign of the Seas," now loading a cargo in Liverpool for Melbourne, to carry a British Mail from the former to the latter port.

---

[1] See despatch to Mr. Marcy, No. 14, Nov. 1, 1853, infra.

The Consul asks for information on the subject, and I would respectfully request to be informed whether the Postmaster General is of opinion that such a right exists. As the vessel will sail from Liverpool on the 3d Sept., I should esteem it a favor if Your Lordship would communicate this information to me in time to transmit it to Liverpool before that day.

I have the honor to be, with great consideration,
Your Lordship's most obedient servant,
(sd.) JAMES BUCHANAN.

THE RIGHT HONORABLE THE EARL OF CLARENDON.
&c. &c. &c.

TO MISS LANE.[1]

CLARENDON HOTEL, LONDON, 26 August, 1853.
MY DEAR HARRIET/
I have received your letter written a few days after my departure from New York, which is mislaid for the moment; and it afforded me great pleasure. It is the only letter which I have yet received from the United States.

I was presented to the queen at Osborne in the Isle of Wight on Tuesday last by the Earl of Clarendon, & delivered her my letter of credence. She has not many personal charms; but is gracious & dignified in her manners & her character is without blemish. The interview was brief. Mr. Ingersoll,[2] who accompanied me to take his leave, & myself lunched at the palace with Lord Clarendon and several of the attachés of Royalty. His conduct towards me is all I could have desired; & Miss Wilcox is a very nice girl.[3] They will pay a short visit to Paris & the continent & return to the United States in October.

You have lost nothing by not coming to England with me. Parliament adjourned on last Saturday; and this was the signal for the nobility & gentry to go to their estates in the country. There they will remain until next February & in the mean time London will be very dull. All gaiety in town is at an end & has been transferred to the estates & country seats throughout the kingdom.

---

[1] Buchanan Papers, private collection. Imperfectly printed in Curtis's Buchanan, II. 100.
[2] Mr. Buchanan's predecessor as minister to England.
[3] A niece of Mr. Ingersoll.

I have not yet procured a house; but hope to do so next week. I have just paid my bill for the first week at this Hotel. I have two rooms & a chamber, have had no company to dine & have dined at home but three days & the amount is £14 7s. 6d., equal to nearly $75.00.

It is my desire to see you happily married, because should I be called away your situation would not be agreeable. Still you would have plenty. Whilst these are my sentiments, however, I desire that you shall exercise your own deliberate judgment in the choice of a husband. View steadily all the consequences, ask the guidance of Heaven & make up your own mind; & I shall be satisfied. A competent independence is a good thing, if it can be obtained with proper affection; though I should not care for fortune, provided the man of your choice was in a thriving & profitable business & possessed a high and fair character. I had not supposed there was any thing serious in the conversation; certainly none of your relatives can interpose any just objection. Be, however, fully persuaded in your own mind & act after due reflection; & may God guide you!

It will require some time to reconcile me to this climate. We have none of the bright & glorious sun & the clear blue sky of the United States; but neither have we the scorching heat, nor the mosquitoes. I have slept comfortably under a blanket ever since I have been here; & almost every man you meet carries an umbrella. The winters, however, are not cold.

Society is in a most artificial position. It is almost impossible for an untitled individual who does not occupy an official position to enter the charmed circle. The richest & most influential merchants & bankers are carefully excluded. It is true as we learned that the niece of a minister at the head of his establishment does not enjoy his rank. At a dinner party, for example, whilst he goes to the head of the table, she must remain at or near the foot. Still, Miss Wilcox has made her way to much consideration, admiration, & respect.

The rage which seems to pervade the people of the United States for visiting Europe is wonderful. It takes up much time at the legation to issue passports. London, however, is but a stopping place. They generally rush to Paris & the continent; & this, too, wisely I have no doubt. I would not myself tarry at London longer than to see the sights. My promise to you shall be kept inviolate; and yet I have no doubt a visit to Europe with an agreeable party would be far more instructive & satisfactory to you than to remain for any considerable length of time with me in London. I thank my stars that you did not come with me, for you would have had a dreary time of it for the next six months.

But the Despatches are to be prepared & the Despatch Bag must close at five o'clock for the steamer of tomorrow. I have time to write no more, but to assure you that I am always your affectionate uncle,

JAMES BUCHANAN.

MISS HARRIET LANE.

Remember me most kindly to all my friends & especially to Miss Hetty, should you still be in Lancaster.

TO MR. POOLE.

(Enclosure in No. 6.[1])

LEGATION &c. 29 August 1853.

JOHN POOLE, ESQ.
    "Lloyd's."

SIR,

I have had the honor of receiving your communication of the 27th inst., enclosing a copy of certain Resolutions adopted by "a Public Meeting of Merchants, Underwriters, Ship Owners, Captains, Officers, and others interested in Navigation, held at the Merchants' Room at Lloyd's, on the subject of the offer made by Lieutenant Maury of the United States Navy on behalf of his Government, to furnish copies of his valuable charts and sailing directions to Masters of British Merchant Ships who shall undertake to furnish the results of their observations in the prescribed form."

You may be assured that I shall esteem it both a pleasure and privilege, in compliance with these resolutions, to become the organ of communicating the thanks of the Meeting to the Government of the United States.

Foreign Commerce, by uniting distant Nations and rendering them mutually dependent, has ever proved to be a powerful means of promoting peace and extending civilization throughout

---

[1] Mr. Buchanan's No. 6, Sept. 6, 1853 (65 MS. Despatches from England), transmits this letter to the Department of State, without comment.

the world. Every improvement, therefore, in the science and practice of Navigation is a benefit to all mankind. In this view of the subject, I feel convinced that the President and people of the United States will learn with peculiar satisfaction that the intelligent and powerful class of British Subjects interested in foreign commerce are disposed to co-operate with the Government of the United States in "collecting and disseminating information relative to the direction of winds and Ocean Currents in all parts of the world," which may shorten the duration and diminish the danger of Voyages, and thus render life and property more secure.

With sentiments of high respect,

I remain truly yours

(Sd.)   JAMES BUCHANAN.

TO BARON DE CETTO.

(Enclosure in No. 7.[1])

LEGATION OF THE U. S. August 29, 1853.

Mr. Buchanan presents his compliments to Baron de Cetto, and has the honor to inform him that he has received instructions from the Government of the United States to conclude a Convention with his Excellency, between the United States of America and the Kingdom of Bavaria, for the mutual extradition of fugitives from justice, similar to that which has recently been concluded between the United States and Prussia, of which Mr. Buchanan has now the honor to transmit a copy.

It affords him pleasure also to inform H. E. Baron de Cetto, that the delay to accede to the wish expressed by him to Mr. Lawrence to conclude such a Convention has been solely occasioned by the doubt which existed whether the Senate of the United States would approve the Convention with Prussia. This doubt having now been removed, Mr. Buchanan is prepared at any time after the present week which may suit H. E. Baron de Cetto's convenience to enter upon the business.

Mr. Buchanan avails himself of this opportunity to assure H. E. Baron de Cetto of his high consideration.

HIS EXCELLENCY BARON DE CETTO,

&c., &c., &c.

---

[1] Despatch to Mr. Marcy, No. 7, Sept. 16, 1853, infra.

FROM LORD CLARENDON.

(Enclosure C. 3. in No. 14.[1])

FOREIGN OFFICE, August 30, 1853.

SIR,

I have the honour to acquaint you that immediately upon the receipt of your letter of the 25th instant, I requested the Post Master General to furnish me with information in regard to the Law by which the Captain of the American Clipper Ship, the "Sovereign of the Seas," had been called upon by the Post Office authorities at Liverpool to carry a British Mail Bag from that Port to Melbourne; and I have now the honor of forwarding to you a copy of a Report from the Post Office, by which you will see that the Master of any Ship, whether British or Foreign, is bound, under a Penalty of Two Hundred Pounds, to convey such a Mail bag on receiving the usual gratuities payable for such service.

I have the honor to be with the highest consideration, Sir,

Your most obedient humble servant

(signed)   CLARENDON.

FROM BARON DE CETTO.

(Enclosure with No. 7.[2])

In reply [to Mr. Buchanan's note of the 29th ultimo] Baron de Cetto begs leave to say that he has heard with much gratification of Mr. Buchanan's being authorized to negotiate and sign the Convention above mentioned, and availing himself of His Excellency's kind offer, he takes the liberty of naming Monday next, if convenient to Mr. Buchanan, for the purpose of their meeting together at the place and at the hour His Excellency may be pleased to appoint.

Baron de Cetto has thus fixed upon an early day with a view of making it possible to settle the affair before his departure from England, which is to take place soon on leave of absence.

Baron de Cetto avails himself of this opportunity to assure Mr. Buchanan of his high consideration.

HILL STREET, BERKELEY SQUARE,
August 31, 1853.

HIS EXCELLENCY JAMES BUCHANAN, Esqre.
&c., &c., &c.

---

[1] Despatch to Mr. Marcy, No. 14, Nov. 1, 1853, infra.
[2] Despatch to Mr. Marcy, No. 7, Sept. 16, 1853, infra.

TO MR. HAWTHORNE.

(Enclosure D. 4. in No. 14.[1])

LEGATION OF UNITED STATES

LONDON, 31 Aug. 1853.

SIR,

Immediately upon the receipt of your favor of the 24th Instant, which was handed to me by Mr. Ingersoll, I addressed a note to Lord Clarendon on the 25th, respecting the claim made by the Post Office authorities at Liverpool to compel the Captain of the American Clipper Ship the " Sovereign of the Seas " to carry a British mail from Liverpool to Melbourne. On last evening I received from the Foreign Office an answer enclosing a report from the Post Office Department on the subject, dated on the 29th, from which I make the following extract:—" I am directed by his Lordship to state to you for the information of the Earl of Clarendon that, in the opinion of the Solicitor to this Department to whom the question has been referred, no master of any vessel, British or Foreign, bound from the Port of Liverpool to Australia could refuse to take a Post letter Bag delivered or tendered to him for conveyance by an officer of the Post Office, without incurring a penalty of £200. The usual gratuities would be payable whether the vessel were British or Foreign."

As I intend to investigate this question, I should be glad that you would inform me, after a careful examination, whether this is the first case of the kind which has occurred at Liverpool. It is presumed that as the British Government have opened their coasting trade to Foreign vessels, they deem it but reasonable that in the enjoyment of this trade those vessels should be subject to the same terms and conditions with British vessels. Whether there exists any Act of Parliament to justify the decision of the Post Office Department will be a subject of immediate investigation. In the mean time, I would advise the Captain of the "Sovereign of the Seas " to receive and carry the mail under protest should he deem this expedient.

Yours very respectfully

(signed)   JAMES BUCHANAN.

NATH. HAWTHORNE, ESQ.

U. S. Consul, Liverpool.

---

[1] See despatch to Mr. Marcy, No. 14, Nov. 1, 1853, infra.

TO MR. MARCY.[1]

(No. 5.)   LEGATION OF THE UNITED STATES.
                              LONDON, 2d September 1853.

SIR,

I have the honor to acknowledge your Despatch No. 8, (of the 18th Aug. 1853,) transmitting a Copy of a Despatch dated 16th Feb. 1853, from Lord John Russell to Mr. Crampton. I have also, since my arrival in London, received your No. 3 (of the 6th July) authorising and instructing me to conclude a Convention, on the part of the United States, with the kingdom of Bavaria, for the mutual Extradition of Fugitives from justice, similar to that recently concluded with Prussia, together with a full power for this purpose. The Baron de Cetto & myself have agreed to meet on Monday next to enter upon this business; and as he is very anxious to conclude the Convention, I do not anticipate any delay or difficulty in accomplishing the object.

I would merely observe that during Mr. Polk's administration, the third Article of the present Convention with Prussia, declaring that " none of the contracting parties shall be bound to deliver up its own citizens or subjects," was considered so wanting in real reciprocity, though reciprocal on its face, that for this, as well as for other reasons which I do not now distinctly recollect, we declined to enter into such a Convention with that Power.

As, however, this concession has already been made to Prussia and other States of the Germanic Confederation, it could not well be denied to Bavaria.

I transmit you copies of two notes from the Earl of Clarendon of the 26th and 30th ultimo, the first announcing that directions had been given, by the General Commanding in Chief, for the immediate discharge of Benjamin Wentworth, a citizen of the United States from her Majesty's Service; and the second, that orders had been given by the Lords Commissioners of the Admiralty for the erection of a Light-House at the " Isaacs " on the Bahama Bank.

I have not yet asked an interview with Lord Clarendon; because I expected to receive by Mr. Sickles a Despatch from you, communicating the views of the President in regard to the stipulations which he would deem indispensable in a Treaty with

---

[1] MSS. Department of State, 65 Despatches from England.

Great Britain for the settlement of the Central American questions; & authorising me, should I deem it expedient, to present a protest to this Government against their establishment of the Colony of the Bay of Islands. In this expectation I have been disappointed; but I shall, notwithstanding, request an interview with his Lordship early next week & report to you the result. At this interview, however, I shall feel somewhat embarrassed, for want of the distinct views of the President on these important subjects.

On Wednesday last, the Turkish Minister at this Court, Mr. Musurus, called to see me, & immediately commenced, with the utmost apparent frankness, to converse on the existing difficulties between the Emperor Nicholas & the Sultan. I observed that I presumed the questions between the two Powers might be considered as settled; because the public Journals asserted, that the modifications proposed by the Sublime Porte to the note agreed upon by the four Powers at Vienna were of a character merely formal, & would, therefore, be accepted by the Emperor. He replied that this was a mistake,—that the modifications were of an important character from which the Sultan would never recede, & they were stated to be merely formal by the French & English Journals, so that the Emperor might the more readily give his assent to them. I asked if the Sultan had required that the Emperor should withdraw his forces from the Danubian provinces as a condition of the settlement. He said not;—but that the Sultan would hold the Mediating Powers responsible for this result.

Since our conversation, these modifications have been published, & although they cannot be said to be merely formal, yet, in my opinion, they contain nothing of a very important character. It was the Turkish Minister's opinion there would be no war; & in this I heartily concur. France & England are so much indisposed to go to war with Russia, that they will find means to avert it, even if the Emperor should refuse to accede to the modifications made by the Sublime Porte, which, however, is not anticipated. It is a remarkable fact that whilst the Governments of both France & England admit that the invasion of the Danubian provinces constituted a casus belli, the question is to be settled by a note from the Sultan which makes no mention whatever of this invasion & requires no stipulation, on the part of the Emperor, that he shall withdraw his forces from these Provinces. I ought to add, that it seems to be confidently believed by the Mediating Powers, that the Emperor will withdraw his forces immediately after his acceptance of the note as modified; & they may have private assurances to this effect. But there will be no war, unless the fanaticism of the Turks should unexpectedly compel the Sultan to commence hostilities.

The Turkish Minister expressed great satisfaction with the conduct of Captain Ingraham in the Koszta affair.

Yours very respectfully,

JAMES BUCHANAN.

HON: WILLIAM L. MARCY,
Secretary of State.

TO MR. BROWN.[1]

LEGATION OF THE UNITED STATES.

LONDON 5 September 1853.

SIR/

I have had the honor to receive the Resolution adopted, on the 30th ultimo, by the American Chamber of Commerce at Liverpool, inviting me to a Banquet to be given by them, as a mark of respect & welcome upon my appointment as Minister of the United States of America to England; & requesting me to name a day when it will best suit my convenience to attend.

Whilst highly & gratefully appreciating this honor, I regret that it is impossible for me, with a due regard to my public duties in London, to say when, if at all, their kind invitation could be accepted. I feel, therefore, constrained respectfully to decline it. In doing this, however, I beg to assure them, that no man in either country estimates more highly than myself the commerce conducted between Liverpool & the United States; & no man more ardently desires that this may long continue to extend itself, in peace & security, & to confer mutual benefits upon both nations.

The period in the world's history seems at length to have arrived when mankind have discovered that narrow & unjust restrictions upon foreign trade most surely defeat their own object, & when selfishness itself is enlisted in favor of a liberal policy. The philanthropist, at the same time, rejoices in the knowledge that the mutual dependence which commerce creates between nations is the surest preventive of war, by rendering

---

[1] Buchanan Papers, Historical Society of Pennsylvania.

peace the interest of all.   For my own part, I firmly believe that the unsettled questions known to exist between Great Britain & the United States, judged alone according to the value of the material interests involved, are not worth six months' suspension of the trade between the two Countries.   It is, therefore, greatly to be desired that these questions should be speedily, honorably & finally adjusted; & that hereafter both nations should enjoy a smooth sea & a cloudless sky for a friendly competition in all the pursuits calculated to enlighten & benefit the human race.   The greatest revolution, so far as the interest of commerce & manufactures is concerned, which has ever been commenced among men, is that now in apparently successful progress in China. Should this terminate in opening a free access to that vast empire of three hundred millions of human beings, the United States & Great Britain will have a harvest presented to them, which, even with all their energy, enterprise & resources, they will scarcely be able to reap.   Then will a noble & generous rivalry, also, spring up between them;—which shall contribute most effectually to promote the cause of Christianity, civilisation & freedom among this ancient & strange people.

　　With sentiments of great respect, I remain,
Your obedient servant
JAMES BUCHANAN.
WILLIAM BROWN ESQUIRE M. P.
　　Chairman &c. &c.

TO THE REV. MR. BUCHANAN.[1]

CLARENDON HOTEL, NEW BOND STREET,

LONDON 8 September 1853.

MY DEAR BROTHER/
　　I am now sitting this evening by a good coal fire thinking of you & all at home kindly.   The change of climate has not been pleasant; though I trust I shall soon be acclimated.   From the night of the day after I left New York, (Aug: 6) I have slept comfortably under a blanket & sometimes under two.   This climate is extremely damp.   It rains very often; & almost every decent looking man you meet carries an umbrella to be prepared

---

[1] Buchanan Papers, Historical Society of Pennsylvania.

for a sudden shower. But if we do not here enjoy the bright suns & clear blue sky of our Country, neither do we suffer from the extremes of heat & cold.

This is the dull season in London. The Nobility & gentry are all in the Country & so they will continue to be until near the meeting of Parliament in February next. This will afford me time to bring up my reckoning & I am glad of it.

The expense of living is great, even beyond any estimate I had formed. Myself & my servant cost me at this Hotel from $80 to $90 per week. I have three rooms. I have been engaged in looking out for a furnished house; but although there are plenty to let, I have not yet found one in all respects suitable.

I regret that circumstances compelled me to accept this mission; yet with the blessing of God, I intend to make the best of it & render myself as comfortable & happy as possible. Independently of the important business there is much to do here; but I think I have been fortunate in the Secretary of Legation & Private Secretary. To be sure, they are somewhat green yet; but they both have capacity & all they want is training.

I shall send you by the next Despatch Bag the London Morning Post of yesterday containing a charge of the Archbishop of Canterbury to his clergy; which I have no doubt will interest you.

The devotion and loyalty of these people to their Queen & "defender of the Faith" is enthusiastic & almost unanimous. Her personal character & conduct are indeed exemplary; but after all, she is little more than a mere pageant, the real power being in the hands of the responsible ministry. My interview with her was but brief. Her manners are gracious & dignified, though she has not many personal charms.

Of the Cabinet Ministers I have only seen the Earl of Clarendon, & Lord Palmerston. With the latter, who came two days [ago] from the Country, I have had a very free & friendly conversation. He is a dashing character & the ablest Debater in the House of Commons.

I hope that ere this James may have commenced his studies, either at Pittsburg or Lancaster.

Last Sunday week I attended Langham Church, a fashionable Episcopal Church, in company with a wealthy Banker & his lady: & was rather pleased with the exercises though the church had something of a Catholic appearance. I confess, however, that when in looking over the Peerage, I found that many of the nobles had from 5 to 20 & even thirty livings in their gift, my Republican spirit was vexed at this abuse.

Last Sunday I went to Great Russell Street to hear Dr. Cummins—a celebrated preacher of the Free Church of Scotland. I, there, felt myself more at home. He did not preach, though we had a good Presbyterian sermon & a running exposition of the chapter which preceded it. We had the old version of David's Psalms; & it would have done Dr. Sample's heart good to hear the style of the singing. I have not the slightest objection to the Episcopal Church in the United States. Far, very far from it; yet early associations attach me to the Presbyterian form. I desire to be a good Christian; & shall make it a point to attend some church every Sunday, unless something particular should prevent.

Please to remember me most kindly to Dr. Sample & the Lightners, with Mrs. Dale. I presume Isaac is now in Washington. Also to Miss Hetty & Eskridge, should you see them. Give my love to Anne Eliza & the children & believe me ever to be your affectionate brother

JAMES BUCHANAN.

REV: EDWARD Y. BUCHANAN.

Please to give the Post to Mrs. Bowman with my kind respects.

FROM MR. HAWTHORNE.

(Enclosure E. 5. in No. 14.[1])

CONSULATE OF THE UNITED STATES.
LIVERPOOL 9th Sept. 1853.

SIR,

Referring to my communication of the 24th Aug., and your reply thereto of the 31st of Aug., I now beg to inform you that, acting on your advice, Capt: Warner, of the "Sovereign of the Seas," received the Letter Bags tendered him by the Post Office, under Protest. Herewith I forward you a copy of the Protest he deemed it proper to make before me.

I cannot find that any previous case of the kind has occurred at Liverpool.

For the voyage to the United States, and until recently American vessels rarely sailed from Liverpool for any other port, the prescribed compensation of two pence a letter was deemed sufficient, and as I understand it was a perquisite of the Captain, no dissatisfaction would be likely to be felt. The raising of the question seems owing to the opening of the Australia and

---

[1] Despatch to Mr. Marcy, No. 14, Nov. 1, 1853, infra.

India trade to American vessels—to the much greater cost of the vessels engaged in it, and the much longer voyage and higher rates of freight, coupled with the facts that the British Government frequently pays large sums for conveyance of the mails to Australia by private vessels, and that a sum so paid would go to the owner of the vessel; and I understand that it was at the instance of the owner of the "Sovereign of the Seas" and his agent that the proposition and objection respecting the carrying of the mails were first made.

What national or higher interests are involved in the question thus raised, you are a better judge of than I can be, but it is desirable that the right in the matter should be settled and understood.

With high respect I have the honor to be

Your obed. servt.

(sd.) N. HAWTHORNE.

TO MISS LANE.[1]

CLARENDON HOTEL, LONDON 15 September 1853.

MY DEAR HARRIET/

On the day before yesterday I received your kind letter of the 28 August, with a letter from Mary which I have already answered. How rejoiced I am that she is contented & happy in San Francisco! I also received your favor of the 18 August in due time. I write to you this evening; because I have important Despatches to prepare for the Department tomorrow, to be sent by Saturday's steamer.

How rejoiced I am that you did not come with me! Perceiving your anxiety, I was several times on the point of saying to you, come along; but you would see nearly as much fashionable society at Wheatland, as you would see here until February or March next. You cannot conceive how dull it is; though personally I am content. The *beau monde* are all at their country-seats or on the continent, there to remain until the meeting of Parliament. But what is worse than all, I have not yet been able to procure a house in which I would consent to live. I have looked at a great many,—the houses of the nobility & gentry; but the furniture in all of them is old, decayed, & wretched & with very few exceptions, they are *very, very dirty*. I can account for this in no other manner than that they are not willing to rent them until the furniture is worn out, & that London is for them like a great watering place from about the first of March until the

---

[1] Buchanan Papers, private collection. Imperfectly printed in Curtis's Buchanan, II. 101–103.

first of August. This hotel, which is the most fashionable in London, is not nearly equal to the first hotels in Philadelphia & New York; & yet the cost of living at it, with two rooms & a chamber is about $90 per week. The enormous expense [here] and the superior attractions [there] drive all the American travellers to Paris & the continent. The *London Times* has taken up the subject & is now daily comparing the superior cheapness & superior accommodations of the Hotels in the United States with those of London. Here there are no *table-d'hôtes* & the house may be full without your knowing who is in it.

I think I have a treasure in the servant (Jackson) I brought with me from New York. If he should only hold out, he is all I could desire.

Mr. Welsh surpasses my expectations as a man of business. Colonel Lawrence, the attaché without pay, is industrious, gentlemanly, & has been highly useful. He knows everybody, & works as though he received $10,000 per annum. I venture to say I have as able & useful a legation as any in London. Lawrence has gone to Scotland in company with Miss Chapman & her father, & I think he is much pleased with her. In truth, she is a nice girl & very handsome. The Chapmans will return immediately to the United States.

The Marchioness of Wellesley is suffering from the dropsy & she, with her sister Lady Stafford, remained a few days at this house. I saw a good deal of them whilst they were here; & they have been very, very kind to me. They love to talk about America & they yet appear to have genuine American hearts. Lady Wellesley lives at Hampton Court,—the old historic palace about fifteen miles from London erected by Cardinal Wolsey, & I am going there to dine with them & see the palace on Saturday. I shall take Sickles & Welsh with me, according to Lady Wellesley's special request, though she does not know them. The Duchess of Leeds is in Scotland.

These three American girls have had a strange fate. Many of their sex have envied them; but I think without cause. They are all childless & would, I verily believe, have been more happy had they been united to independent & intelligent gentlemen in their own country. It is impossible to conceive of a more elegant & accomplished lady than Lady Wellesley; & although bowed down by disease she still retains the relics of her former beauty. Her younger sister, Betsy Caton (Lady Stafford), the belle of belles in her day in America, has become gross & does not retain

a trace of her good looks except a cheerful and animated countenance. She is evidently a fine woman & very much a Catholic
devotee. They are all widows except the Duchess of Leeds.

Rank, rank is every thing in this country. My old friend
of twenty years ago, Mrs. Bates, the wife of the partner of the
great House of Baring Brothers & Co., & then a nice little
Yankee woman who had never been at court, continually talks
to me now about the duchess of this & the countess of that &
the Queen. Lords & Ladies afford her a constant theme. Her
daughter & only child, who will be immensely rich, is the wife of
the Belgian minister, & this has given her a lift. She is still,
however, the same good kind hearted woman she was in the
ancient time; but has grown very large. They are now at their
country-seat at East Sheen in the vicinity of London,—her husband's business preventing her from going far away. I have
now nearly finished my sheet. I have not yet had time to see any
of the Lions. God bless you! Remember me kindly to Mrs.
Hunter. I have written to Clemmie since I have been here.

From yr. affectionate uncle,

JAMES BUCHANAN.

MISS HARRIET LANE.

TO LORD CLARENDON.

(Enclosure F. 6. in No. 14.[1])

UNITED STATES LEGATION.

LONDON, 16 Sept. 1853.

MY LORD,

I have the honor of communicating to you the copy of a
protest made on the 6th inst. before the United States Consul at
Liverpool, by Henry Warner, the Master of the American Ship
" Sovereign of the Seas," against the action of the Post Office
Authorities at that place in compelling him to carry a British
mail to Australia.

The Consul informed me that so far as he can ascertain,
this is the first case of the kind that has ever occurred at Liverpool, and in reporting it to the Government at Washington, I
desire to accompany it with all the necessary explanations.

The Question is one of much interest, particularly to the

---

[1] Despatch to Mr. Marcy, No. 14, Nov. 1, 1853, infra.

owners of our fast sailing Clipper Ships, built at very great expense, who naturally desire to realize all the advantages which fairly belong to them, from the superior swiftness of their vessels.

Under these circumstances, I must beg Your Lordship to procure for me a reference from the Postmaster General to the Act or Acts of Parliament on which the opinion of the Solicitor of that Department, communicated to you, on the 29th ultimo, was founded; that " no master of any vessel, British or Foreign, bound from the Port of Liverpool to Australia, could refuse to take a Post Letter Bag, delivered or tendered to him for conveyance by an Officer of the Post Office, without incurring a penalty of £200." Should this reference be accompanied by a brief explanation concerning the application of the law, and of the penalty to Foreign, as well as to British vessels, it would be still more satisfactory.

If American vessels are required by law, upon clearing from a British Port, to carry British mails to their Ports of destination, it is proper that this should be made known to those interested in the United States, so that they may regulate their conduct accordingly; and thus future trouble be prevented.

I have the honor to be with great consideration
Your Lordship's most obedient servant,
(sd.) JAMES BUCHANAN.

TO MR. MARCY.[1]

(No. 7.)   LEGATION OF THE UNITED STATES.
LONDON, 16th September 1853.
SIR/
I have the honor to acknowledge the receipt of your despatch No. 9, of the 24th ultimo, with the commission of George N. Sanders, Esquire, as Consul of the United States for the Port of London, and to inform you that application has already been made for his Exequatur.

I transmit to you herewith, a convention " for the mutual Extradition of Fugitives from justice, in certain cases," between the United States and Bavaria, which was signed at this Legation on the 12th Instant by Baron de Cetto, the Bavarian Minister in London, and myself. I also transmit a copy of my note to

---
[1] MSS. Department of State, 65 Despatches to England.

Baron de Cetto, of the 29th ultimo, and of his answer of the 31st.[1] These are the only notes of the least importance which passed between us.

Upon examination you will find that this Convention has been drawn in strict conformity with your instructions of the 6th July, and is, in every essential particular, a transcript of our recent Convention on the same subject with Prussia. The verbal variations in the preamble and at the commencement of the first Article were assented to by me in consequence of the strong desire expressed by the Baron, proceeding evidently from national jealousy, that our Convention with Bavaria should not be an exact copy of that with Prussia.

I proposed to him to omit the second article, providing " that the stipulations of this Convention shall be applied to any other State of the Germanic Confederation which may hereafter declare its accession thereto," and asked him whether there were any and what German States who might probably desire to avail themselves of this concession. He answered that Wurtemberg and Hanover and other States might possibly wish to declare their accession to our Convention with Bavaria. I informed him that I had no doubt the Government of the United States would be willing to conclude a similar Convention with either Wurtemberg or Hanover; and that these States could, in my opinion, derive but little benefit from their accession to this Convention, because the act of accession, whatever this might be, must first be ratified by the President and Senate, in order to render it effectual. I also observed that an unhappy misunderstanding now existed between the United States and Austria which might possibly present difficulties to the ratification of a Convention by the President and Senate, which would enable that Power to advance a claim to be placed on the same footing with Bavaria. He replied that I need have no fears on that account. Austria considered herself too great and was too proud to declare her accession to a Convention concluded by any Power but herself. He said he had himself suggested to his Government that the second article might be omitted as unnecessary; but they had objected to it, believing that the United States ought to place Bavaria in this respect on the same footing with Prussia. He added that Austria might at present, if she were so disposed, accede to our Convention with Prussia; and that therefore no

---

[1] For these notes, see the proper dates, supra.

possible inconvenience could result from placing Bavaria on the same footing with that Power.

I informed him that Mr. Polk's administration had serious objections to the conclusion of a Treaty of Extradition with Prussia and the other German States, chiefly because these States insisted upon refusing to deliver up their own subjects who might commit crimes in the United States and escape to their respective countries. He said that the constitution and laws of Bavaria and all the German States prohibited their Governments from surrendering their own subjects to be tried before a foreign jurisdiction, and besides, that the Convention would be strictly reciprocal as it did not require the United States to deliver up their citizens. I observed that this reciprocity was more nominal than real;—whilst the emigration of Bavarian subjects to the United States was very great, but few American citizens visited Bavaria. I said, however, that the Government of the United States had overcome this objection in regard to Prussia and they were willing now to place Bavaria on the same footing.

The Baron is a frank and kind-hearted German, and has been long the Minister at this Court. He seems to be very favorably disposed to our country, and was evidently much gratified that he had signed as Plenipotentiary the first Treaty between Bavaria and the United States. He has obtained a leave of absence for two months, and left London for Munich on Tuesday last, carrying with him the Convention.

I can conceive that serious difficulties may arise from Extradition Conventions, especially when concluded with nations from which there is a large emigration to the United States, by a departure from the rule of surrendering fugitives from justice, no matter to what country they belong, to be tried under the jurisdiction where the crime was committed.

The Emperor of Russia has refused to accept the modifications made by the Sublime Porte to the note of the Four Mediating Powers. Notwithstanding this refusal, I still entertain the opinion expressed to you in my despatch of the 6th instant, that "there will be no war, unless the fanaticism of the Turks should compel the Sultan to commence hostilities." The danger appears to me to be chiefly from this quarter. The Turks have made great preparations; and in doing this have exhausted the resources of the Empire. There are many skilful foreign officers in their service; and they are now probably better prepared for the inevitable struggle than they will be at any future period. Besides, the ancient Mussulman fanaticism has been aroused to the highest pitch against the Russians; and the Turkish troops are anxious to commence hostilities. There is a large and formidable war party in the Divan; and it is believed by many that should the Sultan now be prevailed upon to withdraw his modifications to the note of the mediating Powers and consent to transmit it to Russia in its original form, whilst the Russian troops still occupy Moldavia and Wallachia, his head will be in danger. Still France and Great Britain will exhaust every effort of diplomacy to avert hostilities.

I have lost or mislaid my despatch No. 1, and have never received your No. 4. I would thank you to send me copies of them; and also of all the Consular Regulations of the Department now in force. I have often occasion for these last in my correspondence with our consuls.

I have not yet asked an interview with Lord Clarendon for the purpose of talking over the Central American question, concluding, upon reflection, it was most judicious to await the arrival of the Baltic in the certain expectation that I should then receive your promised instructions together with my full power to conclude a Treaty upon this subject. In this expectation I have been disappointed, and I shall to-morrow ask an interview with his Lordship, though my conversation with him cannot be of that specific and frank character which, I am well persuaded, is best calculated to produce an effect upon this Government.

Yours very respectfully
JAMES BUCHANAN.

HON: WILLIAM L. MARCY
    Secretary of State.

TO MR. MARCY.[1]

(No. 8.)   LEGATION OF THE UNITED STATES.
LONDON, 22 Sept. 1853.

SIR,
    I have the honor to acknowledge the receipt, on the 19th instant, of your despatch, No. 10, of the 2nd, enclosing a copy of the draft of a Treaty submitted to Mr. Crampton on the 1st;

---

[1] MSS. Department of State, 65 Despatches from England.

also of your explanatory communication to him of the same date.

I called on the Earl of Clarendon yesterday at the Foreign Office by appointment.

After mutual salutations, he said he would have called to see me in a friendly way before this time; but his family were in the country and he was with them as much as possible; and whilst in town, they were all worried with the Russian and Turkish question. I answered that I should most probably have called to see him at an earlier day but for this question. I knew how much of their time and attention it occupied, and I had waited until it should be settled; but as this still appeared to be remote, I had determined to wait no longer. He shrugged his shoulders, and observed emphatically that the question now looked squally. They had had a great deal of trouble with it. They had done all they could to save Turkey. The Sultan ought to have been satisfied with the note prepared by the Four Powers. It was true the Emperor of Russia had behaved badly. He had violated existing Treaties, and exposed Europe to the danger of a general war, which, if once commenced, God only knew where it would end.

I remarked that for some time it had appeared to me the danger of war proceeded from the Sultan rather than the Czar;—that the fanaticism of the Turks now seemed to be excited to the very highest degree,—that their army breathed nothing but war against Russia, and that the Sultan might be in personal danger were he now to recede from the modifications he had proposed to the note of the four Powers. His Lordship replied that this was indeed the source of the greatest danger. The Sultan had collected a large body of wild troops from Asia, inspired with fanatical zeal, who would not be willing to return home without a fight; and on both sides they were almost equally barbarians.

I told him that when I was in Russia, twenty years ago, the Emperor had treated me with great personal kindness and had occasionally conversed with me freely; that I considered him one of the ablest men I had ever met, and his manners and conversation were well calculated to give him great personal influence over all those whom he desired to please and conciliate.

His Lordship said this was very true; he was a very able man, had great powers of persuasion, and could render himself very agreeable when he chose.—I proceeded:—when I was in Russia, from the very highest to the lowest, they all looked with intense zeal to the recovery of the Church of St. Sophia, which

they considered the original seat of their holy religion, from the
possession of the Turks;—that, in fact, the Catholic Christians
could not feel greater anxiety for the recovery of St. Peter's at
Rome, were it in the hands of the infidels, than the Greek Christians did to re-possess St. Sophia at Constantinople. Now it
might be a question whether the Emperor Nicholas, all powerful
as he was, after stimulating this religious zeal among his subjects
and taking possession of the Principalities, could with safety retrace his steps.

He said that the Emperor had indeed done all he could to
make his subjects believe that the Greek Church was in danger;
but, his Lordship added, his advices from St. Petersburg were
that the Emperor's efforts had failed. They said there, in regard
to the danger of the Greek Church,—and then he hesitated:—
they said, in plain terms, it is a lie;—it is all a lie.

I expressed my regret at the statement contained in the Post
of this morning, and hoped that it was without foundation. If it
were true, the affair did, indeed, look " squally." He said he had
not seen the Post; he had heard there was an article in it on the
Russian and Turkish question, but had not learned what it contained. I said I would tell him, without any desire to elicit a
response from him, in which, as American Minister, I had no
immediate concern. The statement was that the Russian Government had assigned as one reason for not accepting the note as
modified by the Turks, that the original note prepared by the
Four Powers had, in substance, contained all the concessions
which the Emperor required through Prince Menschikoff, and
that viewing it in this light, the Emperor had been satisfied with
it. This appeared to disturb his Lordship; and from his reply
I understood him to say that the British Government had no
such information; but of this I am not positive. (It would place
both England and France in an awkward predicament if it should
appear that the Emperor and the Sultan both attached the same
meaning to the note of the Four Powers,—a meaning so much
at variance with the professed intention of the British and French
Governments.)

I observed it was fortunate for the cause of peace that the
Danube was between the opposing forces. Yes, said he, if it had
not been for this, they would have been at it long ago.

He was evidently full of the subject; but I took occasion to
change it.

I told him that my principal object in requesting this interview was to inform him that the President of the United States had confided to me the task of settling with him, if this were possible, the questions pending between the two Governments in relation to Central America.   It was not my purpose at this time to enter into any discussion of these questions; but merely to introduce the subject to his notice.

He said he feared we would have great difficulty in settling these questions;—the two Governments seemed to differ widely on this subject.   That for their part, they would gladly get clear of their Mosquito Protectorate,—it was of no advantage to them; but that for a period of two or three hundred years they had exercised this Protectorate, and that the honor of Great Britain required they should not abandon the Mosquitos, without proper attention to their interests.

I replied that upon this point the two Governments did indeed differ widely.   That the American Government was entirely convinced that even if the British Government had formerly any claims to the Mosquito Protectorate, they had entirely and explicitly abandoned them by their Treaties with Spain of 1783 and 1786.   He said there were two opinions on this subject, and that since the date of those Treaties they had resumed their protectorate.   I replied, that this, I believed, they had only done at a recent period.   We then agreed that we would not enter upon the discussion of this or any other of the questions at the present time; for which he was evidently unprepared.

I then told him I would state the fact, that the Senate of the United States, at their last Session, had before them a proclamation dated at Belize in July, 1852, from which it appeared that the British Government had established a new Colony of " The Bay Islands " on the Coast of Honduras, since the date of the Clayton and Bulwer Treaty, and that it seemed to be the opinion of that body, so far as I knew, without dissent, that this Colony had been established in direct violation of that Treaty.   That if this Colony had been established, it would tend very much to complicate the questions between the two Countries.   He answered that he knew nothing about the establishment of such a Colony,—that he was wholly unprepared to say whether it had or had not been established; but would inform me the next time we met.   He then asked what Islands they were.   I told him Ruatan and other smaller Islands in its vicinity.   He said he thought Ruatan had long been in possession of the British.   I observed that this would also be disputed; but in any event, I conceived that the establishment of this Colony, subsequent to the date of the Clayton and Bulwer Treaty, was a plain violation of its terms. I hoped it had not been established. It was not mentioned among their Colonies in the British Imperial Calendar for 1853; and that the Senate had not had before them any official evidence of the fact; but had asked upon such information as seemed to be entirely satisfactory.

He then took a memorandum from me of the proclamation purporting to have been issued on the 17th July, 1852, by "Augustus Frederick Gore, Acting Colonial Secretary." I requested him, if such a Colony had been established, to send me a copy of the official act,—which he promised to do.

His Lordship then branched off, I suppose in consequence of my reference to the proceedings of the Senate in regard to the Bay Islands, & said he was extremely sorry to remark, that the Speakers in our Senate & House of Representatives, particularly the latter, were in the habit of indulging in offensive remarks against Great Britain, calculated to excite unfriendly feelings between the two Countries, which ought always to be good friends. That no member of the House of Lords or House of Commons ever indulged in similar remarks against the United States. If any one of them should attempt to do so, he would meet the strongest marks of reprobation. That in fact it would not be tolerated.

I answered that his Lordship knew well how to make the proper allowance for freedom of discussion in a Legislative Assembly under a free Government. Besides, that unfortunately, ever since my entrance into public life, there had been a continued succession of irritating questions between the two governments, which kept unpleasant feelings alive without intermission. That at the present moment, I was sorry to say, there were many such in existence. Yes, he observed, there was a plentiful crop of them at present, for which he was, also, very sorry;—I continued, it was the desire of the President that all these should be amicably and honorably settled, so that the two countries might make a fresh and propitious start.

I observed, there was one question which had been incessant in its operation and kept alive a constant irritation of feeling in the United States. The Congress of the United States had no more power to interfere with or to abolish the Institution of Slavery in the several States than had the Parliament of Great Britain. He said emphatically he knew that was the case, he knew it well; and yet, I continued, that ever since the establishment of the British Anti-Slavery Society and their associate Societies of Abolitionists in the United States, they had kept up an incessant war upon this subject. These fanatics ought to know and could not but know, that they were adopting the most effectual means of defeating their own avowed object. They had exasperated the feelings of the citizens of the Slave-holding States by their violent and abusive interference in this question, and had thus succeeded in defeating all hopes of emancipation by the only Powers on earth who had any rightful authority over the subject. He observed earnestly, that this was a necessary consequence of their proceedings. I resumed,—Before this Anti-Slavery agitation commenced, about the year 1832 or 1833, a grandson of Mr. Jefferson, Col. Randolph, had introduced into the House of Delegates of Virginia, a proposition for the gradual abolition of Slavery in that important State,—that many of the leading men in the Legislature of Virginia sustained the measure warmly and strongly, that it was deliberately and temperately discussed, and that the mover entertained strong hopes of carrying it at no distant period. In the mean time the British Anti-Slavery Society, and other Societies of a kindred character, had interposed their baneful efforts, and such had been the effect that Col. Randolph himself had assured me, some years ago, he could not now introduce a similar proposition without danger of subjecting himself to personal violence.

I observed that if this question had been left to the citizens of the several sovereign States, to whom it alone belonged, many persons believed that, ere this, laws would have existed in some of the more northern slave-holding States for the gradual abolition of slavery.

We conversed for some time longer in the same strain,—when, just at the moment I was about to proceed, in the execution of your instructions, to ascertain, if possible, the designs of Great Britain in relation to slavery in Cuba, the Earl of Aberdeen was most unfortunately announced. This was the signal to me for retiring. I knew that the attempt would be vain to continue the conversation at this moment—the very crisis of the Russian and Turkish question in which all their feelings are enlisted, whilst the Premier was in waiting for an audience. Lord Clarendon said he was sorry for the interruption,—that he would take the liberty in a few days of addressing me a note requesting me to call at the Foreign Office, when we could continue our conversation; and he expected to be then better posted up than he was at present.

I think I cannot be mistaken in supposing that my conversation on the subject of British interference with Slavery in the United States made a considerable impression on his Lordship.

Lord Clarendon is an experienced and able statesman, whose manners are frank, courteous, and agreeable; but he did not appear to me to possess an intellect of the highest order.

I have received Her Majesty's Exequatur for Mr. George N. Sanders, appointed by the President Consul of the United States for the Port of London.

Yours Very Respectfully,

JAMES BUCHANAN.

HON: WILLIAM L. MARCY
    Secretary of State.

TO MISS LANE.[1]

LEGATION OF THE UNITED STATES.
LONDON 30 September 1853.

MY DEAR HARRIET/

I have a few minutes to spare before the Despatch Bag closes, & I devote them to writing a line to you.   I have received your very kind & acceptable letter of the 14 September from Charlestown, & cordially thank you for the agreeable & interesting information which it contains.

I have not yet obtained a house.   It seems impossible to procure one in every respect suitable for myself & the Legation for less than from $3500 to $4500.   The expense of living in this country exceeds even what I had anticipated.   I paid the Bill for Messrs. Sickles, Welsh, & myself this morning at the Hotel, & it amounted for one week to $150; & we live plainly.   I shall preserve my Hotel Bills as curiosities.

I did not suppose that your name had reached thus far.   I dined the other day at Hampton Court with Ladies Wellesley & Stafford.   Mr. & Mrs. Woodville of Baltimore were present. Mrs. Woodville said she did not know you herself; but her youngest son was well acquainted with you & spoke of you in the

---

[1] Buchanan Papers, private collection.   Imperfectly printed in Curtis's Buchanan, II. 103.

very highest terms. I found she had previously been saying pretty things of you to the two ladies.

Col: Sickles is a very agreeable as well as an able man. He possesses much energy of character, & will make a favorable impression here. I think it will not be long before his lady follows him; & he is evidently very anxious for this result. I am entirely willing;—though not that they should live in the house with me. I understand she is an only child, & so is Col: Sickles. Their respective parents are quite rich, but I do not think that the Col: has a large income.

Mr. Welsh is industrious, agreeable, & performs his duties to my entire satisfaction. He greatly exceeds my expectations.

I shrewdly suspect that Miss Chapman has made a conquest of Col: Lawrence. He went off with her & her father on a visit to Scotland; & I shall not be much surprised if it should be a match, though I know nothing. The Col: is quite deaf, which is very much against him.

She is delighted with her travels, is very handsome, & has a great deal of vivacity. Upon the whole I was much pleased with her.

I am sorry I have not time to write you a longer letter. Remember me very kindly to our friends in Virginia. May God bless you!

Yours very affectionately
JAMES BUCHANAN.

MISS HARRIET LANE.

TO MR. HOLMES.

(Enclosure in No. 26.[1])

UNITED STATES LEGATION.

LONDON, 4 October 1853.

SIR,

I have received your communication of the 18th July with its enclosures, and, also, that of the 20th August with its enclosure, the latter on the 29th ultimo, relating to the arrest and imprisonment of Captain Oliver N. Jenkins, Master of the American Barque " Peytona " at the Cape of Good Hope; and have carefully perused all these documents.

---

[1] Despatch No. 26, March 24, 1854, infra.

In yours of the 18th July you inform me that you " have sent copies of all the documents to the Honorable Secretary of State at Washington." But for this information, I should have promptly answered your first communication. I shall now await instructions from the Department of State, especially as I perceive the case of Captain Jenkins has become a subject of discussion in the public Journals of the United States. In the mean time, however, I deem it proper to make some general suggestions which may be useful to you, without entering into the merits of this particular case.

It is an established principle of public law, that the maritime territory of every State extends to its own ports and to the distance of a marine league from its shores. Within these limits its jurisdiction is absolute and excludes that of every other nation. This jurisdiction is sometimes limited by Treaty, and a portion of it is conferred upon foreign Consuls over the vessels and crews of their respective Nations. Such a Treaty now exists between France and the United States; but we have no similar Treaty with Great Britain.

The proper exercise or the abuse of this jurisdiction is another question; and yet it must be an aggravated case in which one nation could appeal to the Government of another and demand redress for an injury sustained by one of its citizens arising out of a proceeding against him in a Court of Justice. In all my experience I have never known a demand on the Government of the United States for redress arising from the acts and decisions of our Courts of Justice against any Master of a foreign vessel or other person connected with it, within any of our Sea Ports. The Executive branch of our Government is entirely distinct from the Judiciary; and any attempt of the former to interfere with the latter, in any manner whatever, would be a gross violation of duty. Indeed, I do not know that such an attempt has ever been made.

I am far from saying either that a case of this kind may not occur in which it would be the duty of the Government of the United States to interfere nor do I say that the case of Captain Jenkins is not of such a character. There were circumstances attending it, especially in regard to his imprisonment, of a character well calculated to enlist your sympathy and arouse your exertions; and the spirit and energy which you displayed in his behalf are commendable. In any event, they cannot fail to have a good effect. It was a case of cruel and unjust oppression proceeding from a writ of arrest obtained by the perjury of the Plaintiff in the cause and his associates; and yet in justice to the Court, it must be observed, that they quashed the writ and discharged Captain Jenkins, as soon as the true statement of the facts was brought to their knowledge.

Should the Secretary of State instruct me to demand redress for Captain Jenkins from the British Government, I shall do this, in the most effective manner within my power.

Yours very respectfully
(signed)   JAMES BUCHANAN.

G. S. HOLMES, ESQ.
   U. S. Consul, Malta.

TO MR. MARCY.[1]

(No. 10.)   LEGATION OF THE UNITED STATES.

LONDON, 7 October 1853.

SIR,

I have the honor to acknowledge the receipt of your No. 11 of the 12th ultimo, with the Full power, and your No. 13 of the 19th ultimo.   Your No. 12 has not yet arrived, unless the blank envelope containing copies of the Claims Convention between Great Britain and the United States may have been so numbered.

I informed you in my Despatch No. 9 that on the abrupt conclusion of our interview on the 22 ultimo, Lord Clarendon informed me that in a few days he would request me to call at the Foreign Office, when we could continue our conversation.

He has not since made any such request; and I have not deemed it politic or proper as yet to ask another interview.   The truth is, he has been so much occupied with the Turkish question, that I presume he is no " better posted up," to use his own phrase, on the Central American questions than he was at our last interview.

I still continue to be of the opinion that there will be no war unless this should be precipitated by the Turks.   It is understood in high quarters here, that the Emperor Nicholas when at Olmutz manifested pacific dispositions and used pacific expressions which encourage the hope that he may yet yield his pre-

---

[1] MSS. Department of State, 65 Despatches from England.

tensions to such an extent as to satisfy the English and French Governments. It is certain that they will not be very exacting.

I regret that the President has not deemed it expedient to authorize me, in case circumstances should render this advisable, to present a Protest in his name to the British Government, against their colonization of the Bay Islands. That such a colony has been established, although Lord Clarendon was ignorant of the fact, is beyond a reasonable doubt. The truth is that this Government does not seem to understand, certainly it does not appreciate, the importance of the Central American questions. I desired a fair opportunity to present these questions before them in their true light, which such a Protest would have afforded;—because the establishment of this colony violates at the same time their Treaties with Spain of 1783 and 1786, the Monroe Doctrine, and the Clayton and Bulwer Treaty. I shall of course be very glad to receive any information in regard to the Colony of " the Bay Islands " which Mr. Molina may be able to afford.

You inform me that the Government is not aware that Great Britain claims to have full sovereignty over the Belize. I have not yet been able to ascertain the date at which she established a regular Colonial Government over it; but certain it is, that such a Government now exists. I have before me the British Imperial Calendar for 1853, in which among the list of British Colonies is found that of Honduras, with the names of the Superintendent, the Colonial Secretary, the Chief Justice, and those of all the other Officers necessary for its Government. The Calendar of 1845 is the first in which I find the name of a Chief Justice, R. Temple, Esquire, which has since been continued in each successive year. I shall investigate this subject thoroughly; though strange as it may seem, I find it very difficult to obtain any precise information about the Colonies of Great Britain.

No opportunity has yet been afforded me to carry your instructions into effect regarding the projet for the Fishery and Reciprocity Treaty.

Yours very respectfully,

JAMES BUCHANAN.

HON: W. L. MARCY,
    Secretary of State.

_____

TO MISS LANE.[1]

U. S. Legation, London, 14 October 1853.

My dear Harriet/

I have received yours of the 28th ultimo. I did not think I would write to you by to-morrow's steamer; but have now a few minutes left before the closing of the Bag.

I am sorry, truly sorry, that you look upon your trip to England as " the future realisation of a beautiful dream." Like all other dreams, you will be disappointed in the reality. I have never yet met an American, gentleman or lady, who, whatever they may profess, was pleased with London. They all hurry off to Paris, as speedily as possible, unless they have business to detain them here. A proud American who feels himself equal at home to the best does not like to be shut out by an impassable barrier from the best or rather the highest society in this country. My official position will enable me to surmount this barrier; but I feel that it will only be officially. Neither my political antecedents nor the public business entrusted to my charge will make me a favorite with these people : & I shall never play toady to them. It is true I know very few of them as yet. They are all in the Country or on the Continent, where they will continue until the opening of the spring. They pass the spring & part of the summer in London; just reversing the order in our Country.

I get along very comfortably & pleasantly, though I have not yet obtained a house. I find I cannot obtain one at all suitable under £650 per year, equal to $3146; & then I shall have to purchase many articles. The expense of living is great, even much greater than I had anticipated. But enough of this.

Poor Magraw has almost too much good luck,—more than he bargained for.

I still continue to find Messrs. Sickles & Welsh agreeable companions & useful assistants. Mrs. Sickles is very anxious, I believe, to come to England; & it is probable she may do so in the spring. Mr. Sickles will live with me until the arrival of his wife. Both you & myself placed much too low an estimate on Mr. Welsh.

I should be pleased if you would visit Ellen Ward; but you

---

[1] Buchanan Papers, private collection. Imperfectly printed in Curtis's Buchanan, II. 103.

ought not to go so far North much later than this month on account of your health.

I do not think well of your going to Philadelphia to learn French in the house where James Henry boards. Clemmie Pleasonton writes me that they will do all they can to instruct you in speaking that language. You will be far better with them than at a French Boarding House in Philadelphia.

I saw Mr. & Mrs. Haines, Lily's friends, last evening. They left Paris about a week ago. She gave a glowing description of the delights of that City; but said she would be almost tempted to commit suicide, should she be compelled to remain long in London. When you write to Lily, please to give her my love. Remember me very kindly to Mr. Davenport & your relatives, & believe me ever to be

Yours affectionately

JAMES BUCHANAN.

MISS HARRIET LANE.

TO MR. MARCY.[1]

(No. 11.)   LEGATION OF THE UNITED STATES.

LONDON, 18th October 1853.

SIR,

I have the honor to acknowledge the receipt of your Despatch No. 12 of the 21st ultimo, enclosing a number of letters from Professor A. D. Bache, the Superintendent of the U. S. Coast Survey, together with the accompanying reports of the operations of that survey, intended for the principal Continental Ministers resident in England; and it will afford me much satisfaction to have these letters directed and the reports delivered according to your instructions.

I have also received your Despatch No. 14, of the 3d Instant, enclosing the commission of C. W. Dennison as Consul at Demerara, which I have already transmitted to Lord Clarendon for the Queen's Exequatur.

Your very able letter to Mr. Hülsemann, of the 26th ultimo, on the Koszta affair reached London some days ago. Meagre extracts from it have alone been published in the London Journals

---

[1] MSS. Department of State, 65 Despatches from England.

so far as I have observed, without any expression either for or against the doctrines which it enforces. The reason for this doubtless is, that we had received information of the settlement of this affair at Constantinople before your letter arrived in London; and that the Russo-Turkish question is so absorbing here as to swallow up the interest in all other questions. The President's determination not to deliver up Koszta and to sustain Captain Ingraham is approved by every person with whom I have conversed on the subject.

Should the nations of Europe be involved in war, and indeed whether or not, it will become indispensable that either the Department or Congress shall define the protection to be afforded to persons visiting Europe who are merely domiciled aliens in our Country or to those foreigners who have gone a step further and have declared their intention to become American citizens, as against the nations of which they are natives as well as against other Powers. We feel the necessity every day at the Legation for definite rules upon this subject; and the difficulties have sensibly increased since the appearance of your Koszta letter. Should hostilities commence between Turkey and Russia, great numbers of Poles and Hungarians who have declared their intention to become citizens of the United States will apply for passports at this Legation in order to enable them to reach the seat of war. How then ought I to act under such circumstances? I have considered the question with much deliberation, and have determined that it would not be proper for me to assume the grave responsibility, without your explicit instructions, of reversing the rules prescribed by Mr. Everett when Secretary of State, in his Despatches to this Legation No. 6, 11, and 12, of the 13 Nov., 7 December, and 21st December 1852.

Mr. Everett in his Despatch No. 12, whilst denying passports to individuals who have declared their intention to become citizens, says there is no impropriety in authenticating their certificates of declaration by the usual countersign, meaning doubtless the visé. In my opinion, the reasons which he gives for this distinction are inconclusive; and his practice of countersigning such certificates whilst Minister in London was never authorized, so far as I can discover, by the Department of State. The Government of the United States ought not to give its official sanction to any thing which it does not intend to maintain. Regular passports ought either to be granted or refused to foreigners who have declared their intention to become citizens;

without adopting a middle course which may involve themselves as well as the Government in difficulties.

In regard to naturalized citizens of the United States, we are bound by every principle of honor and national faith, whatever may be the consequences, to protect them to the same extent as though they were natives of the soil. In respect to all other persons, I shall await your instructions, acting, in the mean time, upon those of Mr. Everett to which I have already referred.

Yours very respectfully

JAMES BUCHANAN.

HON. WILLIAM L. MARCY
&c. &c. &c. Washington.

TO MR. MARCY.[1]

(*Private.*) UNITED STATES LEGATION,
LONDON, 21 October 1853.

MY DEAR SIR/

I enclose you the within papers, as a mere matter of curiosity, simply because they contain the copy of a grant from the King of the Mosquitos. I have informed the Messrs. Whitington that " there is not the most remote probability, that you will entertain their proposition."

I would thank you to give me the instructions relative to Passports with as little delay as may be convenient. There have been several applications for passports, within the last few days, by individuals who had declared their intention some years ago. We had within the last week almost a scene at the Legation. The excited Poles are under the peculiar protection of Lord Dudley Stuart. He sent one of them to the Legation for a passport who has not been in the United States for several years, who admitted that he had only declared his intention,—that he was no citizen of the United States, & that he desired the Passport in order to reach Turkey. Upon our refusal to grant it, he became somewhat insolent & threatened to appeal to you at Washington.

London is horribly expensive, even more so than I had anticipated. I have not yet obtained a furnished house; but

---

[1] MSS. Department of State, 65 Despatches from England.

expect to accomplish this tomorrow. I have offered £650 for it; but may have to give £700. My calculation is that I shall spend the outfit & salary the first year; & the second $9000 of my own money, less the infit of $2250. But with this personally I am content.

The duties are quite laborious. The number of Consuls who apply to me for information on a variety of subjects is great; & the beauty of it is, that there is not even a copy of the consular instructions in the Legation, from either the Secretary of State or the Secretary of the Treasury, much less any book defining the powers & duties of Consuls. Thanks to my experience in the Department, I have not yet found myself much at a loss.

If any addition should be made to the compensation of Foreign Ministers,—which I would not ask if I were sure this would obtain it,—a house ought to be provided. This could be done at a much cheaper rate on a long lease, than it now costs the minister. Besides, like all other Governments of any consequence, we should have a fixed place & room for the Legation, & the papers would not be tossed about on the arrival of every new Minister. Were it not that we must have two good rooms on the first floor for the Legation, besides a dining room, I could get a good house suitable for myself for £450 or £500.

I do not see how the Russian & Turkish question can now be settled without a little fighting; but they will entertain the hope that it may be settled before the next Spring & that it is now too late in the season for the parties to do each other much harm before that period.

Lord Clarendon has not yet sent for me according to his promise; & with a war impending over them, & absorbed body & soul, as they are, in the question, I have not deemed it discreet to press the Central American questions upon him. I shall ask for an interview early next week, & talk to him about the Reciprocity & Fishery questions & some other matters.

I most sincerely sympathised with Mrs. Marcy & yourself on the loss of your promising son. Pray present to her my kindest & most respectful regards, & believe me to be,

Yours very respectfully

James Buchanan.

Hon. W. L. Marcy.

With Mr. Buchanan's private letter of 21 Octr., 1853.

LONDON 12 Octr. 1853.
2 NEW BROAD ST. CITY.

To His EXCELLENCY THE MINISTER OF STATE &C. FOR FOREIGN AFFAIRS &C. OF THE U. S. OF N. AMERICA.

SIR

I am prepared to sell—for a moderately fair sum, (payable by instalments if so needed and agreed) both or either of the properties whereof I enclose Copy of title &c. and am, in conformity thereto, ready to assign to your Nominee and to give possession accordingly.

This highly important territory, almost free from native occupants, (from not having guarded against the fatal effects of strong drinks and of small-pox!) and presenting a fine field for political and other occupancy &c., must surely be worthy your consideration &c.

The Lake of the more Northern of the two Estates will at trivial Cost afford Harbor &c. for the largest Vessels.

It will be observed that the Grant insures the most perfect freedom to Strangers.

On the Grant comprising the Carratasca Lake &c. the services & obligations required or that can be required have been duly performed & so confirmed; but on the other Grant, the annual tribute must be duly complied with.

Any further information desired will be duly furnished by

Yr. mo. obt. st.

G. T. WHITINGTON.

KNOW ALL MEN PRESENT AND TO COME, That we Robert Charles Frederic of the Mosquito Nation in consideration of the services to us & to our Nation hereafter to be rendered by G. R. B. of the City of London in the Kingdom of England, and of the sum of one hundred Spanish Dollars to us paid by the said G. R. B., the receipt whereof we do hereby acknowledge, with an annual premium of Twenty Dollars: of our own Special act and our own free motion have Given, Granted, and by these present Sealed with Seal of our Realm do give, Grant, & confirm unto the said G. R. B. his heirs & Assigns all that River Waunta Situated and being in or about Latitude 13:33 N. & Longitude 83.32 West, together with the Lagoon and bays, likewise the Rivers commonly called Lyastica and Cocolya with a tract or district of Land adjoining the said Rivers—To wit Ten English Miles, to be computed from each bank of the said Rivers backwards from the mouth of the said River Waunta to the Spanish limits (the said Latitude and Longitude & bearing herein before stated having been taken from the Chart of Commander Owens' late Survey) Together with all Arable lands, Meadows, pastures, Waters, Trees, Wood, underwoods—and the ground & Soil thereof, water, watercourses, Land covered with water, Mines, Minerals, Quarries, Forests, parks, Warrens, Hunting, Fisheries, Towlings, Ways, Customs, Tolls, and Duties, to the said Lands or any part thereof, in any wise appertaining or belonging or of the same or any part thereof deemed or known as part or member with their and every of their appurtances—To Hold & to have the same, unto the said G. R. B. his heirs & Assigns for ever. And we do hereby declare that it shall be lawful for the said G. R. B. his heirs and

Assigns & the inhabitants of the tract or district freely and at all times to pass & repass to & from the said Lands herein before granted & to navigate all Rivers and Waters communicating therewith without the let or hindrance of us or any part of our subjects and to introduce Foreigners to Settle upon and Colonize the said tract or district and to cultivate the Lands thereof. And moreover that it shall be lawful for the sd. G. R. B. his heirs & Assigns in & upon the said Lands to erect any houses & buildings which to him shall seem meet and to Mine for & to get the said Minerals and to carry away the same and to cut down and carry away all Timber & underwood & to hunt and fish and carry away the produce of such huntings & fishings as his & their own proper Goods & Chattels. And further that it shall be lawful for the said G. R. B. his heirs & Assigns to impose and levy all such reasonable dues, customs, and Taxes upon the inhabitants of the sd. tract or district and upon the Merchandize or Goods into or upon the same imported or exported which shall be used or accustomed among European Nations. And lastly we do declare that we will at no time hereafter impose or levy any dues, customs, or Taxes upon the inhabitants of the said Tract or district or their Lands, Goods, and Chattels or upon the Merchandize or Goods into or upon the same imported or exported without the consent of the said G. R. B. his heirs & Assigns, and that we and all our subjects will do all things which may support and cherish the same. Given under our hand & Seal this Twelfth day of December one thousand eight hundred and Thirty-eight and in the Thirteenth year of our Reign.

(Signed.)   ROBERT C. FREDERIC
King of the Mosquito Nation.
Signed & Sealed in the presence
of Three Witnesses.

Be it remembered that on the Twelfth day of December one thousand eight hundred & thirty-eight peaceable and quiet possession of the Land and other Hereditaments within mentioned to be granted and enfeoffed was taken & had by the within named G. R. B., and the sd. Robert Charles Frederic delivered to the sd. G. R. B. to hold to the sd. G. R. B. his heirs & Assigns for ever in the presence of us.

Three Witnesses. Registered 5 March 1840.

[The second grant, though of a distinct tract, is couched in similar terms.]

TO THE REV. MR. BUCHANAN.[1]

[Oct. 21, 1853.]

Took a solitary walk & embodied the ideas I had acquired during the day in language. This fixed them on my mind & gave me a faculty of expression.

I scarcely yet know how I shall like my residence in this Country; but, God willing, I shall make the best of it & do not

---

[1] Buchanan Papers, Historical Society of Pennsylvania.

intend to be miserable. I have not yet got a house but am in a fair way of obtaining one at a rent of £650,—or $3250.—The living here is more extravagant than even I had conceived.

I paid a visit on Saturday last to a gentleman whose estate is in Sussex & remained until Monday. The house was built in the early part of Queen Elisabeth's reign, though it has been in a degree modernised. We attended the Parish Church of Worth Parish,—one of four such churches in Doomsday Book. It was built before the Conquest; but how long before no person can tell. It is venerable from its antiquity & curious as a specimen of church architecture of the olden time. The Saxon arches are entire without regular key stones. Dr. Bethune is its rector,— a descendant of the great Duke of Sully in France, & is also its owner. It descends from father to son. His income from the church, independently of his real estate, is about £1200 per annum. He employs two curates, the one at £60 & the other at £100 per annum. The sermon preached by a stranger from Brighton was a very poor one, so that I was left pretty much to my own reflections.

My thoughts ran upon the numerous successive generations of mortals which had worshiped in this church for nearly a thousand years & the fleeting nature of man. But the Lord endureth forever & is the stay of those who put their trust in him.

I think you acted wisely not to go to Bellefonte & truly rejoice that $150 has been added to your income.

I am sorry Mrs. Musselman has changed her mind. I can give no advice in regard to your purchase of the property. Act wisely & discreetly for yourself upon the best advice. The property will I presume be sold in separate parcels; & if so, would not the house in which Mrs. M. lives suit you the best? We must contrive to raise the money in case of need.

Please to remember me kindly to Dr. Sample & the Messrs. Lightner. I suppose Isaac is by this time in Washington. Give my love to Ann Eliza & all the children & believe me always to be your affectionate brother

JAMES BUCHANAN.

REV: EDWARD Y. BUCHANAN.

TO MISS PARKER.[1]

U. S. LEGATION, LONDON, 21 October 1853.

MY DEAR MISS HETTY/

Your favor of the 11 September was a real treat to me. In the midst of business & numerous engagements, my heart still points to my quiet home at Wheatland. I pray God, that I may enjoy it once more; & if this should be his will, I think I shall never leave it again on public business.

When you write to Mrs. Dunham, please to remember me to her in the kindest & most affectionate terms.

I can assure you I felt quite sorry to hear that we had lost the calf. I had paid so much attention to it myself that I had become attached to it.

I am rejoiced that I could leave Wheatland in charge of a person like yourself in whom I have unbounded confidence. You have indeed faithfully done your duty to me & I shall never forget it. I have always considered you as my kind & much valued friend, & never in any other character. I am happy to learn that you miss me very much & think of me often. My thoughts & feelings towards yourself are exactly the same.

London is a horribly expensive place,—even more so than I had anticipated. My salary will not nearly support me.

Providence which has been heretofore so kind to me has placed me in my present situation, & in it, with his blessing, I am endeavoring to do my duty. I shall make myself as contented & happy as possible.

It has rained almost every day since I reached London. The climate is uncommonly damp; but yet it is healthy. We have the cholera here; but the cases yet have been comparatively few in a population of nearly two millions & an half & have occasioned but little alarm.

Please to remember me very kindly to Father Krider, the Brenners, Mr. Baer & his mother, Mr. Herr & the neighbours, not forgetting Miss Gilfillan.

Should you see my faithful friend Mr. Kautz, also, remember me to him.

Remember me affectionately to Eskridge, your sister Harriet & Aunt Rebecca & all inquiring friends.

---

[1] Buchanan Papers, Historical Society of Pennsylvania.

I hope you will write to me often.　Every little incident of the neighbourhood will be interesting to me.

The Messenger has come for the Despatch Bag & I must close by the assurance that I shall ever be faithfully your friend

JAMES BUCHANAN.

MISS ESTHER PARKER.

TO MR. MARCY.[1]

No. 13.　　LEGATION OF THE UNITED STATES.

LONDON, 28 October, 1853.

SIR/

I deem it proper, however distasteful the subject may be both to you & myself, to relate to you a conversation which I had on Tuesday last with Major General Sir Edward Cust, the Master of Ceremonies at this court, concerning my Court Costume.

I met him at the Traveller's Club, & after an introduction, your circular on this subject became the topic of conversation. He expressed much opposition to my appearance " at Court in the simple dress of an American Citizen."　I said that such was the wish of my own Government; & I intended to conform to it, unless the Queen herself would intimate her desire that I should appear in costume.　In that event, I should feel inclined to comply with her Majesty's wishes.　He said that Her Majesty would not object to receive me at Court in any dress I chose to put on; but whilst he had no authority to speak for her, he yet did not doubt it would be disagreeable to her, if I did not conform to the established usage.　He said, I could not, of course, expect to be invited to Court Balls or Court dinners where all appeared in costume;—that Her Majesty never invited the Bishops to balls not deeming it compatible with their character, but she invited them to concerts: & on these occasions, as a Court dress was not required, I would, also, be invited.　He grew warm by talking; & said, that, whilst the Queen herself would make no objection to my appearance at Court in any dress I thought proper, yet the people of England would consider it *presumption*.

---

[1] MSS. Department of State, 65 Despatches from England.　Inaccurately printed in Curtis's Buchanan, II. 107.

I became somewhat indignant in my turn, & said, that, whilst I entertained the highest respect for Her Majesty & desired to treat her with the deference which was eminently her due, yet it would not make the slightest difference to me, individually, whether I ever appeared at Court.   He stated that, in this Country, an invitation from the Queen was considered a command.   I paid no attention to this remark, but observed that the rules of etiquette at the British Court were more strict even than in Russia.   Senator Douglas of the United States Senate had just returned from St. Petersburg.   When invited to visit the Czar in costume, he informed Count Nesselrode that he could not thus appear.   The Count asked him in what dress he appeared before the President of the United States.   Mr. Douglas answered: In the very dress he then wore.   The Count after consulting the Emperor said that was sufficient; & in this plain dress he visited the Emperor at the palace & on parade & had most agreeable conversations with him, on both occasions.

Sir Edward then expressed his gratification at having thus met me accidentally,—said he had just come to Town for that day & should leave the next morning; but would soon do himself the honor of calling upon me.

Although he disclaimed speaking by the authority of the Queen, yet it appeared both to myself & Col: Lawrence, who was present, that they must have had some conversation in the Court Circle upon the subject.   I entertain this belief the more firmly, as Sir Edward has since talked to a member of this Legation in the same strain.

So, then, from present appearances, it is probable I shall be placed, socially, in Coventry, on this question of dress; because it is certain, that should Her Majesty not invite the American Minister to her Balls & dinners, he will not be invited to the Balls & dinners of her courtiers.   This will be to me personally a matter of not the least importance; but it may deprive me of the opportunity of cultivating friendly social relations with the Ministers & other Courtiers, which I might render available for the purpose of obtaining important information & promoting the success of my mission.

I am exceedingly anxious to appear " at Court in the simple dress of an American Citizen; "—and this not only because it accords with my own taste, but because it is certain, that if the Minister to the Court of St. James should appear in uniform, your circular will become a dead letter in regard to most if not all the other Ministers & chargés of our Country in Europe.

The difficulty in the present case is greatly enhanced by the fact, that the sovereign is a lady, and the devotion of her subjects towards her partakes of a mingled feeling of loyalty & gallantry. Any conduct, therefore, on my part which would look like disrespect towards her personally could not fail to give great offence to the British people.

Should it prove to be impossible for me to conform to the suggestions of the Circular in regard to dress, " without detriment to the public interest " & " without impairing my usefulness to my Country," then I shall certainly & cheerfully be guided by its earnest recommendation & adopt " the nearest approach to it compatible with the due performance of my public duties." This course I pursued from choice whilst Minister in Russia; & this course I should have pursued here without any instructions.

Yours very respectfully

JAMES BUCHANAN.

Hon: WILLIAM L. MARCY,
    Secretary of State.

TO MR. MARCY.[1]

(No. 14.)   LEGATION OF THE UNITED STATES.

LONDON, 1 November, 1853.

On Tuesday last I met the Earl of Clarendon by appointment at the Foreign Office; and, upon the whole, our interview was highly satisfactory.

When I entered, he said he was ashamed to meet me. He ought to have invited me to a meeting at a much earlier period, according to his promise; and the incessant claims upon his time of the Russo-Turkish question had alone prevented.

A conversation ensued in regard to this question, which I do not deem it necessary to state in detail. It proved the perfect understanding and union between France and England, and their determination to sustain the Sultan, at least by their fleets, against the encroachments and demands of Russia. Still it was evident that his Lordship does not yet abandon all hopes of peace. He spoke in emphatic terms against the conduct of the Emperor of Russia and contrasted the high character which he had en-

---

[1] MSS. Department of State, 65 Despatches from England.

joyed but a year ago, for good faith and honor, with that which he now sustained throughout Europe. His Lordship does not seem to apprehend that either Austria or Prussia will render any aid to the Czar in his war against the Sultan.

As bearing upon the question of war, I spoke to him of the apprehensions entertained throughout England of a scarcity of food; and to these he seemed to be sensibly alive, as well he may be. The crop of the present year is a short one, and is far from being yet altogether secured; and the prospects for that of the next year are indeed gloomy. Since my arrival here, it has rained more or less almost every day; and for this cause comparatively but little of the ground has yet been seeded. For the want of accurate statistical information, they can form no near approximation to the amount of this year's crop,—nor that of the supply required from foreign countries,—nor whether the United States will be able to furnish the deficiency. In this state of uncertainty, even the best informed men entertain serious apprehensions of something approaching a famine. Under these circumstances, the prospect of war is any thing but agreeable to British Statesmen.

I come now to the business for which I requested the interview. Under this head, the first topic which I introduced was the claim recently made by the British Post Office upon Captain Warner, the Master of the American Clipper Ship " the Sovereign of the Seas," to carry a British mail from Liverpool to Melbourne under the penalty of £200.

Copies, now enclosed, of the Documents relating to this claim will sufficiently inform you of its history up to the date of our interview, without any observations on my part. These are marked,[1]

A. 1. 24 August 1853. Letter addressed by Nathaniel Hawthorne, Consul of the United States at Liverpool to Mr. Ingersoll, " with the enclosed paper containing extracts of Acts of Parliament relating to the carriage of Letters by ship."

B. 2. 25 August 1853. Mr. Buchanan to the Earl of Clarendon.

C. 3. 30 August 1853. Lord Clarendon to Mr. Buchanan, with a note dated 29 August, addressed by the General Post Office at London to his Lordship.

D. 4. 31 August '53. Mr. Buchanan to Mr. Hawthorne.

---

[1] For the papers here enumerated, see supra, under the respective dates.

E. 5. 9 September '53.   Mr. Hawthorne to Mr. Buchanan, with the Protest of Captain Warner, dated on the 6 September.

F. 6. 16 Sep. '53.   Mr. Buchanan to the Earl of Clarendon.

G. 7. 19 Sep. '53.   The Earl of Clarendon to Mr. Buchanan.

I stated to Lord Clarendon that as the Session of Congress was approaching, I should be glad to communicate to the Secretary of State the information on this subject, which I had requested in my note to him of the 16th ultimo.   It could not prove satisfactory to my Government to receive merely the naked opinion of the Solicitor to the Post Office Department, that American Vessels were bound to carry British Mails from British Ports to Australia, without any reference to the Act or Acts of Parliament creating such an obligation, or any explanations whatever of this opinion.   That such a claim, so far as I could learn, had never before been asserted, and even if the law justified it, we might have expected that some previous notice would have been given before it was enforced.

Lord Clarendon answered, that he doubted himself whether the law did authorise this claim,—it was altogether new to him; and immediately after the receipt of my note of the 16th September he had caused the question to be submitted to the law officers of the Crown.   That their absence from town had occasioned a delay; but he had just received a note from the Post Office Department stating that these officers were divided in opinion on the subject.   He intimated his opinion, in no doubtful terms, that whether the right existed or not, previous notice ought to have been given before its enforcement.

I observed it was true that the Act of Parliament contained expressions broad enough to include all vessels, foreign as well as British, whether bound to a foreign or a British port; but yet in construing this Act, it could scarcely be presumed that Parliament had intended to extend its legislation beyond its own vessels and make it apply to the vessels of foreign countries. If this were really the case, my Government ought to know the fact, and might then, if they thought proper, provide by law to impose similar Postal duties on British vessels clearing from the ports of the United States.

He said this was all fair, and I should have a satisfactory answer with as little delay as possible, reiterating his doubts whether the Post Office Solicitor had placed a correct construction upon the Act of Parliament.

He asked if I was confident that the case of the " Sovereign of the Seas " was the first of the kind. I answered that the Consul at Liverpool had informed me it was the first at that port, and from all I could learn it was the first of the kind that had ever occurred.

I incidentally remarked I had met Captain Porter of the Steamer " Golden Age " a few days ago. She was at Liverpool, and would in a few days proceed to Melbourne, and was said to be the fastest steamer which had ever been built in America. (Then, interrupted his Lordship, if so, she is the fastest in the world.)

The Captain had informed me that the Post Office authorities had demanded that she should carry a British Mail to Australia. Now, my Lord, said I, if it should be the rule that the steamers of the one country shall be compelled by law to carry the mails of the other, what will be the effect of the rule on the steamers of the two Governments sustained at such vast expense chiefly for the purpose of carrying these mails? He said, very true; and his own opinion seems to be decidedly against the right.

I ought to add that Captain Porter thinks he will make a fair profit by carrying the mail to Australia at two pence per letter, the sum allowed by the British law in such cases, provided the Post Office Department shall deal fairly with him; and having heard nothing from him since, I presume he is satisfied.

His Lordship himself then adverted to the subject of the " Bay Islands " and the Central American questions. Perceiving from what he said that he was still not prepared to enter upon the discussion of these questions, I observed it was not my purpose to press them until it should be quite agreeable to him; yet they were very important, and it was highly desirable that they should be settled, if this were possible, without unnecessary delay. I hoped, however, if the British Government had established the Colony of the " Bay Islands," he would be able to furnish me with a copy of the official act, at this time, so that I might transmit it to Washington before the meeting of Congress. He said, these questions were indeed highly important, and that it was his anxious desire they should, if possible, be speedily settled. He then asked me in what manner I thought we had best proceed with the negotiation, and added that he did not himself well understand the questions, and would depend much upon myself for information in regard to them. My Lord, said I, laughingly, this is your first attempt to play the diplomat upon

me; I know you possess a thorough knowledge of the whole
subject.   Indeed, said he, upon my honor, I do not,—I am quite
sincere.   I desire to know your opinion as to the best manner
of our proceeding.   Then, said I, I shall give it to you frankly.
I think when both parties desire to come to an amicable understanding, by far the best mode of accomplishing the object, is
first to talk the whole matter over in a friendly manner.   We
can then soon discover the points on which we agree, and those,
if any, on which we differ.   If we should proceed by addressing
notes to each other, this would produce long delay, and both
parties might feel a sort of necessity to stand by what they had
written.   Now, said I, if you would appoint some day, when
you will have abundance of time, let us hold a free and friendly
conversation, embracing all the questions, and I dare venture to
hope for a favorable result.   He said, he agreed, with his whole
heart, to the plan I had suggested,—he thought it was by far
the best mode of proceeding, and would appoint some day next
week for the conference, of which he would give me sufficient
notice.   He added gayly, " You must not think I was attempting
to play the Diplomat, for in truth I do not understand the subject;
but I shall endeavor to do so before we meet."   He said he had
done his best to get the paper I desired from the Colonial Office,
relating to the " Bay Islands," but had not as yet succeeded;—
he had just received a note from them excusing themselves for
the delay.   He observed that he believed Ruatan was a miserable
little Island that had been occupied for many years by a few
British subjects who had requested the home authorities to give
them some kind of Government.   That their request had been
granted, and that this was entirely a different case from what it
would have been, had they but recently first occupied the Island.
I told him I had no desire to discuss the question at present; but
I must observe, that so far from having occupied it for many
years, I believed it would appear it had been seized from the
State of Honduras by a British Military force so late as 1841.
Mr. Johnston in his Dictionary of Geography, published in 1851,
had stated expressly that the Island had been abandoned by the
English.   But in any event, I conceived that the Clayton and
Bulwer Treaty had disposed of the question of this Island which
was unquestionably a part of Central America.   I then took occasion to observe that the Government of the United States had
no idea of acquiring any territory in Central America.   They
desired only that the small states into which it was divided

should enjoy in peace what belonged to them; the two Governments, each for itself, interposing its good offices to settle the disputed questions of boundary existing between them. That in my opinion neither Great Britain nor the United States had any real interest to pursue a different course, and that in America we had all expected that the Clayton and Bulwer Treaty would produce this happy result. Without this it certainly never would have been ratified.

He said he heartily agreed in the wish expressed by me in favor of these small states; and here the conversation on this subject ended.

I then told him that Governor Marcy had informed me, he had submitted to Mr. Crampton a projet for a Fishery and Reciprocity Treaty, to be submitted to the British Government; and asked him if he had received it. He said he had, and had written to Mr. Crampton that the Treaty did not appear to him to be a reciprocity Treaty. I told him that I had no instructions to negotiate with him on these questions; but I should be most happy to afford him any information in my power in relation to them. I stated, if I were to express an opinion, the American Government might with at least equal justice complain that it would not be a Reciprocity Treaty. Why, said he, you still insist upon giving a bounty to your fishermen, and with this advantage ours cannot fairly compete with them. I replied that a bounty was granted to the Cod Fishery alone, and that it should be borne in mind that these fishermen had to pay a duty of thirty per cent. ad valorem on their salt, from which British fishermen were relieved. That this bounty was but little, if any more than equal to the duty which our fishermen paid upon their salt. That in the Mackerel and Herring fisheries there was no bounty paid, and in regard to these the British fishermen enjoyed a great advantage over the American; inasmuch as the latter paid a duty of thirty per cent. on their salt from which the former were relieved. That the British, from their vicinity to the Fishery grounds, would always possess advantages of which the Americans must necessarily be deprived. The justice of this remark appeared from the fact that the British fisheries were in a flourishing condition, and notwithstanding the duty which they now paid, a large quantity of British caught fish were brought into the markets of the United States, compared with the supply of that article from our own fishermen.

He observed that the British Colonists were of a very dif-

ferent opinion, and complained loudly of what would be the
effect of the Treaty on their fisheries. That he had ordered
tables to be made from official documents shewing what was the
actual state of the trade between the Colonies and the United
States, and these tables would doubtless prove satisfactory to
both Governments, as we should then both know what we were
about.

I stated that the growth and present condition of the British .
Fisheries could be ascertained with certainty from the Treasury
Reports of the United States, and I should be happy to procure
this information for him.

He still repeated that he did not consider the Treaty a
Reciprocity Treaty; but spoke alone of our bounties to the Cod
Fishery, on which he seemed to lay great stress. After repeating to him my explanation on this subject, I expressed the opinion
that the privilege to British Colonial fishermen to supply a population of Twenty-five millions of people, annually increasing at
a rapid rate, with fish free of duty, would of itself be more than
an equivalent for their grant of the shore fisheries to our fishermen; and then observed, that the Treaty would yield to them
great additional advantages in the reciprocal free trade between
the United States and their Colonies. No man could examine
the schedule which it contained, without perceiving these advantages. From this schedule our two important agricultural
articles of Sugar and Tobacco had been omitted, and would still
continue to pay a duty in the Colonies; whilst their grain, flour,
and, I believed, every other agricultural article produced in the
Colonies, would be admitted into the United States, free of duty.

He replied that the Colonists required a duty upon Sugar
and Tobacco to support their Governments; and I answered that
whatever might be the necessity for this duty, the effect would
still be the same on the Tobacco growing and Sugar planting
interests of the United States.

I then proceeded to converse with His Lordship in relation
to your instructions concerning Cuba; and here justice requires
me to remark, that what he said on this subject appeared to be
clear, explicit, and satisfactory.

I commenced by stating, that at the moment when the visit
of the Earl of Aberdeen had terminated our last interview. I
was about, under instructions from my Government, to make an
important enquiry of him, which I would now take the liberty

of making with entire frankness; and that it would then be for him to decide whether he would answer it or not.

I said: "Your Lordship must be fully aware of the deep,— the vital interest which we feel in regard to the condition of the colored population of Cuba. This Island is within sight of our shores; and should a black Government like that of Hayti be established there, it would endanger the peace and domestic security of a large and important portion of our people. To come then to the point:—it has been publicly stated and reiterated over and over again in the United States, that Spain, should she find it impossible to retain the Island, will emancipate the Slaves upon it; and that the British Government is endeavoring to persuade her to pursue this course." I here paused for a reply.

He answered:—"We certainly have no wish, very far from it, to see a Black Government established in Cuba. We have been pressing Spain incessantly to put down the African Slave trade with Cuba; and, I regret to say, without yet having produced the effect which we so much desire. Concha was bad enough in encouraging this trade, but Canedo has proved to be still worse. The temptation to these people, of receiving about thirty dollars a head, on the importation of each slave, has proved irresistible. We now hope for better things. Canedo has been recalled, and a man of fair character (I did not distinctly hear his name) has been appointed; and being a person of great wealth, he will not be exposed to the same temptation as his predecessor. With the exception of urging Spain to abolish the Slave trade and endeavoring to trace out the Emancipados, and do them the justice which good faith requires of us,—and in this last we have had very little success,—we have never had any negotiations of any kind with Spain, or attempted to exercise any influence over her respecting the condition of the slaves in Cuba. We have not the most remote idea, in any event, of ever attempting to acquire Cuba for ourselves. We have, already, too many Colonies,—far more than are profitable to us."

I told him I was very much rejoiced to be able to make this report to my Government. He told me he never would have forgiven me, if, having this upon my mind, I had not frankly made the enquiry which he had as frankly answered. In our intercourse, he hoped there would be the most perfect frankness on both sides. I said, I united in his wish with all my heart, and should always act upon this principle.

We then fell into a desultory conversation, concerning the

Island of Cuba.   In the course of this, I stated to him that the
United States had never had any purpose of acquiring Cuba
except by purchase or by other fair and honorable means.   That
although politically opposed to Mr. Fillmore's administration, I
would do it the justice to declare my conviction that they had
done all they could to prevent the Filibustering Expedition to
that Island.   He answered that he firmly believed this was the
fact.

Finding his Lordship quite willing to converse upon the
subject,—I said that Cuba was wretchedly governed.   The inhabitants were oppressed in every way, under an unmitigated,
irresponsible, and distant despotism.   It was just at our doors,
and the people of the United States could not fail to feel a deep
interest in its fate.   If it were governed as they governed their
North American Colonies, we would be perfectly content that it
should remain in the possession of Spain for an indefinite period.
But our trade with it was shackled by unjust restrictions, and our
general intercourse with it was a source of perpetual annoyance.
He admitted all this to be true, and said he had told Mr. Isturiz,
(the Spanish Minister at this Court) but a few days ago, that if
Spain lost Cuba it would be altogether their own fault, and they
would be indebted for it to the wretched manner in which they
governed the Island.   He added that although Spain did not
deserve it at the hands of the British Government, they still felt a
sympathy for her arising out of their ancient alliances.

I observed that if the oppressions of Spain should produce
an insurrection among the Creoles of Cuba, whilst our Government might not feel disposed to take any part in the struggle as
long as it was confined to the original parties themselves, yet if
other Governments should interfere in the contest on behalf of
Spain, no human power could prevent us from interfering in
favor of the Creoles.   This would be inevitable.   In regard to
the African Slave Trade, we felt as much anxiety to see it suppressed as they could do in Great Britain; and this feeling was
universal throughout our whole country.   Such a feeling was not
only dictated by motives of philanthropy, but by those of self-
protection.   We desired to avoid all possible danger of a Black
Government in Cuba, and we could never witness without great
dissatisfaction a large preponderance of the black over the White
race in that Island.   His Lordship then mentioned he was sorry
to state that some fast sailing clipper ships, built in New York,
had been engaged in carrying on the Slave Trade, and he believed

capital for this purpose had been furnished by merchants of that city, but he would not say that capital had not been, also, furnished for the same purpose by merchants of Liverpool.

I observed that my information did not enable me to speak upon this subject; but this I could say, that if it were known that any individual in the United States had furnished one dollar of capital to build or equip an African Slave Ship, he would be rendered infamous by the act, and would be deserted and proscribed by our whole society, in every portion of the Union.

He replied that such was the feeling in England. Such a man would be detested by all ranks of people.

After some amusing information which his Lordship communicated to me concerning the Queen and Court of Spain, which I do not deem it proper to insert in a Despatch, our long interview terminated.

I have given you the substance, and in many cases, nearly the very words, as they were uttered, of what passed between us; from which you can draw your own conclusions.

One thing is certain:—that whether successful or not in my mission. I anticipate a frank and agreeable official intercourse with Lord Clarendon.

Yours Very Respectfully

JAMES BUCHANAN.

HON. WILLIAM L. MARCY
Secretary of State.

TO MISS LANE.[1]

Private & confidential.

[Undated; about November 1, 1853.]

MY DEAR HARRIET/

I have at length got a house & a good one in an agreeable & sufficiently fashionable locality; but I shall not be able to get possession much before Christmas. Col: Lawrence will go home some time during the present month on the 16th to be married to Miss Chapman, & will return to London with his bride in February next. The opportunity will be so favorable that I am almost inclined to invite you to accompany them. Indeed I would

---

[1] Buchanan Papers, private collection.

do so without hesitation, were it not that I may be *socially* placed
in Coventry here in consequence of Governor Marcy's costume
circular.   I have had a pretty animated conversation on the subject with Sir Edward Cust, the Master of Ceremonies.   He informed me that whilst the Queen would not object to my appearance at Court in any dress I might think proper, yet I could not
expect to be invited to Court Balls & dinners, where all appeared
in costume.   He graciously added, that I would be invited to
Court concerts where the Bishops attended; because a uniform
was not required on such occasions.   Should Her Majesty pursue
this course, it will unquestionably be followed by her courtiers.
Now I would not care a button personally for this social exclusion, but whilst it continues, *I should not be willing to have
you here on any account.*   I need not state what I said to Sir
Edward.   You will not doubt but that I evinced sufficient spirit.

The Queen holds several Levees & Drawing Rooms in the
course of the Season, which does not ordinarily commence until
the beginning of March.   The only distinction between the two
is that at the Levees gentlemen only are admitted; whilst the
Drawing Rooms are intended chiefly for ladies.   No invitations
are extended in either case; but a Court circular is sent by the
Master of Ceremonies to the members of the Diplomatic Corps,
giving them information of the time when they are to be held,
& it is considered their official duty to attend.   It is on these
official occasions that the Queen would receive me, according to
Sir Edward, " in any dress I might choose to put on; " but to
the Court Balls & dinners, according to the same authority, " I
could not expect to be invited."

Should this difficulty be amicably adjusted, then you may
come with Col: Lawrence; otherwise not.   But I have deemed
it proper in the mean time to give you this information.   I shall
write again as soon as I know more of the matter.

I get along very well with the Earl of Clarendon, the Secretary for Foreign Affairs.   Indeed I think our official intercourse
will prove quite agreeable.   I cannot yet form an opinion whether
my mission, in its main objects, will be successful.   The place is
quite laborious.

I pay for my house £700, which is exactly equal to $3388;
but am allowed £80, for office rent, which reduces the amount to
$3000.80.   According to my estimate, the outfit & salary will not
hold out longer than the first year; & I shall have to supply the
deficiency in the second year from my private means.

I shall faithfully keep my promise to you, & this may as well be done in the first as in the second year of my mission, unless the social difficulties should arise which I have reason to apprehend. Still, if you are at all disposed to be seasick, the crossing of the Atlantic in February would be awful. In April it would be much more pleasant, & you would still be in time for the fashionable season. I entrust you with the secret of Col: Lawrence, in the full belief that you will divulge it to no person. I have but a moment before the closing of the Bag, & have only time to add that I am always

Your affectionate uncle
JAMES BUCHANAN.

MISS LANE.

TO MR. MARCY.[1]

(No. 16.)   LEGATION OF THE UNITED STATES.

LONDON, 12 November 1853.

SIR,

I had an interview with Lord Clarendon at the Foreign Office on Monday last, by his own appointment.

His Lordship commenced the conversation by complaining of his incessant labors in endeavoring to settle the Turkish question. I asked him if he believed they would succeed in settling this question, and his answer was, that he really could not say whether there would be peace or war. It was altogether uncertain.

He then observed, he was very much pained to learn that there had been a violent and wholly unfounded article in the Washington Union charging them with an intrigue with Spain to " Africanise " Cuba—he paid no attention to editorials generally, but this editorial derived importance from the fact that the Union was understood to be the Government Organ. I told him this was not the case—that the Union was just about as much the organ of the American administration as the London Times was the organ of the British Government. It was true the Union published official notices and appointments by authority, and gave its support generally to the administration of President Pierce; but the administration had no organ in any other sense

---

[1] MSS. Department of State, 65 Despatches from England.

than I had mentioned, and were not responsible for the editorials of that Journal. Its editorials were its own. He then said several things about the London Times, which it is unnecessary to repeat, disclaiming that it was their organ, and stating wherein its course had annoyed them very much on the Turkish question.

I told him that my last Despatch to Washington would correct the impression extensively entertained in the United States regarding their supposed negotiations with Spain in relation to the colored population of Cuba, as it contained a careful report of our conversation on that subject. For this he expressed his obligations to me, and stated that he had written to Mr. Crampton on the same subject. He added with emphasis there was nothing in the proceedings of the British Government which could affect the United States in the slightest degree that he would not be cheerfully willing to communicate to me without reserve and with the utmost frankness; and that they desired we should be the best friends in the world. He then mentioned that Mr. Crampton had informed him that when he went to see Mr. Marcy on the morning after the article appeared in the Union, the latter had at once declared he knew nothing whatever of this article until after its appearance in print, and that the Administration were in no manner responsible for it.

His Lordship then asked what course I would suggest as the best mode of proceeding with our conferences on the Central American questions;—professing at the same time, as he had done before, that he was not well acquainted with the subject, and assuring me that in making this declaration on a former occasion, he had not been attempting to play the Diplomat. I told him he must have seen that my remark had been merely playful; whereupon a sprightly conversation ensued not worth a repetition.

I then observed that he had stated, in a recent Despatch to Mr. Crampton, that the British Government had on several occasions made overtures to that of the United States for the settlement of these questions; but the administration at Washington were not aware that any distinct overtures of this kind had been presented. It was probable this might have been done in conversations between Mr. Crampton and Mr. Webster or Mr. Everett, but, if so, there was no trace of such overtures in the Department of State. I suggested, therefore, that he should in the first place, as a starting point, state to me clearly and precisely upon what terms the British Government felt disposed to settle these questions. His Lordship made no distinct answer to this suggestion; but asked me if I was not aware of the Agreement which had been entered into between Mr. Webster and Mr. Crampton, on this subject, in April, 1852; and enquired how this would do for a basis of settlement.

I informed him that I was perfectly acquainted with this Agreement. It was now at an end; and I assured him it could not become the basis of a settlement. He inquired my reasons, and I gave them to him at some length.

I stated that this Agreement both recognised and constituted the Mosquito Indians as an Independent Power; which could never be assented to by the United States. That these Indians were incapable of governing themselves; and the consequence would be that they must continue to be under the dominion of the British Government as they had been heretofore. That however much we might like Great Britain, we desired her withdrawal from Central America as speedily as possible. This had been our object in concluding the Clayton and Bulwer Treaty; but unfortunately this object had not as yet been accomplished. Besides, the United States could never recognise the right of Great Britain to a protectorate over the Mosquito Indians.

He then spoke at some length of their ancient and long continued relations with and protectorate of the Mosquitos, adverted to Lord Palmerston's despatch to Mr. Castellon as proving their right, and stated that whilst they earnestly desired to get clear of their protectorate, British honor required that this must be done with a proper regard to the interest and well being of the Mosquitos.

In answer, I briefly presented, with as much clearness and force as I could, their treaties with Spain of 1783 and 1786, and the speech of Lord Thurlow, &c., &c., and proved, at least to my own satisfaction, that they had no right to exercise such a protectorate. I need not repeat my argument, as its main features are embodied in your instructions. Besides, I observed that whatever might have been their rights previously, the Clayton and Bulwer Treaty had expressly prohibited them from exercising any dominion over Central America, and yet, notwithstanding this express prohibition, it was notorious they had continued to exercise exclusive dominion over the whole Mosquito Coast, in the name of a mere shadow, dignified with the title of King of the Mosquitos. That this treaty never would have been ratified by the Senate of the United States, had it not been believed that it would effect their immediate withdrawal from the Mosquito Coast.

The plan of settlement proposed by Lord John Russell, in his despatches to Mr. Crampton of January 19, 1853, next became the subject of conversation : and he enquired what I thought of this plan. I told him that taking the two despatches of that date together, it was difficult to comprehend this plan. It appeared, however, that His Lordship, to use his own expression, desired " to make Mosquito a reality instead of a fiction." And he proposed to do this by establishing a Government over the Mosquito Coast, eventually to become independent both of Great Britain and the United States; but in the mean time, and until it should be able to defend itself, to be under their joint protection.

The first objection to this plan was, that it would be unjust to the Central American States and deprive them of a territory to which, in the opinion of my Government, they were justly entitled.

Besides, independently of this conclusive objection, such an arrangement would perpetuate strife in Central America. These small states, feeling that injustice had been done to them by the arbitrary conduct of the two Governments, would never cease to be dissatisfied, nor discontinue their efforts to have this injustice redressed. In addition, this Territory would become the refuge of the most worthless and lawless population in the world ; and that instead of finally settling the question and restoring peace and harmony to Central America, the two Governments would make confusion worse confounded, and the latter end would be worse than the beginning. To prevent these evils, the best mode was to restore the Central American States to their rights. His Lordship (Russell) had stated that the Mosquito territory extended through six degrees of latitude along the Caribbean Sea from the River Roman to the San Juan, with an indefinite extent inwards, containing thirty or forty thousand Indians. Now, if it were at all necessary to discuss the extent of this Territory, I thought I could prove from their own authors,—their own Government officials, that this territory neither extended to the Roman on the North, nor to the San Juan on the South. The claim reminded me of what Mr. Clay had termed " a vagrant power " when speaking of the incidental power claimed, under the Constitution of the United States, to establish a National Bank.   So this claim was " vagrant " in its character, and could be made to expand or contract, or to embrace any spot along the whole coast, at pleasure.   And in regard to the number of the Indian population:—if his Lordship had stated it at hundreds, instead of thousands, I believed he would have come nearer to the mark.   And then, if my information was correct, they were the most miserable and degraded race of savages on the Continent.   They had been brought into contact with the very worst species of white population, and whilst they had learned all the vices of civilization, they had acquired none of its virtues.   Then as to their King,—it was known he was drunken & worthless.   General Herran, formerly minister from New Granada to the United States, had given me a most ludicrous description of his coronation at Jamaica.   Why, said his Lordship, did they crown him at Jamaica?   Yes, said I, they clothed him with royal robes, I believed, of scarlet, seated him upon a throne, & placed a crown upon his head, whilst the officers of the British Government treated him with mock homage.

He then asked me if I knew the number of Mosquitos on the Coast.   I told him I did not; but spoke from general information.   No census, I presumed, had ever been taken of them; but there were undoubtedly books and documents in London from which information could be derived on this subject.   Here we had some playful conversation concerning the Mosquitos and their King, not proper to be inserted in a grave despatch.

His Lordship then said emphatically that the honor of the British Government absolutely required they should secure some provision for the Mosquitos, and they could not shrink from this duty; but he added they were endeavoring to construct a bridge for the Emperor Nicholas over which he might pass honorably out of the principalities, and asked if we could not assist in constructing a bridge to enable them to pass honorably from the Mosquito protectorate.   He said this could not possibly be done without some provision in the Territory for those Indians who had always been its possessors.   (Here I ought to say, he observed that he would not like to see his allusion to the Emperor Nicholas in print.)   I told him I would make a suggestion upon this subject, (which in fact had just then occurred to me) altogether without authority or instructions from my own Government and without knowing whether it would meet their approbation.   He would, therefore, receive it as such in this free conversation, which he promised to do.

I told him that the principle upon which both the British and American Governments have acted was to consider the Indians within their respective territories as entitled to a qualified right of occupancy. That whilst the sovereignty of these Governments had always been held to embrace the Indian population within their limits, yet it had been the practice of both to extinguish this quasi Indian title by fair purchase before the whites were permitted to settle upon Indian lands. That it was true the Mosquitos had long occupied and roamed over portions of this Territory; and therefore, provided the sovereignty of Nicaragua was clearly recognised and its exclusive right admitted to purchase this occupancy, it was probable that the United States might consent that some territorial provision should be made for these Indians. I did not perceive any valid objection thus to place Nicaragua on the same footing that Great Britain and the United States had always placed themselves in regard to their own Indians; provided all the other questions could be satisfactorily adjusted and the British Government would withdraw from any interference in the concerns of the Mosquitos and leave them as mere occupants within a portion of the Territory of Nicaragua.

I observed that some thing of this kind might constitute a bridge over which they might pass with honor from the Mosquito protectorate; but again disclaimed all authority to make any such proposition.

The idea seemed to strike him with considerable force; and he said that in this view of the subject it would be important to ascertain the number of the Mosquitos, with a view to the extent of the territory within which they might be permitted to remain.

He said the objection to this suggestion was that Nicaragua might not act as Great Britain or the United States would act towards these Indians under similar circumstances, but might cheat them out of their possessions, or expel them by force; and again repeated what he had more than once done before, that the honor of Great Britain required that they should make some provision for these Indians in their own territory, before abandoning them. He stated that probably something might be made of this idea, provided it were stipulated that the Mosquitos should not sell their occupancy to Nicaragua without the approbation of the two Governments. They would take care that those poor Indians should not be cheated, and that the price that they obtained for their lands should be secured to them in such a manner as to do them good. He then made many enquiries of me as to the manner in which our Government had treated the Indians, and to what degree of civilisation they had attained;— all of which I answered.

Here was a pause in the conversation, & I waited for some moments, in expectation that he would introduce the subject of the " Bay Islands." Discovering that this was not his intention, I said, " My Lord, & what of the ' Bay Islands '? " He answered, these Islands were of small importance, & we need not make a Mountain out of a Mole Hill; they had always been in possession of Ruatan, & what they had recently done was merely to give the British subjects settled there a new & more perfect form of government. They had long previously had their magistrates on that Island.

I replied:—" Whatever you may suppose, I can assure you this is the dangerous question; because we firmly believe that the establishment of this Colony is a direct violation of the Clayton & Bulwer Treaty. By your Treaties with Spain of 1783 & 1786, you expressly abandoned all pretensions to this portion of the Continent of Spanish America & its adjacent Islands; & these Treaties were carried into execution. Johnston's Dictionary of Geography, a high authority, published at London in 1851, under the title ' Ruatan,' declared expressly that you had abandoned this Island;[1] & Crowe in ' The Gospel in Central America,' published at London in 1850, states that it was captured from Honduras by the British, so late as 1841. Thus it appears that but a brief period has elapsed since you resumed the possession of Ruatan, after having abandoned it for many years in obedience to your Treaties with Spain."

I then asked his Lordship if he had received Mr. Mason's report to the Senate of the United States, in relation to their new Colony of the " Bay Islands." He answered, he believed it had been sent to him; but intimated that he had never perused it with care. I produced the report & read from it the note on the 5th page, relative to the capture of Ruatan from Honduras; & then offered to leave it with him, which I did, after his expressed wish to that effect. I proceeded:—" Even if it were a fact that you had always been in possession of Ruatan, still your obligation to withdraw from it would, in my opinion, be im-

---

[1] The edition of 1852 is entirely different.

perative, under the Clayton & Bulwer Treaty. What have the United States accomplished by this Treaty? Nothing, literally nothing. So far as we are concerned, it has hitherto proved to be a mere dead letter. It stipulates that you shall not use your alleged protectorate for the purpose of assuming or exercising dominion over any part of Central America & yet it cannot be denied that you still continue to exercise the very same exclusive dominion over the Mosquito territory that you had done before its conclusion.—In regard to Ruatan & the other small Bay Islands, within sight of the coast of the State of Honduras,—all of them clearly Central American Islands,—these are free from the questions arising out of the Mosquito protectorate; and yet you have not withdrawn from them in obedience to the Treaty; but since its date you have not only continued to occupy them & exercise dominion over them, but have actually converted them into a new Colony. Let me assure you that this will be considered a most important question by the Congress & people of the United States; & I have no doubt they will arrive at the same conclusion with the Committee of Foreign Relations of the Senate."

His Lordship then inquired, if we believed the Treaty required them to withdraw from Belize. I replied that this was a question which rested on a somewhat different ground from the others, provided they confined themselves to the boundaries & the terms prescribed by the Treaty of 1786; and I purposely said no more on this branch of the subject.

He asked what was to become of Greytown? And I promptly answered: "Let it be restored to Nicaragua; the two Governments taking ample security from that State to make it a free port, according to the terms of the Treaty."

We then went off into a discursive conversation introduced by his Lordship, about grants which had been made by the Mosquito King to Englishmen & Americans & the Pogais grants on Black River;—which it would be tedious & useless to detail.

In the course of this conversation, I told him that whilst our good mother had been all the time engaged, for one hundred & fifty years, in annexing one possession after the other to her dominions, until the sun now never set upon her empire, she raised her hands with holy horror if the daughter annexed territories adjacent to herself, which came to her in the natural course of events. His Lordship replied:—"Well, you must admit that in this respect you are a chip of the old block." Very true, I observed; but we could not imagine why England should object to our annexations;—we extended the English language, Christianity, liberty, & law wherever we went upon our own continent, & converted uninhabited regions into civilised communities, from the trade with which they derived great advantages. With much similar conversation, especially in regard to the annexation of Texas, this long interview terminated.

Just as I was about to take my departure, I asked him for the Charter of "the Bay Islands," & he handed me the paper which I now enclose. Upon my return home, I found it to be, not the charter, but a proclamation of the Lieutenant Governor of that Colony.

I think I shall not trouble you hereafter with any more such minute details of conversations between Lord Clarendon & myself. You will perceive that it has been my object to impress his Lordship with the serious & even alarming nature of the Central American questions, of which, I am persuaded, he had no just conception. It was for this purpose I felt so anxious to be authorised to protest, in the name of the President, against the establishment of the Colony of "the Bay Islands."

I am now on such free & easy terms with Lord Clarendon that I can say almost what I please to him, in a kind & respectful manner; but I confess nothing would mortify me more than to see our unreserved conversation in print. Besides, this would altogether destroy my usefulness here & make my situation very disagreeable.

I would thank you to inform me what may be the President's opinion of my suggestion to place the Mosquito Indians in the same relation to Nicaragua that our own Indians sustain to the United States. I confess that, after reflection, I can perceive no insurmountable objection to the plan. The most serious difficulty attending it would be to impose any limitation on the right of the Mosquitos to sell or Nicaragua to purchase their lands, such as that suggested by Lord Clarendon. With the consent of Nicaragua, however, which his Lordship does not appear much to regard, the object might be accomplished, if this were the only obstacle in the way to a satisfactory adjustment of all the questions. I hope you will let me hear from you on this subject, at your earliest convenience. Please, also, to inform me of the sequel of the argument between Messrs. Webster & Crampton; & send me a document containing the letter of Lord Palmerston to Mr. Castellon. If you can ascertain what is the probable number of the Mosquito Indians, I should be very glad to know it.

Yours very respectfully

JAMES BUCHANAN.

HON: WILLIAM L. MARCY
    Secretary of State.

(Enclosure in No. 16.)
Recd. from Lord Clarendon at our interview Monday 7 November 1853.

JAMES BUCHANAN.

In the name of Her Majesty Victoria of the United Kingdom of Great Britain and Ireland Queen Defender of the Faith—

PROCLAMATION.

By His Excellency Philip Edmond Wodehouse Esqre. Lieutenant Governor of the Bay Islands. Whereas by letters Patent under the Great Seal of the United Kingdom of Great Britain and Ireland bearing date at Westminster the 26th day of March last past it is directed and enjoined that the said letters Patent be read and proclaimed, And Whereas the said letters have been this day read accordingly, Now therefore we the Lieut. Governor duly appointed under the authority of the said letters Patent do hereby proclaim and declare that Her Majesty Queen Victoria has been pleased to erect the Islands of Ruatan, Bonacca, Utilla, Helena, Barbarat, and Moxat into the Colony of the Bay Islands. And to constitute and appoint the Captain General and Governor in Chief for the time being over the Island of Jamaica to be the Governor and Commander in Chief for the time being of the said Colony.

And Her said Majesty has required and commanded the said Governor to administer the Government of the said Colony, in conformity with the said letters Patent and the instructions to be from time to time given to him and with the Laws to be made and agreed upon by the said Governor with the advice and consent of General Assemblies of the said Colony to be elected in the manner directed by the said letters Patent.

And Her said Majesty has been pleased further to authorize and empower the said Governor by warrant under his hand and seal to constitute and appoint a Lieutenant Governor and also a presiding Magistrate over the said Colony.

Given at Coxon Hole this 2d day of August in the year of Our Lord 1852.

(signed)   P. E. WODEHOUSE.

God save the Queen.

FROM LORD CLARENDON.

(Enclosure in No. 17.[1])

FOREIGN OFFICE, November 19th 1853.

SIR,

I have the honor to refer to your note of the 16th of September enclosing a copy of a protest made before the United States Consul at Liverpool by the master of the American Ship "Sovereign of the Seas" against the action of the Post Office Authorities in compelling him to carry a British Mail to Australia, and requesting to be referred to the Act or Acts of Parliament on which the opinion of the Solicitor of the Post Office was founded, that "no master of any vessel, British or Foreign, bound from the Port of Liverpool to Australia could refuse to take a letter bag tendered to him for conveyance by an officer of the Post Office without incurring a penalty of two hundred pounds."

You also state that you had been informed by the United States Consul that, so far as he could ascertain, this was the first case of the kind which had occurred at Liverpool.

I have, in the first place, to express my regret at the delay which has occurred in answering your communication, owing to circumstances over which this Department had no control; and I have now to state that the United States Consul at Liverpool is mistaken in supposing that the practice complained of by the master of the "Sovereign of the Seas" is new; it has existed, on the contrary, from a period extending as far back as we have any records, and almost every day's "Packet List" contains announcements to the effect "that the Ship letter office will despatch letters under the regulations of the Acts of Parliament," by foreign as well as British Ships; but, after taking the opinion of the law officers of the Crown upon the subject, and having conferred with the Post Master General, it has been considered that the law is not compulsory as respects foreign vessels; and that if captains or owners of such vessels take charge of letter bags, it must be a voluntary act on their part.

Directions to that effect have accordingly been given, to prevent all future cause of complaint; and, in order to explain the course which the Post Office proposes to adopt, I beg to enclose a copy of a letter addressed from that Department to the Agents of the American Ship "Golden Age," who, it appears, made the same objection as the Captain of the "Sovereign of the Seas" to convey the Mail bags.

I have the honor to be, With the highest consideration, Sir,

Your most obedient humble servant,

(sd.)   CLARENDON.

JAMES BUCHANAN, ESQ.
&c. &c. &c.

---

[1] Despatch to Mr. Marcy, No. 17, Nov. 25, 1853, infra.

THE
CHICAGO
PUBLIC LIBRARY

✳
J 108
9

TO MR. MARCY

(No. 17.) LEGATION OF THE UNITED STATES.

LONDON, 25th November 1853.

SIR,

I have the honor to acknowledge the receipt of your Despatches Nos. 16, 17, 18, and 19, respectively.

I have received from Lord Clarendon a communication dated on the 19th instant, enclosing a copy of a note of the 8th instant, from the Post Office Department, London, to Messrs. Deane, Youle & Co., Liverpool, Agents of the " Golden Age," of which I transmit you copies. These terminate the question in our favor, of the claims asserted, and in regard to the "Sovereign of the Seas," enforced, to compel American vessels clearing from British Ports to carry British Mails.

The opinion of the Attorney General, and your Instructions in regard to the Legislative Act of the Colony of New South Wales " for more effectually preventing desertion and other misconduct of Seamen belonging to Foreign Ships," are in accordance with my own anticipations. I shall take care to communicate their substance in an appropriate manner to Lord Clarendon.

I proceed to give you the information concerning Passports requested by your No. 18.

Every passport issued by the Department of State requires the visé of this Legation before the person holding it can proceed from London to any part of the Continent. This visé is a warrant for the French Consul to affix his visé to the same passport which is necessary in proceeding from London to Paris; and so of the appropriate Consuls or Ministers, if the individual desires to proceed directly from London to any other European Country. This duty is generally performed by the Consuls of the respective Governments in London. When American travellers have pre-determined their routes on the Continent, they often obtain visés from the Consuls or Ministers of all the respective Nations, in London, in which they intend to travel.

I transmit you a Blank form of the Passports issued by this Legation. These Passports require the same visés precisely from foreign Consuls and Ministers as are required for the Pass-

---

[1] MSS. Department of State, 65 Despatches from England.

ports issued by the Department of State. There is no difference except that the Legation does not visé its own passports.

The following is the exact form of a visé, whether upon a passport issued by the Department, or on an official certificate of the Declaration of intention of a foreigner to become a citizen of the United States.

No. 350. Vu à la Légation des États Unis d'Amerique, à Londres ce 25th Novembre 1853. Bon pour la France, la Belgique, et partout le Continent.

[Seal]   Pour le Ministre   W. H. Welsh.

In obedience to your Instructions, I always sign original Passports myself. They were formerly signed by the Secretary of Legation or the Clerk of the Mission, for the Minister. I had a new form prepared after my arrival in London. I send a copy of the old form.

This business of granting passports and visés occupies the Clerk of the Mission very often throughout all the business hours of the day. It would be quite impossible for the Minister to attend to it himself personally, without sacrificing the time which ought to be devoted to more important and difficult duties; though he is always at hand to decide any question of difficulty which may arise. Col. Lawrence, the attaché to the Mission, attended to this business in a most satisfactory manner until his recent departure to the United States; and Mr. Welsh now performs this duty in an equally satisfactory manner.

Exequaturs for John C. O'Neill and John Higgins, Esquires, have been obtained and transmitted to these gentlemen with their commissions, at their respective Consulates in Belfast & Cork.

I have just received from the Foreign Office the Exequatur for James H. Williams, Esquire, appointed Consul for the Port of Sydney, which with his commission shall be transmitted to him immediately.

Yours very respectfully
JAMES BUCHANAN.

HON: WILLIAM L. MARCY
    Secretary of State.

TO LIEUTENANT MAURY.[1]

U. S. LEGATION LONDON 25 November 1853.

MY DEAR SIR/

I have received your favor of the 9th Instant & owe you many thanks for the " chart illustrative of the Naval Strength of Great Britain in American waters."

I should gladly serve you in attempting to induce the British Government to adopt the form of the " Abstract Log," recommended by the late Maritime Conference at Brussels &c. &c. &c.; but without instructions from the Department of State, I would not feel justified in entering upon such a negotiation. According to prescribed practice the Foreign Secretary is the only medium of communication between foreign ministers & the other Departments of this Government. I can, therefore, have no direct official communication with the Navy Department or the Board of Trade. Under these circumstances, I should be unwilling to commence the business, unless I could preface my note to Lord Clarendon with the usual phrase, that I have been instructed by my Government to bring the subject to his notice. This might, also, be important to my success. It is for them & not for me to decide whether & how I shall act in this matter. This shall not, however, prevent me from bringing the subject in conversation before the appropriate authorities, whensoever an opportunity may offer.

I should hope that the British authorities, without being urged thereto, by the American Government, would of themselves perceive the value & importance of adopting the recommendation of the Conference at Brussels.

from your friend
very respectfully
JAMES BUCHANAN.

LIEUTENANT M. F. MAURY
of the U. S. Navy.

---

[1] Buchanan Papers, Historical Society of Pennsylvania.

FROM MR. MARCY.[1]

Private.   WASHINGTON Decr. 4th '53.

HON. JAMES BUCHANAN

DEAR SIR: I have received the two private letters with which you have favored me and ought to have acknowledged them before this time. I think you have made an auspicious beginning with Ld. Clarendon and hope the end may fulfil the promises of that beginning. You will see by the date that Congress will assemble to-morrow. The caucus went off quite smoothly last night, much more so than was expected considering the powerful Lobby which were on the ground and were prompt and kind in offering their advice to every M. C. new and old as they came in.

I have made arrangements to have the Message go in the Steamer from Boston which will leave on Wednesday. I venture to predict that you will be highly pleased with it.

I almost regret being confined here, as it prevents me from taking an efficient part in N. Y. in organizing the party for my old friend Dickinson. This is probably one of the reasons that his *hard* friends are so extremely anxious to have the Cabinet broken up. I really do not now see any thing which looks like the happening of such an event. I forbear entering upon political topics, for if you get a sight of the N. Y. Herald or read the Revd. C. Edwards Liston's letters in the London Times you will get—I will not say better—but very different information from that which I could give you.

You will ere long probably see our old Friend, J. Y. Mason. He was delayed (partly by accident) longer than was intended and until so near the time of the meeting of the Senate that it was thought respectful that he should remain for confirmation. The same was the case with Gov. Seymour and R. M. McLane.

I am a little surprised that Mr. Crampton has not yet heard from his government in regard to the Fishery negotiation.

Not long since he read me a passage from a private note of Ld. Clarendon's to him in which there were some civil & complimentary things said of yourself. I ventured to say to Mr. C. that I thought the *liking* was mutual for I was quite sure that your intercourse with Ld. C. had been very agreeable to yourself.

From what Mr. C. said to me about the Sandwich Islands I had a right to infer that G. Britain is a little uneasy about the state of things in them. M. Sartiges exhibits still stronger symptoms of uneasiness on the part of his govt.

I propose to communicate officially with you on that subject before long.

I really hope you will continue to favor me with private letters, for I assure you I read them with much pleasure as I do your excellent Despatches. I cannot in person present as you request your regards to Mrs. Marcy, for she has left me, determined not to return until I get a house to cover her head— a provision for her comfort I have not yet made.

Yours truly

W. L. MARCY.

---

[1] Buchanan Papers, Historical Society of Pennsylvania.

TO MR. MARCY.[1]

U. S. LEGATION, LONDON 9 December 1853.

MY DEAR SIR/

John William Cates, the old & faithful messenger of this Legation, & in many minor matters its factotum, has for eighteen years received £80.00.0. per annum; whilst the expense of living, as well as wages, has in the mean time increased more than 25 per cent. in London. He cannot any longer maintain himself & family on this sum. Indeed, I have been obliged to give my coachman £114 per annum, & he claims other perquisites. I would, therefore, earnestly & respectfully suggest that you should increase his salary to £100.00.0. per annum, & authorise me to pay him this sum from the commencement of the present month. The price of coals has nearly doubled since the approach of winter.

Cates, although a British subject, is a true American, & has so completely identified himself with the Legation, after eighteen years' service, that it would almost break his heart to be compelled to seek other employment.

I do not deem this note of sufficient importance to give it the power of a Despatch, though I desire that it may be filed as the reason for making the increased allowance, which I trust you may think proper to sanction.

No man in London could, until after years' experience, supply the place of Cates. Mr. Everett, I have no doubt, would confirm all I have said about him.

Yours very respectfully

JAMES BUCHANAN.

HON: WILLIAM L. MARCY
    Secretary of State.

---

[1] MSS. Department of State, 65 Despatches from England.

TO MR. LEWIS.[1]

U. S. LEGATION, LONDON, 9 Dec: 1853.

MY DEAR SIR:

Pray write me a long letter, and give me a gossiping account of all matters and things relating to Lancaster, the world in general, and "the rest of mankind." I am sadly in want of such information. Please to direct to me, at the United States Legation, London, care of I. Franklin Pierce, Esquire, Despatch Agent, New York, and pay the postage to that city (New York). Nothing more is necessary.

I believe I shall be able to give you a favorable introduction to the sages of the Law, when you visit England next summer. It has so happened that the Lord Chancellor and the Chief Justice of the Queen's Bench, particularly Lord Campbell, have treated me with great civility and kindness since my arrival in London. The latter has given me a special invitation to visit the Queen's Bench, where he says I shall be received with distinguished honors. What he means by this I do not understand. We have had no conversation on any legal subject, except what incidentally arose from a question of mine as to the period when Lord Holt was Chief Justice, in which I had a meaning. This induced him to speak of the decision in the case of Coggs v. Bernard, in which rusty as I am I felt at home. I then asked him if he was aware Lord Holt had decided that under the law of England negro slaves were merchandise. This was after he had risen from the table of the Duke of Newcastle, where Mrs. Stowe, her book, and American slavery had been a subject of conversation. Upon that occasion I spoke right out, and was agreeably surprised to find that most of the gentlemen at table concurred with me in opinion as to the impropriety and the consequences of their interference on the subject.

" 'Tis distance lends enchantment to the view." In the power and faculty of general conversation, I would be willing to stake Wheatland that the Chief Justice and yourself would excel the Lord Chancellor and the Lord Chief Justice. It is true that in general society they are too polite to converse upon profes-

---

[1] This letter is copied from the original, which was temporarily placed in the editor's hands by Mr. Burton Alva Konkle, who has given passages from it in his Life of Chief Justice Ellis Lewis, 1798–1871, of the First Elective Supreme Court of Pennsylvania.

sional subjects, where I have no doubt they would find themselves at home.

The official costume of the Judges of the Queen's Bench,—large crimson gowns,—is truly ridiculous. That of the Chancellor and Vice Chancellor is far richer, though but little more becoming. In a plain suit of black, I met the Grand Dignitaries, at the Lord Mayor's dinner, all arrayed in their official robes.

If I were twenty years younger, I have no doubt I should be much pleased with a residence at this Court. As it is, I shall endeavor to make the best of it. My heart, however, is still in my native land; and my dream of life is, that I shall pass the remnant of my days, should a merciful Providence prolong them, in retirement at Wheatland. I would now rather have an hour's conversation with Alderman Kautz than with the Lord Chancellor of England.

A few days ago, I went to pay a visit to the Marchioness of Wellesley and Lady Stafford at Hampton Court. The former was very ill with dropsy, and I did not see her. The latter I found in much trepidation in consequence of a notice which she had just received, through the official paper of the Court, to appear before you on the first Monday of January. [Here follows a long passage, carefully crossed out with a pen.] I obliterate this, not because there is anything objectionable in it, but because I have always felt an abhorrence to make any allusion to a Judge about a case before his court, even without expressing my opinion. They asked me to recommend an agent for them for their lands in Pennsylvania, and I suggested the name of our friend Christopher L. Ward.

These ladies have experienced an astonishing fate. They have all married titled noblemen; and no lady stood higher or was more respected at Court than Lady Wellesley. Being the sister-in-law of the Duke of Wellington, and a great favorite with him, she has amused and interested me very much by relating private anecdotes of that remarkable man. She is now a widow, in a dying condition, and has scarcely income sufficient for her support in the rank to which she has been accustomed. Lady Stafford is, also, a widow, and a fine woman; but neither she nor the Duchess of Leeds is at all equal to Lady Wellesley.

I like them all for the strong and ardent American feeling which they still retain. I have no doubt they would have been happier had they remained at home and married independent and worthy American gentlemen.   But enough and far more than enough of this.

The English just reverse our custom in regard to town and country life.   The nobility and gentry visit London only in the summer.   The season, as they call it, commences a few weeks after the meeting of Parliament in February, and terminates with its adjournment in the beginning of August.   All the rest of the year they are upon their estates or roaming over the Continent. If you happen to meet one of them, he will tell you that there is now nobody in town,—a town which contains two millions and a half of people.   They are great sportsmen, and men and women are devoted to exercise in the open air, both on foot and on horseback.   Their ladies are more robust and healthy looking than our own; but they are deficient in that delicacy of beauty for which our countrywomen are so distinguished.   Of course the ministers and officials of the Crown and judges of the courts must be in London after the 1st of November; but they all have a time of it in the country from the adjournment of Parliament up till that day.

I wish I could change the habits of our ladies, and induce them to take more exercise in the open air.   This would contribute both to their health and their beauty.   You never see a lady here on the street in full dress.   With thick shoes and warmly clad, they move at a rapid rate.

I am persuaded that the mass of the people are far, very far behind our own in almost every respect.   The rate of interest and the rate of wages are now so high here that our manufacturers have but little to fear.   The emigration of laborers to America and Australia has produced this effect on labor; but it is a problem which I cannot solve, why money should be so scarce throughout all the commercial nations of the world, notwithstanding the immense production of gold in California and Australia.   Negotiations here in new Rail Road Bonds are at an end for some time to come.

Please to remember me kindly to the Chief Justice and your other associates on the bench.   Also to Hirst, Van Dyke, Tyler, Plitt, Westcott, and all the rest, not forgetting our worthy host, McKibbon.   Present my kindest compliments to Mrs. Lewis, and believe me to be very respectfully

Your friend

JAMES BUCHANAN.

HON. ELLIS LEWIS.

TO GENERAL PORTER.[1]

U. S. LEGATION, LONDON 9 Dec: 1853.

MY DEAR SIR/

"Long looked for come at last." I believe my friends in Pennsylvania have entirely forgotten me. If they knew what a deep interest I take in every thing at home they would surely write to me often. I hope you will give me a long gossiping letter,—cram every thing into it & let me know what is going on behind the scenes. Brawley has never written me a word since I have been in England & my friends at Lancaster have been very chary of their letters. It is true I receive the papers regularly, but they only present the outside. I do not even know whether Frazer & his clique struck Brawley; but presume they did, notwithstanding the coalition, of which I never approved.

I am here like a man in exile, but I shall endeavor to make this exile as agreeable as possible. I cannot yet form an opinion as to whether my mission will be successful; but I shall do my best. I have had several long conversations with Lord Clarendon, the Minister for Foreign affairs, on the subject of it & have spoken as plainly as courtesy would permit. He is a very agreeable man & we are on excellent terms; but the Russian & Turkish question takes up so much of his time, that I have not yet had a fair chance. If the President in his message has spoken plainly in relation to our questions with England, this will render me great assistance. General phrases will be of no service.

It was remarked that at the Lord Mayor's dinner instead of toadying any body myself, I was toadied by Lord Palmerston, —a thing almost unexampled coming from that very able & energetic statesman. The Lord Chancellor said still more; but they do not report the dinner speeches of high dignitaries of the Law. My social position here will be as agreeable as I could desire, unless I shall get into difficulties about the Costume Circular when the Queen begins to hold her Courts, which I apprehend.

The English people, so far as my observation extends, do not like us. Their Public Journals, & particularly the Times, never omit any opportunity of giving us "a rap over the knuckles." This is pretty good evidence of the taste of their readers. They are jealous of us & entertain a vague appre-

---

[1] Buchanan Papers, Historical Society of Pennsylvania.

hension of our progress. And well they may. The rate of
interest & the wages of labor are now nearly as high here as in
the United States. The latter will probably continue so for an
indefinite period, on account of the incessant drain of their laboring population to the United States & Australia. The strikes for
higher wages all over England are a symptom of the times.

The other day at a dinner at the Duke of Newcastle's, Mrs.
Stowe & her book became the subject of conversation, & I did
not mince matters, but spoke right out, *evidently to the satisfaction of a majority of the Company.* The occasion was a proper
one & the necessity justified it. In truth, these people do not
apparently treat me as a stranger. Wherever I have been, after
the first hour I am on free & easy terms with them. They are
now sadly puzzled about the Russian & Turkish question.

Of one thing you may be certain,—that the last crop has
been sadly deficient both in quantity & quality; & they will require
a very large supply from the United States. There will be
great scarcity here before the next harvest; & we have had
scarcely any thing but rain, rain, & very damp weather ever
since my arrival. The consequence may probably be a deficiency
in the next year's crop. I am sorry for them; but " it's an ill
wind that blows nobody good."

The labors of this Legation far exceed my anticipation.
The correspondence with Consuls & others independently of that
with the Department of State is very voluminous, though my
letters are as brief as possible. The compensation is absurdly
deficient; but of this I shall never complain. How I shall rejoice,
should a kind Providence spare my life & restore me to my
native land in health & in peace!

Please to remember me most kindly to Mrs. Porter & give
my love to Lizzie.—Think of me often when assembled in the
back room. Remember me to Brawley, Parke, Judge Dock &
my other friends & believe me to be, very respectfully,

Your friend

JAMES BUCHANAN.

HON: DAVID R. PORTER.

TO MISS LANE.[1]

U. S. LEGATION, LONDON, 9 December 1853.

MY DEAR HARRIET/

I received your favor of the 14th ultimo in due time & thank you for the information it contained, all of which was interesting to me.

In regard to your coming to London with Colonel Lawrence & his lady, should he be married in February next, I have this to say: Your passage at that season of the year would, unless by a happy accident, be stormy & disagreeable, though not dangerous. I have scarcely yet recovered from the effects of the voyage, & should you be as bad a sailor as myself & have a rough passage, it might give your constitution a shock.   The month of April would be a much more agreeable period to cross the Atlantic; & you would still arrive here in time for the most fashionable & longer part of the fashionable season.

It is my duty to inform you that a general conviction prevails here, on the part of Lord Palmerston, the Secretary of the Interior, & the distinguished physicians, as well as among the intelligent people, that the cholera will be very bad in London & other parts of England during the latter part of the next summer & throughout the Autumn.   They are now making extensive preparations & adopting expensive sanitary measures to render the mortality as small as possible.   The London Journals contain articles on the subject almost every day.   Their reason for this conviction is,—that we have just had about as many cases of cholera during the past autumn, as there were during the Autumn in a former year, preceding the season when it raged so extensively & violently.

Now this question will be for your own consideration.   I think it my duty to state the facts; & it will be for you to decide whether you will postpone your visit until the end of the next autumn for this reason, or at least until we shall see whether the gloomy anticipations here are likely to be realized.

I still anticipate difficulty about my costume; but should this occur, it will probably continue throughout my mission.   It is, therefore, no valid reason why you should postpone your visit. In that event you must be prepared to share my fate.   So far

---

[1] Buchanan Papers, private collection.   Inaccurately printed in Curtis's Buchanan, II. 109.

as regards the consequences to myself, I do not care a button for them; but it would mortify me very much to see you treated differently from other ladies in your situation.

If this costume affair should not prove an impediment, I feel that I shall get along very smoothly here.   The fashionable world, with the exception of the high officials, are all out of London, & will remain absent until the last of February or beginning of March.   I have recently been a good deal in the society of those who are now here; & they all seem disposed to treat me very kindly, especially the ladies.   Their hours annoy me very much.   My invitations to dinner among them are all for a quarter before eight, which means about half-past that hour. There is no such thing as sociable visiting here of an evening. This is all done between 2 & 6 o'clock in the afternoon, if such visits may be called sociable.   I asked Lady Palmerston what was meant by the word " early " placed upon her card of invitation for an evening reception, & she informed me it was about ten o'clock.

The habits & customs & business of the world here render these late hours necessary.   But how ridiculous it is in our country, where no such necessity exists, to violate the laws of nature in regard to hours merely to follow the fashions of this country!

Should you be at Mr. Ward's, I would thank you to present my kind love to Miss Ellen.   I hope you will not forget the interests of Eskridge in that quarter.

You inform me that Sallie Grier was & that Jennie Pleasonton was about to be married.

I desire to be remembered with special kindness to Mrs. Jenkins.   I can never forget " the auld lang syne," with her & her family.   Give my love, also, to Kate Reynolds.   Remember me to Miss Hetty, or as you would say, Miss Hettie, for whom I shall ever entertain a warm regard.   I send this letter open to Eskridge so that he may read it and send it to your direction.

From your affectionate uncle,

JAMES BUCHANAN.

MISS HARRIET LANE.

TO MR. FORNEY.[1]

U. S. LEGATION, LONDON,

13 Dec. 1853.

MY DEAR SIR,

"Long looked for come at last." I have received your welcome letter of the 28th ultimo: and now feel the greatest anxiety
to learn that you have been re-elected Clerk. I trust & believe
we shall receive this gratifying intelligence with the President's
message on Monday next.

My social position here will be, in fact is, all that I would
have desired twenty years ago when I was a younger man.
Although they say nobody is in town, I may dine out as often
as I please at 8 o'clock in the evening. Although they are
jealous of us and experience a sort of undefined uneasiness at
our rapid growth in commerce and manufactures, yet when an
American Minister mingles among them with any degree of tact
and talent for conversation, he cannot fail to find himself much
at home. For my own part, I have talked right out, with
prudence but with freedom, as I would do at home. What is
remarkable, I have not met any other Foreign Minister at their
tables, with the exception of a dinner at Lord Palmerston's.
When they speak to me of their friendship for our country, as
they often do, and refer to the mother and the daughter, I
answer that their public journals, and especially the Times, never
fail to give us a "rap over the knuckles" when the occasion
offers, and that this is a strong evidence of public opinion. This
affords me an opportunity which I do not fail to embrace of doing
the President and our Country justice against the New York
correspondent of the Times. In this way, I believe I have
already rendered some service. On more than one occasion Mrs.
Stowe and her book and American Slavery have become topics
of conversation; and I find them more reasonable on this
subject than I had anticipated. I have not yet met the Duchess
of Sutherland.

They speak of the season in London as we speak of the
season at Saratoga. This usually commences about Easter and
terminates on the adjournment of Parliament in August. All
the rest of the year, it is not fashionable to be in town, except for
the members of the Cabinet and the other officials.

My social relations may and probably will undergo a great

---

[1] Buchanan Papers, Historical Society of Pennsylvania.

change after the Queen holds her first Drawing Room. They have talked so much about my costume, that I do not see how it is possible for me to put on gold lace and embroidery. A Court lady asked me the other day if our President had not been a general. I replied, certainly, he had been a good and brave General. Well then, said she, did he not wear the uniform attached to his rank and to distinguish him from other inferior officers and privates? I answered, of course, he did. Well then, she answered, why should not a foreign Minister from your country do the same thing? I gave her the reasons, which it is not necessary to repeat.

I would send for Harriet at once if I could foresee the issue of this affair. I would not care a button about being ostracised myself in the immediate Court Circle; but should be very unwilling to place her in this position. If I should pass through the mill unscathed in plain clothes, I shall have to present Americans at Court in full Court Dress, because for them it is certain they will not relax the rules.

You inform me that the President does not intend to change his Cabinet, and I have not supposed he would. If he should, their successors, whoever they might be, would probably encounter as many difficulties as the present members. I gave the President advice from the bottom of my heart, in December last, in regard to the " launching of his administration." It would probably have been better had he followed it. I have no personal objections to any member of the present Cabinet, and to Davis, Dobbin, and Campbell I am and ought to be warmly attached. I still like Marcy. We got along admirably well, throughout Mr. Polk's administration. I do not think he behaved altogether right to me in the Presidential contest. I now judge of things at home as if I were posterity; and I confess I think Mr. Guthrie committed a great blunder in his letter to Bronson. My influence with the administration is so poor, that my brother informs me the promise of a clerkship has not even been kept to poor Lightner. I am still, notwithstanding, attached to the President, and heartily wish his administration success. You know I have not much confidence in the free soil Democrats of the Buffalo platform. My friends do not write to me, not even from Lancaster. " Out of sight, out of mind." I should forget all, should the President appoint Van Dyke; but he will not do it. With my kindest regards to Mrs. Forney, and a kiss for little Mary, I remain as ever sincerely your friend,

JAMES BUCHANAN.

TO MISS PARKER.[1]

U. S. LEGATION, LONDON 16 December 1853.

MY DEAR MISS HETTY/

I have received your welcome letter of the 24 ultimo. You give me more interesting news than any other friend; & I do hope that you will pass some of the long winter evenings in writing me all about Wheatland, the neighbours, & whatever else you know would be interesting to me. I beg you to take no pains with your letters but write whatever comes uppermost. This I like of all things. My affections are all at home; though I am received & treated here most kindly.

I am glad that you have had interest enough with your two beaus to get them to take Wheatland in hand. It needed it very much; & it was very kind on the part of Mr. Herr & Mr. Baer. Please to thank them in my name. They shall be fully compensated.

I rejoice, also, that Mrs. Fahnestock has consented to stay with you. What a time you & she will have with the bachelor & the widower. Unless Lara has changed very much for the better he is but a poor protector.

Poor old father Kreider! He was an honest, intelligent, & sensible man. He belonged to a generation which have all passed away; & his descendants may be proud of him as well as profit by his example.

I wish I could indulge the hope that I will be at home next summer to enjoy the ice. This, however, is impossible, unless in the ways of a kind Providence, something unexpected should occur. My understanding with General Pierce was not to remain longer than two years; but that I might return home after eighteen months, should I succeed in accomplishing the great objects of my mission. I do not as yet know what may be my luck; but I am trying my best.

I am glad you have got clear of France on peaceable terms. I hope he may have become a better man since he joined the Church. I give myself no trouble about Wheatland, having absolute confidence that you will do all things right. I hope you will not mind the expense of any necessary improvement.

I am very glad to learn that Mr. Weaver still continues to behave himself well & that Jessie is contented & happy. I had

---

[1] Buchanan Papers, Historical Society of Pennsylvania.

not heard a word of them or from them since my departure before I received your letter.

I have but little to say about myself, except that thank God! I am as well as usual & better, I think, than before I left home. The dinner hour here is from 7 till 8 o'clock; & I am obliged to dine out often. The evening parties commence at from 10 to 12. This deranges all my Wheatland habits; & yet when you go to Rome you must do as Rome does. With all this I cannot say but that I enjoy myself in society; & if I were twenty years younger I might relish this kind of life very much. The ladies whom I meet treat me with much civility & kindness.

These late hours are in conformity with all the habits of society here. They cannot well be otherwise. But how ridiculous it is to imitate them in the United States, where the habits & business of the people are altogether different. With us it is a fashion for which there is no reason.

My housekeeper is a Mrs. Sanders,—the lady who has kept house for several of my predecessors. I think she understands her business & is industrious. I am satisfied with her, without being greatly pleased. The man (Jackson) whom I hired accidentally in New York has behaved himself very well. He is very attentive & I think perfectly honest. He is a good looking mulatto, & I have been diverted to witness the attention he receives here where the same prejudices do not exist against color as in the United States. And yet he is homesick & thinks as I do, that there is no place in the world to be compared with our Country.

Please to remember me very kindly to Mrs. Fahnestock & Mrs. Brenner, as well as to the Mrs. Baers, Mr. Herr, & Mr. Baer. Should you be writing to Aunt Rebecca or Harriet, I would thank you to present me kindly to them as well as to Mr. & Mrs. Van Dyke. Do not forget either old Jake or young Jake. I expected ere this to hear of Mrs. B.'s marriage to Mr. Bauman. My sheet is full & I have no more to say but that I remain most sincerely & respectfully your friend,

JAMES BUCHANAN.

MISS ESTHER PARKER.

TO MR. MASON.[1]

Legation of The United States.
                    London 23 December 1853.

My dear Sir/

In your kind note of Aug: 2d you were good enough to promise that you would write to me during my absence. If you could realise the pleasure which letters from home afford me in this foreign land you would not neglect this friendly duty.

My situation here is quite as agreeable as I anticipated. I have been received & treated kindly by the society generally. Lord Clarendon, the Minister for Foreign affairs, is a gentleman of kind & affable manners, with whom it is a pleasure to transact business. Whether I shall succeed in accomplishing the great objects of my mission is as yet quite uncertain. I shall do my best. Twenty years ago I should have enjoyed this mission very much; but between the ages of 42 & 62, a man's tastes & habits undergo a great change. Whilst I am contented here, I should be far more happy in retirement at Wheatland.

These people are jealous of our rapid progress, especially in commerce & manufactures, & entertain a sort of undefined dread of our advancement; but yet with these feelings is intermingled some pride that we owe our origin to them. An American minister possessing some tact & talent for conversation will be always well received in British society. We speak the same language, have read the same books, & had the same history till the period of the Revolution. These are so many links to bind us together; & yet judging from the tone of the Press here & especially of the Mammoth Times, they are far from being friendly to the United States. Still I have always felt myself pretty much at home with them after the first hour & have talked with almost as much freedom at their dinner tables as I would do in Washington City. Mrs. Stowe & her book have occasionally become subjects of conversation, & I have expressed myself freely of their Anti-Slavery Society & its interference in our domestic concerns: & this, generally, with apparent approbation.

The President's message has been well received here, & what is uncommon, has elicited a favorable notice from the Times. This was Tuesday morning. I observe, however, that in an Editorial of the next day it recurs to the everlasting subject of

---

[1] Buchanan Papers, Historical Society of Pennsylvania.

American Slavery, (which these people do not understand) &
the danger arising from it to our Union.

There was a great deficiency in the crop of wheat in this
country at the last harvest, both in quantity & quality; & they
will require a large supply from the United States. I sincerely
pity their condition in this respect; but " it's an ill wind that
blows nobody good."

Please to remember me, in the kindest terms, to Mrs. Mason,
& in the expectation of soon receiving from you a long gossiping
letter about all the world & " the rest of mankind," I remain, as
always,

Sincerely & respectfully your friend

JAMES BUCHANAN.

HON: JNO. THOMSON MASON.[1]

1854.

TO MR. MARCY.[2]

No. 19.   LEGATION OF THE UNITED STATES.

LONDON, 5 January, 1854.

SIR:

I have the honor to acknowledge the receipt of your despatches Nos. 20, 21, 22, and 23, of 19th November and 1st, 3d,
and 16th December respectively.

In reference to your Despatch No. 19, of the 10th November
last, on the subject of the Legislative Act of the Colony of New
South Wales " for more effectually preventing desertion and
other misconduct of seamen belonging to foreign ships," I have
informed Lord Clarendon that the President is unwilling to
express a desire that the Act in question should be enforced
against the crews of ships belonging to the United States. I
have, also, transmitted to him a copy of the opinion of the Attor-

[1] Mr. Mason, a native of Maryland, was a representative in Congress
from that State from 1841 to 1843. In 1851 he was elected by the people a
judge of the court of appeals, a post which he held till 1857, when he resigned
and became collector of the port of Baltimore. (Lanman's Biographical
Annals of the Civil Government of the United States, 276.)

[2] MSS. Department of State, 65 Despatches from England. The principal
part of this despatch is printed in H. Ex. Doc. 1, 34 Cong. 1 Sess. I. 52.

ney General of the 28th October last as containing the reasons
which have caused the President to arrive at this conclusion.
These are certainly sufficient.

I have not deemed it advisable to press the Central American negotiation since my last interview with Lord Clarendon
in November. The causes for this delay have been the unsettled condition of the British Cabinet in consequence of the
resignation of Lord Palmerston and his subsequent withdrawal
of that resignation; the state of the Russo-Turkish question to
which the ministry have been devoting themselves, fruitlessly as
it is now believed to the task of preventing a war between Great
Britain and Russia; and the desire which I felt to receive your
instructions in regard to the suggestion which I had made to
Lord Clarendon that the Mosquito Indians might be placed in the
same relation to Nicaragua that our own Indians sustain to the
United States. Your satisfactory Despatch, No. 21, has removed all doubts on this latter subject.

I have reason to believe that my omission to press the Central American questions at the present most important crisis
between Great Britain and Russia has been properly appreciated
by Lord Clarendon.

On Monday last, however, I addressed His Lordship a note
requesting an interview, to which I have received his answer
appointing to-morrow (Friday), at half past three o'clock, for
our meeting;—too late for the next steamer. Indeed, I had
reason to expect that ere this he would himself have taken the
initiative and have invited me to an interview. In the interview
to-morrow I shall not forget the Fishery and Reciprocity
questions.

I have received the Exequatur for Noble Towner, appointed
Consul at Barbadoes, and have transmitted it to him at his post
together with his commission.

Yours very respectfully

JAMES BUCHANAN.

HON. WM. L. MARCY,
&c. &c. &c. Washington, D. C.

MEMORANDUM, JANUARY 6, 1854,

ON THE CLAYTON-BULWER TREATY.[1]

STATEMENT FOR THE EARL OF CLARENDON.

When the negotiations commenced which resulted in the conclusion of the Clayton & Bulwer Convention of the 19th April, 1850, the British Government were in possession of the whole extensive coast of Central America, sweeping round from the Rio Hondo to the Port & Harbor of San Juan de Nicaragua, except that portion of it between the Sarstoon & Cape Honduras, together with the adjacent Honduras Island of Ruatan.

The Government of the United States seriously contested the claim of Great Britain to any of these possessions, with the single exception of that part of the Belize settlement lying between the Rio Hondo & the Sebun, the usufruct of which, for a special purpose and with a careful reservation of his sovereign rights over it, had been granted by the King of Spain to the British, under the Convention of 1786.

The progress of events had rendered Central America an object of special interest to all the commercial nations of the world, on account of the Rail Roads & Canals then proposed to be constructed through the Isthmus, for the purpose of uniting the Atlantic & Pacific Oceans.

Great Britain & the United States, both having large & valuable possessions on the shores of the Pacific & an extensive trade with the countries beyond, it was natural that the one should desire to prevent the other from being placed in a position to exercise exclusive control, in peace or in war, over any of the grand thoroughfares between the two Oceans.   This was a main feature of the policy which dictated the Clayton & Bulwer Convention.   To place the two Nations on an exact equality, & thus to remove all causes of mutual jealousy, each of them agreed, by this Convention, never to occupy, fortify, or exercise dominion over any portion of Central America.   Both parties adopted this self denying ordinance, for the purpose of terminating serious misunderstandings then existing between them which might have endangered their friendly relations.

---

[1] This memorandum, as here printed, has been compared with the original paper in 65 Despatches from England. It bears this endorsement: "This Memorandum & Statement is to be attached to & made a part of Despatch No. 20 of the 10th January, 1854. J. B." The memorandum is printed in H. Ex. Doc. 1, 34 Cong. 1 Sess. I. 55–64.

Whether the United States acted wisely or not, in relin-quishing their right, as an independent nation, to acquire terri-tory in a region on their own Continent which may become necessary for the security of their communication with their important & valuable possessions on the Pacific, is another & a different question. But they have concluded the Convention;—their faith is pledged, & under such circumstances they never look behind the record.

The language of the Convention is properly mutual, though in regard to the United States, it can only restrain them from making future acquisitions; because it is well known that in point of fact, they were not in the occupation of a foot of terri-tory in Central America. In reference to Great Britain the case is different, & the language applies not only to the future but the past; because she was then in the actual exercise of dominion over a very large portion of the Eastern coast of Central America. Whilst, therefore, the United States had no occupancy to abandon, under the Convention, Great Britain had extensive pos-sessions to restore to the States of Guatemala, Honduras & Nicaragua.

And yet, the British Government, up till the present moment, have not deemed it proper to take the first step towards the per-formance of their obligations under this Convention. They are still in the actual occupancy of nearly the whole coast of Central America, including the Island of Ruatan, in the very same manner that they were before its conclusion. This delay, on their part, surely cannot proceed from any obscurity in the language of the Convention.

The first article declares, that the Government of the United States & Great Britain agree that neither will " occupy, or fortify, or colonize, or assume or exercise any dominion over Nicaragua, Costa Rica, the Mosquito Coast, or any part of Central America." And from abundant caution,—in view of the Mosquito protector-ate, the article proceeds as follows:—" nor will either make use of any protection which either affords or may afford, or any alliance which either has or may have to or with any State or people for the purpose of . . . occupying, fortifying or colonizing Nicaragua, Costa Rica, the Mosquito Coast or any part of Central America, or of assuming or exercising dominion over the same." This rendered into plain English is, that the parties shall not exercise dominion over any part of Central America, either directly or indirectly, either by themselves or in the name of others.

It has been said that the first article of the Convention acknowledged, by implication, the right of Great Britain to the Mosquito protectorate,—a right which the United States have always contested & resisted; a right which would continue to Great Britain that entire control over the Nicaragua Ship canal & the other avenues of communication between the two oceans which it was the very object of the Convention to abolish; and to defeat that equality between the parties in Central America which was its special purpose to secure. Surely the United States could never have been guilty of such a suicidal absurdity.

But admitting, for the sake of argument merely, that the United States have acknowledged the existence of this Protectorate, it would be difficult, restricted in its use, as it has been by the Convention, to conceive for what object of the least importance it could be employed. It assuredly could not be for the purpose of " occupying " " the Mosquito Coast," or " of assuming or exercising dominion over the same," because this has been expressly prohibited by the Convention.

Great Britain has not even retired from the Island of Ruatan, in obedience to the Convention. Here no question can possibly arise from any alleged Mosquito Protectorate. This is clearly a Central American Island belonging to the State of Honduras, & but thirty miles distant from her port of Truxillo. If the Convention plainly embraces any object whatever, this must be Ruatan.

And yet, Great Britain has not only continued to occupy this Island, but since the date of the Convention, she has actually established a colonial Government over it. And not over it alone, but adding thereto five other neighboring Islands, on the Central American Coast, has converted them all into the British Colony of the " Bay Islands." Public sentiment is quite unanimous in the United States, that the establishment of this Colony is a palpable violation both of the letter & the spirit of the Clayton & Bulwer Convention.

Ruatan is well known to be an Island of great value & importance, on account of its excellent harbors, which are rare along that coast. Indeed, it has been described by a Spanish author " as the key of the Bay of Honduras & the focus of the trade of the neighbouring Countries." Such is its commanding Geographical position that Great Britain, in possession of it, could completely arrest the trade of the United States, on its passage to & from the Isthmus. In vain may the Convention have prohibited

Great Britain from erecting or maintaining any fortifications commanding the Nicaragua Canal, or in other portions of Central America, if she shall continue to exercise dominion over " the Bay Islands."

The United States now only ask that this Convention shall be faithfully executed by both parties. They wish that every avenue of communication across the Isthmus shall be opened, not merely for their own benefit, but for that of Great Britain & the whole world. In this respect, they would not, if they could, acquire any peculiar advantages, because these might arouse the jealousy & distrust of other nations.

The rights and duties of the respective parties have been ascertained & determined by the Convention itself; but as the justice of the previous claim of Great Britain to her possessions in Central America has been since asserted in high quarters, it may not be improper to present the views of the Government of the United States upon this subject.

It need scarcely be repeated that the United States have always denied the validity of this claim. They believe that Great Britain has surrendered nothing under the Convention, which she would not voluntarily have done, from her own magnanimity & sense of justice, as soon as the question was brought home to her serious consideration.

It would be a vain labor to trace the history of the connection of Great Britain with the Mosquito shore & other portions of Central America, previous to her Treaties with Spain of 1783 & 1786. This connection doubtless originated from her desire to break down the monopoly of trade which Spain so jealously enforced with her American Colonies, & to introduce into them British manufactures. The attempts of Great Britain to accomplish this object were pertinaciously resisted by Spain, and became the source of continual difficulties between the two Nations. After a long period of strife, these were happily terminated by the Treaties of 1783 & 1786, in as clear and explicit language as was ever employed on any similar occasion; & the history of the time renders the meaning of this language, if possible, still more clear & explicit.

The 6th article of the Treaty of peace of 3d September, 1783, was very distasteful to the King & Cabinet of Great Britain. This abundantly appears from Lord John Russell's " Memorials & correspondence of Charles James Fox." The British Government failing in their efforts to have this Article deferred for six months finally yielded a most reluctant consent to its insertion in the Treaty.

Why this reluctant consent? Because the 6th Article stipulates, that with the exception of the territory between the River Wallis or Belize & the Rio Hondo, within which permission was granted to British subjects to cut Logwood, " all the English who may be dispersed in any other parts, whether on the Spanish Continent, (' Continent Espagnol ') or in any of the Islands whatsoever dependent on the aforesaid Spanish Continent, & for whatever reason it might be, without exception, shall retire within the District which has been above described in the space of Eighteen months, to be computed from the exchange of ratifications." And the Treaty further expressly provides, that the permission granted to cut Logwood " shall not be considered as derogating in any wise from his [Catholic Majesty's] rights of sovereignty " over this Logwood District; and it stipulates, moreover, " that if any fortifications should actually have been heretofore erected within the limits marked out, His Britannic Majesty shall cause them all to be demolished, & he will order his subjects not to build any new ones."

But notwithstanding these provisions, in the opinion of Mr. Fox, it was still in the power of the British Government " to put our [their] own interpretation upon the words ' Continent Espagnol,' & to determine upon prudential considerations whether the Mosquito Shore comes under the description or not."

Hence the necessity for new negotiations which should determine precisely & expressly the territory embraced by the Treaty of 1783. These produced the Convention of the 14th July, 1786; and its very first Article removed every doubt on the subject. This declares that " His Britannic Majesty's subjects, and the other colonists who have hitherto enjoyed the protection of England, shall evacuate the Country of the Mosquitos, as well as the Continent in general and the islands adjacent, without exception," situated beyond the new limits prescribed by the Convention within which British subjects were to be permitted to cut not only logwood but Mahogany and all other wood ; and even this District is " indisputably acknowledged to belong of right to the Crown of Spain."

Thus what was meant by the " Continent Espagnol," in the Treaty of 1783 is defined, beyond all doubt, by the Convention of 1786; and the sovereignty of the Spanish King over the Mosquito Shore, as well as over every other portion of the

Spanish Continent and the Islands adjacent, is expressly recognized.

It was just that Great Britain should interfere to protect the Mosquito Indians against the punishment to which they had exposed themselves as her allies from their legitimate and acknowledged sovereign. The 14th Article of the Convention, therefore, provides that " His Catholic Majesty, prompted solely by motives of humanity, promises to the King of England, that he will not exercise any act of severity against the Mosquitos inhabiting in part the countries which are to be evacuated by virtue of the present Convention, on account of the connections which may have subsisted between the said Indians and the English; and his Britannic Majesty, on his part, will strictly prohibit all his subjects from furnishing arms, or warlike stores to the Indians in general situated upon the frontiers of the Spanish possessions."

British honor required that these Treaties with Spain should be faithfully observed; and from the contemporaneous history, no doubt exists but that this was done; that the orders required by the 15th article of the Convention were issued by the British Government, and that they were strictly carried into execution.

In this connection a reference to the significant proceedings in the House of Lords, on 26th March, 1787, ought not to be omitted. On that day, a motion was made by Lord Rawdon " That the terms of the Convention of July 14, 1786, do not meet the favorable opinion of this House." The motion was discussed at considerable length and with great ability. The task of defending the Ministry on this occasion was undertaken by Lord Chancellor Thurlow, and was most triumphantly performed. He abundantly justified the Ministry for having surrendered the Mosquito Shore to Spain and proved that " the Mosquitos were not our allies;—they were not a people we were bound by Treaty to protect." " His Lordship repelled the argument that the settlement was a regular and legal settlement with some sort of indignation; and so far from agreeing, as had been contended, that we had uniformly remained in the quiet and unquestionable possession of our claim to the territory, he called upon the noble Viscount Stormont to declare, as a man of honor, whether he did not know the contrary."

Lord Rawdon's motion to condemn the Convention was rejected by a vote of 53 to 17.

It is worthy of special remark, that all sides of the House, whether approving or disapproving the Convention, proceeded upon the express admission that it required Great Britain, employing its own language, to " evacuate the Country of the Mosquitos." On this question the House of Lords were unanimous.

At what period, then, did Great Britain renew her claims to "the Country of the Mosquitos, as well as the Continent in general and the Islands adjacent without exception "? It certainly was not in 1801, when under the Treaty of Amiens she acquired the Island of Trinidad from Spain, without any mention whatever of future acquisitions in America. It certainly was not in 1809, when she entered into a Treaty of alliance offensive and defensive with Spain to resist the Emperor Napoleon in his attempts to conquer the Spanish Monarchy. It certainly was not in 1814 when the Commercial Treaties which had previously existed between the two Powers, including, it is presumed, those of 1783 and 1786 were revived. On all these occasions there was no mention, whatever, of any claims of Great Britain to the Mosquito protectorate or to any of the Spanish American territories which she had abandoned.

It was not in 1817 and 1819 when Acts of the British Parliament (57 & 59 Geo. 3rd) distinctly acknowledged that the British settlement at Belize was " not within the territory and dominion of His Majesty," but was merely " a settlement for certain purposes in the possession and under the protection of His Majesty; "—thus evincing a determined purpose to observe with the most scrupulous good faith the Treaties of 1783 and 1786 with Spain.

In the very sensible book of Captain Bonnycastle, of the Corps of British Royal Engineers, on Spanish America, published at London in 1818, he gives no intimation whatever that Great Britain had revived her claim to the Mosquito Protectorate. On the contrary, he describes the Mosquito Shore as " a tract of country which lies along part of the Northern and Eastern shore of Honduras," which had " been claimed by the British." He adds, " the English held this country for eighty years and abandoned it in 1787 and 1788."

Thus matters continued until a considerable period after 1821, in which year the Spanish Provinces composing the Captain Generalship of Guatemala asserted and maintained their independence of Spain. It would be a work of supererogation to attempt to prove, at this period of the world's history, that these

Provinces, having by a successful revolution become independent States, succeeded, within their respective limits, to all the territorial rights of Spain. This will surely not be denied by the British Government, which took so noble and prominent a part in securing the independence of all the Spanish American provinces.

Indeed Great Britain has recorded her adhesion to this principle of international law, in her Treaty of the 26th December, 1826, with Mexico, then recently a revolted Spanish Colony. By this Treaty, so far from claiming any right beyond the usufruct which had been conceded to her under the Convention with Spain of 1786, she recognizes its continued existence and binding effect as between herself and Mexico by obtaining and accepting from the Government of the latter a stipulation that British subjects shall not be " disturbed or molested in the peaceable possession and exercise of whatever rights, privileges, and immunities they have at any time enjoyed within the limits described and laid down " by that Convention. Whether the former Spanish sovereignty over Belize, subject to the British usufruct, reverted of right to Mexico or to Guatemala, may be seriously questioned; but, in either case, this recognition by Great Britain is equally conclusive.

And here it may be appropriate to observe, that Great Britain still continues in possession not only of the District between the Rio Hondo and the Sibun, within which the King of Spain under the Convention of 1786 had granted her a license to cut Mahogany and other woods, but the British settlers have extended this possession south to the River Sarstoon, one degree and a half of latitude beyond " the limits described and laid down " by the Convention. It is presumed that the encroachments of these settlers south of the Sibun have been made without the authority or sanction of the British crown, and that no difficulty will exist in their removal.

Yet in view of all these antecedents, the island of Ruatan, belonging to the state of Honduras and within sight of its shores, was captured in 1841 by Colonel McDonald, then Her Britannic Majesty's Superintendent at Belize, and the flag of Honduras was hauled down and that of Great Britain was hoisted in its place. This small state, incapable of making any effectual resistance, was compelled to submit, and the island has ever since been under British control. What makes this event more remarkable is that, it is believed, a similar act of violence had been committed on Ruatan by the Superintendent of Belize in 1835; but, on complaint by the Federal Government of the Central American states then still in existence, the act was formally disavowed by the British Government and the island was restored to the authorities of the Republic.

No question can exist but that Ruatan was one of the " Islands adjacent " to the American Continent, which had been restored by Great Britain to Spain under the Treaties of 1783 and 1786. Indeed, the most approved British Gazetteers and Geographers, up till the present date, have borne testimony to this fact, apparently without information from that hitherto but little known portion of the world, that the Island had again been seized by Her Majesty's Superintendent at Belize, and was now a possession claimed by Great Britain.

When Great Britain determined to resume her dominion over the Mosquito shore, in the name of a protectorate, is not known with any degree of certainty in the United States. The first information on the subject in the Department of State at Washington was contained in a Despatch of the 20th January, 1842, from William S. Murphy, Esquire, Special Agent of the American Government to Guatemala, in which he states that in a conversation with Colonel McDonald at Belize, the latter had informed him he had discovered and sent documents to England, which caused the British Government to revive their claim to the Mosquito territory.

According to Bonnycastle, the Mosquito shore " lies along part of the Northern and Eastern shore of Honduras," and, by the map which accompanies his work, extends no further south than the mouth of the river Segovia in about 12° North Latitude. This respectable author certainly never could have imagined that it extended south to San Juan de Nicaragua, because he describes this as the principal seaport of Nicaragua on the Caribbean sea; says there are " three portages " between the Lake and the mouth of the River, and " these carrying places are defended, and at one of them is the Fort St. Juan, called also the Castle of Neustra Senora, on a rock and very strong; it has thirty six guns mounted, with a small battery, whose platform is level with the water; and the whole is enclosed on the land side by a ditch and rampart. Its garrison is generally kept up at a hundred infantry, sixteen artillery men, with about sixty of the militia, and is provided with bateaux which row guard every night up and down the stream." Thus it appears that the Spaniards were justly sensible of the importance of defending this outlet from the lake of Nicaragua to the ocean; because as Captain Bonny-castle observes, " This Port [San Juan] is looked upon as the key of the Americas, and with the possession of it and Realejo on the other side of the Lake, the Spanish colonies might be paralyzed by the enemy being then master of the ports of both oceans." He might have added that nearly sixty years ago, on the 26th February, 1796, the Port of San Juan de Nicaragua was established as a Port of Entry of the second class by the King of Spain.

Captain Bonnycastle, as well as the Spaniards, would have been greatly surprised had they been informed that this Port was a part of the dominions of His Majesty the King of the Mosquitos, and that the cities and cultivated territories of Nicaragua surrounding the lakes Nicaragua and Managua had no outlet to the Caribbean sea, except by his gracious permission. It was therefore with profound surprise and regret the Government and people of the United States learned that a British force on the 1st of January, 1848, had expelled the State of Nicaragua from San Juan; had hauled down the Nicaraguan flag, and had raised the Mosquito flag in its place. The ancient name of the Town, San Juan de Nicaragua, which had identified it in all former time as belonging to Nicaragua, was on this occasion changed and thereafter it became Greytown.

These proceedings gave birth to serious apprehensions throughout the United States that Great Britain intended to monopolize for herself the control over the different routes between the Atlantic and Pacific, which, since the acquisition of California, had become of vital importance to the United States. Under this impression it was impossible that the American Government could any longer remain silent and acquiescing spectators of what was passing in Central America.

Mr. Monroe, one of our wisest and most discreet Presidents, announced in a public message to Congress, in December, 1823, that " the American continents, by the free and independent condition which they have assumed and maintained, are henceforth not to be considered subjects for future colonization by any European Powers."

This declaration has since been known throughout the world as " the Monroe doctrine," and has received the public and official sanction of subsequent Presidents, as well as of a very large majority of the American people.

Whilst this doctrine will be maintained whenever in the opinion of Congress the peace and safety of the United States shall render this necessary, yet to have acted upon it in Central America might have brought us into collision with Great Britain, —an event always to be deprecated, and if possible avoided. We can do each other the most good and the most harm of any two nations in the world; and therefore it is our strong mutual interest, as it ought to be our strong mutual desire, to remain the best friends. To settle these dangerous questions, both parties wisely resorted to friendly negotiations, which resulted in the Convention of April, 1850. May this prove to be instrumental in finally adjusting all questions of difficulty between the parties in Central America, and in perpetuating their peace and friendship!

Surely, the Mosquito Indians ought not to prove an obstacle to so happy a consummation. Even if these savages had never been actually subdued by Spain, this would give them no title to rank as an independent state, without violating the principles and the practice of every European Nation, without exception, which has acquired territory on the Continent of America. They all mutually recognized the right of discovery, as well as the title of the discoverer, to a large extent of interior territory, though at the moment occupied by fierce and hostile tribes of Indians. On this principle, the wars, the negotiations, the cessions, and the jurisprudence of these nations were founded. The ultimate dominion and absolute title belonged to themselves, although several of them, and especially Great Britain, conceded to the Indians a right of mere occupancy, which however, could only be extinguished by the authority of the nation within whose dominions these Indians were found. All sales or transfers of territory made by them to third parties were declared to be absolutely void; and this was a merciful rule even for the Indians themselves, because it prevented them from being defrauded by dishonest individuals.

No nation has ever acted more steadily upon these principles than Great Britain; and she has solemnly recognized them in her Treaties with the King of Spain of 1783 and 1786, by admitting his sovereignty over the Mosquitos.

Shall the Mosquito tribe of Indians constitute an exception from this hitherto universal rule? Is there anything in their character or in their civilization which would enable them to perform the duties and sustain the responsibilities of a sovereign state in the family of nations?

Bonnycastle says of them that they " were formerly a very powerful and numerous race of people; but the ravages of rum and the small pox have diminished their number very much." He represents them on the authority of British settlers, as seeming " to have no other religion than the adoration of evil spirits." The same author also states that " the warriors of this tribe are accounted at fifteen hundred." This possibly may have been correct in 1818, when the book was published; but at present serious doubts are entertained whether they reach much more than half that number. The truth is, they are now a debased race and are degraded even below the common Indian standard. They have acquired the worst vices of civilization from their intercourse with the basest class of the whites, without any of its redeeming virtues. The Mosquitos have been thus represented by a writer of authority who has recently enjoyed the best opportunities for personal observation. That they are totally incapable of maintaining an independent civilized Government is beyond all question. Then in regard to their so-called King. Lord Palmerston, in speaking of him to Mr. Rives, in September 1851, says, " they had what was called a King—who, by the bye," he added in a tone of pleasantry, " was as much a King as I or you." And Lord John Russell, in his Despatch to Mr. Crampton of the 19th January, 1853, denominates the Mosquito Government as " a fiction; " and speaks of the King as a person, " whose title and power are, in truth, little better than nominal."

The moment Great Britain shall withdraw from Bluefields, where she now exercises exclusive dominion over the Mosquito shore, the former relations of the Mosquitos to Nicaragua and Honduras, as the successors of Spain, will naturally be restored. When this event shall occur, it is to be hoped that these states in their conduct towards the Mosquitos and the other Indian tribes within their territories will follow the example of Great Britain and the United States. Whilst neither of these has ever acknowledged or permitted any other nation to acknowledge any Indian tribe within their limits as an independent people, they have both recognized the qualified right of such tribes to occupy the soil, and as the advance of the white settlements rendered this necessary have acquired their title by a fair purchase.

Certainly it cannot be desired that this extensive and valuable Central American Coast, on the highway of nations between the Atlantic and the Pacific, should be appropriated to the use of three or four thousand wandering Indians, as an independent

State, who would use it for no other purpose than that of hunting and fishing and savage warfare. If such an event were possible, the Coast would become a retreat for pirates and outlaws of every nation, from whence to infest and disturb the commerce of the world in its transit across the Isthmus. And but little better would be its condition should a new Independent State be established on the Mosquito Shore. Besides, in either event, the present Central American States would deeply feel the injustice which had been done them in depriving them of a portion of their territories. They would never cease in attempts to recover their rights, and thus strife and contention would be perpetuated in that quarter of the world where it is so much the interest, both of Great Britain and the United States, that all territorial questions shall be speedily, satisfactorily, and finally adjusted.

JAMES BUCHANAN.

LONDON, 6 January 1854.

TO MR. MARCY.[1]

No. 20.   LEGATION OF THE UNITED STATES.
LONDON, 10 January 1854.

SIR/
I had a long interview on Friday last with Lord Clarendon, at the Foreign office. We had much desultory & pleasant conversation on various topics but in my report I shall confine myself to the substance of what passed between us in relation to the pending questions between the two Governments.

Some remarks of His Lordship favorable to our naval expedition to Japan introduced the name of Commodore Perry. He then took occasion to repeat to me the handsome things which Sir George Seymour had said to him concerning that gallant officer, as well as his successor Commodore Shubrick, for their conduct on the Fishing grounds during the years 1852 & 1853.

Availing myself of this introduction of the subject, I asked his Lordship what he had done in regard to Secretary Marcy's projet of the Fishery & Reciprocity Treaty communicated to him by Mr. Crampton. His answer was unfavorable to its success.

[1] MSS. Department of State, 65 Despatches from England. The portion of the despatch relating to Central America was printed in H. Ex. Doc. 1, 34 Cong. 1 Sess. I. 52–56.

He said we wanted to drive too hard a bargain with them & one which was unacceptable to Nova Scotia & their other North American Colonies. After endeavoring to convince him, but without apparent success, that the bargain which we had offered was not hard, but in the highest degree liberal, I said, " My Lord, the British Statesman, particularly at the present momentous crisis in the affairs of the world, who shall be instrumental in settling all the questions pending between the two Governments, on fair & honorable terms, & thus converting Great Britain & the United States into nations kindred in friendship, as they already are in blood, will do more for his country, & indeed for both countries, than any Statesman who has arisen in England since the days of Lord Chatham." He interrupted me by a cordial & enthusiastic response to this remark but observed, that the American people seemed to entertain a strong prejudice against England which it would be difficult to remove, & I must admit this was not shared by the English people against the United States. I replied that I could not speak on this subject from personal observation, my intercourse with British society having as yet been comparatively limited; but that in a free country the Public Press necessarily reflected public opinion, and judging by this standard, I could not admit that the British people were very friendly to the United States. Here a conversation intervened of a good-natured character on the relative regard of the people of the two countries for each other;—which I need not repeat.

I then proceeded to remark that there was great danger of serious collision on the Fishing grounds. Under their construction of the Convention of 1818, American fishermen were excluded even from the great Bays or arms of the Sea; whilst under our construction, these fishermen had a clear right to enter all Bays more than six miles wide at their mouth in pursuit of fish. Our fishermen were a class of people always ready & willing to assert what they believed to be their rights; and in consequence a collision might take place any day, which would seriously endanger the peace between the two countries. That this danger ought, if possible, to be avoided.

He said he heartily concurred with me in this opinion; but again repeated his objections, in the same general terms, to your Projet. In answer, I employed such arguments as I thought would be most available in enforcing the reasonable & liberal character of the Projet; but they did not seem to make much impression. Still, he appeared very anxious that some mode should be devised to avert the danger of a collision which might prove less objectionable to the Colonies.

I then told him he knew I had no authority to negotiate upon this subject; but I would make a suggestion on my own responsibility, without in the slightest degree committing my Government, which he might take for what it was worth. He said he would be very glad to hear it;—that whatever was done on this question would necessarily be subjected to a severe criticism from the people of both nations.

I observed: Why not adopt a single article in regard to the Fisheries, for a brief period, which would bear its own justification on its face to the people of both countries? Let this simply state that in consideration of the grant made by Great Britain to the citizens of the United States of the Shore Fisheries, the United States, on their part, grant that British caught fish shall be admitted into their ports free of duty; & that, in addition, there shall be a reciprocal free trade between the British Colonies & the United States in the articles, enumerating them, contained in your schedule.

The thought appeared to strike him favorably; & he asked me to repeat the suggestion, which he took down in writing.

I observed that a simple provision of this kind for a few years would avoid any immediate danger of collision; & I was persuaded that the Colonists, once in the enjoyment of the advantages which such a Treaty must afford, would desire that it should be continued. He said that if they should prove to be dissatisfied, the Treaty might be terminated after a brief period. We then went off into a conversation on the advantages to the Colonists of a free trade in fish, as well as in the other articles enumerated in your schedule, in which I endeavored, as I had done twice before, to convince him of its great virtue to them. The only specific objection which he made to my suggestion was the danger of collision between American & British fishermen, if the former had the right to dry & cure their fish on the shores. This I obviated by stating that without the consent of the owners of the property this right could not be exercised by American fishermen; & that when the question was once settled, the parties would mutually respect each other's rights & not interfere with any previous occupancy.

I am persuaded that it is the strong opposition of the Colonists, and especially those of Nova Scotia, which has prevented the conclusion of your Treaty.

I was somewhat surprised at the apparent favor with which this suggestion was received by Lord Clarendon. This, I am convinced, arose from the clear presentation, in juxtaposition, of the quid pro quo which such an article would exhibit to the Colonists & to the British public. It could not have been from any other cause; inasmuch as the article would assure to American fishermen all the rights specified in the Projet; would relieve us from the embarrassing concession to British fishermen of the right to take fish on our coasts, estuaries, & rivers, as well as from the question of bounties; and, above all, it would waive the claim to the registration in the United States of vessels built in the British provinces,—a claim which ought never to be yielded.

Perhaps I may have gone too far in the suggestion. It was not made until I had clearly ascertained His Lordship's (I think) unreasonable repugnance to your Projet. The discussion, in any event, can have done no harm. On the contrary, I am persuaded it gave him a stronger impression than he had before of the importance of an early settlement of the Fishery question.

I have drawn up such an article as I intended to suggest. At the first, I thought of sending it to his Lordship; but on reflection I concluded this would be going too far. I now transmit it to you. It has not been prepared with much care & is only intended to present the general idea in a more specific form. Perhaps, in the event that your projet should finally fail, something may be made of it; & I might then be able to induce Lord Clarendon to send it to Mr. Crampton for your approbation.

The only objection to the Article which I can conceive is, that it would not confer upon American caught fish the privilege of being imported into the Colonies free of duty. I presume, however, that this privilege would be but of little value to our fishermen. It is, also, possible his Lordship might consent to insert " Fish of all kinds " in the list of free articles, as it is in your schedule; & this would remove the difficulty. This point was not adverted to in our conversation. Still, my impression is, that the favor with which the suggestion seemed to be received was because it presented a substantive consideration for the grant of the shore fisheries, in the free admission of British caught fish into the United States, which was not to be impaired by the reciprocal privilege of admitting American caught fish free of duty into the British provinces. In that I may be mistaken, as, I repeat, there was no allusion whatever to this point.

After our conversation had ended on the Fishery & Reciprocity questions, he informed me that he had presented my suggestion to the Cabinet, that Nicaragua should treat the Mosquitos within her limits as Great Britain & the United States treated their own Indians, under similar circumstances; & they thought, as he had done, that it was highly reasonable. I told him I was glad to learn this, and was happy to inform him I could now state from advices received by the last steamer that you were of the same opinion.

He then asked, in what manner shall we carry this into effect? and intimated that the appointment of Commissioners by the two Governments for this purpose might be the best mode of proceeding. I told him I was not then prepared to express an opinion on the subject; but would take it into consideration. The proportion of territory to be occupied by the Mosquitos, until their title was extinguished by Nicaragua, ought to depend very much upon their number. Lord John Russell had stated this to be thirty or forty thousand, whilst from my information, which was, however, vague, it did not exceed as many hundreds. He replied that Mr. Green, the British Consul & agent at Bluefields, was now in London, & had mentioned to him that my estimate of their number was probably correct in regard to the Mosquitos north of the San Juan, though there might be a thousand more; but that the Mosquitos south of the San Juan were so numerous as to render Lord John's estimate of the whole not excessive. I told him I had never heard that any portion of this tribe resided in Costa Rica, & I thought there must be some mistake in the statement of Mr. Green.

He then asked what we should do with the grants of land which had been made to individuals by the King of the Mosquitos; & I answered, that under the law of all European nations, since the discovery of America, as well as by the uniform practice both of Great Britain & the United States, such grants made by Indians were absolutely void. I also stated to him, somewhat in detail, the decision on this point made by the Supreme Court of the United States, in the case of Johnson v. McIntosh, (8 Wheaton, 543,) to which he appeared to listen with marked attention.

After this, we had a discursive & rambling conversation embracing the Ruatan & Belize questions, the Clayton & Bulwer Treaty, & several other matters, which I do not propose to detail. In the course of it, he stated distinctly that this Treaty was, in their opinion, entirely prospective in its operation & did not require them to abandon any of their possessions in Central America. At this I expressed my astonishment, & we discussed the point, in an earnest but good natured manner.

In regard to Ruatan, he said he had the papers in a box before him to prove their title to that Island; but it would consume too much time to read them, & therefore he had thought of submitting his views to me respecting it in writing. This suggestion pleased me much, as I desired to present to His Lordship a memorandum which I had prepared embracing our whole case in Central America. I told him, therefore, I should be much gratified to receive his views in writing; & at the same time informed him, that without changing our mode of personal conference, I desired, also, to deliver him a written memorandum to which he might at all times refer, containing a statement of the case on the part of my Government. With this he expressed himself to be much pleased. I am sorry that I shall not be able to furnish you a copy of this memorandum by the present steamer.

One incident may be worth particular mention. In the course of the conversation, he said the Bay Islands were but of little value; but if British honor required their retention, they could never be surrendered. I made some playful remark in reference to the idea of British honor being involved in so small an affair. He then became quite earnest on the point of honor, which might, he observed, be as much involved in subjects of little as of great value. To this I assented; but said that when the construction of a Treaty was really doubtful, which I did not admit upon the present occasion, & when the friendly relations between two great countries were at stake, there could, in such a case, be no point of honor involved in the one yielding to the other what was admitted to be of but little value. He replied that in this view of the case I might be correct.

In regard to Belize, there was not the least appearance of yielding on the part of his Lordship. He repudiated the idea with some warmth that any person should suppose they had surrendered this settlement under the Clayton and Bulwer Treaty.

From all that passed, my impression is that, in addition to the Mosquito Shore, they will finally, after a struggle, agree to abandon the Bay Islands; but I am thoroughly convinced they will never consent to surrender Belize,—most certainly not that portion of it the usufruct of which for particular purposes was granted to them by the King of Spain under the Treaties of 1783 and 1786. Johnston, in his general Gazetteer, says that " Belize is now the Depot of British manufactured goods and foreign merchandize designed for Central America. Amount of imports from £400,000 to £500,000; exports about the same. 9000 tons of British shipping employed in the trade."

The time has, therefore, arrived when it becomes indispensable that I should receive the President's instructions on this point. In forming his opinion, it may be worthy of consideration, that the British have been in the actual possession of Belize, under Treaty, for more than seventy years; that no period was fixed when they should withdraw from this possession; that Spain declared war against Great Britain on the 11th October, 1796; that an attack was made from Yucatan on Belize in 1798, which was repelled by the British settlers; and that for nearly a quarter of a century, it has been under a regular colonial Government, without attracting the notice of the United States.

In any event, I shall do my whole duty, in first urging their withdrawal from the whole Colony; and if that should not prove successful, then from the portion of it south of the Sibun; —but what am I to do, in case I shall be unsuccessful in both or either of these particulars? I shall await your answer, with considerable anxiety.

When I pointed out to Lord Clarendon on Bailey's map, which lay before him, the extent of the encroachments which British settlers had made beyond the Treaty limits; his only answer was, in a tone of pleasantry, that we ought not to complain of encroachments, and instanced our acquisition of Texas. I then took occasion to give him information on this subject, for which he thanked me, and said that he had never understood it before.

Returning again to the Mosquitos: am I to consent that they shall continue in the occupation of the territory assigned to them by the agreement between Messrs. Webster and Crampton, of April 30th, 1852, until their title shall be extinguished by Nicaragua? Whether this assignment be unreasonable or not would depend much upon their number. You can doubtless ascertain at Washington whether any considerable number of the tribe inhabit the Country south of the San Juan, as stated by Mr. Green.

In regard to the Mosquitos, the question of the greatest

difficulty would seem to be, in what manner can Great Britain
and the United States interpose, as suggested by Lord Clarendon,
to prevent Nicaragua from depriving these Indians of their right
of occupancy without a fair equivalent? It would seem that
this could be best accomplished by a Treaty with Nicaragua. The
whole detail presents embarrassments which will be annoying
without the consent of Nicaragua; and yet I am persuaded the
British Government care little or nothing for this consent. They
have evidently formed a very unfavorable opinion of that State,
and greatly prefer Costa Rica. It would appear, from what his
Lordship informed me, Mr. Marcoleta had told Mr. Crampton
that Costa Rica is jealous of the influence of Nicaragua with
the United States.

You would naturally desire to know something of His
Majesty the present King of the Mosquitos. I had on a former
occasion stated to Lord Clarendon that he was drunken and
worthless. At this interview his Lordship informed me I was
mistaken; that the present King was a decent and well behaved
youth of between 22 and 23, who resided in Mr. Green's family;
though he believed his late Majesty, to whom I had doubtless
referred, was a bad fellow!

Yours very respectfully

JAMES BUCHANAN.

HON. WM. L. MARCY,
    Secretary of State.

(Enclosure in No. 20.)

In consideration that Her Britannic Majesty, in addition to the liberty secured to American fishermen by the Convention between the parties of October
20th, 1818, hereby grants to the inhabitants of the United States the liberty,
in common with her own subjects, to take fish of every kind on the sea
coasts & shores & in the Bays, harbors, & creeks of all Her Majesty's Atlantic
Colonial possessions & Islands in North America, Newfoundland included,
without being restricted to any distance from the shore: The United States,
on their part, grant that all the fish of every kind caught by British subjects
on the sea coasts & shores & in the Bays, harbors, & creeks of Her Majesty's
said Colonial possessions & Islands, Newfoundland included, shall be admitted
into the Ports of the United States free of duty. And it is furthermore
agreed between the Parties that the following articles, being the growth &
produce of the aforesaid British Colonial possessions & Islands or of the
United States, respectively, shall be reciprocally admitted free of duty into
the Ports of the said Colonial possessions & Islands & into those of the
United States:—to wit, " Grain, flour, & bread stuffs of all kinds," &c. &c. &c.

It is understood, however, that the permission which Her Britannic

Majesty hereby grants to American fishermen to land upon the coasts & shores of all the aforesaid British Colonial possessions & Islands & of their Bays, harbors, & creeks, for the purpose of drying their nets & curing their fish, shall never be construed or employed so as to interfere with the rights of private property, or with British fishermen in the previous occupancy of any part of the said coasts & shores for the same purpose.

TO MR. LEWIS.

(Enclosure in No. 23.[1])

LEGATION OF THE UNITED STATES.

LONDON, January 12, 1854.

SIR,

I have received your favor of the 10th instant, and can most cordially assure you that it will afford me very great pleasure to become the instrument of the " Royal National Institution for the preservation of lives from Shipwreck " in transmitting to my Government the Gold Medallion to be presented to Captain Ludlow, of the American Whaling Ship " Monmouth," in admiration of his noble and persevering exertions in saving one hundred and five persons from the English Emigrant Ship " Meridian," which was wrecked on the Island of Amsterdam on the 24th of August last.

Such a testimonial proceeding from your institution, founded on principles of the purest humanity, will, I dare venture to say, be prized by Captain Ludlow and his family as a most precious treasure; while it may incite other captains to emulate his noble exertions in rescuing their fellow men from a watery grave.

Yours very respectfully

(sd.) JAMES BUCHANAN.

RICHARD LEWIS, ESQ.

Secy. &c. &c. &c.

---

[1] Despatch to Mr. Marcy, No. 23, Feb. 7, 1854, infra.

TO MR. MARCY.[1]

(No. 22.)   LEGATION OF THE UNITED STATES.

LONDON, 20th January 1854.

SIR,

Referring to your Despatch, No. 17, of the 21st October last, I have the honor to inform you that Augustus Nason, of Maine, who had enlisted as a seaman on board Her Majesty's ship Britannia, was discharged from that ship on the 24th December last. I enclose a copy of the Earl of Clarendon's note, communicating this information.

I have, also, received, on the 14th instant, from the Foreign Office, the Commission of John Duffy, Esquire, appointing him Consul to Galway, together with the Queen's Exequatur, both of which have been forwarded to him at his post.

Since the date of my last Despatch, I have heard nothing from Lord Clarendon on the Central American questions, except the formal acknowledgment of " the receipt, on the 14th Instant, of Mr. Buchanan's memorandum, dated the 6th Instant, relative to Central America and Mosquito." I await, with considerable interest, His Lordship's promised exposition of the British title to the Island of Ruatan.

And here I ought to mention that the trouble and confusion incident to my own removal and that of the Legation to the house which I have taken, (No. 56 Harley Street, Cavendish Square) together with other circumstances, which I need not specify, prevented me from having my statement copied for Lord Clarendon until the 13th Instant.

I would refer you to the London Times of yesterday morning and this morning, the latter especially, for significant notices on the Central American questions. I trust that the debates in the Senate may not be of such a character as to embarrass my negotiations on this subject.

Yours very Respectfully

JAMES BUCHANAN.

HON. WILLIAM L. MARCY
    Secretary of State.

---

[1] MSS. Department of State, 65 Despatches from England.

TO LORD CLARENDON.

(Enclosure in No. 23.[1])

FOREIGN OFFICE, LONDON

27th January 1854.

MY LORD,

I have the honor of furnishing you the copy of a letter just received from Nathaniel Hawthorne, Esquire, United States Consul at Liverpool, bearing date on the 26th Instant: Relying with entire confidence on the statements which it contains, I have to request that your Lordship would grant the warrant required by the Act of Parliament to the proper Magistrate or Magistrates at Liverpool, for the arrest of Thomas Hallyman, the second mate, and Henry Shaff, William J. Watson, Ephraim M. Collins, and Jonathan Paramore, Seamen of the American Ship John and Albert, to answer to a charge of assault with intent to commit murder on the chief mate, Charles Sandford, on board the said Ship, off the Ormeshead, about thirty miles from Liverpool, and to be further dealt with according to the provisions of the Tenth Article of the Treaty of Washington, of the 9th August 1842.

I have the honor to be, Very Respectfully,

Your Lordship's Most Obedient Servant

JAMES BUCHANAN.

THE RIGHT HONORABLE, THE EARL OF CLARENDON.

TO MR. MARCY.[2]

(No. 23.)   LEGATION OF THE UNITED STATES.

LONDON, 7th February 1854.

SIR,

I have not yet received from Lord Clarendon his promised statement of the British title to Ruatan. Although I have met him several times in society since the promise was made, he has never once alluded to this statement. I did not introduce the

---

[1] Despatch to Mr. Marcy, No. 23, Feb. 7, 1854, infra.

[2] MSS. Department of State, 65 Despatches from England. The part of this despatch relating to court dress is printed in S. Ex. Doc. 31, 36 Cong. 1 Sess. 16; Curtis's Buchanan, II. 111.

subject, because I knew he would excuse himself on account of the pressure upon his time of the Russo-Turkish question.

This question is decided, at least for the present, and war would seem to be inevitable. The Russian Ministers, both at London and Paris, have demanded and received their passports. Still, many well-informed persons entertain better hopes of peace at the present moment than they have done for several months. These are founded upon assurances said to have been received by this Government, that Austria and Prussia will stand by Great Britain and France in maintaining the independence and integrity of the Ottoman Empire. In my own opinion, nothing can prevent war, unless the two German Powers shall cordially consent to unite their forces with those of Great Britain and France in expelling the Emperor of Russia from the Danubian Principalities; & in that event, it would be the extreme of folly for him to encounter all Europe in arms. I have, however, as yet, seen no evidence that Austria and Prussia will act in this decided manner. On the contrary, the strongest measure which it has yet been suggested these powers would adopt, is that of forcible resistance, in case the Russian troops should pass the Danube.

The people of Great Britain are now almost unanimously in favor of war, unless the Emperor should yield; and the Government are making extensive preparations to carry it on with vigor and effect.

Under these circumstances, the rights and the duties of the United States, as a neutral nation, will become a subject for serious consideration.

In a private letter received from Mr. Schroeder, our Chargé at Stockholm, in December last, he informs me that a copy of the joint declaration of the Swedish, Norwegian, and Danish Governments, embodying, in part or in whole, the principles of the Armed Neutrality of 1780, has been forwarded to the Swedish and Norwegian Chargé d'Affaires at Washington, with instructions to communicate it immediately to the Secretary of State. This has doubtless been done; and Mr. Schroeder assures me that it embraces the principle, that " free ships make free goods."

Should Sweden and Denmark maintain this principle by force, and resist the capture of Swedish and Danish vessels with Russian goods on board, this will bring them into direct and immediate collision with Great Britain and France; because the Judicial tribunals of both the latter powers, as well as the Supreme Court of the United States, have uniformly decided, as a principle of the law of nations, that the goods of an Enemy may be captured on board the vessel of a friend. Great Britain, as a belligerent power, has in all times and under all circumstances maintained this principle; and it is scarcely possible that she will consent to yield it at the present moment to Sweden and Denmark, in favor of the property of Russian subjects.

I shall be glad to learn what are the views of the President on this and the other questions which must necessarily arise, in the course of the approaching war, in regard to our rights and obligations as neutrals, as I desire to be able to speak authoritatively on such subjects.

You will perceive by the London Journals,—The Times, the Morning Post, the News, the Morning Herald, the Spectator, the Examiner, Lloyds, &c., &c., copies of which I send you, that my absence from the House of Lords, at the opening of Parliament, has produced quite a sensation. Indeed, I have found difficulty in preventing this incident from becoming a subject of enquiry and remark in the House of Commons. All this is peculiarly disagreeable to me, and has arisen entirely from an indiscreet and rather offensive remark of the London Times, in the account which that Journal published of the proceedings at the opening of Parliament. But for this, the whole matter would probably have passed away quietly, as I had desired.

Some time after my interview with Sir Edward Cust, the Master of Ceremonies, in October last, (whom I have never since seen) which I reported to you in my Despatch No. 13 of the 28th of October, I determined, after due reflection, neither to wear gold lace nor embroidery at Court; and I did not hesitate to express this determination. The spirit of your circular, as well as my own sense of propriety, brought me to this conclusion. I did not deem it becoming in me, as the Representative of a Republic, to imitate a Court Costume, which may be altogether proper in the Representatives of Royalty. A Minister of the United States should, in my opinion, wear something more in character with our Democratic Institutions than a coat covered with embroidery and gold lace. Besides, after all, this would prove to be but a feeble attempt " to ape foreign fashions; " because, most fortunately, he could not wear the orders and stars which ornament the Coats of other Diplomatists, nor could he, except in rare instances, afford the diamonds, unless hired for the occasion.

At the same time, entertaining a most sincere respect for

the exalted character of the Queen, both as a Sovereign and a lady, I expressed a desire to appear at Court in such a dress as I might suppose would be most agreeable to herself, without departing from the spirit of the Circular.

It was then suggested to me, from a quarter which I do not feel at liberty to mention, that I might assume the civil dress worn by General Washington; but after examining Stewart's Portrait, at the house of a friend, I came to the conclusion that it would not be proper for me to adopt this costume. I observed, " fashions had so changed since the days of Washington, that if I were to put on his dress and appear in it before the Chief Magistrate of my own Country, at one of his receptions, I should render myself a subject of ridicule for life. Besides, it would be considered presumption in me to affect the style of dress of the Father of his Country."

It was in this unsettled state of the question, and before I had adopted any style of dress, that Parliament was opened. If, however, the case had been different and I had anticipated a serious question, prudential reasons would have prevented me from bringing it to issue at the door of the House of Lords. A Court held at the Palace would, for many reasons, be a much more appropriate place for such a purpose.

Under these circumstances, I received, on the Sunday morning before the Tuesday on which Parliament met, a printed circular from Sir Edward Cust, similar to that which I have no doubt was addressed to all the other foreign Ministers, inviting me to attend the opening of the session. The following is extracted from this circular. " No one can be admitted into the Diplomatic Tribune, or in the body of the House, but in full Court Dress."

Now, from all the attending circumstances, I do not feel disposed to yield to the idea that any disrespect was intended by this circular, either to my country or myself. Since I came to London, I have received such attentions from high official personages as to render this quite improbable. What may be the final result of the question, I cannot clearly foresee, but I do not anticipate any serious difficulties.

For the purpose of bringing to your notice the discrepancy existing between the Legislation of Great Britain and that of the United States, to carry into effect the 10th (Extradition) Article of the Treaty between the Parties, of the 9th August, 1842, I transmit to you copies of an application made by me under this Treaty and of the warrant issued by Lord Palmerston.[1] Upon examination of the Act of Parliament of the 22nd August, 1843, (6 and 7 Victoria) you will find that the requisition must be made " by the authority of the United States," and that no British Magistrate is authorised to take any step in the arrest of a Fugitive from Justice until he shall have first received a warrant for that purpose, issued " by one of Her Majesty's Principal Secretaries of State."   The consequence must be the escape, at least in some cases, of such fugitives before a warrant can be obtained from London; and this would have been the result on the present occasion, had not the police of Liverpool voluntarily held the fugitives in custody for several days.

I transmit herewith a Gold Medallion, unanimously voted by " the Committee of Management of the Royal National Institution for the preservation of lives from Shipwreck," " to Captain Ludlow of the American Whaling Ship, *Monmouth,* in admiration of his noble and persevering exertions in saving one hundred and five persons from the English Emigrant Ship *Meridian,* which was wrecked on the Island of Amsterdam, on the 24th August last;" and I have the honor to request that you will cause this Medallion to be delivered to the brave and benevolent Captain.   As I have acknowledged its receipt, I would thank you to inform me of its delivery.   For further particulars, I refer you to the correspondence between Richard Lewis, Esquire, the Secretary of the Institution, and myself, marked A. B. C. & D.[2]

I have this moment received your Despatch No. 27, of the 20th January last, together with the Commission of Thomas Steere, Esquire, as Consul for the Port of Dundee, to which immediate attention shall be given.

Yours Very Respectfully

JAMES BUCHANAN.

HON. W. L. MARCY
    Secretary of State.

---

[1] To Lord Clarendon, Jan. 27, 1854, supra.
[2] See Mr. Buchanan to Mr. Lewis, Jan. 12, 1854, supra.   The rest of the enclosures are not given.

TO MR. LEON.

(Enclosure in No. 24.[1])

LEGATION OF THE UNITED STATES.

LONDON, 9 February 1854.

SIR,

I have just received and hasten to answer your favor of the 4th instant.

It is impossible for me, in the present want of information as to the course which Russia may pursue, in regard to neutral Commerce, in the war which would seem to be impending, to furnish precise answers to your questions. Under the law of nations, as expounded by British and American Tribunals, the goods of an American Citizen, if not domiciled in a foreign country, found on board of a British vessel, would be restored by a Russian Prize Court to their owner. In the language of Chancellor Kent: " The two distinct propositions, that enemies' goods found on board a neutral ship of war, and that the goods of a neutral found on board of an enemy's vessel, were to be restored, have been explicitly incorporated into the jurisprudence of the United States, and declared by the Supreme Court to be founded in the law of Nations."

It will, therefore, be very important that in such cases as you mention, the clearest evidence possible should be found on board the British ship of the American ownership of the goods. Of what particulars this evidence ought to consist, it is impossible for me to give you accurate information at the present moment.

I ought to add, that if you are domiciled in this country and are here conducting a mercantile business, though an American Citizen, the goods belonging to this establishment would be liable to capture and condemnation in the very same manner as though you were a British subject. Such is the settled law both of Great Britain and the United States.

Yours very respectfully

(sd.) JAMES BUCHANAN.

MR. A. LEON.

---

[1] Despatch to Mr. Marcy, No. 24, Feb. 10, 1854, infra.

TO MR. BRIGHT.[1]

U. S. LEGATION, LONDON,

9 Feby. 1854.

MY DEAR SIR,

I owe you many thanks for your kind note of yesterday, & feel much gratified that you have refrained from introducing the subject to the notice of the House.

I know not whether I shall be received at Court in any dress I could wear, with propriety, at a reception by the President of the United States. If not, my strong desire to become instrumental in settling the serious questions pending between the two Countries causes me earnestly to hope, that I shall not encounter any possible embarrassment which might arise from the call of public attention to a matter comparatively so unimportant as my absence from the opening of Parliament, a Levee, or a Drawing Room.

With sentiments etc.

(sd)   JAMES BUCHANAN.

JOHN BRIGHT, ESQ. M. P.[2]

---

[1] Buchanan Papers, Historical Society of Pennsylvania.

[2] Mr. Bright's letter (now among the Buchanan Papers, Historical Society of Pennsylvania), to which the foregoing is a reply, is as follows:

REFORM CLUB Feby 8. 54.

MY DEAR SIR,

I spoke to Lord John Russell at the meeting of the House on the day on which I called upon you—all I could extract from him was that he had written to Lord Clarendon on the subject—but he seemed not to wish anything to be said in the House. I therefore abstained from saying anything, in accordance with what I thought was your own desire under these circumstances—tho' I must say I was silent against my own judgment.

I would have called upon you again, but I think I shall take up less of your valuable time by sending this note.

Believe me to be with great respect

Yours faithfully

JOHN BRIGHT.

THE HONBLE. JAMES BUCHANAN
56 Harley St.

TO MR. MARCY.[1]

(No. 24.) LEGATION OF THE UNITED STATES.

LONDON, 10th February 1854.

SIR,

I have the honor to transmit you the copy of a letter of the 20th January from the Chamber of Commerce of Newcastle upon Tyne, together with the copy of the answer thereto, dated on the 29th ultimo; and to request that you would submit them to the Secretary of the Treasury.

I also enclose an extract from my letter to August Belmont, Esquire, our Chargé d'Affaires at the Hague, in answer to inquiries made by him; and the copy of a letter addressed by me on yesterday to Mr. A. Leon,[2] an American citizen at Sheffield, in answer to a letter from him of the 4th Instant.

As the views which I have presented in these letters, on important international questions, may assume a practical character, in the event of war between Russia and Great Britain and France, I should be glad to learn that they had received your approbation. Should you entertain different opinions, you will, of course, furnish me instructions accordingly.

I have said, in my letter to Mr. Belmont, that " I shall not approach Lord Clarendon for the purpose of obtaining from the British Government a declaration in favor of the principle that ' free ships make free goods,' without instructions from my Government." Whilst I am fully sensible of the great benefits which would result to our neutral commerce should the belligerents act upon this principle, I yet feel reluctant, without the authority of the President, to interfere in the matter and thus furnish a precedent which, in his opinion, might by possibility hereafter prove embarrassing to our country. Still, in view of the great and immediate advantages to our commerce, circumstances may arise which will induce me to assume the responsibility of speaking to Lord Clarendon on the subject; and therefore I trust I may have your instructions upon it by the first returning steamer. It is certain that Sweden, Denmark, the Netherlands, and, I believe, Prussia, are all anxious that the belligerents, during the apparently approaching war, should carry into effect the principle that " free ships make free goods."

---

[1] MSS. Department of State, 65 Despatches from England.

[2] Letter to Mr. Leon, Feb. 9, 1854, supra.

I transmit you the copy of a letter which I have this moment received from Joseph Hume, Esquire, Member of Parliament, which from the importance of its contents to our commercial interests, as well as the character of the writer, will, I know, secure your immediate attention.

I have not yet received from Lord Clarendon the promised statement of the British title to Ruatan, and I begin to believe that he may have found it difficult to answer my own statement in regard to that Island.

Yours very respectfully

JAMES BUCHANAN.

HON: WILLIAM L. MARCY,
    Secretary of State.

(Enclosure in No. 24.)

[Extract from a letter to August Belmont, Esquire, United States Chargé d'Affaires at the Hague, in answer to enquiries from him.]

" I shall not approach Lord Clarendon for the purpose of obtaining from the British Government a declaration in favor of the principle that ' free ships make free goods,' without instructions from my Government. I have written to Gov. Marcy on the subject of our neutral rights and obligations, and I enclose you an extract from my Despatch of yesterday. . . .

" We have entered into several Treaties with weak Powers, establishing the principle that as between the parties " free ships shall make free goods," in some with and in others without modifications. It has hitherto been the policy of our Government to change the law of Nations in this particular. We have succeeded with the weak; but not with the strong. Russia refused, in 1832, to make such a Treaty with us. What would now be the consequence resulting from these Treaties in case we were at war with England? Why, British goods would be protected from capture on board the vessels of those Nations with whom we have such unqualified Treaties, whilst American goods, on board the very same vessels, would be subject to capture by our enemy. If the strong maritime Powers would adopt the principle, I should hail it as a benefit to neutral Commerce, and as a most desirable change in the law of Nations; but until such powers shall agree to make the change, I cannot perceive the advantage to our Country of concluding any such Treaties with the weaker Nations. If England and France would now agree to this just and enlightened policy, and issue a declaration that the flag shall protect the property, I have no doubt the United States would gladly follow the example, in case they should become a belligerent. I, therefore, wish Baron Bentinck entire success in his efforts with Lord Clarendon."

Dated, 8th February 1854.

UNITED STATES LEGATION AT LONDON.

(Enclosure in No. 24.)

BRYANSTON SQ. 10 Feby. 1854.

DEAR SIR,

I formerly received from the Secretary to the Marine at Washington a copy of his publications on public Light houses and on the experiments made

on Coals for Steamers and on Gas for Light houses, which were placed in
the hands of the Government here, and I cannot get them back.

I wish, in writing to Washington, that you would ask the Secretary of
the Marine to send me a copy of all the publications on the above subjects
of *Light houses, Coals,* and *Gas,* as I am pressing the Government *to abolish
Light house dues,* and to assimilate the system to that of the United States.

There is a letter from your Predecessor " on the subject of English Light
dues, on American Ships," and, with your assistance, I am sanguine to think
that the Government will be induced to abolish them.

Since January, 1854, a reduction of ¾ths of the coasting light dues on
ships has been effected. My opinion being that a similar reduction should be
made on all foreign traders, I propose, as soon as I receive a complete set
of the papers from the United States I now ask for, to bring the subject
before the House of Commons with the object of reduction or of the abolition of Light house dues altogether. If you refer to the letter of your
Predecessor on this subject to Lord Palmerston, you will see the importance
of my motion to the trade of both countries.

I hope you received the Parliamentary papers I sent you, whilst I remain
Your obd. Servt.

(sd.)   Joseph Hume.

N. B. Your Government are in possession of the Reports on Light
Houses of 1834/5 and of 1845, by Committees of which I was Chairman, and
of which I sent copies, as in them will appear the object I have in view.

TO MISS LANE.[1]

Legation of the United States,

London, 18 February 1854.

My dear Harriet/

According to my calculation, Captain West will leave New
York for Liverpool in the Atlantic on Saturday the 29th April;
& it is my particular desire that you should come with him, *under
his special care,* in preference to any other person. I shall send
this letter open to Captain West; & if he should transmit it to
you with a line stating that he will take charge of the freight you
may then consider the matter settled. I shall meet you, God
willing, at Liverpool.

I have no doubt that the lady whom you mention in yours of
the 2d instant would be an agreeable companion, & should she
come in the Atlantic at the same time with yourself it is all very
well; but even in that event, I desire that you should be under the
special care of Captain West. He is a near relative of our old

---

[1] Buchanan Papers, private collection; Curtis's Buchanan, II. 112.

friend, Redmond Conyngham; & I have the most perfect confidence in him both as a gentleman & a sailor. He stays at the Astor House when at New York; & you had better stop there with your brother when about to embark.

Had he been coming out two weeks earlier in April I should have been better pleased; but on no account would I have consented to your voyage until near the middle of that month.

Yours affectionately,

James Buchanan.

Miss Harriet Lane.

FROM MR. HAWTHORNE.[1]

(Enclosure C in No. 26.[1])

Consulate of The United States.

Liverpool, 20 February 1854.

Sir,

Referring to my communication to you of the 31 January, I have now to inform you, that in a final examination, had on Saturday, of the persons charged with an assault with intent to commit murder on board the American Ship " John & Albert," the Magistrate has decided, that the evidence of criminality is insufficient against any of them except Jonathan Paramore, whom he has committed to Gaol, to be dealt with according to the provisions of the Treaty, and has discharged the others from custody. His certificate to this effect will be sent by Post to-day to the Secretary of State, Lord Palmerston.

I presume that nothing now remains to be done but to obtain the Secretary of State's Warrant for the Prisoner's extradition; and if this can be in Liverpool by Wednesday morning, he can be sent back in the " John & Albert," which sails for Charleston on Wednesday, and the Captain, Higgins Crowell, may be designated to receive him.

It is very desirable that he should be sent in the " John & Albert," as the two principal witnesses are the Cook and Steward of that vessel, and there being no Law under which I could oblige any other Captain to take him, there might be some difficulty in finding another conveyance within the time allowed by Law.

With great respect, I have the honor to be

Your obed. Sert.

(sd.)   N. Hawthorne.

To His Ex: James Buchanan
&c. &c. &c.

---

[1] Despatch to Mr. Marcy, No. 26, March 24, 1854, infra.

TO LORD PALMERSTON.

(Enclosure D in No. 26.[1])

LEGATION OF THE UNITED STATES.

LONDON, 21 February 1854.

MY LORD/

Referring to the Warrant which your Lordship granted on the 28th ultimo for the apprehension of Thomas Hallyman and others, under the 10th Article of the Treaty of Washington of August 9th, 1842, and the Act of Parliament of 6 & 7 Victoria, Cap. 76, giving effect thereto, I have the honor to communicate to your Lordship the copy of a letter which I have just received from Nathaniel Hawthorne, Esquire, Consul of the United States at Liverpool, dated on yesterday, and to request, for the reasons therein stated, that your Lordship would issue your Warrant, under the said Treaty and Act of Parliament, ordering Jonathan Paramore to be delivered to Captain Higgins Crowell, of the Ship " John & Albert," that he may be conveyed therein to the United States, there to be tried for the crime of assault with intent to commit murder within the jurisdiction of the same.

I have the honor to be

Your Lordship's Most obd. Servant

(signed)   JAMES BUCHANAN.

To the RIGHT HONL. LORD VISCOUNT PALMERSTON
&c. &c. &c.

TO MISS LANE.[2]

LEGATION OF THE UNITED STATES.

LONDON, 21 February 1854.

MY DEAR HARRIET/

I have received your letter of the 2d Instant & am truly rejoiced to learn that you have recovered your usual good health. I hope you will take good care of yourself in Washington & not expose yourself to a relapse.

I intended to write you a long letter to-day; but an unexpected pressure of business will prevent me from doing this before the Despatch Bag closes. I now write merely to inform you

---

[1] Despatch to Mr. Marcy, No. 26, March 24, 1854, infra.

[2] Buchanan Papers, private collection; Curtis's Buchanan, II. 113.

that I have made every arrangement for your passage with Captain West in the Atlantic either on Saturday the 15th, or Saturday the 29th April. He does not at present know which; but will inform you on his arrival in New York. He will leave Liverpool to-morrow. And let me assure you that this is the very best arrangement which could be made for you. You will be quite independent & under the special charge of the captain. You will discover that you will thus enjoy many advantages. If you have friends or acquaintances coming out at the same time this is all very well; *but let not this prevent you from putting yourself under the special charge of Captain West & you can say that this is my arrangement.* I wish you to inform me whether you will leave New York on the 15th or 29th April, so that I may make arrangements accordingly. In either event, I shall, God willing, meet you at Liverpool. I shall write to Eskridge by the next steamer & direct him to provide for your passage. You will, of course, have no dresses made in the United States. I am not a very close observer or an accurate judge; but I think the ladies here of the very highest rank do not dress as expensively, with the exception of jewels, as those in the United States.

I dined on Wednesday last with the Queen, at Buckingham Palace. Both she & Prince Albert were remarkably civil, & I had quite a conversation with each of them separately. But the question of costume still remains; & from this I anticipate nothing but trouble in several directions. I was invited " in frock dress " to the dinner, & of course I had no difficulty. To-morrow will be the first levee of the Queen, & my appearance there in a suit of plain clothes will, I have no doubt, produce quite a sensation & become a subject of gossip for the whole court.

I wish very much that I could obtain an autograph of General Washington for the Countess of Clarendon. She has been very civil to me & like our friend Laura is a collector of autographs. She is very anxious to obtain such an autograph & I have promised to do my best to procure it for her. Perhaps Mr. Pleasonton could help me to one.

The first wish of my heart is to see you comfortably & respectably settled in life; but ardently as I desire this, you ought never to marry any person for whom you think you would not have a proper degree of affection. You inform me of your conquest, & I trust it may be of such a character as will produce

good fruit.   But I have time to say no more, except to request
that you will give my love to Laura & Clemmie, & my kindest
regards to Mr. Pleasonton & also to Mr. & Mrs. Slidell & Mr. &
Mrs. Thomson of New Jersey.

Ever yours affectionately,

James Buchanan.

Miss Harriet Lane.

TO MR. MARCY.[1]

(No. 25.)   Legation of The United States.

London, 24 February 1854.

Sir,

    I have the honor to acknowledge the receipt of your
Despatch of the 7th instant informing me that you had increased
the salary of John Miller, the Agent of this Legation, from
Eight hundred to one thousand dollars.   Mr. Miller is an old
and faithful public servant, but from age has become rather
inefficient in the discharge of his duties.   I was not aware that
he had applied for an increase of salary.

    I have transmitted to Messrs. Baring Brothers & Co. your
letter to them increasing the contingent expenses of this Legation from $2800 to $3000, to meet the corresponding increase in
Mr. Miller's salary.

    I have received from the Foreign Office the Exequatur of
Thomas Steere, Esquire, United States Consul at Dundee,
together with his Commission, and have forwarded both to him
at his Post.

    I had an interview with Lord Clarendon at the Foreign
Office on Monday last, the 17th Instant.   From the pressure of
the war question with Russia and his engagements at the commencement of the Session of Parliament, he was not then prepared to proceed with our negotiations.   Indeed, I scarcely expected that he would be, but I deemed it advisable to remind
him of their urgency and importance.   I told him that the Session of Congress was rapidly passing away and before its adjournment the President would certainly expect to be able to
communicate to them the result of the negotiation in regard to
the Central American Questions.   Besides, I observed that the

---

[1] MSS. Department of State, 65 Despatches from England.   The most of
this despatch is printed in H. Ex. Doc. 103, 33 Cong. 1 Sess. 7–9, 19–20.

Fishing Season was approaching and there would be great danger of collision on the Fishing grounds, should not the question, in the mean time, be adjusted.   After some conversation on these subjects, not of sufficient importance to repeat, he promised that at as early a day as his pressing engagements would permit, he should send for me and then be prepared to go thoroughly into the different questions.   Nothing was said, on either side, of his Lordship's promised statement of the British title to the Island of Ruatan.   I did not deem it prudent, at the moment, to remind him of his unperformed promise.

I then enquired of His Lordship, whether the British Government had yet determined upon the course they would pursue, during the impending war, in regard to neutrals;—whether they would adhere to their old rule of capturing the goods of an enemy on board the vessel of a friend, or adopt the rule of " free ships free goods," observing that it was of great importance to my countrymen engaged in commerce that they should know the decision on this point as speedily as possible.   He said that the question was then under the consideration of the Cabinet and had not yet been decided; but I should be the very first person to whom he would communicate the result.   Intimating a desire to converse with me informally and unofficially upon the subject, I informed him that I had no instructions whatever from my own Government in relation to it, but as an individual, I was willing frankly to express my opinions.   From what passed between us, I should consider it a breach of confidence in me to report his private opinions on a question still pending before the Cabinet Council and on which its members are probably divided.   I can, however, have no objection to repeat to you the substance of my own observations.

I said that the Supreme Court of the United States had adopted, in common with their own courts, the principle that a belligerent had a right, under the law of nations, to capture the goods of an enemy on board the vessel of a friend, and that he was bound to restore the goods of a friend captured on board the vessel of an enemy.   That, from a very early period of our history, we had sought in favor of neutral commerce to change this rule by Treaties with different nations; and instead thereof, to adopt the principle that the flag should protect the property under it, with the exception of contraband of war.   That the right of search was at best an odious right and ought to be restricted as much as possible.   There was always danger from its exercise of involving the Neutral in serious difficulty with the Belligerent. The captain of a British Man of War or privateer would meet an American vessel upon the ocean and board her for the purpose of ascertaining whether she was the carrier of enemy's property. Such individuals, especially, as their own interest was deeply involved in the question, were not always the most competent persons to conduct an investigation of this character. They were too prone to feel might and forget right. On the other hand the American Captain of the vessel searched would necessarily be indignant at what he might believe to be the unjust and arbitrary conduct of the searching officer. Hence bad blood would be the result and constant and dangerous reclamations would arise between the two nations.

I need not inform his Lordship that our past history had fully justified such apprehensions. On the other hand, if the rule that " free ships shall make free goods " were established, the search of the Boarding Officer would be confined to the ascertainment of the simple facts, whether the flag was bona fide American, and whether articles contraband of war were on board. He would have no investigations to make into the ownership of the cargo. If, superadded to this rule, the corresponding rule were adopted that " enemy's ships shall make enemy's goods," the Belligerent would gain nearly as much by the latter as he had lost by the former; and this would be no hardship on the neutral owner of such goods, because he would place them on board an enemy's vessel with his eyes open and fully sensible of the risk of capture. I observed that the Government of the United States had not, to my recollection, made any Treaties recently on the principle of " Free ships free goods; " and the only reason, I presumed, was, that until the strong maritime nations, such as Great Britain, France, and Russia, should consent to enter into such Treaties, it would be but of little avail to conclude them with the minor powers.

This I believe is a fair summary of all I said at different times in the course of a somewhat protracted conversation, and I hope it may meet your approbation.

I shall not be astonished if the British Government should yield their long cherished principle and adopt the rule that the flag shall protect the cargo. I know positively that Sweden and Norway, Denmark, the Netherlands, and Prussia are urging this upon them; but what I did not know, until the day before yesterday, was that the Government of France was pursuing the same course. I have the information from Count Walewsky, the French Ambassador, himself. In this connection I feel it to be my duty to say, that the correspondence of Mr. Schroeder, our Chargé d'Affaires at Stockholm, a gentleman with whom I am not personally acquainted, has furnished me the earliest and most accurate information of the proceedings of the Northern Powers on questions which may affect the neutral interests of the United States.

Lord Clarendon referred to our Neutrality Law [of April 20th, 1818] in terms of high commendation, and pronounced it superior to their own, especially in regard to Privateers. They are evidently apprehensive that Russian privateers may be fitted out in the ports of the United States, to cruise against their commerce, though in words his Lordship expressed no such apprehension. Would it not be advisable, after the war shall have fairly commenced, for the President to issue his proclamation calling upon the proper official authorities to be vigilant in executing this law? This could not fail to prove satisfactory to all the Belligerents.

In the course of conversation with Lord Clarendon, I made an appeal to him in favor of the pardon of Smith O'Brien, on condition that he would go to the United States; stating, at the same time, that this proceeded entirely from myself as an individual, and without instructions from my Government. He said he felt much obliged to me for the suggestion,—expressed the opinion that Mr. O'Brien could do them no harm in the United States, remarked that he had been Lord Lieutenant of Ireland when the proceedings against him had occurred and knew all about him;—and concluded by stating he would embrace the very first opportunity to consult the other members of the Cabinet on the subject of his pardon. You may, therefore, judge how much I felt gratified when on opening the " Times " yesterday [Thursday] morning, I discovered that Lord Palmerston had stated in the House of Commons, on the preceding night, in answer to an enquiry of Mr. Beamish, " that the question of extending the clemency of the Crown to Mr. Smith O'Brien had been under the consideration of the Government. Other persons in the same category, (he observed) had thought fit to break their parole; but Mr. O'Brien, whatever had been his faults and his crime, had acted, in this respect, like a gentleman, and it was the intention of the Government to advise the Crown to extend to him, as an act of clemency, permission to place himself in the same situation as that in which those other persons had placed themselves by a violation of their pledges."

The question of Court Costume has been finally settled to my entire satisfaction. I appeared at the Queen's Levee, on Wednesday last, in the very dress which you have often seen me wear at the President's Levees, with the exception of a very plain black handled and black hilted dress sword; and my reception was all that I could have desired. I am confident they are as well pleased as myself that this small affair has ended. I have never felt prouder, as a citizen of my country, than when I stood amidst the brilliant circle of foreign ministers and other Court dignitaries, " in the simple dress of an American Citizen." I think I cannot be mistaken in saying that the preponderance of public opinion in England is decidedly in favor of the Circular. Many of the most distinguished liberal members of Parliament have never appeared at Court, simply because they would not consent to wear the prescribed costume.

I have purposely avoided to mention the names of those with whom I have had interviews on this subject, lest it might expose them to censorious remarks hereafter; but having mentioned that of Sir Edward Cust, the Master of Ceremonies, in my despatch No. 13 of the 28th of October last, it is but an act of simple justice to state, that at the Court on Wednesday last, his attentions to me were of the kindest and most marked character and have placed me under many obligations.

In the matter of the sword, I yielded, without reluctance, to the earnest suggestion of a high official character, who said that a sword, at all the Courts of the world, was considered merely as the mark of a gentleman, and although he did not mention the Queen's name, yet it was evident from the whole conversation, that this was desired as a token of respect to Her Majesty. He had on a former occasion expressed the hope that I would wear something indicating my official position, and not appear at Court, to employ his own language, in the dress I wore upon the street. I told him promptly I should comply with his suggestion, and that, in wearing a sword at Court, as an evidence of the very high regard which I felt for her Majesty, I should do nothing inconsistent with my own character, as an American Citizen, or that of my country. I might have added that as the " simple dress of an American Citizen " is exactly that of the upper Court servants, it was my purpose, from the beginning, to wear something which would distinguish me from them. At the first I had thought of United States buttons, but a plain dress sword has a more manly and less gaudy appearance. I hope I am now done with this subject forever.

Upon the request of Lord Raglan, the Master General of the Ordnance, and Commander in Chief of the British forces destined to serve against Russia, I have given Col. Burn of the Royal Artillery a letter of introduction to the Secretary of War. The object of his mission to the United States is, in the language of his Lordship, " to visit the Government small arms manufactories in that country & any other establishments of the same nature, or of machinery that it may be interesting and instructive to look at." For several reasons, it is desirable that Col. Burn should be treated with kindness and attention by the President and Cabinet. In this manner we shall have the opportunity of reciprocating the liberal conduct of the British Government to our own officers and countrymen on similar occasions. Col. Burn will leave Liverpool by the Steamer of to-morrow. I enclose you a copy of my note in answer to that of Lord Raglan, which you will please to hand to the Secretary of War. I am well acquainted with his Lordship, but have never seen Colonel Burn.   Yours very respectfully

JAMES BUCHANAN.

HON. W. L. MARCY,
    &c. &c. &c.

TO MISS LANE.[1]

LEGATION OF THE UNITED STATES.
LONDON 24 February 1854.

MY DEAR HARRIET/

Mr. Peabody handed me at the dinner table the enclosed, which he made me promise to send to you. Mr. Macalester has mentioned your name to him.

The dress question, after much difficulty, has been finally & satisfactorily settled. I appeared at the Levee on Wednesday last, in just such a dress as I have worn at the President's one hundred times. A Black coat, white waist-coat & cravat & black pantaloons & dress boots, with the addition of a very plain black-handled & black-hilted dress sword. This to gratify them who

---

[1] Buchanan Papers, private collection; Curtis's Buchanan, II. 114.

had yielded so much & to distinguish me from the Upper Court servants.　I knew that I would be received in any dress I might wear; but could not have anticipated that I should be received in so kind & distinguished a manner.　Having yielded, they did not do things by halves.　As I approached the Queen, an arch but benevolent smile lit up her countenance;—as much as to say, you are the first man who ever appeared before me at Court in such a dress.　I must confess that I never felt more proud of being an American, than when I stood in that brilliant circle, " in the simple dress of an American citizen."　I have no doubt the Circular is popular with a majority of the people of England.　Indeed, many of the most distinguished members of Parliament have never been at court, because they would not wear the prescribed costume.

I find lying on the table before me a note from the Duchess of Somerset which possibly Laura might be glad to have as an autograph.　She prides herself on being descended in a direct line from Robert the Third of Scotland.

With my love to Laura & Clemmie & my best regards to Mr. Pleasonton, I remain, in haste, yours affectionately

JAMES BUCHANAN.

P. S.　I have not had time to write to Eskridge by this steamer; but shall do so by the next.

TO MISS LANE.[1]

LEGATION OF THE UNITED STATES.

LONDON 10 March 1854.

MY DEAR HARRIET/

I have received yours of the 16th ultimo from Philadelphia & am rejoiced to learn from yourself that your health has been entirely restored.　For several reasons I should have been glad you had gone to Washington at an early period of the winter as I desired & I hope you went there as you said you would the week after the date of your letter.

You have not mentioned the name of Miss Wilcox in any of your letters, & from this I presume you have not made her

---

[1] Buchanan Papers, private collection.　Imperfectly printed in Curtis's Buchanan, II. 114.

acquaintance. I regret this, because she was much esteemed among her acquaintances here, & many persons whom you will meet will make inquiries of you concerning her. It is strange she did not call to see you, if that be the fact. She talked of you to me.

I shall soon expect to learn from you whether you will leave New York with Captain West for Liverpool on the 15th or 29th April. God willing, I shall meet you at Liverpool. I should be very glad if Mrs. Commodore Perry would accompany you. I am well acquainted with her & esteem her highly. Still I repeat my desire that in any event you should come with Captain West on one of the two days designated.

I have no news of any importance to communicate. I am getting along here smoothly & comfortably, determined to make the best of a situation not very agreeable to me. My health has absolutely required that I should decline many 7½ & 8 o'clock dinner invitations, & evening parties commencing at 10½ & 11 o'clock.

I venture to predict that you will not be much pleased with London, & I desire that you should not be disappointed. You must not anticipate too much, except from seeing the sights. These are numerous & interesting from their historical associations. I have been making inquiries concerning a maid for you.

Please to remember me, in the kindest terms, to Mr. Pleasonton & give my love to Laura & Clemmie. . . . Ever yours affectionately,

JAMES BUCHANAN.

MISS HARRIET LANE.

TO MR. FARNUM.

(Enclosure B in No. 26.[1])

UNITED STATES LEGATION.

LONDON, 14 March 1854.

SIR,

Your letter of the 15th December last concerning the ill-fated Barque " Peytona " was received at the Legation on the 28th Ultimo. I had already heard much of this vessel from the Cape of Good Hope.

---

[1] Despatch to Mr. Marcy, No. 26, March 24, 1854, infra.

From the circumstances which you state and to which I need not specially refer, it is evident that Captain Jenkins had no other alternative than that of abandoning the vessel for the benefit of those whom it might concern.

It seems that the Bottomry Bond for the sum of $1964, executed by the Captain at Bahia, in April last, at the ruinous rate of 50 per cent. interest, was put in suit before the Vice Admiralty Court at St. Louis; and that Captain Jenkins contested the jurisdiction of the Court. The Court, however, decided, and no doubt correctly, that they had jurisdiction. Indeed, after the Barque had been abandoned and the voyage broken up, the Bottomry Bond would have become a nullity had its payment not been enforced by the Vice Admiralty Court. After the decision of the question of jurisdiction, you state that " Captain Jenkins abandoned all other action in the matter; " and from this moment forward he paid no attention either to the Bottomry suit or any of the other suits brought against him.

In this he violated his duty both to his owners and the underwriters. He ought to have contested, by the employment of Counsel and all the means in his power, the justice and fairness of the Bottomry Bond and of all the other claims put in suit, if he deemed them unjust and unfair. This was his duty as the Master of the " Peytona; " and he had no justifiable excuse for abandoning this duty and " leaving it to higher authority at home to decide whether the action of the Court was right or wrong."

Nothing can be clearer than the jurisdiction of the Vice Admiralty Court. I shall make an extract for your use of what I have written upon this subject on the 4th October last, concerning the same Captain Jenkins, to Gideon S. Holmes, Esquire, Consul of the United States at the Cape of Good Hope.

[Here, inserted Extract from letter beginning at " It is an established principle," etc. and ending with " nor do I say that the case of Captain Jenkins is not of such a character," etc.]

It appears that on the 16th November last, the Barque " Peytona " was sold at Public Auction under a decree of the Court of Vice Admiralty for the sum of $9501, " a very high price " in your opinion.

Now in order properly to raise any question for redress against the British Government, on this part of the case, it will be necessary for you to obtain a copy of the decree of the Court stating to whom and in what manner the proceeds of the sale have been distributed. On the face of this decree, an inference may be drawn whether this money was unjustly and lawlessly distributed, as you state in general terms, among parties not entitled to receive it.

It will also be the duty of Captain Jenkins to furnish an accurate statement to the parties interested of the disposition of the Cargo as well as of the vessel.   In order to do this, he should obtain certified copies of the proceedings of the Court in all the suits brought against himself or his vessel, in which he has unfortunately suffered judgments to be entered by default.

When these statements shall be furnished to the parties interested, in the United States, they may appeal, should they deem this advisable, to the State Department at Washington, and in the event that the Secretary shall consider it a proper case for a demand for redress against the British Government, I shall cheerfully present the claim in the best manner in my power. Upon your vague and general statement, I am sorry to say I can make no such demand.

Yours very respectfully

JAMES BUCHANAN.

GEORGE H. FARNUM, ESQ.
U. S. Consul, Mauritius.

MEMORANDUM.[1]

Thursday, March 16, 1854.

Called at the Foreign Office by the invitation of Lord Clarendon. He presented me a printed treaty in blank, which he proposed should be executed by Great Britain, France and the United States. The chief object of it was that all captains of privateers and their crews should be considered and punished as pirates, who, being subjects or citizens of one of the three nations who were neutral, should cruise against either of the others when belligerent. The object undoubtedly was to prevent Americans from taking service in Russian privateers during the

---

[1] Curtis's Buchanan, II. 128-130. Curtis, in a note to this memorandum, says: "I find in Mr. Buchanan's private memorandum book the account of this matter in his handwriting, given in the text." The manuscript to which Curtis refers has apparently been lost, probably in the fire in which a number of the Buchanan papers were destroyed.

present war.   We had much conversation on the subject, which I do not mean to repeat, this memorandum being merely intended to refresh my own memory.   His lordship had before him a list of the different treaties between the United States and other nations on this subject.

I was somewhat taken by surprise, though I stated my objections pretty clearly to such a treaty.   Not having done justice to the subject in my own opinion, I requested and obtained an interview for the next day, when I stated them more fully and clearly.   The heads were as follows:

1. It would be a violation of our neutrality in the war to agree with France and England that American citizens who served on board Russian privateers should be punished as pirates. To prevent this, Russia should become a party to the treaty, which, under existing circumstances, was impossible.

2. Our treaties only embraced a person of either nation who should take commissions as privateers and *did not extend to the crew.*   Sailors were a thoughtless race, and it would be cruel and unjust to punish them as pirates for taking such service, when they often might do it from want and necessity.

3. The British law claims all who are born as British subjects to be British subjects forever.   We naturalize them and protect them as American citizens.   If the treaty were concluded, and a British cruiser should capture a Russian privateer with a naturalized Irishman on board, what would be the consequence?   The British law could not punish him as an American citizen under the treaty, because it would regard him as a British subject.   It might hang him for high treason; and such an event would produce a collision between the two countries.   The old and dangerous question would then be presented in one of its worst aspects.

4. Whilst such a treaty might be justly executed by such nations as Great Britain and the United States, would it be just, wise or humane to agree that their sailors who took service on board a privateer should be summarily tried and executed as pirates by several powers which could be named?

5. *Cui bono* should Great Britain make such a treaty with France during the existing war.   If no neutral power should enter into it with them, it could have no effect during its continuance.

6. The time may possibly come when Great Britain, in a war with the despotisms of Europe, might find it to be exceed-

ingly to her interest to employ American sailors on board her privateers, and such a treaty would render this impossible. Why should she unnecessarily bind her hands?

7. The objections of the United States to enter into entangling alliances with European nations.

8. By the law of nations, as expounded both in British and American courts, a commission to a privateer, regularly issued by a belligerent nation, protects both the captain and the crew from punishment as pirates. Would the different commercial nations of the earth be willing to change this law as you propose, especially in regard to the crew? Would it be proper to do so in regard to the latter?

After I had stated these objections at some length on Friday, the 17th of March, Lord Clarendon observed that when some of them were stated the day before, they had struck him with so much force after reflection, that he had come to the office from the House of Lords at night and written them down and sent them to Sir James Graham. In his own opinion the treaty ought not to be concluded, and if the cabinet came to this conclusion the affair should drop, and I agreed I would not write to the Department on the subject. If otherwise, and the treaty should be presented to the Government of the United States, then I was to report our conversation.

In the conversation Lord Clarendon said they were more solicitous to be on good terms with the United States than any other nation, and that the project had not yet been communicated even to France.

(Vide 1 Kent's Commentaries, 100. United States Statutes at large, 175, Act of March 3d, 1847, to provide for the punishment of piracy in certain cases. Mr. Polk's message to Congress of December 8, 1846.)

General conversation about privateering.

The object of the treaty was to change the law of nations in this respect, and Lord Clarendon said that if England, France and the United States should enter into it, the others would soon follow. The project contained a stipulation that the person who took a commission as a privateer should give security that he would not employ any persons as sailors on board who were not subjects or citizens of the nation granting the commission.

March 22, 1854. At her majesty's drawing-room this day, Lord Clarendon told me that they had given up the project of the treaty, etc., etc.

TO MR. MARCY.[1]

(No. 25.)   LEGATION OF THE UNITED STATES.

LONDON, 17 March, 1854.

SIR,

Lord Clarendon sent for me yesterday, and in compliance with his promise read me the declaration which had been prepared for Her Majesty, specifying the course she had determined to pursue towards Neutral Commerce, during the present war. It announces distinctly not only that the Neutral flag shall protect the cargo, except in cases of contraband, but that the goods of neutrals captured on board an enemy's vessel shall be restored to their owners. It fully adopts the principle that " free ships shall make free goods; " and also secures from confiscation the property of a friend found on board the vessel of an enemy.

The declaration on the subject of blockades, so far as I could understand it from the reading, is entirely unexceptionable and in conformity with the doctrines which have always been maintained by the Government of the United States.

Her Majesty, also, declares that she will issue no commissions to Privateers or letters of marque during the war.

His Lordship then asked me how I was pleased with it; and I stated my approbation of it in strong terms. I said that in one particular it was more liberal towards neutral commerce than I had ventured to hope, and this was in restoring the goods of a friend though captured on the vessel of an enemy. He remarked that they had encountered great difficulties in overcoming their practice for so long a period of years and their unvarying judicial decisions; but that modern civilization required a relaxation in the former severe rules, and that war should be conducted with as little injury to neutrals as was compatible with the interest and safety of Belligerents. He also observed that he had repeated the conversation which he had held with me on these subjects to the Cabinet Council, and this had much influence in inducing them to adopt their present liberal policy towards neutrals. He then expressed the hope that their course would prove satisfactory to the Government of the United States; and I assured him that I had no doubt it would prove highly gratifying to them.

---

[1] MSS. Department of State, 65 Despatches from England. Extract printed in H. Ex. Doc. 103, 33 Cong. 1 Sess. 9-10.

I asked if I were at liberty, in anticipation of the publication of Her Majesty's declaration, to communicate its substance to yourself; and he replied certainly I was. He had not shewn it to any foreign Minister except myself, nor did he intend to do so. It had not yet undergone the last revision of the Cabinet; but the principles stated in it had received their final approbation and would not be changed.

If our shipping interest in the United States should feel as anxious upon this subject as American owners of vessels in this country, you may deem it advisable to publish a notice of the practice which will be observed by Great Britain and France towards neutrals during the continuance of the present war; and to this I can perceive no objection.

The commercial world here, I think, overestimate the danger of the capture of British Merchant vessels by Russian Privateers; and the rate of insurance is high in proportion. The effect of this, however, will be to give our vessels a great advantage over British vessels in the carrying trade. It is unfortunate that as yet we have no Minister in St. Petersburg, as I learn by a letter from our Consul there of the 9th Instant received this morning. Should Russia be prevailed upon to adopt the liberal policy towards neutrals announced in the Queen's declaration, we may expect a harvest for our carrying trade such as it has never before experienced. I could almost wish myself to be in St. Petersburg for a fortnight.

In the course of the conversation with His Lordship, I playfully observed that as Great Britain and France did not seem to be content to confine themselves to the regulation of the balance of power in Europe, but were willing to extend their care to our "hemisphere," it might become necessary for us to ally ourselves with Russia for the purpose of counteracting their designs; and I then asked him if he had read the remarks made by General Cass in the Senate on his speech in the House of Lords. He said he had not read the remarks but the substance of them had been reported to him; that he was very much astonished how any person could suppose they were intended to have the least bearing on the United States; it was evident they were only intended to refer to the joint action of the two Powers on the River Plata and in that region of South America.

I then said, "I desire to put a distinct question to your Lordship which I have no doubt from what you have already said you will be willing to answer *totidem verbis:*—Have Great

Britain and France entered into any Treaty or understanding
of any kind whatever concerning Cuba, or in relation either to
the present or the prospective condition of that island?" He
replied, "I shall answer you in *totidem verbis:* Great Britain
and France have not entered into any Treaty or understanding,
direct or indirect, of any kind whatever concerning Cuba or in
relation to the present or prospective condition of Cuba; we have
never even thought of such a thing, nor have we the least intention to adopt any such course."

I told him the answer of His Lordship was entirely satisfactory and could not fail to prove highly gratifying to the President. I should communicate it to Governor Marcy by Saturday's
Steamer; and he replied, he would feel much obliged to me
for doing so. I observed that I had not myself placed the construction on his speech in the House of Lords which General
Cass had done; but I might add that a very able and excellent
gentleman now in the Foreign Diplomatic Service of the United
States in Europe had come to a similar conclusion with the General and had written me seriously on the subject. I referred to
Judge Mason though I did not mention his name.

Believing this to be a convenient opportunity to say something about the Sandwich Islands, I remarked that if the Public
Journals were to be credited, there was at least one particular
in which Great Britain and France appeared to be acting in
concert in such a manner as might possibly affect the interests
of the United States. I had noticed that Mr. Crampton and the
Count de Sartiges had gone together to the Department of State
and protested against our acquisition of these Islands. In reply
he said he believed there had been an attempt to revolutionize
the Sandwich Islands, for the purpose of annexing them to the
United States, which was headed by Dr. Judd, but this had
failed. I said I thought I could venture to assure him that the
Government of the United States had neither directly nor indirectly instigated this movement; to which he assented. One
thing, however, I said was certain. Those Islands had been
almost completely Americanized. A very large portion of their
inhabitants were American Citizens, and should the people of
the Islands Voluntarily express a desire to be annexed to the
United States, in all human probability their request would be
granted by Congress. To this he gave me no satisfactory reply,
nor did he express any disapprobation; and I did not deem it
advisable at the moment to press the subject further. I shall

resume it again, in a cautious manner, on the first favorable opportunity, without committing my Government.

Whilst deeply convinced of the very great advantages which would result to our country from the possession of these Islands, I yet cannot be insensible to the fact that their great distance and their inability to support a sufficient population to defend themselves against a great Naval Power, such as England or France, would render them the only Vulnerable point of our territory. In these respects, they differ altogether from Cuba, which, besides, is a necessity.

I again pressed upon his Lordship the importance of prosecuting our Central American conferences to a conclusion, informing him that at Washington they would now be expecting from me by every steamer a definitive report on the subject. He again apologized for his delay, on account of the pressure upon him of the war questions; but promised *emphatically* that in a very few days he would send for me and seriously resume our conferences. I hope that, in the meantime, I may hear from the Department. The Collins Steamer which was to have left New York on Saturday the 4th Instant, has not yet arrived.

Neither did I forget the Fishery question and the danger of collision on the Fishing grounds, should he not furnish Mr. Crampton instructions which would enable him to settle it before the commencement of the approaching season.

I have been sent for to the Foreign Office in relation to another matter, about which if deemed necessary I shall write you by the next steamer, and so must omit for the present several things which I had intended to communicate.

I shall now barely mention that Baron de Cetto, the Bavarian Minister, returned to London some time since with the Treaty ratified by the King, and is very anxious to learn that it has been confirmed by the Senate. He fears that the time may be suffered to elapse within which the ratifications are to be exchanged.

Yours very respectfully

JAMES BUCHANAN.

HON. WM. L. MARCY,
    Secretary of State.

TO MR. MARCY.[1]

(No. 26.)   LEGATION OF THE UNITED STATES.
LONDON, 24 March 1854.

SIR: In my last Despatch, No. 25, of the 17th Instant, I omitted, for want of time, to refer to the conversation between Lord Clarendon & myself on the general subject of Privateering. He did not propose the conclusion of a Treaty between Great Britain & the United States for its suppression; but he expressed a strong opinion against it, as inconsistent with modern civilisation & liable to great abuses. He spoke in highly complimentary terms of the Treaties of the United States with different nations, stipulating that if one of the parties be neutral & the other belligerent, the subjects of the neutral accepting commissions as Privateers to cruise against the other, from the opposing Belligerent, shall be punished as pirates.

These ideas were doubtless suggested to his mind by the apprehension felt here that Americans will, during the existing war, accept commissions from the Emperor of Russia, & that our sailors will be employed to cruise against British commerce.

In short, although his Lordship did not propose a Treaty between the two Governments for the total suppression of Privateering, it was evident that this was his drift.

In answer, I admitted that the practice of Privateering was subject to great abuses; but it did not seem to me possible, under existing circumstances, for the United States to agree to its suppression, unless the great naval Powers would go one step further & consent that war against private property should be abolished altogether upon the ocean, as it had already been upon the land. There was nothing really different in principle or morality between the act of a regular cruiser and that of a Privateer, in robbing a Merchant vessel upon the Ocean & confiscating the property of private individuals on board, for the benefit of the Captor.

But how would the suppression of Privateering, without going further, operate upon the United States? Suppose, for example, we should again unfortunately be engaged in a war with Great Britain, which I earnestly hoped might never be the case, to what a situation must we be reduced, if we should

---

[1] MSS. Department of State, 65 Despatches from England. The part relating to neutral rights is printed in H. Ex. Doc. 103, 33 Cong. 1 Sess. 10-11.

consent to abolish Privateering? The navy of Great Britain was vastly superior to that of the United States in the number of vessels of war. They could send Cruisers into every sea to capture our Merchant vessels; whilst the number of our Cruisers was comparatively so small as to render anything like equality, in this respect, impossible. The only means which we would possess to counterbalance, in some degree, their far greater numerical strength would be to convert our Merchant vessels, cast out of employment by the war, into Privateers, & endeavor, by their assistance, to inflict as much injury on British as they would be able to inflict on American commerce. The genuine dictate of Christianity & civilisation would be to abolish war against private property upon the ocean altogether & only employ the navies of the world in public warfare against the enemy, as their armies were now employed;—& to this principle thus extended it was highly probable the Government of the United States would not object.

Here the conversation on this particular subject ended in a good natured manner; & I am anxious to learn whether what I have said in relation to it meets your approbation.

The French Consul in London gave us notice some weeks ago that, by order of his Government, he would thereafter refuse to add his visé to that of this Legation on Certificates of the Declaration of intention made by individuals to become Citizens of the United States. Such Certificates viséed by this Legation are, therefore, no longer of any avail, in enabling their holders to proceed from Great Britain to France.

The Department ought to know that there is a Notary Public in New York, by name, J. B. Nones, who issues Passports in considerable numbers for the fee of three dollars each. Many of these have been exhibited at the Legation. This is a downright imposition, & ought, if possible, to be prevented. In several instances, it has subjected ignorant individuals, not citizens of the United States, who have arrived here relying upon these Passports, to considerable loss & inconvenience.

Referring to my Despatch No. 23, of the 7th February last, I have the honor of transmitting to you copies of the final proceedings, in the case of the extradition of John Paramore, ending with Lord Palmerston's warrant of the 21st February last for his delivery to the agent of the Government of the United States.

My correspondence with our Consuls in different portions of the British Empire has become quite voluminous. Some of

the questions propounded to me are important, whilst the Legation possesses no books furnishing information on Consular
duties.   I shall supply myself with the necessary works at my
own expense; but I have one request to make of the Department.
We already have in the Library of the Legation the Reports of
the decisions of the Supreme Court of the United States up to
11th Wheaton, inclusive.   My request is that you would cause
to be sent to the Legation the succeeding volumes of these Reports till the present time, together with the latest & best general
index of their contents.   They would prove useful at all times;
but during the existing war, they would seem to be almost indispensable.   Why the Department should have ceased to send the
volumes after Eleventh Wheaton is unaccountable.

You will probably have several claims for indemnity on the
British Government before you, arising out of the incidents of
the unfortunate Bark, Peytona, Captain Oliver N. Jenkins
master, which sailed from New York on the 9th day of February,
1853, bound for Melbourne, which she never reached.   For this
reason, I transmit to you copies of two letters from myself in
relation to this vessel, the one addressed to Gideon S. Holmes,
Esquire, United States Consul at the Cape of Good Hope, on the
4th October last, & the other to George H. Farnum, Esquire, our
Consul at the Mauritius, on the 14th Instant, in answer to communications from them.

Several applications have been made to me to represent to
the President the propriety of appointing a Consul at Newcastle
upon Tyne.   Mr. Christian Allhausen, one of the largest manufacturers & most influential inhabitants of that Town, called
upon me a few days ago in behalf of himself & his fellow towns-
men, upon the subject; & from his representations of its increased
& increasing trade & the inconvenience experienced for the want
of a Consul upon the spot, it is my belief that such an appointment would be judicious.

Yours very respectfully

JAMES BUCHANAN.

HON: WILLIAM L. MARCY
    Secretary of State.

ENCLOSURES.

(A.)   Letter to Gideon S. Holmes, Esq. [See Oct. 4, 1853, supra.]
(B.)   Letter to George H. Farnum, Esq. [See March 14, supra.]
(C.)   Letter from N. Hawthorne, Esq. [See Feb. 20, 1854, supra.]
(D.)   Letter to Lord Palmerston. [See Feb. 21, 1854, supra.]
(E.)   Letter from Lord Palmerston. [Formal; not printed.]
(F.)   Warrant of Extradition. [Not printed.]

TO MR. MARCY.[1]

(No. 27.) LEGATION OF THE UNITED STATES.

LONDON, 31 March 1854.

SIR,

I have the honor to acknowledge the receipt of your Despatches Nos. 28, 29, and 30, of the 7th, 11th, and 15th Instants, respectively; and at this moment Mr. Winslow has arrived, on his way to Madrid, and has delivered me your Despatch No. 30 of the 17th Instant.

I also forward you the Copy of a note from Lord Clarendon, of the 29th Instant, communicating to me the " Copy of a message sent by the Queen to both Houses of Parliament respecting the impending hostilities with Russia, together with a supplement to the London Gazette, containing Her Majesty's declarations on the same subject," both of which I now transmit.

You will perceive that Her Majesty's Declaration concerning the commerce of Neutrals is substantially the same as that which I informed you it would be in my Despatch of the 17th Instant. It has given great satisfaction to the Diplomatic Representatives of Neutral Nations in London and to none more than to myself. Indeed, it is far more liberal than I had any reason to expect it would have been, judging from the Judicial decisions and the past history of this country.

Yours Very Respectfully

JAMES BUCHANAN.

HON: WILLIAM L. MARCY
Secretary of State.

---

[1] MSS. Department of State, 65 Despatches from England. Extract printed in H. Ex. Doc. 103, 33 Cong. 1 Sess. 11-12.

SPEECH, APRIL 6, 1854,

AT A BANQUET TO LORD ELGIN.[1]

At a splendid banquet given in London, on the evening of the 6th instant, to Lord Elgin, governor-general of Canada, Mr. Buchanan was present, and responded to a toast by the Earl of Ellesmere as follows.

The Earl of Ellesmere, in highly complimentary terms, proposed, " The Health of his Excellency the American Minister; " and, in doing so, referred to his own recent visit to the United States, to the hospitable reception which he received there, and to the impression which all that he had seen in the western world had left upon him.

Mr. Buchanan then rose and said: My lords and gentlemen, I came to England anticipating that I might find myself a stranger in a strange land; but after the first hour, I have never failed to feel myself at home in any society of Englishmen which it has been my good fortune to meet. In the name of my countrymen, I thank your lordship (the Earl of Ellesmere) most cordially for the kind sentiment which you have proposed in favor of my country, and myself as its representative; and my gratitude is due to this large and distinguished company for the enthusiasm with which that sentiment has been received. This honor will be fully appreciated on the other side of the Atlantic. If my countrymen themselves could have selected the individual by whom such gracious and kind words should be spoken, I am persuaded their choice would have fallen upon the noble Earl. He has been amongst us; he has seen us at home, and has been

> " To our virtues very kind
> And to our faults a little blind."

There are thousands on the other side of the Atlantic who will respond to the universal sentiment of approbation in this country, when they learn that his sovereign has conferred upon him one of the highest and proudest marks of distinction which it was in her power to bestow. May he long live to enjoy it! Certain I am that the penalty denounced by the motto of the

---

[1] Reprinted in the Washington *Daily Union,* April 23, 1854, with Mr. Buchanan's corrections, from the London *Morning Post* of April 7, 1854; enclosed by Mr. Buchanan with his letter to President Pierce, April 7, 1854, *infra.*

garter will never reach either his head or his heart. And here I ought, perhaps, to stop. We have been taught that after-dinner speeches are dangerous; and prudence might, on ordinary occasions, dictate that I should proceed no further. If, however, at a public dinner given to Lord Elgin, as governor-general of Canada, I should make no reference to his merits, I would expose myself to the condemnation of my own countrymen. Under his enlightened government, her Majesty's North American provinces have realized the blessings of a wise, prudent, and prosperous administration; and we of the neighboring nation, though jealous of our rights, have reason to be abundantly satisfied with his just and friendly conduct towards ourselves. He has known how to reconcile his devotion to her Majesty's service with a proper regard to the rights and interests of the kindred and neighboring people. Would to Heaven we had such governors-general in all the European colonies in the vicinity of the United States! His lordship had solved one of the most difficult problems of statesmanship. He has been able, successfully and satisfactorily, to administer, amidst many difficulties, a colonial government over a free people. This is an easy task where the commands of a despot are law to his obedient subjects; but not so in a colony where the people feel that they possess the rights and privileges of native-born Britons. And now what shall I say in reply to the wish so earnestly expressed by his lordship, that he might never live to see the bonds of friendship interrupted between the kindred nations? Had I not imagined that my own humble instrumentality might contribute in some small degree to remove existing causes of dissension between the two countries, and to confirm and perpetuate their mutual friendship, I should not have enjoyed the privilege of addressing you this day as the minister of my country. It is my most earnest desire that the two nations, kindred as they are in point of blood, should be equally kindred in each other's affections. And why should they not be? We have many free principles in common which it would be tedious to enumerate; we speak the same language, we read the same books, and we both enjoy a free press, without which liberty in any country would soon become an empty name. We claim your old masters to be our property as much as yours, and, thank God! our people are able to read and appreciate them. Every child born in most of our States has the same right to receive a good and useful common-school education as to breathe his native air or to drink from his native fountains. Why, then, should any jealousy exist between us? There have never been two nations on the face of the earth whose material interests are so closely identified. Commercially speaking, the progress of the United States has proved nearly as beneficial to Great Britain as to ourselves. The extension of our possessions on the continent of America, from the purchase of Louisiana to the present moment—an extension which has been accomplished, whatever may be said to the contrary, upon pure principles of honor and justice—has in the very same degree extended British commerce and manufactures. Though not blessed with a poetic imagination, I look forward with confident hope to the day when the English language, which is the language of Christian, civil, and political freedom, will be the language of the larger portion of the habitable globe. No people speaking this language can ever become the willing instruments of despotic power. These great results, in the destiny of the future, are to be peacefully accomplished by the energy, enterprise, and indomitable perseverance of the British and American races. I do not confine myself to the Anglo-Saxon race alone, because a large, respectable, and useful portion of the population of my country have sprung from the Irish, the German, and other European stocks. I am myself, whatever may be my merits or my faults, the son of a native-born Irishman, and I am proud of my descent. With your indulgent patience, I cannot suffer this occasion to pass without expressing my gratification with her Majesty's wise and liberal declaration in favor of neutral commercial rights during the existing war. It is worthy of the civilization of the nineteenth century, and worthy of the best constitutional sovereign who has ever sat upon the proud and powerful throne of Great Britain. The time will arrive when war against private property upon the ocean will be entirely proscribed by all civilized nations, as it has already been upon the land, and when the gallant commanders of the navies of the world will esteem it as great a disgrace to rob a peaceful merchant vessel upon the seas as the general of an army would now do to plunder the private house of an unoffending citizen. [Loud cheers.]

TO PRESIDENT PIERCE.[1]

LEGATION OF THE UNITED STATES.

LONDON 7 April 1854.

MY DEAR SIR/

I thank you cordially for your kind letter of the 22d February & 13 March. I am truly rejoiced that you approve my conduct as minister to this Country & that you have expressed your approbation in such emphatic & friendly terms. In my future course I shall endeavor to deserve your good opinion, & should I succeed in this, I shall feel certain that it will not be withheld. I can say with sincerity, that I have no other public object in view than that of closing my mission here with honor to myself & advantage to my Country, & then retiring to my peaceful home. And I beg to remind you of your kind promise that you will permit me to do this, after two years' service.

When you open the envelope of this letter, you will be surprised to find that it contains some remarks of mine taken from the London Morning Post at the dinner given to the Earl of Elgin.[2] These I have corrected so as to make them conform exactly *in substance* with what I did say. In almost every part of them they were hailed by the audience with loud applause. I would thank you to give them to our good friend Forney & request him to have them *correctly* published in the Union with as little delay as possible.

I am invited here to all sorts of public dinners & am urged to attend them. In almost every instance I have declined; but it was impossible for me under the circumstances, to decline that given to Lord Elgin. He has been exceedingly kind & attentive to me; & I trust I may be able to convert my intercourse with him to good account for my Country.

And here I would respectfully intimate that the Union, in good policy, ought not to be so severe in its strictures against this Country. The Times has changed its course, since my arrival, in regard to yourself & your administration, both of which I have never failed to defend & support in British Society. I think the effect has been favorable. Lord Clarendon has several times alluded to articles in the Union. Now if faith is to be reposed in his Lordship's declarations, & I have no doubt of their

---

[1] MSS. Department of State, 65 Despatches from England.

[2] See Speech, April 6, 1854, supra.

sincerity, Great Britain has no Treaty or understanding with Spain in regard to Cuba; nor has she any Treaty or understanding with France in regard to that Island, nor the least idea, at present, of entering into any such engagements.   Although I am not informed of your particular policy in regard to the means of acquiring this Island, yet I have shaped my course, ever since I have been in London, with a view of reconciling Great Britain to that great object.   A portion of my remarks at Lord Elgin's dinner was intended to convince the people of Great Britain that the extension of the United States could not fail to benefit them. In the Earl of Ellesmere the United States have a good friend; & without living in this Aristocratic Country, you can scarcely appreciate the value of the friendship of a nobleman so rich, so highly connected, so intelligent, & so influential.   A word in his praise in the Union would be well received & well deserved. I have had a long talk with him this morning on the Fishery question, & have no doubt what I said will be conveyed to the proper quarter.—I am inclined to doubt the friendship of Mr. Crampton for our Country.   Am I correct?   I should be sorry to harbor unjust suspicions against him, because I like the man.

I purposely made no reply to Lord Ellesmere's remarks in relation to their war with Russia.   They commence this war with enthusiasm & with almost perfect unanimity; & yet no man has been able to tell me what precise objects they mean to accomplish by it beneficial to themselves.   " Shadows, clouds, & darkness " rest upon the future, & the complications to which it may give birth, in the present state of Europe, no man can foresee.   Let us hope that it may eventuate in favor of the cause of human liberty.   John Bull is a pugnacious animal & is ever ready for a fight, though he grumbles at paying the Bill.   I am persuaded that the present popularity of the war in England arises from his desire to take the part of the weak against the strong,—the feeble against the powerful.   The Ministry have been reluctantly forced into it; & such is the opinion of the Turk. The Emperor of Russia has certainly behaved badly.   He has violated solemn Treaties; but these Treaties were guaranteed by Austria & Prussia as well as by England; and yet England is in the forefront of the battle, whilst her associates having a greater interest in the question than herself remain neutral.   *The French alliance will not last forever.*

I have made it a point to read that part of your letter to Sanders which relates to himself & to endeavor to convince him of your continued friendship, not, I trust, without effect.   He certainly has made a good & useful officer; & his influence is great with the leaders of the revolutionary party from the different Nations of Europe now assembled in London.   I am glad you have determined not to be in a hurry in sending a new nomination to the Senate.   In respect to the individual whom you may select to fill his place, I have nothing to say; but should esteem it a favor *that you should know him personally to be the right kind of a man*.   It is now one of the best offices, if not the very best, in your gift.

I cannot close this long letter without cordially & gratefully thanking you for the appointment of Van Dyke.   You will find him to be true & faithful.   He serves his friends with all his heart.

Col: Sickles & Mr. Welsh both desire to be very kindly remembered to you.   Please to present my warmest regards to Mrs. Pierce, whom I shall ever kindly remember.   My niece, Miss Lane, in her last letter, speaks of her much & in the proper spirit.

Reciprocating with all my heart your friendly sentiments towards myself, I remain always, very respectfully, your friend

JAMES BUCHANAN.

HIS EXCELLENCY, FRANKLIN PIERCE.

TO MR. MARCY.[1]

(No. 28.)   LEGATION OF THE UNITED STATES.

LONDON, 11th April 1854.

SIR,

On the 30th March, I received a card from Messrs. Stanislaus Worcell, Anthony Zabicki, and Leo Zienkowicz, " the Deputation of the Polish Central Democratic Committee " in London, requesting me to appoint a day on which I would grant them an audience.   In answer, I deemed it prudent to address them the following note, dated Friday, 31 March:—" Mr. Buchanan presents his respectful compliments to the gentlemen composing the deputation of the Polish Democratic Committee, and will be happy to receive them at his house, on Wednesday next, at 12

---

[1] MSS. Department of State, 65 Despatches from England.

o'clock. In the mean time, he should esteem it a favor, if they would intimate to him the topics on which they desire to converse, so that he may be prepared to conduct the interview in a manner satisfactory to both parties."

In reply, I received a note from them on the 2nd Instant, which I now have the honor of transmitting.

The interview took place on the 3rd Instant, according to appointment, when the Deputation, consisting of the gentlemen whom I have already named, delivered me the enclosed memorial, with the request that I would forward it to the President of the United States. This duty I assured them it would afford me pleasure to perform, as well as to communicate to them the President's answer.

The Deputation remained with me but a short time. Mr. Worcell, the Chairman, presented in conversation, very briefly, some of the views which, on perusal, I discovered were contained at length in the memorial. He appears to be a discreet, sensible, and gentlemanly individual. The other two members of the Deputation participated but little in the conversation, and for my own part I was almost entirely a listener. You will find the memorial to be a very interesting paper.

It is certain that the Partition of Poland by Russia, Austria, and Prussia was a deliberate act of high-handed robbery and cruel oppression, without a parallel, at least in Modern History; and every friend of liberty,—nay, every friend of simple justice, must hope that an over-ruling Providence, in his own good time, will redress the outrage and vindicate the right. Whether that time is so near at hand as the Polish Central Democratic Committee believe, is questionable. Let us hope for the best.

Of course you will consider this memorial, from its very nature, as strictly confidential.[1]

Yours Very Respectfully,

JAMES BUCHANAN.

HON: WILLIAM L. MARCY,
　　Secretary of State.

---

[1] This memorial, addressed to the President of the United States, is an interesting document, but fills twenty closely written pages.

TO MR. MARCY.[1]

(No. 29.)   LEGATION OF THE UNITED STATES.

LONDON, 14 April 1854.

SIR/

On Sunday last, I received a note from Lord Clarendon appointing Tuesday, the 11th Instant, at the Foreign Office, for our often promised but long delayed interview on the Central American questions.   In his note he says,—" I must again apologise for the delay that has unavoidably taken place & again thank you for your patience."

Upon our meeting, after the first salutations, his Lordship, referring to my statement of the 6th January last, inquired whether in his reply he should treat it as official or as informal. I told him he had perhaps better consider it as official, though viewed in either light it was substantially the same.   Hitherto, I said, I had occupied more time in our conferences than my share, & had, in addition, submitted to him three months ago a long statement of our case in writing; & I now was truly rejoiced that my Government was about to learn, in an authentic form, what steps the British Government intended to take in execution of the Clayton & Bulwer Treaty.   He then clearly & distinctly announced, that they considered the Treaty as entirely prospective in its operation & not as interfering with any of their existing possessions in Central America.   I replied that according to this construction, Lord Palmerston had put himself to much unnecessary trouble in insisting upon an acknowledgment from Mr. Clayton, before the exchange of ratifications, that the provisions of the Treaty did not embrace Belize.   Instead of this, he ought to have desired that this possession should, as well as the rest, enjoy the benefits of the Treaty.

Here a discursive conversation succeeded which I need not repeat, as I am to receive, " *in a very few days,*" his Lordship's answer to my statement, which will doubtless present the views of the British Government more fully & authentically than a report of this rambling conversation.   Lord Clarendon throughout seemed confused & embarrassed, & spoke more like a man under the superior influence of others than with the freedom & ease which had characterised his manner on former occasions. Still, his embarrassment may have arisen from what I venture

---

[1] MSS. Department of State, 65 Despatches from England.

to call their absurd construction of the Treaty.   I fear that Lord
Palmerston is in the back ground.

I then determined that, in conformity with the spirit of your
Despatch of the 11th ultimo, I would have a plain conversation
with his Lordship on the Fishery question.—I said I had observed a statement in a New York Journal that Governor Marcy
& Mr. Crampton were on the point of concluding a Treaty to
settle this question, & I should be rejoiced to learn that the statement was well founded.   He asked what provisions this Treaty
was supposed to contain; & I answered that the Journal did
not enter into particulars.   He observed he was sorry to say
there could not be any foundation for this report, as he had
informed Mr. Crampton some time ago that Governor Marcy's
projet could not be accepted by the British Government, without
material alterations.   It had encountered the decided opposition
of the British Colonies, whose interests they were bound to
consult.   I stated that the question of the Fisheries was a most
serious question & well worthy of his Lordship's profound attention.   The destinies impending over the civilised world, at the
present moment, seemed to be full of danger; & complications
already existed which human sagacity could neither foresee nor
avoid.   In addition to existing embarrassments I should not be
astonished, on any day, to learn that a collision had actually taken
place on the Fishery grounds between Her Majesty's Cruisers &
our Fishing vessels.   If in such a collision American blood
should be shed, this would excite & electrify our whole population
& might produce the most unhappy consequences.   That after
our fishermen had enjoyed, for a quarter of a century, the right
to fish in the large & open bays along the coasts of the British
North American Provinces, under what we believed to be a
correct construction of the Convention of 1818, the British
Government had suddenly & without proper previous notice sent
a naval force to arrest us in the exercise of this right & to enforce
a new construction of the Treaty.   Had General Jackson then
been President, an immediate collision would have been inevitable.
If they should still persist in this construction of the Convention
& attempt to prevent our fishermen from taking fish in the open
bays, a collision, during the present season, could hardly be
avoided.   This right the American Government will claim for
them & feel itself bound to maintain at any hazard.   These
fishermen had manifested a disposition, during the last season, to
arm their vessels & maintain by force what they believed to be

their rights; but in consequence of the interposition of our Government, they were prevented from pursuing this course, in the hope that the negotiations then pending would lead to a satisfactory result.   After this hope shall have been abandoned, it would be difficult to restrain them from arming in their own defence.   I also informed him I had held a conversation on this subject with Lord Ellesmere, who was sensibly alive to the dangers of a collision & was most anxious to prevent such a catastrophe, if possible.   He understood the subject perfectly, his son having commanded one of the British cruisers during the last two seasons, whose disagreeable duty it was to pursue American Fishing vessels & prevent them from passing the line which had been prescribed for them by the British Government.

His Lordship listened to me with marked attention, & seemed solemnly impressed with what I had said.   He entirely agreed with me that a destiny did indeed appear to threaten the civilised nations of the world which human prudence & honest efforts had in vain endeavored to avert.   He spoke in the highest terms of Lord Ellesmere, & said he was as anxious as his Lordship could be to prevent a collision & to settle the question.—He then asked, whether I had received any answer from Governor Marcy with respect to the suggestion which had been made by me for a temporary settlement of this question.   I told him I need scarcely repeat that this suggestion had been made without instructions, & was dictated solely by a desire to avoid the dangerous consequences of a collision on the Fishing grounds; & that it was not made until I had ascertained from him that a more general & permanent arrangement was probably out of the question.   Premising this, I said I had heard from Governor Marcy on the subject; & if nothing better & more permanent could be accomplished, he would be willing, in order to ward off impending danger, to enter into an arrangement substantially such as I had suggested.   Whilst in manner expressing his gratification with the information, he seemed carefully to avoid any committal;—again spoke of the opposition of the Colonies, & said they would object to any arrangement which did not embrace reciprocal trade, thus in fact returning to the original projet.

I told him I believed it was Nova Scotia which chiefly opposed the settlement of the Fishery question; & if I had been correctly informed, the Nova Scotians caught but few fish & had comparatively but little interest in the matter.   He said he believed this was the fact; but that I was mistaken in supposing that the other Colonies did not share the same feelings with Nova Scotia, & he specially mentioned Canada.

I could have wished at the moment I had possessed authority to propose to conclude a Treaty with him immediately, based upon my suggestion which he had appeared to regard with so much solicitude & favor. As it was, I deemed it expedient to say that should he determine to instruct Mr. Crampton to enter into such a Treaty with Governor Marcy, I would write to the Governor & other official friends & advise the acceptance of the offer as a temporary measure, in view of the threatening crisis.

It is worthy of remark that Mr. Hincks has not called upon me since his arrival in England.

I then changed the subject, & told his Lordship that his speech concerning their " happy accord with France " had produced a decided sensation throughout the United States; & I took from my pocket your Despatch of the 11th ultimo & read to him its first paragraph, ending with the sentence: " The answers received from them," &c. &c. He said he was sorry that the Americans were ever ready to place an unfavorable construction upon what was said or done in England. That in his speech, as he had already assured me, he had not the most remote intention or idea of referring to our country. The only reference he had in view was to the joint action of France & England in regard to the navigation of the Plata, the Paraguay, the Amazon, & other rivers, & to the countries of South America bordering upon them; & that this action was equally beneficial to the commerce of the United States as to their own commerce.

I observed in reply that he was mistaken in supposing that any disposition existed on the other side of the Atlantic to place an unfavorable construction upon his speech. On the contrary, I believed that at the present moment a more friendly feeling existed in the United States towards this country than had done at any former period. (Here he interrupted me & expressed his satisfaction at this statement.) Whilst I could say for myself I had not at the time placed a construction upon his remarks unfriendly to the United States, yet after a careful examination of his language, I was not surprised that others had arrived at a different conclusion. I observed that Governor Marcy was a clear-headed, sagacious, able, & sound-judging man, without any prejudice whatever against either England or himself; & yet it appeared that he had understood his Lordship's remarks as having a direct bearing on the United States. In reply he expressed his concurrence in the estimate which I had placed on the Governor's character.

And here I urged upon his Lordship the importance & necessity, with a view to the preservation of our friendly relations, if nothing better could be accomplished, of causing instructions to be immediately issued to their cruisers not to attempt to exclude our fishermen from the open bays along the coasts of their North American Colonies; but to this, I am sorry to say, he gave me no satisfactory answer.

We then had some conversation about the Russian war & other topics, in which, however, he did not forget again to call my attention to the danger that Russian Privateers might be fitted out in the Ports of the United States; & I stated my belief that no serious grounds existed for this apprehension, observing that our neutrality law would be faithfully executed. He then asked me, in evident connection with the subject of Privateering, if I was acquainted with an American gentleman by the name of M'Kay who had recently been in London. I told him I was,— he was a large ship builder in New York, & had constructed vessels for the Emperor of Russia. I had received from this very gentleman the most positive assurances that there was not the least reason to apprehend that Russian Privateers would be fitted out in our Ports, & that certainly no attempt of this kind had been made when he left the United States. I added, presuming they were aware of the fact, that Mr. M'Kay had gone to Russia for the purpose of purchasing hemp, an article indispensable to his calling. He told me he could not procure it in London; & that it was his intention to have it conveyed from St. Petersburg by land to the nearest Prussian Port, & from thence ship it in a neutral vessel to the United States. Yes, he said, this would be done, under their declaration in favor of neutrals;— that they had surrendered a great deal under this declaration,— without it, they could have prevented Russia from having any foreign market for her important staples, & thus have produced much distress among the landed proprietors & made them far more strongly feel the necessity for peace.

As I took my leave & when at the door, his Lordship told me playfully not to write too strongly to Governor Marcy of what had occurred at this interview.

I have time to make but one or two remarks in conclusion.

From my own careful observation, as well as from the information of others, I am convinced that a more friendly feeling
towards the United States exists among the mass of the English
people than has ever done at any former period. They would
deprecate nothing so much as a war with our Country; & they
are wholly unconscious of the serious difficulties existing between
the two Governments. How is a knowledge of these to be
brought home to them? In no other manner than by the publication of official documents in the United States; because these &
these only will be republished in England. Speeches in Congress,
however able & eloquent, are not republished in the Journals of
this Country. I am satisfied that if any mode could be devised
of bringing the true state of our relations with Great Britain to
the knowledge of the British people, public opinion would operate
powerfully in favor of a prompt, fair, & peaceful settlement of
the questions in dispute. It was public opinion that, in my judgment, forced the Ministry into the existing war. Without this
resort, I confess I indulge in no bright hopes of the settlement
of the questions entrusted to my management. The Coalition
Ministry are too timid & cautious to do what is right without
external support. They are now anxious & apprehensive in
regard to the consequences to this Country of the war with
Russia, & the uncertain & wavering policy of Austria & Prussia
gives them much uneasiness.

I have the honor to acknowledge the receipt of your Despatches Nos. 32 & 33, both of the 20th ultimo.

Yours very respectfully

JAMES BUCHANAN.

HON: WILLIAM L. MARCY,
    Secretary of State.

TO MR. MARCY.[1]

(No. 30.)   LEGATION OF THE UNITED STATES.

LONDON, 21 April 1854.

SIR,

On the 19th instant I received a note from Governor Kossuth, of which the following is a copy:

---

[1] MSS. Department of State, 65 Despatches from England.

Sir,

The object of my present communication is to solicit the favor of an early interview for the purpose of presenting a Memorial from myself to the President of the United States, and of requesting Your Excellency to transmit it to the Cabinet at Washington; to support with your authority its contents, if they meet your approbation, and to communicate in due time to me the answer from your Government.

I have the honor to be &c. &c. &c.

In consequence of this request Mr. Kossuth called upon me by appointment at 2 o'clock to day, and delivered me the enclosed Memorial to the President which I now have the honor to transmit.[1]   The interview was brief; and I expressed no opinion to him whatever on the points embraced by it.   Indeed, I had no accurate knowledge of what these were until I had read it over after his departure.   I have been a careful and deeply interested observer of the progress of events in Europe since my arrival in this country, though I have preserved a discreet caution in the expression of my opinions.   Whilst clouds and darkness rest upon the future, still, in certain probable contingencies, the oppressed people in different European Nations may rise against their oppressors with fair prospects of success.

It is to be hoped that the existing complications may result in such a reorganization of at least some of the States in Europe as will relieve the downtrodden people from the oppression under which they now suffer from Nationalities foreign to themselves which they detest.   Hungary, Poland, and Italy ought to be independent of Russia and Austria; even with a view to the much applauded European doctrine of the balance of Power.   Should the people of all or either of these nations rise against either Russia or Austria and establish a regular de facto Government with a reasonable prospect that they will be able to maintain it, I have no doubt the President would according to our uniform practice cheerfully adopt the proper measures to recognise their independence.   From the high character of our country, such a recognition would afford them powerful moral aid in the struggle, without giving just cause of offence to the Powers endeavoring to hold them in subjection.   This opinion, however, I did not express to Mr. Kossuth, deeming it proper, in my situation, to relieve the President from any embarrassment which an expression of opinion on my part might cast in his way.   One thing is

---

[1] The memorial, which is addressed to the President of the United States, fills twelve large pages.

certain. The revolutionary leaders in London are now inspired by the highest hopes. This I learn, not from themselves, but from others in their confidence. They profess that they only await the declaration of Austria in favor of one or the other of the belligerents, or even to remain neutral, to make a prompt and decided movement.

Yours very respectfully

JAMES BUCHANAN.

HON: WILLIAM L. MARCY
    Secretary of State.

TO LORD CLARENDON.

(Enclosure B in No. 32.[1])

UNITED STATES LEGATION

LONDON, 25 April 1854.

The undersigned, Envoy Extraordinary and Minister Plenipotentiary of the United States, has the honor of bringing under the notice of the Earl of Clarendon, Her Majesty's Principal Secretary of State for Foreign Affairs, the case of ten prisoners now confined on board the American Ship " Sovereign of the Seas " lying in the Port of London, charged with the crime of mutiny. The names of these prisoners are George Sutters, John Benson, Henry Bundy, George Hall, Irvine Lowry, William Watts, Peter Sturman, George Davidson, James Bartlett, and Augustus Holme.

The " Sovereign of the Seas " has recently arrived at this Port from Melbourne. Whilst on her passage and when on the high seas on the 17th March last, the persons named rose in mutiny against Henry Warner of New York, the Master.

Upon the arrival of the vessel in the Port of London, George N. Sanders, Esquire, the Consul of the United States, in pursuance of his general Instructions proceeded to take the Depositions of Witnesses for the purpose of ascertaining the facts in an authentic form. Copies of these Depositions the undersigned has now the honor to transmit, which do not seem to leave any doubt as to the guilt of the prisoners.

The next step prescribed to Consul Sanders by his Instructions was " to apply to the local Authorities for means of securing

---

[1] Despatch to Mr. Marcy, No. 32, May 12, 1854, infra.

the offenders while they remain in Port, and to provide the means of sending them without delay to the United States for trial." Application was accordingly made, on yesterday, by the Consul to the local Authorities, who refused to afford him the necessary aid, on the plea that they possessed no jurisdiction. If this be the case, the necessary consequences will be not only that these Mutineers shall escape punishment and be let loose upon society, but that the numerous American vessels trading between Great Britain and Australia, with the property of British Merchants aboard, will be in danger of becoming a prey to Mutiny, punishment for this crime being rendered impossible. The " Sovereign of the Seas " does not return to the United States, Captain Warner being now engaged in shipping a cargo for Melbourne; and it has thus become necessary that the Prisoners shall be discharged, if lawful authority should not be granted to secure them, until the Consul can send them for trial to an American Port.

The undersigned, therefore, under the circumstances, respectfully requests that the Earl of Clarendon would cause the proper local Authorities to interfere for the purpose of enabling the American Consul to perform his duty; but if this cannot be done, that his Lordship would so inform the undersigned that the Prisoners may be discharged without delay.

The undersigned avails himself of this opportunity to assure the Earl of Clarendon of his distinguished consideration

(signed)   JAMES BUCHANAN.

THE RIGHT HON. THE EARL OF CLARENDON
&c. &c. &c. &c.

FROM LORD CLARENDON.

(Enclosure C in No. 32.[1])

FOREIGN OFFICE, May 2, 1854.

SIR,

I have the honor to acquaint you that I am informed by the Secretary of State for the Home Department that in the case of the mutinous seamen of the " Sovereign of the Seas," to which you called my attention in your note of the 25th ultimo, there is no ground upon which an English Magistrate can exercise jurisdiction.

The mutinous conduct complained of by the Captain took place on the High Seas, and on board of an American Ship, and must, therefore, be con-

---

[1] Despatch to Mr. Marcy, No. 32, May 12, 1854, infra.

sidered in point of law to have occurred in the Territories of the United
States, where alone the matter can properly be adjudicated upon.

I have the honor to be with the highest consideration, Sir,

Your Most obedt. humble servant

(signed)   CLARENDON.

JAMES BUCHANAN, ESQ.
&c. &c. &c.

TO MR. MARCY.[1]

(No. 31.)   LEGATION OF THE UNITED STATES.

LONDON, 5 May 1854.

SIR: Late on Tuesday evening last, I received the long-
promised & long-delayed Statement of Lord Clarendon on the
Central American questions, dated on the 2d Instant, a copy of
which I have now the honor to transmit.[2] Accompanying this
Statement I also received a private note from His Lordship
apologizing " for the further delay that has taken place owing
to the Easter Holidays & the necessity of consulting some of my
[his] colleagues who were out of town."

The labor of assisting to copy this statement in season for
to-morrow's steamer, with other pressing engagements, has left
me no time, at the present moment, to make any extended remarks on its character. You will perceive that it is rambling &
inconclusive in its arguments, & its style is not equal to what
might have been expected from Lord Clarendon. For this the
cause & not the advocate is probably responsible.

But whatever may be the merits or defects of the Statement
as a composition, it would seem to put an end to any reasonable
hope of arriving at a satisfactory understanding with the Government of Great Britain as to the true meaning of the Clayton &
Bulwer Convention;—or even of effecting any compromise of
the Central American questions which the United States could
with honor accept. Although the task of answering it is not
difficult, I shall be in no hurry to perform this duty, at least until
after I shall have learned the President's views in answer to my
earnest request for instructions in relation to certain of these
questions, contained in Despatch No. 20, of the 10th January last.

---

[1] MSS. Department of State, 66 Despatches from England. An extract is
printed in H. Ex. Doc. 1, 34 Cong. 1 Sess. I. 65.

[2] This statement is printed in H. Ex. Doc. 1, 34 Cong. 1 Sess. I. 80-93,
and elsewhere.

These instructions I have for some time been anxiously awaiting. Without having first received them, I should be unwilling to offer the counter-propositions, on behalf of my Government, to those of the British Government, which will doubtless be expected.

We ought now to place ourselves upon record in regard to the Central American questions upon such principles as may challenge the approbation of the civilized world.

Yours very respectfully

JAMES BUCHANAN.

HON: WILLIAM L. MARCY
    Secretary of State.

TO MR. MARCY.[1]

No. [32.]   LEGATION OF THE UNITED STATES.

LONDON, 12 May 1854.

SIR,

I have the honor to acknowledge the receipt of your Despatches Nos. 34, 35, 36, 37, and 38, of the 6th, 13th, 14th, 22nd, and 27th April respectively. May I ask it as a favor that you would acknowledge the receipt of my Despatches when you have occasion to write?

I owe you many thanks for your prompt attention in forwarding me the Reports of the decisions of the Supreme Court of the United States since 11th Wheaton, together with the digested Index. These have already arrived, and will prove to be very useful, not only to the Legation but to General Thomas.

I am gratified to learn, from your Despatch No. 35, that the President will not consent to enter into a Treaty with Great Britain and France stipulating " that the subjects or citizens of the party being a Neutral, who shall accept Commissions or letters of Marque, and engage in the Privateer service, the other being a belligerent, may be treated as Pirates." I have been aware for some time that the Governments of these two Countries desire to conclude such a Treaty with the United States, but it appears to me the objections to it are insuperable. These, as they have occurred to my own mind, I had been prepared to submit to you at considerable length, but since the arrival of your Despatch, I shall merely advert to them in general terms.

---

[1] MSS. Department of State, 66 Despatches from England.

1. During the pendency of the present war, it would be a violation of our Neutrality to agree with Great Britain and France that American Citizens who may serve on board of Russian Privateers shall be punished as Pirates.

2. Our Treaties with other powers embrace American Citizens only who shall accept Commissions as Privateers; *but do not extend to the Crew.* Sailors are a thoughtless race, and peculiarly deserve the protection of the Government; and it would be cruel and unjust to hang them as pirates for enlisting in such service, when they might be constrained to do this from necessity.

3. The British law claims all who are born British subjects to be British subjects forever. If the Treaty were concluded and a British Cruiser should capture a Russian Privateer with a Naturalized American Citizen on board, what would be the consequence? The British law could not punish him as an American Citizen under the Treaty, because it would regard him as a British subject. It might hang him for high Treason; and such an event would produce an immediate collision between the two countries. The old and dangerous question would then be revived in one of its worst aspects.

4. The time may arrive when the United States shall require the services of foreign sailors on board their own Privateers; and would it be wise to deprive ourselves of their services by establishing a principle which would render them Pirates for enlisting in our service? In point of fact, we have now in a great degree to depend upon foreign sailors to man both our vessels of War and of Commerce.

5. Such a Treaty with Great Britain and France might prove to be an entangling and dangerous alliance.

6. Under the law of Nations as expounded both by British and American Courts, a commission to a Privateer, regularly issued by a Belligerent nation, protects both the Captain and the Crew from punishment as Pirates. Would it be proper for us, then, to expose our own Citizens to be tried and punished as Pirates by a foreign and often prejudiced jurisdiction for such an offence? By our Neutrality law of 1818, we have gone further than any other nation,—but not too far, in punishing breaches of Neutrality, before our own Tribunals; and with this foreign nations ought to be satisfied.

7. There is no safe mean for us between preserving the rights of maritime war upon the Ocean as they exist and abolishing all war, whether by Privateers or regular Cruisers, against

private property upon the Ocean, as has already been done upon the land. To the latter, for one, I should cheerfully consent; but until this can be adopted, it would be suicidal in us, with our small Navy, to cripple ourselves in manning Privateers, should this become necessary in a contest with any great Naval Power.

I beg leave to call your attention to the enclosed copies of letters, marked, A, B, and C;[1] the first from Consul Sanders to Mr. Buchanan, dated April 22nd, 1854,—the second from Mr. Buchanan to Lord Clarendon, dated April 25th,—and the third from Lord Clarendon to Mr. Buchanan, dated May 2nd. The mutineers therein mentioned have all escaped punishment.

I presume there can be no doubt but that the decision of the Secretary of the State for the Home Department is correct, and that no law of England would justify the local Magistrates in the exercise of jurisdiction in such cases. I am satisfied that there is a correspondent want of jurisdiction in our Magistrates over mutiny and other offences committed in a British vessel on the high seas.

The number of American vessels now engaged in the carrying trade between Great Britain and her Colonies renders this a serious evil. Any crime whatever committed in these vessels on the high seas is almost certain to escape punishment; because their masters will not abandon a profitable trade to carry offenders home for trial.

In conversing with Lord Clarendon, the day after the receipt of his note of the 2nd Instant, he stated to me that the British Government had made a proposition to our Government, in the time of Mr. Lawrence, under which such offenders could be secured and sent home for trial and punishment, but this had been rejected. I said I was not aware any such proposition had been made. He stated that he would send me a copy of Mr. Lawrence's letter; whereupon on the next day I received a note from him of which the following is a copy.

GROSVENOR CRESCENT May 4/54.

My DEAR MR. BUCHANAN,

The letter to which I alluded yesterday was, I find upon enquiry, from yourself, and dated Dec. 28/53, in answer to our proposal with respect to the means of apprehending foreign seamen, deserters, in New South Wales. You declined acceding to it upon grounds stated by the Attorney General.

---

[1] Papers B and C are printed supra under April 25 and May 2, 1854, respectively. Paper A is merely a letter of Mr. Sanders transmitting to Mr. Buchanan the depositions.

I made a mistake in saying that the proposal had been general, but if it had, the constitutional objection stated by the Attorney General would have applied equally,—a Treaty would be necessary for the purpose. I am not acquainted with the Treaty you have with France on this subject, but shall look at it, as a similar one with us might perhaps be of advantage to both Countries.

In examining our Conventions with France, I find that deserters from our vessels are not to be delivered up in the ports of France, if they be French Citizens. Such a provision could not be inserted in a similar Treaty with Great Britain; because then under their principle of perpetual allegiance they might refuse to surrender Naturalized Citizens of the United States who had deserted. If any Treaty should be concluded with Great Britain, the provision ought to apply to all deserters without reference to their Country. The fact of desertion ought alone to be the test of delivery. But comparatively few of the sailors on our Merchant vessels trading between Great Britain and her Colonies are American Citizens.

But whilst our Fishery Convention of 1818 and the Clayton and Bulwer Convention with Great Britain are both violated, ought we, for the present, to enter into any other Treaty with that Power? This is a serious question. I fear we shall have cause to regret the Claims Convention, although I am convinced that both Judge Upham and General Thomas have been doing and will continue to do their whole duty. It was unfortunate that it provided for the session of the Commissioners in London.

I have not been inattentive to the subject of your Despatch No. 38, received last night. Large quantities of grain and other articles have been purchased in Russia by the subjects of several Neutral Powers in Europe, whose representatives here have urged upon the British Government that they should grant permission to export these articles from Russian Ports, notwithstanding the blockade. This permission has hitherto been refused. I shall without delay bring your instructions to the knowledge of Lord Clarendon, and urge the justice and propriety of them with all the arguments in my power.

Yours very Respectfully

JAMES BUCHANAN.

HON. W. L. MARCY
    Secretary of State.

FROM THE MARQUIS OF BREADALBANE.[1]

ST. JAMES'S PALACE, May 17, 1854.

The Lord Chamberlain presents his compliments to The American Minister, &, fearing from what Sir Edward Cust said to him this morning, that there may be some misunderstanding as to the dress to be worn, this evening, at the Court Ball, begs to inform His Excellency that the dress worn is exactly the same as that worn at The Queen's Drawing Room, and that the regulations are that no persons can be admitted into Buckingham Palace this evening, unless they are in uniform, or Court Dress, or in that which has been conceded to His Excellency & the members of the Legation of the United States, as worn by His Excellency at the Drawing Room, namely breeches, buckle, & sword.

The Lord Chamberlain did himself the honor to call upon The American Minister this afternoon, but not having found him at home, begs now to make this communication to him.

TO LORD CLARENDON.

(Enclosure in No. 33.[2])   [May 19, 1854.]

The Undersigned, Envoy Extraordinary and Minister Plenipotentiary of the United States, has been instructed by his Government to ascertain from the Earl of Clarendon, Her Majesty's Principal Secretary of State for Foreign Affairs, what will be the character of the Blockade of the Russian Ports which Great Britain and France propose to establish, so far as the rights of American Citizens are concerned.

The Government of the Undersigned has received, with peculiar satisfaction, the Declaration of Her Britannic Majesty that she is " desirous of rendering the war as little onerous as possible to the Powers with whom she remains at peace." Placing implicit confidence in this declaration, he is encouraged to believe, that the blockade of the Russian Ports will be conducted in such a manner as not to prevent the exportation of property which had been bona fide acquired by American Citizens before its commencement.

According to the regular course of the trade of the United States with Russia, and because of the great distance between the two Countries, American Merchants have been in the habit, through their Agents, of purchasing Russian productions in the

---

[1] Buchanan Papers, Historical Society of Pennsylvania.
[2] Despatch to Mr. Marcy, No. 33, May 19, 1854, infra.

Autumn and Winter, and of sending vessels in the succeeding Spring to carry them to American Ports. Purchases of this kind have been made to a considerable extent during the last Autumn and Winter, in good faith, before the blockade,—and even before it was believed in the United States that the differences between Great Britain and Russia would terminate in hostilities. This property, belonging to American Citizens, for which they have paid the full value, is now lying at St. Petersburg and other Russian Ports in the Baltic. It is manifest that to force such property to remain there can do no possible injury to Russia. The injury inflicted would be confined exclusively to the Citizens of a friendly Power. The property may be injured or destroyed in Russian Ports; but if it should, Russia will sustain no loss, whilst innocent neutrals may be ruined.

The Undersigned is even ignorant, at this day, whether a blockade of the Russian Ports exists, and if so, when it commenced; no notification of it having yet, to his knowledge, been officially published. On this point he begs leave to ask for information.

It is presumed that an American vessel having her cargo on board at the commencement of the blockade will be permitted to pass out through the blockading Squadron; because this is a neutral right clearly established by the law of Nations. The same reason will apply to an American vessel in port, though not actually laden before the blockade, provided her cargo had been previously purchased by American Citizens. It would be a measure of extreme severity to compel a vessel to depart in ballast, leaving the neutral cargo behind for which she had been sent from the other side of the Atlantic.

Then, in regard to an American vessel which had not actually reached Port at the commencement of the blockade, but had cleared out from the United States before its existence was known, the Undersigned conceives the principle to be the same, provided always her cargo had been fairly and bona fide purchased by American Citizens at a previous period.

It may be said that were Great Britain to adopt this rule, it might give rise to frauds; but these could be easily guarded against so far as the United States are concerned. Indeed, our distance from the scene of action and the annual freezing of the Baltic, rendering it necessary that purchases of Russian goods should be made so long in advance of the time when they can be carried away, are circumstances which, in themselves, would almost entirely relieve such transactions from any suspicion that the purchases had been made after the commencement of the blockade. From the very nature of the trade, therefore, it could be easily ascertained when the Russian goods had been ordered, where the purchases were made, and when the price was paid. In fact, in many instances, these payments are made through the agency of London Bankers. The American Consul at St. Petersburg, if need be, under the supervision of the American Minister there, could ascertain and verify the facts in a manner which could not fail to prove satisfactory to the British Government.

If American Citizens, under these peculiar circumstances, shall be compelled to leave their property in Russian Ports, it would be difficult to conceive what will be the practical advantages to neutrals of Her Majesty's wise and satisfactory Declaration in favor of their rights. The Russian Ports will doubtless be all blockaded; and in that event, neutral trade with Russia will be entirely prohibited. Except for the noble precedent, it is in vain that Free Ships shall make free goods, and that the goods of a Friend, captured on board the vessel of an Enemy, shall be restored, if the Enemy's ports are all sealed against neutral commerce. Of this, however, the undersigned does not complain. Belligerents have their rights, under the law of Nations, which must be respected by Neutrals. But he respectfully suggests, that this blockade ought not to deprive Neutrals, and especially a distant Neutral, like the United States, of the power to carry away property from the belligerent Country which had been honestly purchased, and for which the price had been fairly paid, before the existence of the blockade, or any notification of it, had been published.

The Undersigned, knowing his Government to be sincerely desirous of avoiding every difficulty which might possibly arise between the two Countries out of the existing war, respectfully requests that Her Majesty's Principal Secretary of State for Foreign Affairs would furnish him, at as early a day as may be convenient, the necessary information on the points suggested in the present communication. If, in addition to this, the undersigned could be informed when the blockade of the Russian Ports actually commenced, if, indeed, it has already commenced, and what instructions have been given to Her Majesty's Cruisers in regard to their treatment of Neutral vessels, so that these vessels may be placed upon their guard, this might obviate all causes of future complaint.

The Undersigned avails himself of this opportunity to renew to the Earl of Clarendon the assurance of his distinguished consideration.

(signed) JAMES BUCHANAN.

UNITED STATES LEGATION
LONDON 19th May 1854.

TO THE RIGHT HONORABLE THE EARL OF CLARENDON
&c. &c. &c. Foreign Office.

TO MR. MARCY.[1]

No. 33. LEGATION OF THE UNITED STATES.

LONDON, 19 May 1854.

SIR/

I met Lord Clarendon, on the day before yesterday, by appointment at the Foreign Office, for the purpose of urging upon him the views presented in your Despatch No. 38, of the 27th ultimo, in reference to the Blockade of the Russian Ports as affecting American Vessels; & I read the greater portion of it to him, as the most appropriate introduction to our conversation. I need not detail this conversation, as you will find the substance of what I said in relation to the subject embraced in the enclosed copy of a note which I have just addressed to his Lordship.[2] In this you will perceive that I have not referred to your suggestion that American vessels might be permitted to depart from Russian Ports *with cargoes* purchased *after the Blockade had commenced;* because I had ascertained to an absolute certainty, from our conversation, that this permission would not be granted. I may add that a considerable part of my note consists of answers to objections made by him, in conversation, to the grant of such permission to vessels whose cargoes had been purchased *before the commencement of the Blockade.*

Neither is it necessary for me to repeat his verbal remarks; because he has promised me a speedy answer in writing to the points which I have presented to him by my note of to-day, & this will be more authentic. I may say, however, in general terms, that I fear there is but little reason to expect that Great Britain & France, in their Blockade of the Russian Ports, will

---

[1] MSS. Department of State, 66 Despatches from England.
[2] The preceding paper.

grant any thing more to neutrals than is required by the Law of Nations. On one point he spoke positively, & that is, that they would not, under any circumstances, grant special licenses to individuals to carry on any trade whatever with Russia. All should be treated alike. Indeed, I have known this for some time, & have, on more than one occasion, given this information to American Merchants. His Lordship observed that great abuses had arisen from these Licenses during their last war; & they had determined to have nothing more to do with them. They had such an understanding with the French Government. Neither of them would grant Licenses; & if both had not adopted this rule, great abuses must have been the consequence. You will thus be enabled to give a positive answer to the applications of Mr. J. M. Forbes & the Messrs. Cunningham, of Boston.

I asked if his Lordship had yet received a copy of your answer of the 28th ultimo to Mr. Crampton's note of the 21st, communicating Her Majesty's Declaration in regard to the conduct to be observed towards Neutrals during the existing war. He said he had not; whereupon I read it to him, believing it to be an excellent & appropriate document. Upon completing the following sentence:—" Notwithstanding the sincere gratification which Her Majesty's declaration has given to the President, it would have been enhanced if the rule alluded to had been announced as one which would be observed not only in the present, but in every future war in which Great Britain shall be a party," —he interrupted me & said, " This will make no difference; the precedent has now been set, & it will not be departed from in future wars."

After I had finished the reading, he referred to the subject of the impressment of seamen, & said he was glad this had passed away;—they could no longer impress their own sailors in their own ports. I told him I was much gratified at his remark; as any attempt to revive the practice of impressment on board of American vessels could not fail to produce an immediate collision between the two Countries.

Public opinion in this Country would not now tolerate a Press Gang. There is no occasion for a Treaty on this subject. Indeed such a Treaty could scarcely be framed which would not, at least by some remote implication, admit that a reasonable pretext had existed for the exercise of this cruel, lawless, & arbitrary power on board of American vessels. I should as soon think of asking Great Britain to declare by Treaty that she would not seize individuals upon our own soil & carry them into captivity, as that she would not impress American Seamen on board of our Merchant vessels.

We also had some conversation about the Mosquito Coast & the Island of Ruatan, in reference to portions of his Statement of the 2d Instant. I shall not repeat this, having doubtless already wearied you with too many conversations on Central American Affairs which have hitherto resulted in nothing. I might, however, say, judging from the tenor of his remarks, that I would again have cause to entertain some hopes of settling these questions, had I not been discouraged by past experience. I await with anxiety the instructions which I have requested in relation to Central America.

Lord Clarendon asked me how the case of the Black Warrior was getting along at Madrid, & I told him I did not know. I had heard nothing from there that was satisfactory. He said he had received a letter from Madrid that morning, & a prospect now existed that it would be amicably settled. The Spanish Government, I understood him to say, had offered to remit the fine & restore the property seized, & the remaining questions were about the indemnity & the amount. Mr. Soulé, when he received this proposition, had expressed himself satisfied with it so far as it went, & thought it afforded reason to believe that the question would be satisfactorily adjusted. I expressed my gratification at the information, & embraced the occasion to make a brief statement of the case of the Black Warrior to him, as I understood it from the published documents. I also informed him that this was but one of many cases of injustice, vexation, & oppression on the part of the Cuban Authorities against Citizens of the United States. He replied that British subjects had, also, on many occasions suffered from the unjust & arbitrary conduct of the Authorities, & spoke in terms of severity against both them & those of Old Spain.

I give you this information for what it is worth; though you, most probably, will have far more correct information from Mr. Soulé. His Lordship did not mention his authority; but he seemed to attach entire credit to it.

I have the honor to acknowledge the receipt of your Despatch No. 39, of the 2d Instant.

Yours very respectfully,
JAMES BUCHANAN.

HON: WILLIAM L. MARCY
      Secretary of State.

TO MR. SLIDELL.[1]

U. S. LEGATION, LONDON, 23 May 1854.

MY DEAR SIR,

I received on yesterday, per the Arabia, your very brief note of the 14th Instant: accompanied by your very able speech, which I have perused for the second [time] with great care and deep interest.

My correspondence with the State Department has been quite voluminous: but yet I have not perceived that either through the columns of the Union or in any other manner the information which I have communicated has reached the Public. Of this I do not complain. Governor Marcy has, doubtless, good reasons for what you call his "reticence." I wish, however, you had seen this correspondence before you made your speech. Without, however, violating any duty or principle of honor, I may say that Lord Clarendon, both in public and in private, has constantly and in the most emphatic terms denied the construction placed upon his ill-guarded speech, in the United States, and has given every assurance which man could give that they had no Treaty or understanding with France and Spain relative to the future condition of Cuba. This I would not say *even to you* if his declarations had been confined to myself. Neither do I believe from what I know to be the feelings of the liberal party in this Country, and from the utter ruin in which many of its manufactures would be involved by a war with the United States, that our acquisition of Cuba, in a fair and honorable manner, would produce such a war. In fact the public mind of this country is gradually preparing itself for such an event; and on all suitable occasions I speak of it as what must naturally happen. Indeed, it has more than once been foreshadowed in the columns of the "Daily News," with whose Editor I am well acquainted, as well as in other Papers.

The feelings of the Emperor of France, however, may be very different. The Empress is, in heart and soul, a Spaniard, and I am inclined to believe that France or rather *he* would look upon our acquisition of Cuba with much more hostile feelings than England. Should the Union of the two powers be successful in humbling Russia, then there might be serious danger of

---

[1] From an unsigned copy among the Buchanan Papers of the Historical Society of Pennsylvania.

an alliance between them to preserve Cuba to Spain. We ought certainly to be prepared for such an event, although I am convinced that no such alliance exists or is even in contemplation at the present moment.

I am wholly ignorant whether our administration has adopted any measures to acquire Cuba by purchase. If they have, the knowledge of them is confined I think to Mr. Soulé. I presented and reiterated to the President before I left the United States a plan for accomplishing this purpose first suggested to me by Mr. Belmont, which I understood at the time was favorably received. Mr. Belmont, after sounding influential individuals, still thinks it would work well, and undoubtedly the present would seem to be a favorable moment for making the attempt; but in order to afford a chance of success, the influence of the large capitalists of Europe having an interest in Spanish Bonds must be enlisted.—From information derived from Lord Clarendon, as well as from what was stated the other night in the House of Commons by Lord John Russell, it is highly probable the case of the " Black Warrior " will be finally adjusted upon fair and satisfactory terms. I gave Governor Marcy by the last steamer the information I had received from Lord Clarendon on the subject, and the declaration of Lord John, which I know from himself was founded on that information. has satisfied the public mind here.

If ever my Despatches should be submitted to your Committee of Foreign Relations, you will find what difficulties we had to encounter in prevailing upon the British Government to adopt the principle of " free ships free goods " during the existing war. I spoke very freely and plainly to them on the subject, and when they had finally resolved to adopt the principle, I was the first person to whom they communicated their resolution; and some time before their Declaration was promulgated in London I communicated the substance of it, by their consent, to Governor Marcy. It might, therefore, have been known in Washington before it was known in London. " During the existing war " means nothing but to let themselves down gradually. It is now freely admitted, even by the London Times, they can never take a step backwards in future wars;—as it is that impressment is gone forever. Indeed, a Press Gang would now not be tolerated by public opinion even in Great Britain. In our Discussions, Privateering was several times a subject of conversation; and my remark at Lord Elgin's dinner was intended as a public "clincher" to what I had said in private conversation against any arrangement either to abolish privateering "per se," or to deprive ourselves of any legitimate means justified by the law of nations to carry it on with effect, *unless war upon the ocean against private property was abolished altogether, as it has been upon the land.* This was perfectly understood by those present. Since, however, I have abandoned all idea of being a candidate for the Presidency, misconstructions of my own conduct are not much regarded by myself, knowing that the truth will at last prevail.

For the United States to abolish Privateering on any other condition would be a suicidal act. What would be the consequences of such a measure in case of war with Great Britain? Her Navy is vastly superior to that of the United States in the number of vessels of war. She could send National cruisers into every sea to capture our Merchant vessels: whilst the number of our cruisers would be comparatively so small as to render any thing like equality in this respect impossible. The only means which we possess to counterbalance their far greater numerical strength would be to convert our Merchant vessels, cast out of employment by the war, into Privateers; and in this manner we might inflict as much injury on British as they would be able to inflict on American Commerce. Besides, there is nothing really different in principle or morality between the act of a regular cruiser and that of a Privateer in robbing a Merchant vessel upon the ocean. The general dictate of Christianity and civilization would be to abolish war against private property upon the ocean altogether and employ the navies of the world in public warfare against the enemy as the armies are now employed. This, which would afford perfect security to our commerce in war as well as in peace, and be "a consummation devoutly to be wished," the British Government are far from being prepared to adopt. It is the best answer, however, which can possibly be made to any offer of theirs to abolish Privateering. They must go the whole, or we ought not to stir a step.

I have on more than one occasion been obliged to declare that I knew nothing either from Washington or Madrid concerning the case of the "Black Warrior," except what I have seen in the public journals. In this respect, the practice of our Government is so different from that of all others, that although my declarations have been received with courtesy, yet it was pretty evident they were considered as merely diplomatic.

TO MR. MASON.[1]

U. S. LEGATION
LONDON 30 May 1854.

MY DEAR SIR/

I ought long since to have answered your kind letter of the 20th February last; but the pressure of business of various kinds is so great upon this Legation as to leave but little time for private & friendly correspondence. In the conclusion of your letter you express the hope that I may soon return home. Would that this hope could be realised! I agreed with the President to remain here for two years, & I intend to fulfil my engagement & in the mean time make myself as contented & happy as possible. This period will not end until August, 1855. But my desire to return home does not proceed from any idea of future political advancement. Even if " there were three or four Presidential terms in me," not one of them should be " gotten out." *I shall not again be a candidate for the Presidency.*

This I say after mature reflection, & valued friends like yourself ought to know it & be able to shape their political course accordingly. This determination proceeds neither from mortification nor disappointment. The world has been a good & indulgent world to me, & I have already enjoyed more honors & offices than I ever deserved. My friends & my party have been faithful & true to me, as I shall ever be, I trust, to them. But I was 63 years of age on the 23d April last, & should I be elected President, I would be nearly *three score & ten* before the completion of the term. I think a wise man & one who desires to be a Christian ought to prefer retirement during the short remnant of days which a man at my age can reasonably expect. Besides, I have always thought it a melancholy spectacle to witness old men on the political arena struggling with younger competitors for the honors & offices of this world, as though it were to be their everlasting abode. I have been near enough the Presidency to know that it is " a crown of thorns," & although the most distinguished position in the world, it is not worth what it costs. Its labors & anxieties have become so great as to destroy the best constitutions of younger men than myself. But enough & more than enough of this.

---

[1] Buchanan Papers, Historical Society of Pennsylvania.

You mention that it was argued before you that a white witness ought to be excluded from giving testimony in favor of the freedom of a negro; because he would not get his per diem in case the cause should be decided in favor of the master. This reminds me of a conversation I had a few days ago with Sir Frederick Pollock, the Chief Baron of the Exchequer. He informed me that their practice of examining the parties to a cause had worked admirably & beneficially; & he highly applauded the example which had been set them in America in this particular, which he said they had followed. I am on terms of familiar acquaintance with him, the Lord Chancellor, & the Lord Chief Justice; but whilst I find them all to be highly intellectual & agreeable, I only say the truth when I assert that the more distinguished Judges of our Courts would compare advantageously in society with any of these high dignitaries of the law. Of course I do not speak of their legal qualifications; because I have been so long out of the practice of the law, that I am not adequate to form an opinion on this subject.

We are now in the midst of what is called the " London season." The nobility & gentry do not consider London as their home, & they remain here only from Easter until the adjournment of Parliament about the end of July. During this season they make a toil of a pleasure. The almost daily dinners at 8 o'clock & the numerous evening parties commencing near eleven are too much for my constitution; but as my niece is now with me, I must go out much oftener than I would do under other circumstances. I long for Wheatland.

Please to tell Mrs. Mason that she ought to pity the sorrows of a poor old bachelor, rather than condemn him for his misfortune. Present her my kindest & best respects, & believe me always to be your friend

JAMES BUCHANAN.

HON: JNO. THOMSON MASON.

TO MR. MARCY.[1]

No. 34.   LEGATION OF THE UNITED STATES.
                            LONDON, 2nd June 1854.

SIR,

Since the date of my note to Lord Clarendon of the 19th ultimo, I have had conferences with His Lordship and also with Sir James Graham, the First Lord of the Admiralty; and from these I feel authorised to say that Great Britain and France will eventually relax their blockade of the Russian Ports, so far as to permit American Vessels to enter these Ports for the purpose of carrying away Russian goods which had been purchased by American Citizens before the existence of the blockade. I have been requested by Lord Clarendon to furnish him a list of the American Vessels which desire to enter the Port of Cronstadt for this purpose; but upon application to the House of Baring, Brothers & Co., Mr. Russell Sturgis, one of the partners of the firm, informed me that after a thorough examination of their own transactions, as well as a strict enquiry from other Houses in London connected with the American-Russian trade, they know of no such vessels. He also informed me that the quantity of Russian goods owned by American Citizens, now in Russian Ports, is comparatively very small, as our merchants, apprehending the war and blockade, did not make their usual purchases last winter.

The "Flying Childers," belonging to J. M. Forbes, and the "Sherwood," belonging to Cunningham Brothers, concerning which you addressed me in your Despatch No. 38, of the 27th April last, both left Cronstadt with full cargoes on the 15th May; and at that date this Port was not blockaded. There have been other American Vessels which might have entered and departed in a similar manner, but these, apprehending danger, have carried their cargoes to Neutral Ports in the Baltic. I have advised such of them as applied to me to proceed directly for Cronstadt; and it would be time enough for them to change their destination and enter a Neutral Port, when met by a Cruiser of the Blockading Squadron and warned of the existence of the blockade. I give this advice, because the British Government have not yet made any public notification of the Blockade in the London Gazette or otherwise; and because I did not believe

---

[1] MSS. Department of State, 66 Despatches from England.

that any actual blockade of Cronstadt existed.   Only one of three vessels, the " Dublin " from New Orleans, has taken my advice. She sailed from the harbor of Cork for Cronstadt on the 22nd ultimo, and although this was a late period, I shall not be astonished if she should succeed in entering and leaving that Port before it shall be actually blockaded.

Since the date of my note to Lord Clarendon, the Representatives of other Neutral Powers, whose subjects own large quantities of grain and other articles now in the Russian·Ports of the Baltic, have renewed their applications for permission to export them; and notwithstanding repeated decisions of this Government to the contrary, I am inclined to believe such permission will be eventually granted.   One of them has appealed earnestly to me not to inform Lord Clarendon at the present moment that American Citizens do not appear any longer to have an interest in the question.

*   *   *   *   *   *   *   *   *   *

Yours very respectfully,

JAMES BUCHANAN.

HON. WILLIAM L. MARCY
    Secretary of State.

TO LORD CLARENDON.

(Enclosure in No. 35.[1])
(No. 5.)   LEGATION OF THE UNITED STATES.

LONDON 22 June 1854.

MY LORD/

I have had the honor to receive your note of the 20th Instant transmitting to me " three copies of notification inserted in the London Gazette of the 13th and 16th Instant, announcing the establishment, by the combined British and French Naval forces, of Blockades of the Danube and of the Russian Ports, Places, Creeks, and Havens in the Baltic therein specified." [2]

In compliance with your request, I shall transmit copies of these notifications to my Government by the next steamer.

For the present, I shall content myself with a single remark

---

[1] Despatch to Mr. Marcy, No. 35, June 23, 1854, infra.
[2] This and other notices of blockade may be found in the British and Foreign State Papers.

upon the character of the notification of the 16th Instant. This is not a blockade of a single Russian Port, or of a specified number of Russian Ports, with a declaration that there is a sufficient force at their entrance to prevent communication, but it purports to be a blockade of all "ports, roads, havens, or creeks," extending for hundreds of miles in continuous lines over the Baltic, the Gulf of Finland, and the Gulf of Bothnia. In its effect it would seem rather to be a general interdict of all neutral trade and communication with Russia, than such a blockade of particular Ports as has hitherto been usual in the practice of Nations.

Yours very respectfully,
(signed)   James Buchanan.

The Right Hon. The Earl of Clarendon,
&c. &c. &c.

TO MR. MARCY.[1]

No. 35.   Legation of The United States.

London, 23 June 1854.

Sir,

I have the honor of enclosing to you the copy of a communication which I have received from the Commissioners under the Convention for the settlement of outstanding claims between the United States and Great Britain, proposing an extension of the period for closing the Commission from the 15th September, 1854, till 15th January, 1855. I also transmit a copy of the projet of the Article which they have prepared for this purpose.

Upon a consultation with Lord Clarendon on the subject, we arrived at the conclusion that, in view of the great number of cases before the Commission, it would be a wise precaution to extend the period for six instead of four months, though it is proper to observe that Judge Upham, the American Commissioner, who is very anxious to return home, still believes it possible to close the business of the Commission on the 15th January, 1855. Notwithstanding this opinion, however, I respectfully suggest, as my deliberate judgment, that the Commission should be extended until the 15th March.

Lord Clarendon will immediately transmit to Mr. Crampton

---

[1] MSS. Department of State, 66 Despatches from England.

a communication similar to this, so that the Article may be concluded between him and yourself, should you deem this advisable, and be submitted to the Senate before its adjournment.

Under your instructions of the 2nd July last, I was directed to advise with the Commissioner and Agent on the part of the United States, in regard to the performance of their duties. This has brought me into frequent official communication with both these gentlemen, and I am very happy to be able to state, that so far as I can judge, they have discharged their duties with industry, fidelity, and ability. It has been no fault of theirs that it is now manifestly impossible to terminate the business of the Commission on 15th September.

I also transmit to you the copy of a note which I have received from Lord Clarendon, dated on the 20th Instant, communicating three copies (two of which I send to you) of the notification of the blockade, by the combined British and French Naval forces, " of the Danube and of the Russian Ports, Places, Creeks, and havens in the Baltic," together with my acknowledgment, on the 22nd Instant, of the receipt of the same. To this I have added a single remark on the character of the Blockade, which I trust may meet your approbation.[1]

I desire again to call your attention to the Bavarian Treaty, about which Baron de Cetto manifests much anxiety.

I have the honor to acknowledge the receipt of your Despatches Nos. 40 and 41, of the 17th and 23rd ultimo.

I have received the Exequatur of Robert L. Loughead, appointed Consul of the United States for the Port of Dublin, and this, together with his commission, I have forwarded to him at his post.

Your despatch No. 41, of the 23rd Ultimo, respecting our Postal relations with Great Britain, did not reach me until the 20th Instant. I presume that the reason of this delay was, that it must have been among the contents of a Despatch bag directed to this Legation and entrusted to Mr. Drake, as Bearer of Despatches, who, instead of leaving it with our Consul at Southampton, carried it on with him to Berlin. Your instructions on this subject shall receive due attention.

Yours Very Respectfully
James Buchanan.

To Hon. William L. Marcy
    Secretary of State.

---

[1] Mr. Buchanan to Lord Clarendon, June 22, 1854, supra.

FROM LORD CLARENDON.

(Enclosure in No. 36.[1])   [July 4, 1854.]

The undersigned, Her Britannic Majesty's Principal Secretary of State for Foreign Affairs, has hitherto deferred replying in detail to the note which Mr. Buchanan, Envoy Extraordinary & Minister Plenipotentiary from the United States of America, addressed to him on the 19th ultimo, in the hope that some means might be devised whereby the exemptions from the effect of Blockades of Russian Ports to be established by Her Majesty's Naval forces, requested by Mr. Buchanan in favour of the Mercantile Marine of the United States, might be granted without such an abandonment of the Belligerent right of Blockade as might very much impair its efficiency as a hostile measure; & it is a satisfaction to the undersigned to feel assured by the communications which have passed between Mr. Buchanan & himself that, although as stated in his letter to Mr. Buchanan of the 23d Instant Her Majesty's Government were unable to allow Messrs. Cameron & Brand of New York to remove from St. Petersburg, in a neutral vessel to be sent thither for that purpose, a cargo of flax purchased by them in the year 1853, the case of those parties is the only one of the kind in which citizens of the United States are interested, wherein the parties will be inconvenienced by the strict enforcement by Great Britain & France of the Belligerent right of Blockade as recognised by the United States no less than by this Country.

Under these circumstances the Undersigned might perhaps abstain from any lengthened reply to Mr. Buchanan's note of the 19th May, but as in that note Mr. Buchanan throws out various suggestions in regard to the general principles on which Maritime blockade may be enforced, the Undersigned thinks it may be more satisfactory to Mr. Buchanan to be made acquainted in detail with the views of Her Majesty's Government on those points.

Her Majesty's Government readily admit that it is consistent with Maritime law that an American vessel having a cargo on board at the commencement of a Blockade should be permitted to pass out through the Blockading squadron, but they cannot subscribe to the extension of that doctrine suggested by Mr. Buchanan, that an American vessel in port, though not actually laden before the Blockade commenced, provided her cargo had been previously purchased by American Citizens, should equally be permitted to pass out with such cargo through the Blockading Squadron. In this refusal the British Government are borne out by the best authorities on questions of international law, & the Undersigned need only cite Mr. Wheaton & Chancellor Kent to satisfy Mr. Buchanan that the soundness of the doctrines maintained in England is recognised by those distinguished jurists of the United States.

Mr. Wheaton, in his " Elements of International Law," Volume II., pages 244, 245, says,—" With respect to violating a Blockade by coming *out* with a cargo, the time of shipment is very material; for although it might be hard to refuse a neutral liberty to retire with a cargo already laden, & by that act already become neutral property, yet after the commencement

---

[1] Despatch to Mr. Marcy, No. 36, July 11, 1854, infra.

of a Blockade a neutral cannot be allowed to interpose in any way to assist the exportation of the property of the enemy." . . . "A neutral ship departing can only take away a cargo bona fide purchased & delivered before the commencement of the Blockade; if she afterwards take on board a cargo, it is a violation of the Blockade." . . . "After the commencement of a Blockade, a neutral is no longer at liberty to make any purchase in that Port."

In his Commentaries, Volume I., page 148, Chancellor Kent says,—"The object of a Blockade is not merely to prevent the importation of supplies, but to prevent export as well as import, & to cut off all communications of commerce with the Blockaded Port. The act of egress is as culpable as the act of ingress, if it be done fraudulently; & a ship coming out of a Blockaded port is, in the first instance, liable to seizure, & to obtain a release the party must give satisfactory proof of the innocence of his intention. But according to modern usage, a Blockade does not rightfully extend to a neutral vessel found in port when the Blockade was instituted, nor prevent her coming out with the cargo bona fide purchased & laden on board before the commencement of the Blockade."

Her Majesty's Government are equally unable to admit the principle contended for by Mr. Buchanan, that an American Vessel which had not actually reached Port at the commencement of the Blockade, but had cleared out from the United States before its existence was known, should be allowed to enter through the Blockade & to pass out, provided always her cargo had been fairly & bona fide purchased by American Citizens at a previous period.

The Undersigned must observe, in the first place, that the course of trade with Russia to which Mr. Buchanan adverts as justifying this principle is not peculiar to the United States, but is common to many other nations, especially Great Britain & the Hanse Towns, whose subjects have made large advances upon & payments for Russian produce, by which they may be great losers in consequence of the war.

But as regards the bearing of international law on this principle, the Undersigned would beg leave to observe that, in the view of the British Government, all that an American vessel would be entitled to under the circumstances stated by Mr. Buchanan would be *actual notice* or warning of the blockade having been established; but even that notice or warning is not to be sought for off the Port blockaded.

Chancellor Kent, in his Commentaries, Volume I., page 150, says with reference to this particular point,—"Some relaxation was very reasonably given to this rule in its application to distant voyages from America; and ships sailing for Europe before knowledge of the blockade reached them were entitled to notice even at the blockaded Port. If they sailed after notice, they might sail on a contingent destination for the blockaded Port with the purpose of calling for information at some European port, and be allowed the benefit of such contingent destination to be rendered definite by the information. But in no case is the information as to the existence of the Blockade to be sought for at the mouth of the Port."

Mr. Wheaton also says, in his Elements of International Law, Volume II., page 233,—"Where the vessel sails from a country lying sufficiently near to the blockaded Port to have constant information of the state of the blockade, whether it is continued or is relaxed, no special notice is necessary; for the public declaration in this case implies notice to the party after sufficient time has elapsed to receive the declaration at the Port whence the vessel sails. But when the country lies at such a distance that the inhabitants cannot have this constant information, they may lawfully send their vessels conjecturally, upon the expectation of finding the Blockade broken up after it has existed for a considerable time. In this case the party has a right to make a fair enquiry whether the blockade be determined or not, and consequently cannot be involved in the Penalties affixed to a violation of it, unless upon such enquiry he receives notice of the existence of the Blockade."

With reference to Mr. Buchanan's enquiry as to what instructions have been given to Her Majesty's Cruisers in regard to their treatment of Neutral vessels, the Undersigned has the honor to state generally that Her Majesty's Cruisers will doubtless in all cases of blockade be guided by the established law and practice of Nations as regulated and interpreted by the decisions of the Prize Courts of Great Britain and of the United States, "which" (says Chancellor Kent, Commentaries, page 149) "are distinguished for general coincidence and harmony in their principles."

The Undersigned has purposely confined himself in this note to citing Writers of the United States as authorities for the doctrines of International Law applicable to the points adverted to by Mr. Buchanan; but he need scarcely add that the opinions expressed by those distinguished Jurists are identical with those on the same points which are to be found in the Works of the best European Authorities.

The undersigned requests Mr. Buchanan to accept the assurances of his highest consideration.

(signed)　Clarendon.

Foreign Office, July 4th 1854.

TO MR. MARCY.[1]

No. 36.　Legation of The United States.

London, 11 July 1854.

Sir,

I have the honor to acknowledge the receipt of your Despatches Nos. 42, 43, and 44 of the 12th, 26th, and 27th June respectively.

I am now busily employed in preparing a reply to Lord Clarendon's Statement on Central American Affairs, in accordance with your instructions of the 12th ultimo. For this purpose the materials in my possession are abundant.

---

[1] MSS. Department of State, 66 Despatches from England. The third paragraph of this despatch, relating to the postal convention, is printed in S. Ex. Doc. 73, 33 Cong. 2 Sess. 60.

Until I shall dispose of this business, it is not my purpose to commence negotiations on the subject of our Postal Convention with Great Britain. After a review of the correspondence upon this subject, I entertain the opinion of Mr. Lawrence, that a recognition of our just claims can be obtained from the British Government only by giving the notice to annul the existing Convention. Nevertheless, in obedience to your instructions, I shall renew our solicitations. Great Britain never voluntarily yields an advantage.

I feel much obliged to you for the information communicated concerning the case of the Black Warrior. I am on very friendly terms with the Chevalier Comyn, the present Acting Chargé d'Affaires of Spain in this Country, who has read me copies of some of Mr. Soulé's notes to Mr. Calderon and his answers, as well as given me information communicated by the latter of some particulars in the conduct of our Minister of which the Spanish Government think they have cause to complain. Without knowing the fact, I have no doubt that all these things have been regularly communicated to the Governments of France and England, but whether in accordance with the wishes of the Spanish Government I do not know. Chevalier Comyn expresses a strong personal desire that Commissioners might be sent by the United States to Madrid. In selecting these Commissioners, I trust the President will take care that one of them at least shall be a perfect Master of either the Spanish or French language. The former would be preferable.

In regard to the mode of acquiring Cuba, I have expressed my views fully to the President in a letter dated 11 December, 1852, and directed to him at Concord, as well as in several conversations with him when I was last in Washington, and especially in reference to the appointment of Mr. Belmont, who I considered might be rendered very useful in accomplishing the object. I shall by no means despair of success, should the plan indicated in my letter and conversation be steadily pursued in concert. It would be manifestly the interest of the holders of the Spanish debt, as well as of Spain herself, that the Island should be ceded to the United States for a fair pecuniary consideration. Nor do I believe that this Government would interpose any serious obstacles. I am not now certain that I was correct in the statement contained in my letter to the President, that Queen Christina does hold " very large possessions " in Cuba; but it is certain that she derives a large annual income from its revenue. She is very avaricious, and in order to secure success it might be necessary to conciliate her interests.

I transmit to you a copy of the note of Lord Clarendon to me dated July 4th, 1854,[1] in answer to mine of the 19th May last. This long delayed answer is different from what might have been expected, from my conversations with him and Sir James Graham, and from what I have some reason to believe it would have been if the interests of the United States had been seriously involved. Messrs. Cameron and Brand, referred to in the note, had an ample opportunity to withdraw their goods from St. Petersburg, had they been able to procure a neutral vessel to bring them away. The latter, now in Dundee, made this inability the ground of his application to obtain a special license, which has not been granted in any case, and he is entirely satisfied that every thing has been done for him which was possible.—I have not heard it intimated in any quarter that the French and English Governments would consider coal as an article contraband of war, nor do I believe they have any such purpose. Indeed, they could have no object in raising such a question, as all the Ports of Russia have been blockaded. Nevertheless, I shall mention the subject incidentally to Lord Clarendon, speaking of coal not being contraband as a matter of course.—France and England might as well have declared, in a sweeping clause, that they had blockaded all the coasts of Russia, both in Europe and Asia. Their declaration much resembles the old orders in Council and the Berlin and Milan Decrees.

Yours very respectfully

JAMES BUCHANAN.

P. S. I may probably answer some of the points in Lord Clarendon's note.

HON. WILLIAM L. MARCY
&c. &c. &c. Washington.

---

[1] This note is given, under the proper date, supra.

TO MR. MARCY.[1]

No. 37.   LEGATION OF THE UNITED STATES.

LONDON, 14 July 1854.

SIR,

I herewith transmit to you a copy of a note addressed to me by Lord Clarendon on the 12th Instant, enclosing copies of the "Supplement to the London Gazette of Tuesday the 11th of July," 1854, announcing further blockades of Russian Ports in the Gulf of Finland, by the combined British and French Naval forces. Two of the three copies of this notification sent to me are now forwarded for your information.

Yours very Respectfully

JAMES BUCHANAN.

To HON. WILLIAM L. MARCY

Secretary of State.

TO MR. MARCY.[1]

No. 38.   LEGATION OF THE UNITED STATES.

LONDON, July 21, 1854.

SIR,

The success of the Spanish insurrection is an event of such importance to the United States, that I have sent a Telegraphic Despatch announcing it to Mr. Hawthorne at Liverpool, to be telegraphed from Halifax to you at Washington. In this way the news may most probably reach you before the adjournment of Congress.

The misgovernment of the Administration of the Queen, as well as the serious objections to her personal character, have produced this Revolution. The elements, however, which compose the revolutionary party are of a very heterogeneous character. They consist of Absolutists, liberal Monarchists, and Republicans. In all human probability, these different factions will eventually come to blows with each other; and Spain will present, as she has so often done, a scene of anarchy and confusion. The great question for the United States is, what influence will this Revolution exercise upon Cuba? There is every reason to believe it will produce a corresponding revolution in

---

[1] MSS. Department of State, 66 Despatches from England.

that Island; and if the Cubans are wise, they will seize the present propitious moment to relieve themselves from the Spanish yoke and declare their Independence.

There is one fact of which you ought to be apprised. Colonel Sickles, the Secretary of this Legation, has derived it from frequent conversations in London with a Spaniard of high character, now at Barcelona at the head of the Republican party in Spain, whose name I do not feel myself at liberty to mention. It is the intention of that party, should they obtain the reins of Government, to imitate the example of the French Republicans, and emancipate the Slaves in Cuba; and all the arguments which the Colonel could employ were urged in vain against the adoption of such a course. It was also distinctly stated by this gentleman, that the British Anti-Slavery Society had offered the Republicans of Spain the funds necessary to create a Revolution, provided they would enter into an agreement, in case of success, to emancipate the Slaves. This offer was rejected, as he said, because of their detestation and distrust of Great Britain.

Under these circumstances, it will be for the Government at Washington to decide whether they ought to take any steps to give a direction to the impending Revolution in Cuba.

In haste, Yours Very Respectfully

JAMES BUCHANAN.

HON. WILLIAM L. MARCY
    Secretary of State.

TO LORD CLARENDON.[1]

(Enclosure with Mr. Buchanan's No. 39.[2])

[July 22, 1854.]

REMARKS IN REPLY TO LORD CLARENDON'S STATEMENT OF
MAY 2ND, 1854.

It would not seem necessary to extend these remarks by pointing out what might be deemed inaccuracies in Lord Clarendon's introductory resumé of the points in Mr. Buchanan's statement of 6th January, 1854, nor of the order in which these

---

[1] MSS. Department of State, 66 Despatches from England; H. Ex. Doc. 1, 34 Cong. 1 Sess. I. 93.

[2] Despatch to Mr. Marcy, No. 39, July 25, 1854, infra.

points have been presented. It is sufficient to observe that the
6th and last point of this resumé, embracing the true construction of the Convention of April 19th, 1850, and which was the
first discussed in Mr. Buchanan's statement, being by far the
most important, it is entitled to precedence.

The American Government cordially reciprocates the desire
expressed by that of Great Britain " to live on intimate terms and
friendly relations " with the United States. Strong bonds of
interest and affinity ought to unite the two nations in perpetual
peace and friendship. Mr. Buchanan, therefore, deplores the
unhappy misunderstanding which exists between them, in regard
to the construction of a Convention which it was believed, on
the part of the American Government, would terminate all their
pre-existing difficulties in Central America. How unfortunate
would it be if this Convention instead of settling, should only
complicate these difficulties!

In replying to the British statement, whilst it has become
his duty to maintain the proposition that Great Britain has
failed to carry into effect the provisions of the Convention—
a subject in its nature intrinsically delicate—he will endeavor
to perform the task in a manner consistent with the exalted respect which he entertains for the Government of Great Britain.

The rights and the duties of the parties must be regulated
by the first article of the Convention of 19th April, 1850, and
these observations shall, therefore, be primarily directed to the
ascertainment of its true meaning. The following is a copy of
its text: " The Governments of the United States and Great
Britain hereby declare, that neither the one nor the other will
ever obtain or maintain for itself any exclusive control over the
said ship Canal; agreeing that neither will ever erect or maintain
any fortifications commanding the same or in the vicinity thereof,
or occupy, or fortify, or colonize, or assume or exercise any
dominion over, Nicaragua, Costa Rica, the Mosquito coast, or any
part of Central America; nor will either make use of any protection which either affords or may afford, or any alliance which
either has or may have, to or with any state or people, for the
purpose of erecting or maintaining any such fortifications, or of
occupying, fortifying, or colonizing Nicaragua, Costa Rica, the
Mosquito coast, or any part of Central America, or of assuming
or exercising dominion over the same; nor will the United
States or Great Britain take advantage of any intimacy, or use
any alliance, connexion, or influence that either may possess

with any state or Government through whose territory the said canal may pass, for the purpose of acquiring or holding, directly or indirectly, for the citizens or subjects of the one, any rights or advantages in regard to Commerce or Navigation through the said canal which shall not be offered on the same terms to the citizens or subjects of the other."

In the course of these remarks it is proposed to maintain that this article requires Great Britain to withdraw from the possession of Ruatan and the other Bay Islands; the Mosquito coast; and the territory between the Sibun and the Sarstoon. The Belize settlement will demand a separate consideration.

What then is the fair construction of the article? It embraces two objects. 1. It declares that neither of the parties shall ever acquire any exclusive control over the ship canal to be constructed between the Atlantic and the Pacific, by the route of the River San Juan de Nicaragua, and that neither of them shall ever erect or maintain any fortifications commanding the same or in the vicinity thereof. In regard to this stipulation, no disagreement is known to exist between the parties. But the article proceeds further in its mutually self-denying policy, and. in the second place, declares that neither of the parties will " occupy, or fortify, or colonize, or assume or exercise any dominion over, Nicaragua, Costa Rica, the Mosquito Coast, or any part of Central America."

We now reach the true point. Does this language require that Great Britain shall withdraw from her existing possessions in Central America, including " the Mosquito Coast"? The language peculiarly applicable to this coast will find a more appropriate place in a subsequent portion of these remarks.

If any individual enters into a solemn and explicit agreement that he will not " occupy " any given tract of country then actually occupied by him, can any proposition be clearer, than that he is bound by his agreement to withdraw from such occupancy? Were this not the case, these words would have no meaning, and the agreement would become a mere nullity. Nay more, in its effect, it would amount to a confirmation of the party in the possession of that very territory which he had bound himself not to occupy, and would practically be equivalent to an agreement that he should remain in possession—a contradiction in terms. It is difficult to comment on language which appears so plain, or to offer arguments to prove that the meaning of words is not directly opposite to their well known signification.

And yet the British Government consider that the Convention interferes with none of their existing possessions in Central America;—that it is entirely prospective in its nature and merely prohibits them from making new acquisitions. If this be the case, then it amounts to a recognition of their right, on the part of the American Government, to all the possessions which they already hold; whilst the United States have bound themselves, by the very same instrument, never under any circumstances to acquire the possession of a foot of territory in Central America. The mutuality of the Convention would thus be entirely destroyed; and whilst Great Britain may continue to hold nearly the whole Eastern Coast of Central America, the United States have abandoned the right, for all future time, to acquire any territory or to receive into the American Union any of the states in that portion of their own Continent. This self-imposed prohibition was the great objection to the Treaty in the United States, at the time of its conclusion, and was powerfully urged by some of the best men in the country. Had it then been imagined that whilst it prohibited the United States from acquiring territory under any possible circumstances, in a portion of America through which their thoroughfares to California and Oregon must pass, the Convention at the same time permitted Great Britain to remain in the occupancy of all her existing possessions in that region, Mr. Buchanan expresses the confident conviction that there would not have been a single vote in the American Senate in favor of its ratification. In every discussion, it was taken for granted that the Convention required Great Britain to withdraw from these possessions, and thus place the parties upon an exact equality in Central America. Upon this construction of the Convention there was quite as great an unanimity of opinion as existed in the House of Lords, that the Convention with Spain of 1786 required Great Britain to withdraw from the Mosquito Protectorate.

There is the strongest reason to believe that the same construction was placed upon the Convention by the Government of Great Britain at the time of its conclusion. If this were not the case, why their strenuous efforts, before the ratifications were exchanged, to have the British settlement of Belize specially excepted from its operation? Upon the opposite construction of the Convention, it ought to have been their desire to place that settlement under its protection, and thus secure Great Britain in its occupancy.

The conduct of the Government of Great Britain, on this occasion, can be satisfactorily accounted for only upon the principle that, perceiving the language of the Convention to be sufficiently explicit and comprehensive to embrace Belize, they must have made these efforts to prevent the necessity of their withdrawal from that settlement. And as no attempt was made to except any other of their possessions from its operation, the rule that expressio unius est exclusio alterius applies to the case, and amounts to an admission that they were bound to withdraw from all their other Central American possessions.

If this be the true construction of the Convention, as well as its manifest spirit, then let us apply it to the objects it was intended to embrace. And first of Ruatan—thus for the present disembarrassing ourselves from the Mosquito Protectorate.

It is not denied by the British statement that Ruatan " is clearly a Central American Island," " and but thirty miles distant from the [Honduras] Port of Truxillo." Indeed, it was impossible that this could be denied. Why then is this Island not embraced by the Convention? The only reason given for it is the allegation that Ruatan and the adjacent Islands were dependencies of Belize and were protected from the operation of the Convention by Mr. Clayton's declaration of the 4th July, 1850. Now admitting for the sake of argument that this declaration is binding on the United States, to what does it amount? Its language is very explicit. The Convention was not understood by either of the negotiators, says Mr. Clayton, " to include the British settlement in Honduras (commonly called British Honduras, as distinct from the state of Honduras) *nor the small Islands in the neighborhood of that settlement which may be known as its dependencies.*"

" The small Islands in the neighborhood of that settlement " —what are they? These are undoubtedly Cayo Casina and " the cluster of small islands " on the coast at the distance of " three leagues from the river Sibun " particularly specified in the British Convention with Spain of 1786. Indeed, the same construction would seem clearly to have been placed upon this Convention by the British Minister at Washington in his letter to Mr. Clayton of the 7th of January, 1854—a copy of which is doubtless in the possession of Lord Clarendon. It would be a strained construction of Mr. Clayton's carefully guarded language to make his " small islands in the neighborhood " embrace the comparatively large and very important Island of Ruatan, with its excellent harbors, not in the neighborhood but hundreds of miles distant; an island represented " as the Key of the Bay of Honduras and the focus of the trade of the neighboring countries," which is considerably larger, according to Captain Henderson, than many of the West India Islands in cultivation; and in its soil and natural advantages not inferior to any of them. This would be to make the dependency far more valuable than the principal, and to engraft an absolute sovereignty upon a mere usufruct. And here it may be proper to observe that the quotation " Island dependencies " in the British statement, if intended to be made from any part of Mr. Clayton's declaration, is an incorrect quotation. His language is not " Island dependencies," but " small islands in the neighborhood " of Belize. This Island is then clearly a Central American Island in the neighborhood, not of Belize, but of the state of Honduras; and in the language of Mr. Clayton's statement, so much relied upon, is one of " the proper dependencies " of that State, and is, therefore, embraced by the Treaty. Indeed, it would be little short of an absurdity for Mr. Clayton to have excepted, as it is contended he ought to have done, from his declaration, including only " the small Islands in the neighborhood " of Belize, the distant, large, and valuable island of Ruatan. And yet it is alleged, from his omission to do this, that Great Britain was justified " in deeming that her claim to Ruatan as a part of the Belize settlement was not about to be disputed! "

The British statement seems to attach considerable importance to the fact, but why it is difficult to conceive, that " Mr. Buchanan in his statement observes that Ruatan was occupied in 1850 by Great Britain." It was for the very reason that not only Ruatan but nearly the whole Eastern Coast of Central America was occupied by Great Britain that the Government of the United States was so anxious to conclude a Convention requiring her to withdraw from this occupation. It was for this reason that the United States, as an ample consideration for this withdrawal, bound themselves never to occupy any portion of Central America. But for this agreement to withdraw, the United States, in self defence, would have been compelled to accept cessions of territory in Central America; because without such territory, Great Britain would have been left in a position absolutely to command not only the projected canal by the Lake Nicaragua, but all other Canals and Railroads which may be constructed through any part of the Isthmus. The Convention was, therefore, not confined to this single route, but extended its protection " to any other practicable communications, whether by Canal or Railway, across the Isthmus which connects North and South America." Both parties were to stand aloof, and neither of them was to occupy territory in the vicinity of any of these routes, much less an Island, which, from its position and excellent harbors, would enable a strong naval Power in possession of it to close any canals or Rail Roads which might be constructed across the Isthmus.

Now, whether Great Britain was in the occupation of Ruatan at the date of the Convention by a good or by a bad title cannot make the least difference in regard to the construction of that instrument. The case might have been different, had the question arisen between her and the State of Honduras. The question between the United States and Great Britain, however, is not as to the validity of her title, but, no matter what it may have been, whether she has not agreed to abandon her occupation under this title. Not what was the state of things before, but what she agreed it should become after the conclusion of the Convention. Still, out of deference to the British statement, which contends that the British title was good to this island at the conclusion of the Convention, it is but proper to examine the reasons on which this claim was founded.

Ancient possession is invoked to sustain this claim, and it is said that " it is well known that [in] 1742 the English were formally settled at Ruatan; " but in reply it may be stated that this possession was speedily abandoned. We are informed by Rees's Cyclopædia, published in London in 1819, that " the English in the year 1742 formed a settlement here [in Ruatan] for the purpose of carrying on the logwood trade, *but it was soon abandoned.*"

In answer to the map published by Jeffries, in 1796, cited by Lord Clarendon, it may be observed, that there is another copy of the very same map in the British Museum, published in the same year, on which Ruatan is not colored as a British possession. At the date of this map, more than a half a century ago, the Geography of that portion of America was comparatively but little known. For this reason, the map published at London, in 1851, "by James Wyld, Geographer to the Queen," " of the West India and Bahama Islands, with the adjacent coasts of Yucatan, Honduras, Caraccas," &c., also to be found in the British Museum, is of much higher authority, and upon its face Ruatan and the other Bay Islands are assigned to Honduras. The same view is presented by the same author on a former "map of the West India and Bahama Islands," &c., published in 1849, and now in possession of the Legation. ·

It may also be confidently asserted, as a well known historical fact, that if the English were in the occupation of Ruatan at the date of the Treaty with Spain of 1786, they abandoned it immediately thereafter in obedience to that Treaty. Brooke's General Gazetteer, published at London in 1853, distinctly states this fact. It says, "this beautiful Island, partially covered with wood, was once in possession of the English, who fortified its excellent harbor, *but abandoned it when they withdrew from the Mosquito shore.*" And Johnson, in his Dictionary of Geography, published in London in 1851 and 1852, describes it as an Island off the North Coast of Central America, "*formerly belonging to the English.*" "Near its southern extremity is a good harbor, with batteries erected by the English during their former occupation."

At what period, then, after the Convention of 1786 did this Island cease to be Spanish and become English? It is admitted by Captain Henderson, an officer of the British Army, in his "Account of the British settlement of Honduras," an authority which will not be disputed, that it was still a Spanish Island in 1804. The next we hear of it is, that it was in the possession of Honduras as the successor of Spain in 1830, whilst the confederation of the Central American states still continued to exist, and was, in that year, (not in 1835, as in the former statement) captured from that state by the British forces; but was soon afterward restored. The following extract from Crowe's "Gospel in Central America," an able and interesting work prepared after personal observation, and published in London in 1850, gives a correct account of the transaction. The author says "1830. The only notable breach upon peace and good order was the seizure of the Island of Ruatan in the Bay of Honduras, by the authorities of the neighboring British settlement. But upon complaint by the federal Government the act of the Superintendent of Belize was theoretically disallowed by his Government, though it has since been practically repeated in precisely the same quarter and under the sanction of the same Power." There is other evidence of a similar character in the possession of Mr. Buchanan, but as it proceeds from American sources, it is deemed best to let the facts, especially as they have not been contradicted by the British statement, rest upon the authority of a British author of highly respectable character. The author then proceeds to speak in indignant terms of its second capture and annexation in 1841, denouncing it as an " inglorious revolution."

Lord Clarendon, in his statement, admits that this Island and that of Bonacca " have doubtless been at various times left unoccupied and at others claimed or held by other Powers; " but says, " it is certain that in 1838, 1839, and 1840 [it ought to have been in 1841] Great Britain not only asserted her right to the same, but declared her intention to maintain that right by force."

That is, in substance, that Great Britain captured this Island from Honduras in 1841, and expelled the troops of that state from it, and now maintains that this capture gives her title. It is impossible that Great Britain can claim this Island by the right of conquest, because the capture was made in a time of profound peace. She cannot convert the very act of which Honduras complains, as a wrong and an outrage, into the foundation of British title. Of the manner in which the seizure of Ruatan was made by the superintendent of Belize, in 1841, Mr. Crowe speaks in the following language:

" As he expected, Colonel Macdonald found only a few inhabitants, under care of a sergeant, and a small detachment of soldiers belonging to the state of Honduras. These being incapable of resistance, he proceeded to haul down the flag of the Republic and to hoist that of Great Britain in its stead. No sooner, however, had he re-embarked, than he had the mortification of seeing the Union Jack replaced by the blue and white stripes of Honduras. He subsequently returned, and completed the inglorious revolution, by taking such precautions and making such threats as he thought necessary."

The British statement contests the principle that the Central American Provinces, having by a successful revolution become independent states, succeeded within their respective limits to all the territorial rights of Spain.

As the statement presents no reason for denying this principle, it is not deemed necessary to assign reasons in its support in addition to those of the former American statement. The principle cannot, it is conceived, be successfully controverted. Were any third Power permitted to interpose and seize that portion of territory which the emancipated colony could not defend, all Powers might exercise the same right, and thus the utmost confusion and injustice would follow. If Great Britain could seize Ruatan, France might have taken possession of another portion of Honduras, and the United States of a part of San Salvador; and thus a successful revolution, instead of proving a benefit to those who had asserted and maintained their independence, would give rise to a general scramble among the nations for a proportion of the spoil.

But the British statement not only denies that her Treaty with Mexico of the 26th of December, 1826, is a recognition of the principle asserted, but maintains that it proves the contrary.

At the date of this Treaty Great Britain was in possession, for special purposes, of the usufruct of Belize, which she had acquired from Spain under the Treaty of 1786. Upon what other principle could she have solicited and obtained from Mexico an agreement that British subjects should not be disturbed in the enjoyment of this limited usufruct, unless upon the principle that Mexico had inherited the sovereign rights of old Spain over the Belize settlement? Had she then intended to claim this settlement in absolute sovereignty, she never would have sought and obtained from Mexico a continuance of her special license. The idea of an absolute owner asking a special permission to use his own property in a particular manner, from a person in whom he recognizes no title, would be, to say the least, a novelty, if not an absurdity. Greatly to her credit and her good faith, however, Great Britain agreed to hold under Mexico in the very same manner she had held under old Spain, and thus clearly recognized the rights of Mexico.

How does the British statement answer this argument? It says that the Treaty "simply stipulates that British subjects should not be worse off under Mexico independent than under Mexico when a Spanish province." And "it was natural in recognizing the independence of Mexico that Great Britain should make such a stipulation." It was certainly natural that she should do this, but only on the principle that Mexico might otherwise have asserted her rights as the successor of Old Spain, and at any moment have terminated the license.

The British statement observes that, since the capture of the island, in 1841, no attempt has been made by Honduras to recapture it; and that the Commandant of Truxillo, when on two or three occasions complaints had been made to him for redress against the settlers of Ruatan, had referred them to Belize, telling them that the island was British. But what inference can be drawn from these facts? Honduras from her feebleness has been compelled to submit, and to resort to the only remedy which the weak have against the powerful. Complaints and protestations against the act, which she has never ceased to make, have been her only resource. How ridiculous it would have been for her to have attempted to recapture this island from Great Britain! And the Commandant of Truxillo would, as a matter of course, refer complaints against the settlers in Ruatan to Great Britain for redress,—the Power in possession, and the only power in existence which could apply the remedy.

If, therefore, the question depending had been between Great Britain and Honduras, and the point to be decided by an impartial umpire were, which of the two Powers held the best title to the Island, there could be but little doubt, it is conceived, what would be his decision. But, as before remarked, the question is not between these parties, but between Great Britain and the United States. Its decision does not depend upon the validity or invalidity of the British title, but whether Great Britain has bound herself by Treaty with the United States not " to occupy, or fortify, or colonize, or assume or exercise any dominion over " Ruatan. Under these circumstances, it was not the duty of the United States, as is alleged, at the conclusion of the Convention of 1850, to have formally contested the title of Great Britain to this island. Such a course could only have produced useless irritation. It was sufficient for them to know that Great Britain, being in the occupation of it, no matter by what title, had agreed to withdraw from this occupation.

But " Her Majesty's Government cannot admit that an alteration in the internal form of Government of these Islands is a violation of the Treaty, or affords a just cause of remonstrance to the United States." What are the facts of the case? When the Treaty was concluded, Great Britain was simply in the occupation of Ruatan under the capture made by Colonel Macdonald. She had established no regular form of Government over its few inhabitants, who, to say the least, were of a very heterogeneous character. She had then taken but the first step, and this in the face of the remonstrances of Honduras, towards the appropriation of the Island. No trouble could have been anticipated by the United States in regard to this island. No doubt could have been entertained but that Great Britain would promptly withdraw from it after the conclusion of the Treaty. Her relation towards Ruatan at this time was merely that of a simple occupant. From this occupancy it was easy to retire, and the Island would then have naturally reverted to Honduras. Instead, however, of taking one step backward, the Government of Great Britain has since taken a stride forward, and has proceeded to establish a regular colonial government over it. But this is not all. They have not confined themselves to Ruatan alone, but have embraced within their colony five other Central American Islands off the coast of the state of Honduras. One of these, Bonacca, says Bonnycastle, is an island about sixty miles in circumference, and is supposed to be the first island which Columbus discovered on his fourth voyage. It was not known, however, in the United States, that the British Government had ever made claim to any of these five Central American Islands, previous to the proclamation announcing their colonization. Indeed, the British statement nowhere asserts that any of them had ever been occupied, at any period, by Great Britain, before their incorporation with Ruatan and the establishment in 1851 of the Colony of the " Bay Islands."

In this manner has the feeble state of Honduras been deprived of every valuable island along her coast, and this is now completely commanded by the impending power of Great Britain.

The Government of the United States view the establishment of the colony of the " Bay Islands " in a still more unfavorable light than they do the omission on the part of the British Government to carry the provisions of the Treaty into effect. They feel this to be the commission of a positive act in " palpable violation both of the letter and the spirit of the Clayton and Bulwer Convention."

2. THE MOSQUITO PROTECTORATE.

It does not seem necessary to add arguments to those of the former American statement, for the purpose of proving that the Mosquito Protectorate has been abolished by the Convention. This point has nowhere been directly met throughout the British statement, by arguments drawn from the body of the Treaty itself. These remarks shall, therefore, be confined to the topics presented in the British statement.

In this discussion, as in the case of the Bay Islands, it ought ever to be borne in mind that it is the true construction of the

Convention which is mainly to be ascertained & enforced, & not the historical circumstances & events which either preceded or followed its conclusion.

The admission is noticed with satisfaction, that the United States had not, under the Convention, acknowledged the existence of the British Protectorate in Mosquito. This relieves the argument from much embarrassment & the American negotiator from the imputation of having done an act which would have been condemned by his Country.

It is also repeatedly admitted that although the British Government (to employ its own language) " did not, by the Treaty of 1850, abandon the right of Great Britain to protect the Mosquitos, yet it did intend to reduce & limit that right." Had the statement proceeded one step further & specified in what manner & to what extent the British Government intended to reduce & limit this right, the controversy on this point might, then, for all practical purposes, have been settled. Why? Because Lord Clarendon must have resorted to the Convention itself for the limitations imposed on the Protectorate; & this would have informed him that it shall never be used for the purpose of " occupying " " the Mosquito Coast " " or of assuming or exercising dominion over the same." Let Great Britain no longer employ it for these purposes,—let her cease to occupy this Coast & exercise dominion over it, & although not all the Convention requires, yet for every essential object this would prove sufficient.

The British statement, strangely enough, first proceeds to discuss at considerable length what it terms " the spirit " of the Treaty, which, it says, " must always be inferred from the circumstances under which it takes place; " & afterwards, in a very few lines, disposes of the great question of the true construction of its language. This entirely reverses the natural order of things. Vattel informs us, in his Chapter on " The interpretation of Treaties," that " the first general maxim of interpretation is, that *it is not allowable to interpret what has no need of interpretation.* When a deed is worded in clear & precise terms, —when its meaning is evident & leads to no absurd conclusion,— there can be no reason for refusing to admit the meaning which such deed naturally presents. To go elsewhere in search of conjectures in order to restrict or extend it, is but an attempt to elude it. If this dangerous method be once admitted, there will be no deed which it will not render useless."

It was, therefore, incumbent upon the British statement, first, to prove that the language of the Convention is obscure,—a most difficult task,—before it could properly resort to extraneous circumstances to explain its meaning. Nevertheless, following the order of the statement, a reply shall first be given to the circumstances adduced.

But, as preliminary to these, the statement branches off into a declaration " that Mr. Buchanan confounds the two conditions of a Sovereignty & a Protectorate, & under this error treats the agreement ' not to colonize, nor occupy, nor fortify, nor assume, nor exercise dominion over,' as including an agreement not to protect." Now, admitting for the sake of argument that these words do not include " an agreement not to protect," they do at least limit this protection so that it cannot be employed for the purpose of occupying or exercising dominion over the Mosquito coast. Let this be granted, & the United States need ask but little more.

No foundation, however, is to be found in Mr. Buchanan's statement for the criticism that he had confounded two things so distinct in their nature as " a Sovereignty & a Protectorate." Indeed, he does not even use the word " Sovereignty " in connection with this topic, throughout his whole statement. On the contrary, he has carefully confined himself to the language of the Convention itself, & employed only the words " occupy " " or assume or exercise dominion."

The American Government have never treated the Protectorate claimed by Great Britain as one which could be recognized by public law. They well knew, from the savage & degraded character of the Mosquito Indians, that no Treaty of Protection could exist between Her Britannic Majesty & the King of the Mosquitos such as is recognized among civilized Nations. Under such a Treaty, the protected Power reserves to itself the right of administering its own Government,—a right which it was impossible for the Mosquitos to exercise. This nominal Protectorate must, therefore, from the nature of things, be an absolute submission of these Indians to the British Government, which, in fact, it has ever been. For these reasons, the American statement has everywhere treated Great Britain as in possession of the Mosquito coast & in the exercise of dominion over it, in the same manner as though she were its undisputed owner; & has contended that she is bound by the Treaty to withdraw from this possession & the exercise of this dominion. This is the substance.

All the rest is mere form. In this point of view, it is wholly immaterial whether the relations of the Mosquito Indians towards Great Britain be called a Protectorate, a Submission, or by any other name. The great object of the Convention, as understood by the Government of the United States, is, that she should cease to occupy the Mosquito coast, no matter by what name, or under what claim, it is retained.

The leading, indeed, it may almost be said, the only circumstance adduced to illustrate " the spirit " of the Convention, & to bear upon its construction, is a correspondence which took place at London, in November, 1849, between Mr. Lawrence & Lord Palmerston. It is thus sought to convert this preliminary correspondence, which occurred months before the Convention was concluded, between different individuals, into the means of changing & limiting the meaning of the language afterwards employed by the actual Negotiators. By such means, all agreements between private parties & all Treaties between Sovereign States might be annulled. When the final agreement is once concluded, the preliminaries become useless. Like the scaffolding of a building, they are cast aside after the edifice has been erected.

But even if such a process were legitimate, there is nothing in this correspondence which, so far from weakening, does not fortify the construction placed upon the Convention by the Government of the United States. Mr. Lawrence first asks Lord Palmerston, as the primary object, " whether the British Government intends to occupy or colonize Nicaragua, Costa Rica, the Mosquito coast, or any part of Central America; " and then inquires " whether the British Government will unite with the United States in guaranteeing the neutrality of a ship canal, railway, or other communication, to be opened to the world & common to all nations." In reply, Lord Palmerston says " that Her Majesty's Government do not intend to occupy or colonize Nicaragua, Costa Rica, the Mosquito coast, or any part of Central America; " & he also gave an equally satisfactory answer to the second inquiry of Mr. Lawrence.

Now, what inference does the British statement draw from this language? It is, that as the correspondence, which is alleged to have been before the negotiators, does not refer to the Mosquito Protectorate by name, therefore, they must have intended that this should remain untouched by the Treaty. But no inference can prevail against a positive fact. If the correspondence be silent in regard to the Protectorate, not so the Convention. This expressly embraces it, & declares, " nor will either [of the parties] make use of any protection which either affords or may afford, or any alliance which either has or may have, to or with any state or people, for the purpose of (erecting or maintaining any such fortifications or of) occupying, fortifying, or colonizing Nicaragua, Costa Rica, the Mosquito coast, or any part of Central America, or of assuming or exercising dominion over the same."

But even if the Convention had not contained this express stipulation in regard to the Mosquito Protectorate, & had simply provided for carrying into effect the intention expressed by Mr. Lawrence & Lord Palmerston that neither of the parties should " occupy or colonize " " the Mosquito coast," this would, it is conceived, have been abundantly sufficient to bind Great Britain to withdraw from its occupation. In point of fact, it resulted from abundant caution alone that the clause just quoted from the Convention was superadded, prohibiting Great Britain, whether under the name of a " Protection " or " Alliance," from " occupying " " the Mosquito coast," " or of assuming or exercising dominion over the same."

In reference to the " literal meaning of the Convention," which is certainly the main point, the British statement occupies but a few lines & avoids any direct discussion of the language which it employs. Indeed, the construction for which the Government of the United States contends is substantially admitted. The statement, after quoting the provisions of the article & asserting that it " clearly acknowledges the possibility of Great Britain or the United States affording protection to Mosquito or any Central American State," concedes that whilst it was not the intention of the parties to prohibit or abolish, it was their intention " to limit & restrict such Protectorate." Let there be no dispute about words on so grave a question. How did the Convention limit & restrict this Protectorate? It does this, as before observed, by prohibiting both parties from using " any protection which either affords," for the purpose of occupying or exercising dominion over the Mosquito coast.

Throughout that portion of the argument arising out of the correspondence between Mr. Lawrence & Lord Palmerston, & indeed in other parts of it, the British statement has treated the joint protection of the two Governments to the Nicaragua Canal as though this were the principal & almost the only feature of the

Convention. Such expressions as these are employed:—"The mere Protectorate of Great Britain, stripped of those attributes which affected the construction & the freedom of the proposed canal, was of small consequence to the United States." It is again treated as "a matter of indifference, so far as the canal is concerned, as to whether the Port & Town of San Juan are under the modified Protectorate of Great Britain or under the Government of Nicaragua." And again:—"The practical difference between Great Britain & the United States, with regard to the only mutually important portion of Mosquito, namely that portion to which the construction & condition of the canal, which formed the origin & basis of the Treaty of 1850, applies, is very small indeed," &c. &c.

These are but very partial & limited expositions of the motives which gave birth to the Convention. It consecrated a policy far more extended & liberal. The Convention was not confined to a single route, but embraced all the routes, whether for rail-roads or canals, throughout Central America. To employ its own language, it agreed to extend the protection of the two Governments, "by Treaty stipulations, to any other practicable communications, whether by canal or rail-way, across the Isthmus which connects North & South America, & especially to the inter-oceanic communications, should the same prove to be practicable, whether by canal or rail-way, which are now proposed to be established by the way of Tehuantepec or Panama." Over all such routes Great Britain & the United States have bound themselves to cast the ægis of their protection, not for their own exclusive benefit, but for that of all the commercial nations of the earth. It was to avoid all jealousies between themselves, as well as those which might arise against either or both on the part of other nations, that they agreed, not merely that neither of them would erect fortifications on the single route of the San Juan, or in its neighbourhood, but, also, that neither would directly, or by virtue of any Protectorate or Alliance, "occupy, or fortify, or colonize, or assume or exercise any dominion over, Nicaragua, Costa Rica, the Mosquito Coast, or any part of Central America." Without this latter provision the former would have been vain. The prohibition of occupation was, therefore, co-extensive with the whole territory over which such canals or Rail-roads might pass.

Viewing the Treaty in the light of its own extended & liberal provisions, it was a matter of some surprise that the

British statement should have confined itself merely to a proposition for the two Governments to enter into some arrangement whereby Great Britain may withdraw her Protectorate from the Port & Harbor of Greytown & the Northern Bank of the San Juan, thus leaving the residue of the Mosquito coast in its present condition.

The Government of the United States can become a party to no such arrangement. It stands upon the Treaty which it has already concluded, firmly believing that under this Great Britain should, more than four years ago, have ceased to occupy or exercise dominion over the whole & every part of the Mosquito coast. It cannot, therefore, now enter into any new stipulation confined to the Port of Greytown & the Northern bank of the San Juan. Such an agreement could only lead to fresh complications, & besides, would be a tacit admission, which the United States cannot make, that the Convention of 1850 did not embrace the entire Mosquito coast, as well as every other portion of Central America. All that the Government of the United States deem it proper to do, under existing circumstances, is to persist in their efforts to induce Great Britain to withdraw from the entire coast. This object once accomplished, the Treaty will then have its full & beneficent effect. The two Powers can then proceed in harmony to procure from the proper Central American States the establishment of two free Ports, one at each end of the canal, & successfully to interpose their good offices to settle all existing disputes concerning boundaries between these States. It is manifest, however, that nothing of this kind can be accomplished,— there can be no settlement of Central American affairs whilst Great Britain shall persist in expressing a determination to remain in possession, under the name of a Protectorate, of the whole coast of Nicaragua on the Caribbean Sea.

The Earl of Clarendon has been already informed, that the Government of the United States, from motives of humanity, are willing to unite with Great Britain in inducing the State of Nicaragua to assign a suitable portion of her territory for the occupation of the miserable remnant of the Mosquito Tribe. This, however, upon the principle always recognized by Great Britain & the United States, in the treatment of their own Indians, that the ultimate dominion & absolute sovereignty belong to Nicaragua; the Mosquitos having a right of mere occupancy, to be extinguished only by the State of Nicaragua.

How unfortunate is the condition of Nicaragua! Her title

to all the territory embraced within the limits of the ancient Province of that name is perfect. This she has acquired not only by a successful revolution, but she holds it under a solemn Treaty with Spain. This Treaty, concluded at Madrid on the 25th July, 1850, recognizes her sovereignty & independence, as well as her right " over the American territory situated between the Atlantic & Pacific sea," & " from sea to sea," " with its adjacent Islands, known before under the denomination of Province of Nicaragua, now Republic of the same name." And yet her Eastern coast is covered, in its whole extent, by the Mosquito Protectorate, & she is deprived of every outlet to the Caribbean Sea. Her Port of San Juan has been seized by British troops, & that of Bluefields is the residence of the King of the Mosquitos & the seat of the British dominion.

An effort has been made to assimilate the case of the British Protectorate over the Mosquitos to that of Englishmen & Americans acting as Ministers to the King of the Sandwich Islands. But there is no parallel between the cases. The inhabitants of the Sandwich Islands are not degraded savages, but a Christian people, & the Government of their King has been recognized by the principal Powers of the earth. He possesses the right to select foreigners for his ministers, as other sovereigns have frequently done; but these, in the exercise of their functions, are totally independent of their own Governments.

It is alleged that a British Consul or agent resides in Mosquito, who " may oftentimes be called upon to give his opinion or advice to the Mosquito Government." But it is notorious, & from the degraded character of the Indians it cannot be otherwise, that the Mosquito Government is exclusively the British Government, exercised through the agency of this Consul. It is through him that the British Government, in the name of this mere shadow of a King, captures the Sea Ports of his neighbours, by the employment of British forces alone, & exercises dominion over the entire so called Mosquito Coast. We have the nothingness of the Mosquito Government & the King graphically delineated by two eminent British statesmen of the present Cabinet. Truly this Government is but a " *fiction*," whilst that of Great Britain is the substantial reality.

The British statement, after defining the general distinction between " sovereignty " & " defence or protection," presents the consequences which might arise if an agreement " not to occupy or exercise dominion " should prohibit either party from the performance of certain enumerated acts, either for or against the Central American States. As these remarks are merely hypothetical & do not seem to have any direct bearing upon the great question pending between the parties, it is deemed unnecessary to prolong this statement by a reply to them seriatim. They may be well or ill founded; but it is inconceivable in what manner they bear upon the simple question under the Treaty,—which is, shall Great Britain continue to occupy or exercise dominion over the Mosquito Coast?—not what acts she may perform, without a violation of the Convention, after she shall have withdrawn from this occupation & the exercise of this dominion.

Opinions are referred to, said to have been expressed by Mr. Webster concerning the Convention; but this is to be expounded according to its own text, & not by the mere incidental dicta of any man, no matter how eminent.

And here all has been said which either directly or remotely touches the merits of the Mosquito question; but as several other topics have been introduced, it would be improper to pass them over in silence.

The statement declares, in reference to the Mosquito Protectorate, that Great Britain " will not enter into any explanation or defence of her conduct with respect to acts committed by her nearly forty years ago." Be it so. Such an explanation is not solicited by the United States. Still it is but just to observe, that the British Government first set the example of discussing their ancient right to the Mosquito Protectorate; & this is the only reason given in the former American statement for presenting " the views of the Government of the United States on the subject."

It is highly satisfactory, however, to observe, that the British statement, instead of relying upon acts of the English on the Mosquito Coast for centuries, limits these within a period of less than forty years anterior to the present date. It is possible that the former American statement may have done some good in effecting this change, by causing Lord Clarendon to re-examine the Treaties of 1783 & 1786 & to refer to the history of the time, in which additional proof has been found, not now necessary to be presented, in confirmation of the construction placed upon these Treaties by the American Government.

It would still have been interesting, as a historical fact, to learn at what time, " nearly forty years ago," under what circumstances, & upon what terms Great Britain again entered upon

Mosquito, after having acknowledged the sovereignty of Spain over it, in 1783 & 1786, & surrendered it to that Power.

The British statement proceeds to allege, that, since the peace of 1815, Old Spain had never raised any question with the British Government respecting the Mosquito Protectorate. This is doubtless the case, because Old Spain, from the intimate relations of friendship which had existed between the two Governments since their Treaty of Alliance in 1809, could not have suspected that Great Britain was renewing her connection with the Mosquitos; & soon after " the acts committed by her nearly forty years ago," the Spanish American Revolutionary war commenced, which would naturally prevent the Spanish Government from bestowing its attention on a matter so comparatively unimportant.

The statement then denies that, by the British Treaty with Mexico of 1826, Great Britain had recognized the right of the Central American States, having achieved their independence, to the territories respectively included within their boundaries, as these had formerly existed under Old Spain. As this point has been discussed in a former portion of the present statement, it is not now necessary to add any thing to what has already been said.

But, again, argues the British statement, even supposing that these States did inherit the rights of Old Spain, they made no remonstrance " for many years, after the Protectorate of Great Britain over Mosquito had been a fact well known to them."

Surely the British Government does not mean to contend that the omission of these feeble States, agitated, in the first place, by a Revolutionary War & afterwards by domestic dissensions, to make such remonstrances, would confer upon Great Britain the right to deprive them of their territory. Besides, if it were necessary to go into the question, it might be proved that not many but only a few years had elapsed before these States did remonstrate against the encroachments of Great Britain.

The statement next asserts, that although the Government of the United States, in 1842, knew of the existence of the British Protectorate, yet they did not complain of it until 1849. And from this what is to be inferred? The United States had no right, under any Treaty with Great Britain, to interfere in this question, until April, 1850. But even if they had been directly interested in the territory, as Nicaragua was, is there any Statute of Limitations among nations, which, after six years of unlawful possession, deprives the true owner of his territorial rights?

Had the United States interfered in this question before the conclusion of the Convention of 1850, this could only have been done under the Monroe doctrine; & then they would have been informed, as they have already been in the British statement, that this doctrine " can only be viewed as the dictum of the distinguished personage who delivered it; but Her Majesty's Government cannot admit that doctrine as an international axiom which ought to regulate the conduct of European States."

But it must not be inferred, from what has been said, that, without this Convention, the Government of the United States would not have eventually interfered, in obedience to the Monroe doctrine, to prevent, if possible, any portion of Central America from being permanently occupied or colonized by Great Britain.

Neither is Lord Clarendon correct in supposing that this doctrine is but the mere " dictum " of its distinguished author. True, it has never been formally sanctioned by Congress; but when first announced, more than thirty years ago, it was hailed with enthusiastic approbation by the American people; & since that period different Presidents of the United States have repeated it, in their messages to Congress, & always with unmistakable indications of public approbation.

If the occasion required, Mr. Buchanan would cheerfully undertake the task of justifying the wisdom & sound policy of the Monroe doctrine, in reference to the nations of Europe, as well as to those on the American Continent.

The British statement proceeds to enumerate several instances, commencing in November, 1847, extracted from the report of Mr. Clayton to the President, in July, 1850, in which no answers were returned by the Government of the United States to appeals made by, or on behalf of, the State of Nicaragua for our interference to arrest the progress of British encroachments in Central America.

Surely the war then pending between the United States & Mexico was sufficient to account for this temporary omission, without attributing it to any indifference to the proceedings of Great Britain against Nicaragua.

But even before this war was finally terminated by a Treaty of peace, & after the capture of San Juan by the British forces, President Polk, in April, 1848, gave a public pledge to the world, in strong terms, of his adherence to the Monroe doctrine, as he had already done in two previous Messages. Besides, in December, 1847, he asked an appropriation from Congress to enable him to send a Minister to Guatemala; & this Minister was accordingly despatched with instructions, which have been published, having distinctly in view the adoption of measures necessary to give effect to this doctrine in Central America.

The British statement, whilst admitting that, under the former principles & practice of European Nations in regard to their treatment of the Indian races, the Mosquitos would have no right to rank as an independent State, yet indicates that Great Britain has changed her conduct in this respect. As examples of great changes in other respects which have occurred in modern times, & as an excuse or justification for her own change, the British statement cites the suppression of the African Slave Trade & the establishment of the Republic of Liberia. Neither of these would seem to be very wonderful. They both occurred in the natural progress of events, from the advance of civilization & the efforts of wise & benevolent men. But the British Government will have performed a miracle if they can convert the debased & degraded race of Mosquito Indians, such as they have been described without contradiction in the American statement, into citizens or subjects of a really independent & sovereign nation.

The British statement, also, declines to furnish " the grounds on which Her Majesty's Government made the capture of San Juan de Nicaragua," & it is, therefore, scarcely necessary to pursue this branch of the subject. If it were, it would be easy to add proofs to those contained in the former American statement, that this was never a Mosquito Port, in any sense, but always, together with the River San Juan, rightfully belonged to Spain, & afterwards to Nicaragua. Reference might be made to the Report of Sir William Wise, the Commander of the British Ship of war, Sophie, who visited the coast in 1820, & also to that of Mr. Orlando Roberts, who was carried as a prisoner up the San Juan in 1821. The latter describes the Fort, to which Captain Bonnycastle had referred, as then still mounting twelve pieces of large cannon & containing accommodations for one hundred men.

The two chapters of Crowe's Central America, entitled " British Encroachments," might also be cited. Of these the author presents a striking history, from the time of the numerous & formidable but unsuccessful expedition of Great Britain against Spain, in 1780, for the purpose of wresting from that Power the Port & River of San Juan, until they were finally captured from Nicaragua, in 1848, & then first became a part of the Mosquito Protectorate.

3.   THE TERRITORY BETWEEN THE SIBUN & THE SARSTOON.

The next portion of Central America which demands attention is the territory between the Rivers Sibun & Sarstoon. Over this territory the British settlers from Belize have been encroaching for several years; but this, it was believed, without the authority or sanction of the British Government. It now appears that Great Britain claims the territory, & declines to withdraw from its occupation, in obedience to the Convention.

In regard to it, the question need not be discussed whether the Convention embraces the entire Isthmus, geographically known as Central America, or is confined to the five States which formerly composed the Republic of that name. In either sense, the country between the Sibun & the Sarstoon is included within Central America. This territory is a part of the Province of Vera Paz, all of which constitutes an integral portion of the State of Guatemala. At the date of the Treaty of 1786, & until the Spanish dominion terminated, the territory South of the Sibun was included within the ancient Kingdom of Guatemala, of which, with the exception of Chiapas, the confederated Republic was composed. This, as a geographical fact, it is presumed, will not be denied.

The British statement contends that Mr. Clayton's declaration of the 4 July, 1850, not only embraces the settlement of Belize proper, under the Treaty with Spain, but covers the territory South of it, between the Sibun & the Sarstoon.

The language employed by Mr. Clayton is,—"The British settlement in Honduras." Now, while such a settlement exists, under the Treaty of 1786, to which this language is precisely applicable, it would be a most strained construction to extend its application beyond the Treaty limits & make it protect the encroachments of British settlers over a larger territory than that included within the settlement itself.

Besides, Mr. Clayton states, in a subsequent part of the same document, that the Convention of 1850 " was understood to apply to and does include all the Central American States of Guatemala, Honduras, San Salvador, Nicaragua, and Costa Rica, with their just limits and proper dependencies."

Then, under this declaration itself, the territory in question, being within "the just limits" of the state of Guatemala, is expressly embraced by the Convention.

Lord Clarendon considers himself "more warranted" in concluding that Mr. Clayton's statement applies to this territory, "from the fact that the United States had in 1847 sent a Consul to the settlement, which consul had received his Exequatur from the British Government; a circumstance," says his Lordship, "which constitutes a recognition by the United States Government of the settlement of British Honduras under Her Majesty, as it then existed."

Now, it would be easy to prove that a Consul is never sent to a whole settlement or to an entire nation, but only to a single port, for the purpose of superintending the Commerce at that Port, and therefore that no inference could be drawn from the fact that the United States had sent a Consul to the Port of Belize, within the Treaty limits, in favor of the claim of Great Britain to a country far beyond these limits; but this would not be sufficient for the occasion. Mr. Buchanan emphatically denies the proposition that the appointment of a Consul to Belize was any, even the slightest, recognition of the right of Great Britain to this very port.

A Consul is an officer appointed to reside in a foreign Country for the purpose of facilitating, extending, and protecting the trade of his nation with that Country. Such officers follow foreign trade wherever it may go, and afford protection to it, no matter whether the ports to which they are sent be in the possession of the rightful owner or a usurper. The appointment of a Consul recognizes nothing more than the *de facto* possession of the Port by the Power from which his Exequatur is received. Such an appointment does not, in the slightest degree, interfere with the question of the right [*de jure*] of this Power to be in possession. This has ever been, and this must ever be, the law and practice of modern commercial nations. If it were otherwise, then, before the appointment of a Consul, the government of a nation must first carefully inquire whether the party in possession be the rightful owner of the Port; and if they determine against its right, then their commerce with it must either cease altogether or remain without Consular protection. This would be a novel doctrine to maintain in the present age of commercial progress.

The law and practice of nations have for a long period been

clear on this point; because Consuls are mere commercial and not political agents. At the present time, even the appointment of a public minister is wisely considered as a recognition of nothing more than the *de facto* possession of the Power to which he is accredited.

The British statement claims the territory between the Sibun and the Sarstoon by right of conquest, and observes " that the Treaty of 1786 was put an end to by a subsequent state of war " with Spain, and " that during that war the boundaries of the British settlement in question were enlarged," and that, the subsequent Treaty of peace not having revived the Treaties of 1783 and 1786, Great Britain is entitled to retain this territory.

It may be observed that the statement does not mention at what period the boundaries of the British settlement were enlarged. If this took place, as it is believed it did, after the date of the Treaty of alliance between Great Britain and Spain, in 1809, which terminated the war, then this argument falls to the ground. If before 1809, Great Britain, when concluding this Treaty, ought to have informed Spain that she intended to convert the encroachments of the settlers in Belize on Spanish territory into an absolute right. That she did not then intend to pursue such a course towards an ally in distress is clear from her subsequent conduct.

In 1814 Great Britain revived all her pre-existing Commercial Treaties with Spain; and what is the privilege granted to her by the Treaty of 1786, of cutting mahogany, logwood, and other dye woods on Spanish territory, thus enabling her to extend British commerce in these articles, but a commercial privilege?

So far from the Treaty of 1786 being " put an end to " by the war, its continued existence, in 1817 and 1819, was recognized by acts of the British Parliament. These declare, in so many words, that Belize was " not within the territory and dominion of his Majesty," but was merely " a settlement for certain purposes, in the possession and under the protection of His Majesty."

For the nature of this " settlement " and a knowledge of these " certain purposes," we can refer nowhere except to the Treaties of 1783 and 1786.

In addition to these acts of Parliament, it is proper here to repeat that so late as 1826, Great Britain has, by her Treaty with Mexico, acknowledged the continued existence and binding force of the Treaty of 1786.

But no matter what may be the nature of the British claim to the country between the Sibun and the Sarstoon, the observation already made in reference to the Bay Islands and the Mosquito Coast must be reiterated, that the great question does not turn upon the validity of this claim previous to the Convention of 1850, but upon the facts that Great Britain has bound herself, by this Convention, not to occupy any part of Central America nor to exercise dominion over it, and that the territory in question is within Central America, even under the most limited construction of these words. In regard to Belize proper, confined within its legitimate boundaries, under the Treaties of 1783 & 1786, & limited to the usufruct specified in these Treaties, it is necessary to say but a few words. The Government of the United States will not for the present insist upon the withdrawal of Great Britain from this settlement, provided all the other questions between the two Governments concerning Central America can be amicably adjusted. It has been influenced to pursue this course, partly by the declaration of Mr. Clayton of the 4th of July, 1850, but mainly in consequence of the extension of the license granted by Mexico to Great Britain under the Treaty of 1826, which that Republic has yet taken no steps to terminate.

It is, however, distinctly to be understood, that the Government of the United States acknowledge no claim of Great Britain within Belize, except the temporary " liberty of making use of the wood of the different kinds, the fruits, and other produce in their natural state," fully recognizing that the former " Spanish sovereignty over the country " now belongs either to Guatemala or Mexico.

In conclusion, the Government of the United States most cordially and earnestly unite in the desire expressed by " Her Majesty's Government not only to maintain the Convention of 1850 intact, but to consolidate and strengthen it by strengthening and consolidating the friendly relations which it was calculated to cement and perpetuate." Under these mutual feelings, it is deeply to be regretted that the two Governments entertain opinions so widely different in regard to its true effect and meaning.

(signed) JAMES BUCHANAN.

UNITED STATES LEGATION
LONDON, 22 July 1854.

TO MR. MARCY.[1]

(No. 39.)   LEGATION OF THE UNITED STATES.

LONDON, July 25th, 1854.

SIR: I have the honor to transmit to you a copy of my " Remarks in reply to Lord Clarendon's Statement of May 2nd, 1854," the original having been sent to his Lordship on the 22nd Instant.

I regret their length; but I found it impossible, such were the number of topics introduced in the British Statement, to render them shorter. I trust they may meet the approbation of the President and yourself.

JAMES BUCHANAN.

HONL. WM. L. MARCY, &c., &c., &c.

FROM MR. MARCY.[2]

Private & Confidential.

WASHINGTON, August 8th, 1854.

HON: JAMES BUCHANAN.

SIR: Your " Remarks " in reply to Lord Clarendon's statement of the 2nd of May were received here yesterday and read in Cabinet. There is but one opinion among us in regard to them. They are exceedingly able. Your positions are so well sustained by an array of facts and cogency of argument that it seems to us to be impossible to shake them.

The occurrence at Greytown is an embarrassing affair. The place merited chastisement, but the severity of the one inflicted exceeded our expectations. The Government will, however, I think, stand by Capt. Hollins.

Will Great Britain interfere in the matter? If she does, her course will tend to bring Central American affairs to a crisis. I am glad your reply to Lord Clarendon was in before the news of the bombardment of Greytown was received at London.

The Reciprocity & Fishery Treaty has not only passed the Senate by a strong vote, but the law requisite to give it effect was passed by Congress.

We are not sorry to be relieved from the presence of Congress for a few months. That body did not see fit to put at the disposal of the Executive extraordinary means for the adjustment of our difficulties with Spain.

Yours sincerely,

W. L. MARCY.

---

[1] MSS. Department of State, 66 Despatches from England; H. Ex. Doc. 1, 34 Cong. 1 Sess. I. 69.

[2] Buchanan Papers, Historical Society of Pennsylvania.

FROM PRESIDENT PIERCE.[1]

WASHINGTON, Aug. 12, 1854.

MY DEAR SIR—

Altho' Mr. Sickles is to return to the Legation by the Steamer which will leave New York next week on Saturday, I cannot permit the Wednesday's Steamer to depart without expressing my admiration of your argument on the Central American question, and my acknowledgments for the honor you are reflecting upon our Country.

Mr. Sickles' visit at this time is, on several grounds, very opportune, and if he has participated in the pleasure he has conferred, he will have no occasion to regret it. Altho' you will be sorry to part, as I regret to have you, with Mr. Sanders, you will be glad to meet again yr. old acquaintance and friend Genl. Campbell, who, with his family, will probably go out in the same steamer which will bear this.

Mr. Sickles will return with despatches for yourself, Mr. Mason, & Mr. Soulé, and will have much to communicate verbally with regard to home and other affairs. Please to present my kindest regards to yr. niece Miss Lane.

Yr. friend,

FRANK. PIERCE.

HON. JAS. BUCHANAN.
    London.

TO LORD CLARENDON.

(Enclosure in No. 53.[2])

UNITED STATES LEGATION,

LONDON 15 August 1854.

The undersigned, Envoy Extraordinary and Minister Plenipotentiary of the United States, has the honor of presenting to the Earl of Clarendon, Her Majesty's Principal Secretary of State for Foreign Affairs, the claim for indemnity of George W. Colson, Master of the American Ship " Moses Kimball," who has been imprisoned and fined by the Mayor and two Magistrates of Newport, Monmouthshire, on the first instant, for an assault alleged to have been committed by him on one of his own sailors, in his own vessel, whilst she was off the Coast of France, between Cape Hève and Cape Barfleur. The Magistrates overruled the plea of Captain Colson that they had no jurisdiction, and thus disregarded the undoubted principle of public law that an offence committed on board of an American

---

[1] Buchanan Papers, Historical Society of Pennsylvania.
[2] Despatch to Mr. Marcy, No. 53, December 29, 1854, infra.

ship when on the high seas can alone be tried and punished by an American tribunal. Under these circumstances Captain Colson claims that the sum of £16.16.0. which he has been actually compelled to pay in fine, costs, and attorney's fee shall be refunded to him. He might claim an indemnity for his unlawful imprisonment and detention at Newport; but this he consents to waive.

The undersigned transmits to the Earl of Clarendon copies of two communications received from Captain Colson bearing date on the 8th & 10th instant, which fully explain the nature of his case.

The undersigned avails himself of this opportunity to renew to the Earl of Clarendon the assurance of his distinguished consideration.

(Signed)   JAMES BUCHANAN.

THE RIGHT HON. THE EARL OF CLARENDON,
&c. &c. &c.

TO MR. MARCY.[1]

No. 40.   LEGATION OF THE UNITED STATES.

LONDON, 18th August 1854.

SIR,

I have the honor to acknowledge the receipt of your Despatches No. 45, on the first instant, Nos. 47, 48, 49, and 50 on the 14th Instant, and No. 51 on the 16th instant. Your No. 46 has not yet come to hand.

I had an interview on Tuesday last with Lord Clarendon, respecting several Consular and other matters of comparatively small importance which are constantly demanding the attention of this Legation; and I embraced the occasion to introduce the subject of the existing Postal relations between the two Countries.

In complying with your instructions, No. 41, I did not deem it advisable, after two recent & positive refusals, to make a third formal proposition to the British Government to convey the closed mails between the United States and France, through England, at a rate not exceeding 12½ cents per ounce.

---

[1] MSS. Department of State, 66 Despatches from England. Paragraphs 2-5, inclusive, of this despatch, relating to the postal convention, are printed in S. Ex. Doc. 73, 33 Cong. 2 Sess. 60.

The first of these refusals will be found in the note of Lord Palmerston to Mr. Lawrence of October 14th, 1851, and the second in that of Lord Clarendon to Mr. Ingersoll of May 27th, 1853. Without any change of circumstances, and recollecting that Lords Palmerston and Clarendon are still members of the British Cabinet and Lord Canning still Post Master General, I deemed it proper first to ascertain, if possible, whether there was any probable prospect of success, before submitting another formal proposition.

Taking this view of my duty, I had a general conversation with Lord Clarendon on the subject of the existing Postal Convention, which it is evident he would be unwilling to see annulled. The result was, that I am to converse with Lord Canning, the Post Master General, and his secretary, Mr. Rowland Hill, and ascertain whether we can come to any agreement. Lord Canning, however, has left England for a month in his yacht, and Mr. Hill has within the last few days had a severe attack of Asiatic Cholera; so that it will be some time before I can have an interview with either of them. I confess, however, I expect but little from such an interview; and I do most cordially coincide in the opinion expressed and reiterated by Mr. Lawrence, even before the second refusal, in his note to Mr. Webster of the 30th April, 1852, that " when I look at the circumstances under which this negotiation has been conducted and at the fact that the British Office is a great gainer by the continuance of the present state of things, I cannot but again respectfully but strongly advise that the notice to annul the Convention be given at once." A strong intimation that the Convention would be annulled unless the British Government should comply with our proposal has already been tried in vain. The notice once given, the state of the case will be changed, and it will then be for them to decide whether they will abandon all the advantages they enjoy under the Convention, rather than convey the mails between the United States and France through England at the same rate we convey their mails to Canada through the United States. Until this question shall be presented to them in a distinct form, it is my opinion they will hold on to their present advantageous position.

In reference to your instruction to ascertain from Lord Clarendon whether the British Government considered coal as an article contraband of war,—he stated that coal was not in their opinion generally contraband, but was one of the articles which might become so, if evidently intended for warlike purposes. For example, if a neutral vessel were found conveying coal to an enemy's port to be used to propel his war steamers, he thought this would convert it into contraband.

Sir James Graham has stated in the House of Commons " that coals will be regarded by our cruisers as one of the articles *ancipitis usus,* not necessarily contraband, but liable to detention under circumstances that warrant suspicion of their being applied to the military or naval uses of the enemy." Vide Edinburgh Review for July, 1854, pages 201 & 202,—Title, " The orders in Council on Trade during War."

On the receipt of your Despatch No. 51, on the 16th Instant, I sent a copy of it to Lord Clarendon accompanied by a note in which I expressed the hope that his Lordship would enable me to communicate to the Secretary of State, by Saturday's steamer, that orders had been sent by the British Government to the authorities in the Colonies not to molest American Fishermen in using at once the privileges secured to them by the Treaty. I also cordially congratulated him " upon the final settlement of the Fishery Question, which has for so many years threatened to produce serious difficulties between our two Countries; " and expressed the wish that they might ever be friends. Lord Clarendon in answer under date of the 17th Instant says:

I have requested the Colonial Office and the Admiralty to send out instructions to-morrow that will secure to American fishermen at once the privileges of the Treaty.

I lost not a moment in informing the Queen of the intelligence that arrived yesterday. She says in answer to-day that she considers the Treaty most important, and that it has given her the sincerest satisfaction.

Lord Clarendon is evidently very much gratified with the Treaty, and it will probably secure to Lord Elgin a Marquisate or a Dukedom, if not the Governor Generalship of India, to which it is said he aspires. One cause of the favor with which it is regarded in this Country, is the belief that Canada, having acquired by it a free trade with the United States in her most valuable productions, will feel no desire to change her allegiance and annex herself to the American Union.

I send you two copies of a notification, inserted in a supplement to the London Gazette of the 11th Instant, containing a further announcement relating to blockades of Russian Ports in the Baltic, which Lord Clarendon requests me under date of the 15th instant to transmit to my Government, " in order that it may through that channel become known to the citizens of the United States."

I have watched with deep interest the progress of the Revolution in Spain, without being able to form any decided opinion as to what will be its final result. It is certain, however, I think, that we have only yet witnessed "the beginning of the end." Those who know Espartero best, whilst they concur in representing him as a man of pure integrity and patriotism and personally brave as his own sword, yet say that he wants the energy, industry, and moral courage required by the crisis. It is evident that the Revolution is proceeding. Although Espartero's Cabinet have decided that a Constituent Cortes consisting of only one branch shall be elected, under the extended right of suffrage granted by the Constitution of 1837, and that the Queen Mother shall be kept in confinement and tried before this Cortes, yet the people do not seem to be satisfied with these concessions. The Juntas still exercise their revolutionary powers, and no person here pretends to predict what a day may bring forth in Spain. It is an incomprehensible Country. It might be worth the time for you to examine the leading Editorial of the Times of this morning on the subject.

In the course of conversation with Lord Clarendon on Tuesday last, I observed that, the Reciprocity Treaty having been concluded, they ought now to settle the Central American questions and thus remove every subject out of the way which might threaten serious difficulties between the two Countries. He said that the burning of Greytown was not well calculated to lead to such a result. I replied that I thought this act with all its attendant circumstances shewed conclusively the necessity of restoring the Town to Nicaragua, under which alone a regular and orderly Government could be established. In that event, Great Britain and the United States might proceed together, in pursuance of the Clayton & Bulwer Convention, in procuring the establishment of two free Ports, one on the Atlantic and the other on the Pacific. He replied that we seemed to be very partial to Nicaragua. And I said this was not the case,—we only advocated her claims because we believed she had the right on her side. He informed me that Mr. Crampton had written to him that he had conversed with you in regard to the burning of Greytown; but that you had informed him the Cabinet were at the moment (I think he said) in session on the subject, and that you could then say nothing decisive about it. I told him that I had seen the instructions from yourself and Secretary Dobbin in the Public Papers; and it was evident from them that Captain Hollins had exceeded his instructions and had no authority to proceed to such extremities.

It cannot be denied that this act of Captain Hollins in burning a town which had been deserted by its population, and in destroying indiscriminately the private property not only of its inhabitants but of the citizens of other Countries, has produced a most unfavorable impression in England. Whilst those unfriendly to us denounce it in savage terms, as the London Times did a few days ago, our friends regret it extremely. From the very first, I undertook to express my firm conviction that it was an act done without authority, and I await with confidence its disavowal by the Government. At the same time, I shall be most happy to learn any circumstances which will palliate the conduct of Captain Hollins in proceeding from the bombardment to the burning the town.

Great Britain, it is true, has no right to regard it as a place under her protection, and should she make any claims upon our Government in this character, on account of the act of Captain Hollins, we ought to resist them to the last extremity. In my opinion, however, the British Government will not attempt to pursue such a course.

I have this moment returned from the Foreign Office, where Lord Clarendon and myself exchanged the ratifications of the Convention for the extension of the period limited for the duration of the Mixed Commission under the Claims Convention of the 8th February, 1853, and I now have the honor of transmitting to you through the Despatch Bag, according to your instructions, the copy of the Convention ratified by Her Britannic Majesty together with the proper certificate.

Yours very respectfully

JAMES BUCHANAN.

HON: WILLIAM L. MARCY,
    Secretary of State.

TO MR. MARCY.[1]

Private & Confidential.

LEGATION OF THE U. S.

LONDON, 25 Aug. 1854.

MY DEAR SIR,

I have received yours of the 8th inst., and am much gratified to learn that the President and Cabinet are satisfied with the remarks in reply to Lord Clarendon on Central American affairs. I am sorry, however, to be informed that the Government will, you think, stand by Captain Hollins. I have read every thing with care in regard to that affair, and with the strongest disposition to excuse or justify him for burning Greytown;—and I still hope that after more mature reflection the Government will not adopt the act.

There are many things which pass here in social conversation that you ought to know; and yet I should consider it highly improper to record them in a Despatch. Lord Clarendon & myself have many jokes together.

Some time ago we met, and the son and grandson of Tippoo Saib, rigged out in their gorgeous Eastern Costume, were in the Company. I said to his Lordship, I hope you pay well for this finery. The annexation of Seringapatam deserves a large pension to Tippoo's descendants. Yes, he said, it was worth something handsome, and they paid these people a goodly pension;—adding that *he supposed they would also have to pension His Majesty the King of the Mosquitos.* I said I was glad to hear it. This would be the best mode of getting clear of him. Since that time we have had a conversation of similar character, but not so direct.

I was with him but a very few minutes on Friday last the 18th Instant, and this at a late hour, when we exchanged the ratifications.[2] After the ceremony was over and when I got up to take my leave, he repeated what he had written, but in still stronger terms, of the Queen's gratification and pleasure at the conclusion of the Reciprocity Treaty. I said to him, My Lord, the Queen may well be pleased. You have got every thing your own way in this Treaty and have secured the allegiance of

---

[1] Buchanan Papers, Historical Society of Pennsylvania.

[2] Of the convention of July 17, 1854, extending the duration of the claims commission under the convention of Feb. 8, 1853.

Canada for a long time to come. You might now by addressing me a note of twelve lines settle the Central American Questions; then every thing would be adjusted between the two governments and we would make a new and fair start, and nothing I thought could occur to interrupt our friendship. He said, if I were to do this, our American cousins would say, we have discovered the mode of dealing with the British—we went down to Greytown and *smashed* it, whereupon they became alarmed and gave us all we wanted. I told him I must go and have a long talk with Lord Aberdeen himself on Central American Affairs. I had already conversed with him on the subject at the Frenchman's dinner. Lord Aberdeen had always been disposed to treat America fairly, and such was his character in the United States. Lord Clarendon then seized me by the lapels of my coat and shook me, and said, " I am as good a friend of the United States as Lord Aberdeen, or any man in the three Kingdoms." I replied I entertained no doubt that his feelings were equally friendly with those of Lord Aberdeen; but they did not bring forth fruit.

You will admit that I ought not to write these things in a Despatch and hardly in a private letter, but still it may be of some consequence you should know them.

At the date of my last Despatch I did not believe that Great Britain, *in the character of Mosquito Protector,* would interfere in the Greytown affair. From an article in the " Times " this morning I fear I was mistaken. Should she attempt to interfere in this character through me, I shall at once inform Lord Clarendon that we cannot in any manner or form recognise her in that capacity.

TO MR. MARCY.[1]

No. 41.   LEGATION OF THE UNITED STATES.

LONDON, 25 August 1854.

SIR/

I have the honor to acknowledge the receipt of your Despatches Nos. 52 & 53, of the 7th & 8th Instant, respectively.

I transmit you the copy of a note received from Lord Clarendon, dated on the 19th Instant, in which he states, in reply to mine of the 16th Instant, that Her Majesty's ratification of

---

[1] MSS. Department of State, 66 Despatches from England.

the Fishery & Reciprocity Treaty " was sent last night, (the 18th) to Her Majesty's Minister at Washington, & that by the same Mail directions will have been sent to the British Colonial & Naval Authorities not to molest American Fishermen in using at once the privileges secured to them by the Treaty."

I have received the Exequatur for George A. Brandreth, Esquire, appointed Consul of the United States for Plymouth, & this, together with his commission, I have forwarded to him at his post.

Yours very respectfully
JAMES BUCHANAN.

HON: WILLIAM L. MARCY,
    Secretary of State.

TO PRESIDENT PIERCE.[1]

U. S. LEGATION,
LONDON 1 Sept. 1854.

MY DEAR SIR,

I have received your favor of the 12th ultimo and am truly gratified to learn that my "remarks" in answer to Lord Clarendon, on the Central American Questions, have received your approbation. It was not difficult to advocate a course so just.

Col. Sickles has returned, but I have seen very little of him since his arrival. He brought with him the Despatch to which you refer. I can not for myself discover what benefit will result from a meeting between Mr. Soulé, Mr. Mason, and myself. I perceive that you expect from it " useful information and suggestions," but it is impossible for me to devise any other plan for the acquisition of Cuba in which I could be useful than what I have already fully presented to you. We are willing to purchase, and our object is to induce them to sell. One great means of accomplishing this object is to bring the creditors of Spain into our views by an appeal to their self-interest. The best agent for this purpose with whom I am acquainted would be Mr. Belmont, and it was for this reason that I so strongly urged his appointment. Besides, I should deem it to be unfortunate for Mr. Soulé to be absent from his mission at the present crisis in the affairs of Spain. He might thus miss the " golden

---

[1] Buchanan Papers, Historical Society of Pennsylvania.

opportunity." I am glad, therefore, that our *meeting for mere consultation and not for decisive action* is left to his discretion.

I am truly sorry for Sanders, to whom and to whose family I have become attached,—certainly not on account of any past services or future expectations. He is active and energetic, and was capable of rendering service both to the Legation and the Country. The Consulate at London is the best office, pecuniarily speaking, in your gift; and ought at this centre of the Commercial and political world to be filled by a first rate man.

I send you as an object of curiosity a recent letter in four languages written by Sanders to the President of the Federal Council in Switzerland on the subject of the right of asylum. I knew not his intention to write such a letter until I saw it in the London Times. It has created quite a sensation throughout Europe, and has been more extensively translated and republished than any American document except the President's Message.

I also send you a few of the stamps prepared for imposing on the United States " Taxation without representation." They were presented to me as a curiosity by the head of the Excise office, who in his note observes that " the arbitrary attempt happily failed, and led to the independence of your Country and the prosperity of America and the Parent State. May their cordial relations long continue! "

I am getting along here "as well as could be expected." I should get along better and I think more successfully but for the attacks of the Union. Please to tell Forney that he is quite too belligerent to be politic. Still my heart is at home, and I anticipate my return to my native land in another year with unalloyed pleasure. I am heartily tired of public life, and hope to pass the remnant of my days, after the termination of my present mission, in tranquillity and retirement. Miss Lane desires me to present her kindest regards to Mrs. Pierce and yourself. With sentiments of the highest regard, I remain, very respectfully

Your friend
(Signed)   JAMES BUCHANAN.

HIS EX. FRANKLIN PIERCE.

P. S. Since the foregoing was written, I have had a long conversation with Col: Sickles, and am sorry to say this has not changed my views concerning the policy of a meeting between Mr. Mason, Mr. Soulé, and myself; nevertheless, I shall write nothing to either of them on the subject. No more unsuitable place than Paris could be devised for such a meeting. The French espionage is perfect and all-pervading, and all its eyes would be upon us. Every object which you have in view can, in my opinion, be accomplished by correspondence.

Should you deem it proper to cause me to be specifically instructed to that effect, and furnish me with the necessary means from the Treasury, to be strictly accounted for, I think I could, with the assistance of Mr. Belmont, ascertain the names and places of residence of the principal Spanish Bond holders and probably induce them to unite in an effort to prevail on the Spanish Government to sell Cuba to the United States. Capital and Capitalists, however, are proverbially timid, and nothing of this kind ought to be attempted until after the éclat by the public journals to Col. Sickles' journey to Paris and Madrid shall have passed away. Matters of this kind, in order to be successful in Europe, must be conducted with secrecy and caution.

According to the Times of to-day, Espartero's ministry have entered office with a deficit of £6,000,000 sterling left by their predecessors, and with the revenues of Cuba anticipated for two years and an half. From present appearances, the party in favor of constitutional monarchy will prevail, and in that event, the slaves will not be emancipated as it is supposed they would be were the Republicans in power.

TO MR. ELY.

(Enclosed with No. 44.[1])
LEGATION OF THE UNITED STATES.
LONDON, 28th Septr. 1854.

SIR:

I have received your favor of the 31st of July and regret that I cannot give it a more satisfactory answer. Many similar complaints have reached me from different quarters; but without a Consular Convention between Great Britain and the United States, such as we have with France, these cannot be redressed.

The only provision in any existing Treaty between the two Countries in regard to Consuls is to be found in the 4th Article

---

[1] Despatch to Mr. Marcy, No. 44, September 29, 1854, infra.

of the Convention of the 3d July, 1815. This merely provides that "it shall be free for each of the two contracting parties, respectively, to appoint Consuls for the protection of trade, to reside in the dominions and territories of the other party," &c., without conferring upon them any power whatever either of an executive or judicial character; and neither the laws of Great Britain nor the United States, in the absence of a Treaty Stipulation, supply this defect. The consequence is, that no provision exists on either side for the restoration of deserters. The Act of Congress of March 2d, 1829, is confined expressly to the Consuls and Vice Consuls "of any foreign Government *having a treaty with the United States stipulating for the restoration of seamen deserting*" "while in any port of the United States."

Then, again, the Consuls of the United States ought unquestionably to possess the exclusive power of deciding "differences which may arise, either at sea or in port, (to use the language of our Consular Convention with France) between the captain, officers, and crew, without exception, particularly in reference to the adjustment of wages and the execution of contracts;" and the local authorities in British Ports ought to be bound, as in France, to carry these decisions into effect. This, I regret to say, is not the case.

A case has recently occurred in London, under the 35th Article of the 5th Section of the Consular Instructions. A mutiny had been committed on board of an American vessel on the high seas; and our Consul at London, having complied with all the necessary preliminaries, applied "to the local authorities for means of securing the offenders while they remain in port, and to procure the means of sending them, without delay, to the United States for trial." The local authorities refused to interfere, and their refusal was sanctioned on an appeal to the highest authority, on the principle that there was no law in existence which would warrant such an interference. The consequence was that the mutineers escaped.

The men to which you refer who were guilty of the assault and battery with intent to kill on the Master and Second Officer of the Ship Napoleon, *as this offence was committed, not upon the high seas, but within the Port of Bombay,* might have been tried and punished by the British Court at that place having jurisdiction of such offences. There is no principle of public law better settled than that the maritime territory of every state extends to its own Ports and to the distance of a marine league from its shores.   Within these limits, its jurisdiction is absolute and excludes that of every other nation.   In the very strong language of Lord John Russell, whilst Minister for Foreign Affairs, in a note addressed to Mr. Ingersoll, my predecessor, of the 24th day of January, 1853, " a merchant vessel of one country within the waters of another country is, with all the persons on board, as fully and entirely liable to the laws and jurisdiction of the country within whose waters the ship is, as if that ship and those persons were high and dry upon the land of such country."

The necessity for a Consular Convention between the United States and Great Britain is becoming more apparent every day, and I trust that ere long such a Convention may be concluded. In the mean time, I have no advice to give but that you should, as a matter of international courtesy, obtain from the local authorities all the assistance within your power in the performance of your duties, which I regret you cannot demand as a matter of right.

Yours very respectfully

(Sd.)   JAMES BUCHANAN.

EDWARD ELY, ESQ.,
   Consul U. States, at Bombay.

———

TO MR. MARCY.[1]

No. 44.   LEGATION OF THE UNITED STATES.

LONDON, 29 September 1854.

SIR/

The numerous complaints of our Consuls from different Ports throughout Her Majesty's dominions, with the detail of which I shall not trouble you, seem to render a Consular Convention between the two Governments indispensable.   As a specimen both of the nature of these complaints & the answer I am obliged to give them, I transmit the copy of a letter which I yesterday addressed to Mr. Edward Ely, our Consul at Bombay.[2]

Indeed, since the trade has been opened to our vessels between the British Ports in Europe & those in Australia & other

---

[1] MSS. Department of State, 66 Despatches from England.
[2] To Mr. Ely, Sept. 28, 1854, supra.

British possessions in the East, such a Convention is imperatively required. A great number of American vessels are now employed in this trade, & from necessity these are navigated by sailors of all nations,—many of them desperate characters. Does such a vessel enter any British Port, the crew may desert with perfect impunity; & what is worse, should a mutiny or other crime have been committed on board, whilst on the high seas, the criminal is placed beyond the reach of punishment, & must be discharged. It cannot be long before British freighters will hesitate to employ American vessels in this trade; because they have no security for their property against the acts of lawless men, whom nothing but the fear of punishment will restrain.

Several of the Consuls who have written to me assert that the local authorities in American Ports do aid British Consuls in securing & restoring deserters from British Ships; & upon enquiry, I am informed this is the case both in New York & Philadelphia. I have not learned whether aid is given by our authorities to prevent the escape of offenders who have committed crimes on board of British Vessels on the high seas, & to send them to a British Port for trial.

It is important that I should know what has been the practice in our Ports in such cases. It seems to be certain, at least, that there has been a want of reciprocity in British Ports, in regard to deserters.

I have examined our Consular Convention with France, & can perceive no objection to a similar Convention with Great Britain, except that under its Ninth Article deserters are not to be restored, *if they be citizens of the Country where the demand is made*. Should this clause be inserted in a Treaty with Great Britain, they might, under their decision of perpetual allegiance, refuse to surrender a seaman born in the Queen's dominions, who had become an adopted citizen of the United States. This we could not tolerate.

But why make such an exception? Is it not just that a sailor, no matter what may be his nation, should be compelled to perform his contract? Why should a British subject or an American Citizen be released from this obligation & permitted to desert with impunity, especially when such a license may cost the lives of the passengers & remaining crew, as well as the loss of the vessel? By striking from the 9th Article the words, " *not being citizens of the Country where the demand is made,*" the difficulty would be removed. Whether in the one form or the other, however, I am persuaded, the conclusion of a Consular Convention with Great Britain cannot long be delayed.

It is, to say the least, doubtful whether our Convention with France provides for the case mentioned in the 35th Article of the 5th Section of the Consular Instructions; & on this subject all doubt ought to be removed in a Convention with Great Britain. Should such a Convention be concluded, it ought to contain a clear & positive stipulation, requiring the local authorities to furnish the necessary aid to the Consuls of both Governments to enable them to send home for trial those accused of having committed offences on the high seas against the laws of the respective Countries, under the circumstances stated in this 35th Article.

My position here & my correspondence with our Consuls at British Ports have impressed me with the great importance to our navigation & commerce of a Consular Convention with Great Britain. Should you entertain a similar opinion, then you might, with the President's approbation, either negotiate with Mr. Crampton or leave the matter to Lord Clarendon & myself. To me it is indifferent which course shall be pursued. If the latter, I would thank you to express an opinion, whether the words, "*not being citizens of the Country where the demand is made,*" should be inserted in the Convention, with such other instructions as you may deem advisable.

I have the honor to acknowledge the receipt of your Despatches Nos. 57, 58, & 59, of the 24th Ultimo & the 9th & 14th Instant, respectively.

In regard to your Despatch No. 58, you have left to my discretion whether I shall present to Lord Clarendon the claim of Major Wigg against the British Government (which comes to me unaccompanied by a single voucher) for spoliations committed on the property of his Grandfather more than seventy years ago by the British forces, during the American Revolution. I do not think that a claim like this, whatever may have been its original justice, ought to be presented, when we know that not the most remote probability exists that it will be allowed. After the Treaty of Peace of 1783, a subsequent war, a second Treaty of Peace, & numerous Treaties respecting claims, & when the injury to the property was public & notorious at the time it was committed, it is now, in my opinion, too late in the day to invoke the interposition of our Government in favor of this claim. Should all the injuries done to private property by the British forces throughout the Revolutionary war & during & since that period in all portions of the world be allowed, this would break down the Treasury of Great Britain. If, however, you should think differently & instruct me accordingly, I shall, as in duty bound, obey, without hesitation.

Yours very respectfully

JAMES BUCHANAN.

HON: WILLIAM L. MARCY,
    Secretary of State.

TO MRS. BAKER.[1]

LEGATION OF THE UNITED STATES.

LONDON 6 October 1854.

MY DEAR MARY/

I received your letter in due time of the 14th July, & should have answered it long ere this, but that I knew Harriet wrote to you regularly. I wrote to you soon after my arrival in London; but you have never acknowledged that letter, & as you have said nothing about it in yours of the 14th July, I fear it has miscarried.

If I do not write often it is not because you are not freshly and most kindly remembered. Indeed, I feel great anxiety about your health & prosperity, & am rejoiced that you appear to be happy in San Francisco. You are often, very often, a subject of conversation between Harriet & myself.

We set out for Belgium to-morrow where I have important public business to transact. I take Harriet along to enable her to see a little of the Continent; & I may perhaps have time to accompany her along the Rhine. I cannot be long absent, because the business of this Legation is incessant, important, & laborious.

Thank God I have been enjoying my usual health here, & am treated quite as kindly as I could have expected. And yet I long to return home, but must remain nearly another year to fulfil my engagement with the President when I most reluctantly consented to accept the mission. Should a kind Providence prolong my days, I hope to pass the remnant of them in tranquillity & retirement at Wheatland. I have been kindly treated by the world, but am heartily sick of public life. Besides, a wise

---

[1] Buchanan Papers, private collection.

man ought to desire to pass some time in privacy before his inevitable doom.

Please to remember me, in the kindest terms, to Mr. Peyton, Governor Foote, Mr. & Mrs. Stanley, Mrs. Greenhow & her daughters, & also to Mr. and Mrs. Beale.

I hope to be able to take Harriet on a short visit to Paris before her return to the United States.

I have but little time to write to-day after my Despatches, & determined not to let another Post for California pass without writing.

Remember me kindly to Mr. Baker, & believe me to be with warm & sincere affection & regard

Your uncle

JAMES BUCHANAN.

MRS. GEORGE W. BAKER.

TO MR. MARCY.[1]

No. 45.   LEGATION OF THE UNITED STATES.

LONDON, 6 October 1854.

SIR:

In obedience to your instructions, No. 56, of the 16th August last, I intend to leave London to-morrow morning for the purpose of meeting Mr. Soulé and Mr. Mason, by appointment, at Ostend on Monday next.

In my Despatch No. 51, of the 25th August, I informed you that I had received and forwarded to Plymouth the Commission and Exequatur of George A. Brandreth, Esquire. On the 25th September, the envelope containing these documents, with the accompanying letter, has been returned to me by the Post, with the remarks endorsed, " Not called for,"—" Not known." We have heard nothing of or from Mr. Brandreth at the Legation.

I have the honor of transmitting you two copies of a notification of the Blockade of certain Russian Ports by the British and French fleets, extracted from the London Gazette of September 29, 1854, which I received last evening with a Note dated yesterday from Lord Clarendon, requesting that I would transmit them

---

[1] MSS. Department of State, 66 Despatches from England.

to my Government, " in order that it may through that channel become known to the citizens of the United States."

Yours very respectfully,

JAMES BUCHANAN.

HON: WILLIAM L. MARCY,
    Secretary of State.

THE OSTEND REPORT.[1]

AIX-LA-CHAPELLE, October 18th, 1854.

TO THE HON. WM. L. MARCY,
    Secretary of State.

SIR: The undersigned, in compliance with the wish expressed by the President in the several confidential despatches you have addressed to us respectively to that effect, have met in conference, first at Ostend, in Belgium, on the 9th, 10th, and 11th instant, and then at Aix-la-Chapelle, in Prussia, on the days next following, up to the date hereof.

There has been a full and unreserved interchange of views and sentiments between us, which, we are most happy to inform you, has resulted in a cordial coincidence of opinion on the grave and important subjects submitted to our consideration.

We have arrived at the conclusion and are thoroughly convinced that an immediate and earnest effort ought to be made by the Government of the United States to purchase Cuba from Spain, at any price for which it can be obtained, not exceeding the sum of one hundred and twenty millions of dollars.

The proposal should, in our opinion, be made in such a manner as to be presented, through the necessary diplomatic forms, to the Supreme Constituent Cortes about to assemble. On this momentous question, in which the people both of Spain and the United States are so deeply interested, all our proceedings ought to be open, frank, and public. They should be of such a character as to challenge the approbation of the World.

We firmly believe that, in the progress of human events, the time has arrived when the vital interests of Spain are as seriously involved in the sale as those of the United States in the purchase

---

[1] MSS. Department of State, 66 Despatches from England. Printed in H. Ex. Doc. 93, 33 Cong. 2 Sess. 127–132; Horton's Buchanan, 392–399. An extract is given in Curtis's Buchanan, II. 139.

of the Island, and that the transaction will prove equally honorable to both nations.

Under these circumstances, we cannot anticipate a failure, unless, possibly, through the malign influence of foreign Powers who possess no right whatever to interfere in the matter.

We proceed to state some of the reasons which have brought us to this conclusion; and, for the sake of clearness, we shall specify them under two distinct heads:

1. The United States ought, if practicable, to purchase Cuba with as little delay as possible.

2. The probability is great that the Government and Cortes of Spain will prove willing to sell it, because this would essentially promote the highest and best interests of the Spanish people.

Then—1. It must be clear to every reflecting mind that, from the peculiarity of its geographical position and the considerations attendant on it, Cuba is as necessary to the North American Republic as any of its present members, and that it belongs naturally to that great family of States of which the Union is the Providential Nursery.

From its locality it commands the mouth of the Mississippi and the immense and annually increasing trade which must seek this avenue to the ocean.

On the numerous navigable streams, measuring an aggregate course of some thirty thousand miles, which disembogue themselves through this magnificent river into the Gulf of Mexico, the increase of the population, within the last ten years, amounts to more than that of the entire Union at the time Louisiana was annexed to it.

The natural and main outlet of the products of this entire population, the highway of their direct intercourse with the Atlantic and the Pacific States, can never be secure, but must ever be endangered whilst Cuba is a dependency of a distant Power, in whose possession it has proved to be a source of constant annoyance and embarrassment to their interests.

Indeed, the Union can never enjoy repose, nor possess reliable security, as long as Cuba is not embraced within its boundaries.

Its immediate acquisition by our Government is of paramount importance, and we cannot doubt but that it is a consummation devoutly wished for by its inhabitants.

The intercourse which its proximity to our coasts begets and encourages between them and the citizens of the United States has, in the progress of time, so united their interests and blended their fortunes, that they now look upon each other as if they were one people and had but one destiny.

Considerations exist which render delay in the acquisition of this Island exceedingly dangerous to the United States.

The system of emigration and labor lately organized within its limits, and the tyranny and oppression which characterize its immediate rulers, threaten an insurrection, at every moment, which may result in direful consequences to the American People.

Cuba has thus become to us an unceasing danger, and a permanent cause of anxiety and alarm.

But we need not enlarge on these topics. It can scarcely be apprehended that foreign Powers, in violation of international law, would interpose their influence with Spain to prevent our acquisition of the Island. Its inhabitants are now suffering under the worst of all possible Governments,—that of absolute despotism, delegated by a distant Power to irresponsible agents who are changed at short intervals, and who are tempted to improve the brief opportunity thus afforded to accumulate fortunes by the basest means.

As long as this system shall endure, humanity may in vain demand the suppression of the African Slave trade in the Island. This is rendered impossible whilst that infamous traffic remains an irresistible temptation and a source of immense profit to needy and avaricious officials who, to attain their end, scruple not to trample the most sacred principles under foot.

The Spanish Government at home may be well disposed, but experience has proved that it cannot control these remote depositories of its power.

Besides, the commercial nations of the world cannot fail to perceive and appreciate the great advantages which would result to their people from a dissolution of the forced and unnatural connection between Spain and Cuba, and the annexation of the latter to the United States. The trade of England and France with Cuba would, in that event, assume at once an important and profitable character, and rapidly extend with the increasing population and prosperity of the Island.

2. But if the United States and every commercial nation would be benefited by this transfer, the interests of Spain would also be greatly and essentially promoted.

She cannot but see that such a sum of money as we are

willing to pay for the Island would effect in the development of her vast natural resources.

Two thirds of this sum, if employed in the construction of a system of Railroads, would ultimately prove a source of greater wealth to the Spanish people than that opened to their vision by Cortes.   Their prosperity would date from the ratification of the Treaty of cession.   France has already constructed continuous lines of Railways from Havre, Marseilles, Valenciennes, and Strasbourg, via Paris, to the Spanish frontier, and anxiously awaits the day when Spain shall find herself in a condition to extend these roads, through her Northern provinces, to Madrid, Seville, Cadiz, Malaga, and the frontiers of Portugal.

This object once accomplished, Spain would become a centre of attraction for the travelling world and secure a permanent and profitable market for her various productions.   Her fields, under the stimulus given to industry by remunerating prices, would teem with cereal grain, and her vineyards would bring forth a vastly increased quantity of choice wines.   Spain would speedily become, what a bountiful Providence intended she should be, one of the first Nations of Continental Europe, rich, powerful, and contented.

Whilst two thirds of the price of the Island would be ample for the completion of her most important public improvements, she might, with the remaining forty millions, satisfy the demands now pressing so heavily upon her credit, and create a sinking fund which would gradually relieve her from the overwhelming debt now paralysing her energies.

Such is her present wretched financial condition, that her best bonds are sold, upon her own Bourse, at about one third of their par value; whilst another class, on which she pays no interest, have but a nominal value and are quoted at about one sixth of the amount for which they were issued.   Besides, these latter are held principally by British creditors, who may, from day to day, obtain the effective interposition of their own Government, for the purpose of coercing payment.   Intimations to that effect have been already thrown out from high quarters, and unless some new source of revenue shall enable Spain to provide for such exigencies, it is not improbable that they may be realized.

Should Spain reject the present golden opportunity for developing her resources and removing her present financial embarrassments, it may never again return.

Cuba, in its palmiest days, never yielded her Exchequer,

after deducting the expenses of its Government, a clear annual income of more than a million and a half of dollars. These expenses have increased to such a degree as to leave a deficit chargeable on the Treasury of Spain to the amount of six hundred thousand dollars.

In a pecuniary point of view, therefore, the Island is an encumbrance instead of a source of profit to the Mother Country.

Under no probable circumstances can Cuba ever yield to Spain one per cent. on the large amount which the United States are willing to pay for its acquisition.

But Spain is in imminent danger of losing Cuba without remuneration.

Extreme oppression, it is now universally admitted, justifies any people in endeavoring to relieve themselves from the yoke of their oppressors. The sufferings which the corrupt, arbitrary, and unrelenting local administration necessarily entails upon the inhabitants of Cuba cannot fail to stimulate and keep alive that spirit of resistance and revolution against Spain which has of late years been so often manifested. In this condition of affairs, it is vain to expect that the sympathies of the people of the United States will not be warmly enlisted in favor of their oppressed neighbors.

We know that the President is justly inflexible in his determination to execute the neutrality laws, but should the Cubans themselves rise in revolt against the oppressions which they suffer, no human power could prevent citizens of the United States and liberal minded men of other countries from rushing to their assistance.

Besides, the present is an age of adventure, in which restless and daring spirits abound in every portion of the world.

It is not improbable, therefore, that Cuba may be wrested from Spain by a successful revolution; and in that event, she will lose both the Island and the price which we are now willing to pay for it—a price far beyond what was ever paid by one people to another for any province.

It may also be here remarked that the settlement of this vexed question, by the cession of Cuba to the United States, would forever prevent the dangerous complications between nations to which it may otherwise give birth.

It is certain that, should the Cubans themselves organize an insurrection against the Spanish Government, and should other independent nations come to the aid of Spain in the contest, no human power could, in our opinion, prevent the people and Government of the United States from taking part in such a civil war in support of their neighbors and friends.

But if Spain, deaf to the voice of her own interest, and actuated by stubborn pride and a false sense of honor, should refuse to sell Cuba to the United States, then the question will arise, what ought to be the course of the American Government under such circumstances?

Self-preservation is the first law of nature, with States as well as with individuals. All nations have, at different periods, acted upon this maxim. Although it has been made the pretext for committing flagrant injustice, as in the partition of Poland and other similar cases which history records, yet the principle itself, though often abused, has always been recognized.

The United States have never acquired a foot of territory, except by fair purchase, or, as in the case of Texas, upon the free and voluntary application of the people of that independent State, who desired to blend their destinies with our own.

Even our acquisitions from Mexico are no exception to this rule, because, although we might have claimed them by the right of conquest in a just way, yet we purchased them for what was then considered by both parties a full and ample equivalent.

Our past history forbids that we should acquire the Island of Cuba without the consent of Spain, unless justified by the great law of self-preservation. We must in any event preserve our own conscious rectitude and our own self-respect.

Whilst pursuing this course, we can afford to disregard the censures of the world to which we have been so often and so unjustly exposed.

After we shall have offered Spain a price for Cuba, far beyond its present value, and this shall have been refused, it will then be time to consider the question, does Cuba in the possession of Spain seriously endanger our internal peace and the existence of our cherished Union?

Should this question be answered in the affirmative, then, by every law human and Divine, we shall be justified in wresting it from Spain, if we possess the power; and this, upon the very same principle that would justify an individual in tearing down the burning house of his neighbor, if there were no other means of preventing the flames from destroying his own home.

Under such circumstances, we ought neither to count the

cost, nor regard the odds which Spain might enlist against us. We forbear to enter into the question, whether the present condition of the Island would justify such a measure. We should, however, be recreant to our duty, be unworthy of our gallant forefathers, and commit base treason against our posterity, should we permit Cuba to be Africanized and become a second St. Domingo, with all its attendant horrors to the white race, and suffer the flames to extend to our neighboring shores, seriously to endanger or actually to consume the fair fabric of our Union.

We fear that the course and current of events are rapidly tending towards such a catastrophe. We, however, hope for the best, though we ought certainly to be prepared for the worst.

We also forbear to investigate the present condition of the questions at issue between the United States and Spain.

A long series of injuries to our people have been committed in Cuba by Spanish officials, and are unredressed. But recently a most flagrant outrage on the rights of American citizens, and on the flag of the United States, was perpetrated in the harbor of Havana, under circumstances which without immediate redress would have justified a resort to measures of war, in vindication of national honor. That outrage is not only unatoned, but the Spanish Government has deliberately sanctioned the acts of its subordinates and assumed the responsibility attaching to them.

Nothing could more impressively teach us the danger to which those peaceful relations it has ever been the policy of the United States to cherish with foreign nations are constantly exposed than the circumstances of that case.

Situated as Spain and the United States are, the latter have forborne to resort to extreme measures. But this course cannot, with due regard to their own dignity as an independent nation, continue; and our recommendations, now submitted, are dictated by the firm belief that the cession of Cuba to the United States, with stipulations as beneficial to Spain as those suggested, is the only effective mode of settling all past differences and of securing the two countries against future collisions.

We have already witnessed the happy results for both countries which followed a similar arrangement in regard to Florida.

Yours very respectfully,

JAMES BUCHANAN.
J. Y. MASON.
PIERRE SOULÉ.

TO MR. MARCY.[1]

No. 46.   LEGATION OF THE UNITED STATES.
                                        LONDON, 23 October 1854.

SIR/

I have the honor to inform you that I returned to this Legation on Saturday the 21st Instant, after a fortnight's absence, from the conference between Mr. Mason, Mr. Soulé, & myself, held first at Ostend, & afterwards at Aix La Chapelle. Our joint Despatch to you dated at the latter City, on the 18th Instant, will make known to you fully the result of our deliberations. As this has already been transmitted to you by Duncan K. M'Rae, Esquire, U. S. Consul at Paris, whom Mr. Soulé selected for this purpose, it has become unnecessary for me to prepare & send another copy.

                            Yours very respectfully
                                        JAMES BUCHANAN.

HON: WILLIAM L. MARCY
    Secretary of State.

TO MR. MARCY.[1]

No. 47.   LEGATION OF THE UNITED STATES.
                                        LONDON, 31 October 1854.

SIR,

I visited the Foreign Office on Friday afternoon last, for the purpose of paying my respects to Lord Clarendon, not having seen him for several weeks. In soliciting the interview, I informed him that I had no " business of the least importance " to bring to his notice. His Lordship was thus left free to introduce what topics he pleased. He very soon adverted to the recent " Congress of American Ministers on the Continent," which has given rise to so many absurd surmises and reports. We had much agreeable bagatelle upon this subject, in which I treated in the jesting manner they deserved the various ridiculous rumors concerning the Conference which had found their way into the public Prints. Still, he manifested considerable anxiety to learn something of the objects of our meeting and the nature of our proceedings. I told him nothing could be more natural and proper, under the circumstances, than the desire of the Adminis-

---

[1] MSS. Department of State, 66 Despatches from England.

tration at Washington that Mr. Mason and myself should meet
Mr. Soulé and advise with him in regard to the existing relations
which he had in charge, between Spain and the United States.
It was true that far more éclat than was necessary had been
given to this very simple and informal affair; and I assured him
there was no foundation for his remark that Mr. Dudley Mann,
the Assistant Secretary of State, had been sent out by you to
preside at our meeting. He had not the least connection with
it, and had, in fact, returned to the United States before it took
place. I said it would be improper for me to give him any information in regard to our proceedings. This was a secret
which belonged exclusively to the Administration at Washington,
but still I might assure him that nothing had transpired which
ought to give the slightest offence to the British Government.
They might differ in opinion from the members of the Conference in certain points, but so far as I was personally concerned,
I should be quite willing to see our proceedings published in the
London Times. He then expressed a strong desire, (with which
I was not displeased) to know why we were so anxious to
acquire Cuba. I told him the constant danger that Cuba might
be " Africanized," and become a second St. Domingo, thus
threatening our domestic security, was one principal cause of
our anxiety. He replied that he felt confident there was not the
slightest danger of any such results. I then added that the
people of the Valley of the Mississippi, whose numerous navigable rivers in their courses measured some thirty thousand
miles, had scarcely any other outlet for their productions, to the
Ocean, than through the Mississippi, and that the Island commanded its mouth. From the position of Cuba, therefore, we
felt a deep interest in its acquisition, but this only on fair and
honorable terms. We were opposed to all filibustering expeditions; but we would give a price for the Island, which would
enable Spain, now in a state of hopeless bankruptcy, to develop
her resources by constructing a system of National Rail-Roads
and to make provision for restoring her credit and paying the
interest due to the holders of her Bonds. The conversation then
branched off upon the conduct of Mr. Soulé at Madrid, which
I defended, employing for this purpose the information he had
furnished me; and Lord Clarendon recounted unfounded charges
which had been made against him by the Spanish press whilst he
was Minister in Spain, illustrative of the suspicious character of
the people of that Country.

His Lordship then, with much apparent anxiety, expressed his deep regret that the President had again sent Captain Hollins in command of a naval force to Grey Town, and his serious apprehension, from the character of the Captain, that there might be a collision between the parties at that place. I told him I had not heard from you that Captain Hollins had been sent, and expressed some doubt upon the subject, as the reports in the Public papers had been contradictory. He said, nevertheless, it was certain,—that at the first the President had determined not to send him back again, but had afterwards changed his mind, on the solicitation of his friends. I told him I did not apprehend any danger of collision between the forces, as I entertained a perfect confidence that his instructions had been prudently and carefully prepared, and I doubted not the British Government had pursued a similar course. It was possible that if he and Captain Jolly should meet, they might have a personal conflict, but this could not involve the peace of the two Countries. After some further general conversation upon this subject, His Lordship next adverted to our acquisition of the Sandwich Islands. He said that a Treaty had already been concluded for this purpose, and that when Mr. Crampton spoke to you upon the subject, you had informed him that if these Islands should be offered to the United States, they would be accepted. I told him that here again he had the advantage of me. I had heard from you neither of the existence of the Treaty, nor that it would be sanctioned by the President. His Lordship manifested more feeling upon this subject than I could have anticipated. He said the Government of Great Britain had refused to accept a cession of the Sandwich Islands when it was offered in 1843. That they had supposed it was perfectly understood among the Commercial Powers chiefly interested, that these Islands were to remain independent, the vessels of each having free access upon equal terms to their Ports. That he understood the Government of the United States had been perfectly content with this arrangement. Of course, having no recent instructions and no authentic information, I waived this subject for a future occasion.

And here it is my duty to observe that I fear the annexation of these Islands, at the present moment, may result in serious consequences. After having been a close observer for more than a year in England, I am now convinced that both this Government and People earnestly desire to preserve peaceful and friendly relations with the United States. They would make many sacrifices rather than go to war with us. In my opinion, Louis Napoleon is not inspired by similar sentiments. As a despot, he regards the existence and the rapid advance of the Republic of the United States as a standing censure upon his usurpation and his tyranny. He has annihilated liberty in France, and looks upon its existence in our Country with extreme jealousy. He is bold, wary, and unscrupulous. Knowing that our naval force is comparatively insignificant, though of the very best material, it would be altogether in consistency with his character to attempt to humble us by one of those bold strokes in which he so much delights, and to declare that we shall not have the Sandwich Islands. In vain might we justly say to him that under the law of Nations, the people of the Sandwich Islands had a right to cede them, and we had a right to accept this cession, without the interference of any third Power. His past history proves how little such considerations would influence his conduct.

And here I am sorry to observe that I believe him to be the controlling spirit of the Alliance. His influence over the Counsels of Great Britain is very great, if not commanding. I do not think there is any heart love between them, yet she dreads the consequences of a rupture with France. It is, therefore, not improbable that he might be able to induce Great Britain to unite with him in an attempt to prevent us from acquiring the Sandwich Islands.

The allies have already sustained an immense loss of human life in the Crimea, both by battle and by disease. That they will eventually capture Sebastopol is generally believed; but this will be accomplished by a great additional sacrifice of human life. No well informed person, however, believes that the capture of Sebastopol will terminate the war, or that the Czar, in that event, would yield to the terms which Great Britain and France are disposed to dictate. Indeed, they can do him but little more harm. But in case of a rupture between us and the Allies, or, what is more probable, between us and France alone, he could render us but very little service. The contest would be one purely by sea; because no European Power, it is presumed, would commit the folly of landing forces on our Continent, although I have been informed that individuals near the Emperor Napoleon express the belief that the Union is ready to fall to pieces on the Slavery question.

I have felt it to be my duty to throw out these suggestions in order that you may be prepared for any contingency. I believe we might acquire Cuba with far less danger of serious consequences than would result from the acquisition of the Sandwich Islands. For the former we ought to be willing, if necessary, to risk a war. It is questionable whether we ought to do this for the latter. The former we could defend, with the assistance of its population, whilst the defence of the latter, from their great distance, and the feebleness of each of the separate Islands, and our inability to send troops to their assistance, would be attended with great difficulty. Besides, it is worthy of consideration whether the annexation of the Islands might not raise a clamor in France and England against our annexing propensities, and produce a concert between these Powers, which I am convinced does not exist at present, to prevent our acquisition of Cuba,—which is a necessity.

Lord Clarendon next adverted to our proposed Protectorate of the Dominican Republic and our acquisition of Samana. I told him I had heard nothing from you on this subject, and therefore presumed that the object of our Government, if there were any truth in the report, was to acquire a Naval Station in the West Indies, of which we were greatly in need, such as we already had in the Mediterranean. I send you the Morning Post of Friday last, containing a leading Editorial on this subject. This Journal is supposed to be the organ of Lord Palmerston, and it certainly always defends and eulogises him.

We then had a conversation respecting a Consular Convention, which His Lordship will have no difficulty in concluding. The want of it is a cause of great labor and annoyance to this Legation, and, what is much more important, injuriously affects our Navigating & Commercial interests throughout the British Empire.

Here I rose to leave, determined not to introduce the subject of the recent refusal of the French authorities at Calais to permit Mr. Soulé to enter France. His Lordship, however, asked me if I knew any cause for this refusal, and expressed a fear that Mr. Soulé might have said or done something to give serious offence to the Emperor of the French.

This afforded me an opportunity, which I embraced, of speaking my mind freely on this act of the French Government.

I said that, unexplained, it could be viewed in no other light than a deliberate insult to the United States. I recollected no example in modern times of the refusal of one Country to grant to the Public Minister of another Country, whilst peaceful relations subsisted between them, the right of passage to the Court where he had been accredited.   Mr. Soulé was travelling under a Passport from Mr. Pacheco, the Spanish Minister for foreign affairs, and was on his return to Spain, after a brief visit to London.   He had received no previous notice of the intention of the French Government to refuse him a passage.   The information was first communicated to him by the Commissary of Police of Calais.   Even admitting, which I did not for a moment believe, that Mr. Soulé had said or done something to give just offence to the French Emperor, this would be no justification or excuse for the denial of a passage to him as the Minister of a friendly Nation.   It was impossible that Louis Napoleon, whilst exercising despotic power over thirty-six millions of Frenchmen, and with the system of espionage which existed in France, could say that his Government would be in danger from permitting Mr. Soulé to pass through his dominions to Spain.   As the case at present appeared, I could view it in no other light than a premeditated insult to the Government of my Country.   We were a young Nation, and could not afford to submit patiently to such an indignity; and I was persuaded, however much the people of the United States might be divided on domestic questions, they would to a man resent any insult to the National honor.   That in my opinion, if a suitable atonement were not made for this act, or if satisfactory reasons were not given for it, which I did not consider possible, Mr. Mason would be justified in demanding his Passports.   I might, also, add that I had come to the knowledge of other circumstances which, in connection with the recent overt act, induced me to apprehend that the French Emperor indulged hostile feelings towards the United States.

His Lordship appeared to be deeply impressed with what I had said, and, laying his hand upon his heart, declared upon his honor that he knew I was mistaken in attributing to Louis Napoleon unfriendly sentiments towards the United States.   On the contrary, he knew that the Emperor was desirous of maintaining and cultivating the most friendly relations with our Country,—of this I might feel well assured.

This conversation took place on Friday, and on Monday, the 30th, there appeared in the Times a leading and significant editorial on the subject.   To this I would specially refer you.   I now learn that Mr. Mason addressed his note to the French Minister for Foreign Affairs on the 27th Instant; and I cannot doubt that this article was prepared with a reference to that note and probably to my conversation with Lord Clarendon.

The plot thickens, and it will require all your skill to navigate the Ship of State successfully through the breakers. But she is a gallant vessel and will triumphantly weather the storm.

Even the audacity of the French Emperor will hesitate before coming to extremities with the United States. He will be unwilling to risk the consequences which might result to himself from the loss to the Bourgeoisie of his good city of Paris and other cities of the immense purchases of expensive articles of French manufacture made by our wealthy and extravagant citizens. These, according to current report, surpass those of any other nation. This species of trade is altogether for the benefit of French manufacturers and shop keepers, without any corresponding advantages to our Country. Its sudden interruption might raise a storm about Louis Napoleon which he would not be able to weather.

Lord Clarendon and myself had then some conversation about our Central American difficulties, from which I might infer an increased disposition to settle them. I shall not repeat it, because its character was not such as to inspire me with any great degree of confidence, and I have already sufficiently troubled you on this matter.

Yours Very Respectfully

JAMES BUCHANAN.

HON. WILLIAM L. MARCY
    Secretary of State.

P. S.   I have the honor to acknowledge the receipt of your Despatches, Nos. 60 & 61, of the 27th September & 2d October, respectively.

TO MR. MARCY.[1]

LEGATION OF THE UNITED STATES.
LONDON 3 November 1854.
¼ to 6 P. M.

MY DEAR SIR,

It is with much pleasure I inform you that the French Government have revoked the order refusing Mr. Soulé permis-

---

[1] MSS. Department of State, 66 Despatches from England.

sion to enter France. This information is official & authentic; but I have not time to give you the particulars before the closing of the Despatch Bag. Great credit is due to Mr. Mason for the able, discreet, & judicious manner in which he has conducted this affair.

Mr. Soulé will leave here on his return to Madrid, via Calais & Paris, on Monday next.

Yours very respectfully
JAMES BUCHANAN.

HON: WILLIAM L. MARCY.

TO MR. MARCY.[1]

No. 48.   LEGATION OF THE UNITED STATES.
LONDON 3 November 1854.

SIR/

I have the honor to inform you that on Wednesday last, the first Instant, the Baron de Cetto & myself met & exchanged the Ratifications of the Convention for the mutual extradition of criminals, fugitives from justice, which had been concluded at London on the 12th September, 1853, between the United States & Bavaria.

I now transmit you, through the Despatch Bag, according to your instructions, the copy of this Convention ratified by the King of Bavaria which I received from the Baron in exchange for the copy ratified by the President, together with a certificate of the Exchange of Ratifications.

I also send a translation from the German into English of His Bavarian Majesty's act of Ratification, furnished me by Baron de Cetto.

Yours very respectfully,
JAMES BUCHANAN.

HON: WILLIAM L. MARCY
    Secretary of State.

---

[1] MSS. Department of State, 66 Despatches from England.

TO MISS LANE.[1]

LEGATION OF THE UNITED STATES.
LONDON 4 Nov: 1854.

MY DEAR HARRIET/.

I have little to say, but General Thomas presents so good an opportunity that I must write a line. We are getting on as usual. You are not included in the invitation to the Lord Mayor's Dinner. But the present Lady Mayoress says she will take you under her wing. I do think you ought to be smuggled in.

I dine to-day at Col: Lawrence's.

The new cook has come & promises rather fairly.

Judge Mason has proved himself to be fully equal to the Soulé occasion. I wrote a few lines to Gov. Marcy last night after I heard the news; which I hope he may publish. They do Mason justice. They went in the Despatch Bag. Moran promises fairly. I have got him at work. He is willing, & in a short time will relieve me greatly. Cobden & Bright dined with me yesterday. They were greatly pleased at Mason's victory.

Yours affectionately
JAMES BUCHANAN.

MISS HARRIET LANE.

TO MR. MARCY.[2]

No. 49.   LEGATION OF THE UNITED STATES.
LONDON, 21 November, 1854.

SIR:

I have the honor to acknowledge the receipt of your Despatches Nos. 62, 63, 64, and 65, of the 26th and 31st ultimo, and of the 2d Inst., respectively.

Having learned that Lord Canning had returned from Paris and resumed the duties of his office, I addressed him a

----

[1] Buchanan Papers, private collection.

[2] MSS. Department of State, 66 Despatches from England. The parts of this despatch relating to the postal convention are published in S. Ex. Doc. 73, 33 Cong. 2 Sess. 61–63. The suggestion of arbitration as to the Clayton-Bulwer treaty is printed in S. Ex. Doc. 35, 34 Cong. 1 Sess. 246. The passage relating to the cases of the "Hudson" and the "Washington" is printed in S. Ex. Doc. 19, 42 Cong. 2 Sess. 12.

note on the 7th Instant, expressing a desire to converse with him
" on the subject of the present Postal relations between Great
Britain and the United States, especially in regard to the expense
of transporting American Mails through this Country to France,
when compared with the correlative expense of transmitting
Mails through the United States to Canada," and requesting him
to designate a time when I might wait upon him at the General
Post Office for this purpose. On the next day I received a note
from his Lordship appointing Saturday, the 11th Instant, for
our interview.

We accordingly met and had a long conversation, in which
I pressed the arguments which had been employed by my predecessors to induce the British Government to reduce their rate to
12½ cents per ounce for the conveyance of our closed mails
through England to France; and his Lordship, in answer, repeated the objections which he had urged against this measure,
through Lord Clarendon, in the communication to Mr. Ingersoll
of May 27th, 1853. It would be useless to repeat this conversation. It is sufficient to observe, that I could not infer from it
the slightest indication that he intended to depart from the
decisions which had been announced in this communication and
in that from Lord Palmerston to Mr. Lawrence of the 14th
October, 1851.

There was nothing new, except that he informed me that
whilst recently in Paris he had endeavored in vain to make
such an arrangement with the French Postal authorities as
would enable the British Government to reduce the transit rate
for carrying our mails to the point which would be acceptable
to us, without being unjust to British subjects. That M. Drouyn
de L'Huys had stated this was impossible, and had at the same
time intimated that the French Government had then before
them a proposition from our Government on the same subject,
which Lord Canning inferred did not meet with any favor. His
Lordship said he was anxious to know from Drouyn de L'Huys
the nature of this proposition; but deemed it indelicate to ask.
I informed him that, if I were acquainted with it, I should cheerfully communicate its purport to him; but I had received no
information from my Government on the subject. We did not,
however, consider that their Postal relations with France, whatever they might be, could justify them in charging more for
carrying our mails through England to France than we charged
them for carrying their mails through the United States to Can-

ada. And that it would be most unfortunate, after all matters in relation to their North American possessions had been adjusted by the Reciprocity Treaty between the two Governments to their entire satisfaction, that we should get up a petty war of retaliatory Post Office restrictions, which could not fail injuriously to affect these Provinces. He referred to Mr. Bancroft's memorandum of November, 1848, to shew the nature of our existing Postal Convention. I answered that the Convention itself afforded us a remedy in the provision which would enable the United States Government to terminate it after a year's notice.

His Lordship also informed me that he had endeavored, whilst in France, to have the rates of Postage reduced on letters between France and England from the present rates of 8d. and 10d. to 3d. and 4d., England however agreeing to adopt the ¼ ounce standard which prevailed in France. He had hopes of success in this effort; and when informed of the decision of the French Government, he would let me know the result.

I told him, I had brought with me a letter from our Postmaster General to the Secretary of State (that of the 19th July, 1853) in which the whole of this subject was clearly and ably presented, and I would leave this with him, if I could entertain the hope that it might produce any change in his views. He said if I would leave it, he would be most happy to give it a careful consideration. I told him he could return it to me when convenient.

In the course of the interview, I expressed my willingness to unite with him in giving the invitation to France required by the 12th article of the Postal Treaty; but he expressed a confident belief, from his recent interview with the French Postal Authorities, that they would not accede to our wishes. He said that Monsieur Stourm, the Director General of Posts, had emphatically declared that they could not reduce their postal rates to the standard either of the United States or Great Britain;— that their service was much more costly than that in either of these countries, and the expense which they incurred in the delivery of letters throughout France, to all persons to whom they were directed, was very great.

It is doubtless the policy of France, under its present Government, to discourage instead of encouraging private correspondence. Besides, their present revenue falls so far short of their expenses, that it is confidently asserted they must speedily negotiate a new loan of four or five hundred millions of francs.

On Friday last, I called upon Lord Clarendon by his own invitation on a matter wholly personal to him and myself. The conversation between us branched off, as it usually does, to matters and things in general. In the course of it, I observed an increasing disposition to settle the Central American questions upon satisfactory terms, of which several slight indications had been previously given; and yet I cannot express the opinion that this disposition will result in any decided action. He informed me that he had some time since prepared an answer to my statement of the 22d July last; but not caring to have the last word, he had hitherto omitted to send it.

I feel confident there would not be the least difficulty in arriving at a satisfactory adjustment of the Mosquito question. The point of difficulty with the British Government is the Bay Islands. In the course of the conversation he intimated that it might be desirable to have the opinion of a third Power on the true construction of the Convention. To this I playfully observed that it would now be difficult to find an impartial umpire, as they had gone to war with our arbitrator, the Emperor of Russia. This was, however, but a mere intimation on his part. I then urged upon him as strongly as I could the reasons which, I thought, ought to induce the British Government to relinquish the Bay Islands to Honduras. He replied that these Islands were not of the least value to Great Britain; and the only question with them was whether the national honor did not forbid this course.

He is evidently apprehensive that the conduct of Captain Hollins, on his return to Greytown, may lead to some new complications. I told him I had great faith in your sound judgment and prudence, and had no doubt your instructions to the Captain would fully justify this opinion, though I had not the least knowledge of what they were.

I am happy to believe that we shall soon know the final determination of the British Government on the Central American questions. Should Lord Clarendon send the answer to my statement which he informed me he had prepared, I presume it will be decisive.

The very great freedom with which we converse whenever we meet, and the excellent opinion which I entertain of his Lordship, forbid me to report what he says, unless upon official interviews. Indeed, I would consider it dishonorable. Suffice it to observe, that upon all suitable occasions I never fail to say something in favor of my own country. The Island of Cuba,—the balance of power in Europe,—the resistance which we would make to the application of this doctrine to America,—the threats thrown out in some of the British Journals that England and France would regulate us after they had done with Russia,—the visits of inquiry and discovery of Messrs. Crampton and Sartiges to yourself, &c., &c., &c., are topics upon which I often comment.

I gave him as graphical an account as I could of your interview with these gentlemen on Dominican affairs.

I entertain not the least doubt of the warm and friendly feelings of Lord Clarendon towards the United States. I wish I could say as much for his colleague, Lord Palmerston. The Morning Post, believed to be his organ, is incessant in its abuse of the United States. Scarcely a week passes that it does not contain disparaging remarks upon our Country. I will quote the last example from its Saturday's number. In an article on the subject of withdrawing the British Troops from Canada for the purpose of reinforcing the army in the Crimea, it observes:—
" It is, therefore, necessary that Canada should have some means of self defence,—some regularly organized force,—always available not only to maintain internal peace, but sufficient, at least, to garrison its strong places, *if its neighbour should, in any complication of affairs, inconveniently extend that doctrine of annexation, which is only to be equalled in its dishonesty by that repudiation principle which is so much in vogue in some of the States."*

Notwithstanding these and similar remarks from different quarters, I have no doubt that the bone and sinew of this country sincerely desire to maintain the most peaceful and friendly relations with the United States.

The present war against Russia is emphatically a war of the British people. The more its difficulties and dangers increase, the more determined they seem to be to prosecute it with determined perseverance to a successful conclusion. I am fully persuaded that the present Ministry could not make peace with Russia, on any terms which the Emperor would be likely to accept, without being forced by public opinion to retire.

In reference to your No. 60, of the 27th September last,— I have not yet made a demand for indemnity from the British Government on behalf of the owners of the " Hudson " and the

"Washington," according to your instructions. This delay has been occasioned solely by the receipt of your favor of the 8th October, in which you inform me that Mr. Crampton had presented you a copy of a despatch from Lord Clarendon relative to the occurrences at the Falkland Islands, in reply to your note of the 1 July, which is in effect a demand for indemnity; and that you would soon probably communicate with me on this affair. I did not think it advisable to complete my note asking indemnity from the British Government without a copy of this despatch from Lord Clarendon, and either a copy of the documents or of the statement of the facts made out from them to which you refer in your note to Mr. Crampton. I await your further instructions.

Yours very respectfully,

JAMES BUCHANAN.

HON. WILLIAM L. MARCY,
    Secretary of State.

P. S. I have been agreeably surprised in receiving a private note from Lord Canning, who, in returning " Mr. Campbell's letter with many thanks," informs me that he hopes " to be able to make a proposal to you [me] in regard to the subject of our late conversation (the Rates of Transit) which may be acceptable to the Government of the United States and which will not be dependent upon the French Post Office. Some little time will elapse before I shall be able to communicate with you upon it; but I will let you know as soon as I can do so." I need scarcely add that this proposal when received shall be immediately communicated to you.

TO MR. MARCY.[1]

No. 50.   LEGATION OF THE UNITED STATES.
LONDON, 28 November 1854.
SIR :

I had the honor of receiving, on yesterday, your Despatch No. 66, of the 14th Instant, together with a copy of your Despatch to Mr. Soulé of the 13th Instant, transmitted for my information. The original Despatch to Mr. Soulé was received at the same time, with a note from Mr. Hunter, as follows, " If

---

[1] MSS. Department of State, 66 Despatches from England.

Mr. Soulé should be in London, please hand him the enclosed. If, however, he should have started for Spain, please forward it to him."

I have already sent this Despatch to Mr. Mason to be forwarded from Paris; because the opportunities are very rare of sending any communication direct from London to Madrid; and I do not know any trustworthy person here whom I could employ as a Special Bearer of Despatches, even if I possessed the authority to draw upon the Bankers of the United States, in London, for his expenses and services. Of course, such a Despatch cannot be entrusted to the Mail.

I transmit you two copies of a notification extracted from the London Gazette, which I have received from Lord Clarendon, together with a copy of his Lordship's note in which they were inclosed. You will observe that whilst this notification announces the raising of the blockade of certain Russian Ports therein specified,[1] the note expresses " the intention of the allied Governments in the event of the continuance of the war with Russia, to institute a strict blockade of the Enemy's Ports, from the earliest period next Spring when ships of war can resume their Station."

On the 24 Instant, Count Kielmansegge, the Hanoverian Minister at this Court, called upon me to ascertain whether it was probable the Government of the United States would consent to conclude a Convention of Extradition, for the mutual delivery of criminals, with Hanover, similar to that which existed between us and Prussia; and whether we would be willing to extend the list of criminals to be surrendered to certain other cases. I told him that from our very friendly relations with Hanover, I had reason to believe the President would be willing to place Hanover in this respect upon the same footing with Prussia and Bavaria; but I did not think he would consent to extend the Convention to new offences. After some further conversation we parted, he promising to send me his request in writing and I stating that I would communicate it to the Secretary of State by the next Steamer. I now send you his note and memorandum of the 25th Instant, and request that you will enable me to answer them as soon as may be convenient.

I herewith return the paper containing the letters of Denis Cassidy and Judge Kane, of the 28th October last, to the Hon:

---

[1] " Russian ports in the Gulf of Bothnia."

Mr. Florence, with the endorsement of the latter, which you transmitted to me with your Despatch No. 64, of the 31st ultimo. I do this because, without the usual testimony under oath of the parent to the age of his son, it would certainly be in vain to attempt to obtain his discharge from the British Service as a minor at the time of his enlistment.   When I shall be furnished with this proof, and a letter from Mr. Florence or Judge Kane, in favor of the father's character, which I can submit to Lord Clarendon, it will afford me great pleasure to use my best efforts to secure the son's discharge; and the British Government upon the submission of the proper proof have been liberal in granting such applications.   The father's letter does not even state the name of his son.   As he enlisted under an assumed name, and when it would seem he was nearly of age, the proof ought to be as clear as possible.

Yours very respectfully
JAMES BUCHANAN.

HON : WILLIAM L. MARCY
    Secretary of State.

TO MR. FORNEY.[1]

LEGATION OF THE UNITED STATES.
LONDON 14 December 1854.

MY DEAR SIR/
    I have received your two letters of the 27th ultimo; & whilst I feel deeply mortified that any portion of my letter to you, in its nature private & confidential, should have reached the public, I do not harbor the slightest suspicion that you intended this result in communicating its contents to third persons.   I feel that such a suspicion would do you wrong & great injustice.

It is well known to the President & many other friends, that I was strongly against the separation of the questions between us & England; & that it was my firm conviction *that both ought to have been settled together* either at London or at Washington.   The public revelation of my well known opinion on this subject, therefore, only distresses me for the reason that its repetition by me whilst in the employment of the Government, except

---

[1] Buchanan Papers, Historical Society of Pennsylvania.

to a private friend who like yourself had previously known it, would not be consistent with the proprieties of my position.

But what shall I say of Sickles? You are the only person in the world to whom I have ever written a word which could by possibility do him an injury. I am warmly & strongly attached to him. He is a man of fine talents, of excellent manners, & of a brave & loyal temper. My personal relations with him have been every thing I could desire. It is true that it is almost essential the Secretary of this Legation should be able to write a fair recording hand; & in this respect he is deficient, & has not, therefore, been able to render me all the assistance I could have desired; yet no human consideration would have induced me to mention this circumstance, could I for a moment have supposed it possible it would find its way to the public. In fact Col: Sickles possesses qualifications both of mind & manners for a much higher place than that of Secretary of Legation. To-morrow's steamer will bear him to the United States. Both his professional & private interests at the present moment require that he should return to New York. When he left this with his family in July last, he would have remained at home but for the earnest request of the President that he should bear Despatches to Mr. Soulé at Madrid. He leaves the Legation entirely upon his own suggestion; though after his determination had been communicated to me, with the reasons, it received my approbation.

You have been entirely misinformed as to the intention of Mr. Sanders "to set up a campaign paper" for me. No person knows better than he my firm & unchanged purpose not to be a candidate for the Presidency & my determination to make this publicly known upon the first suitable occasion.

I am sorry that the President or his immediate friends should imagine that it was possible I could oppose him whilst holding an office under him, even if I were so disposed. I entertain no such disposition. On the contrary, it has almost daily fallen to my lot to defend him in society here as well as the Cabinet against the charges in the American papers. These people so little know our Institutions that many of them believe he & the Cabinet ought to resign, the recent elections having gone against them; just as a British ministry would resign under similar circumstances.

I was much surprised to learn from your letter that Mr. Sanders had circulated "his French & Swiss letters" under seal or stamp of the American Legation at London; & "that the official covers of his French letters have been received by the President." I had not the most remote idea that such a thing existed until I received your letter, & I am obliged to you for the information. I presume Governor Marcy will write to me on this subject. I am now inquiring about it. It is impossible, I think, that either the seal or the official stamp of the Legation could thus have been used; but there is a stamp in the office commonly used to verify the papers sent to the Despatch agent from the Legation. I as yet, however, know nothing accurately of the matter.

The present war with Russia is a war of the masses,—of the British people. It is especially a war of those who from their liberal & progressive sentiments are most strongly inclined to favor our country. Their only apprehension is that the Government from dynastic prepossessions have not conducted it & will not conduct it with as much vigor as they ought to have done. Whether rightly or wrongly, the British Liberals believe that it is a war to promote progress & free principles. Hence they receive with somewhat embittered feelings the news that " their cousins on the other side of the Atlantic " sympathize with Russia. We do not stand as well with the popular element in England as we did six months ago.

Rest assured, my dear Sir, you are entirely mistaken in regard to any change of feeling on my part towards yourself, as Col: Sickles can abundantly satisfy you.

With the kindest regards of Miss Lane & myself for Mrs. Forney, I remain sincerely & respectfully your friend

JAMES BUCHANAN.

COL: JOHN W. FORNEY.

TO MR. MARCY.[1]

No. 51.   LEGATION OF THE UNITED STATES.

LONDON, 15 December 1854.

SIR/

Tomorrow's Liverpool Steamer will bear Colonel Sickles, the Secretary of this Legation, to the United States. Both his professional & private interests render this course imperative, & it

[1] MSS. Department of State, 66 Despatches from England.

has received my approbation.   When he returned with his family
to New York in July last, it was then his intention to remain at
home; but he yielded to the request of the President that he
should bear your instructions respecting the conference of Ministers to Mr. Soulé at Madrid, & orally furnish that gentleman
such explanations of the views of the administration as could be
more fully & satisfactorily communicated in this manner than
by writing.

Our intercourse has uniformly been of the most agreeable
& friendly character, & he carries with him my best wishes for
his future welfare.

At the request of Mr. Paul Harro Harring, I transmit you a
communication, dated on the 2d Instant, addressed to me, complaining of the violation of his rights as an American Citizen
travelling with a Passport from the State Department, by the
authorities in Denmark & at Hamburg.   Ere this can reach the
Department, you will doubtless have received information on this
subject from Mr. Bedinger & our Consul at Hamburg.   From
the statement of Mr. Harring, his case would seem to be of a
serious character.

I transmit two copies of the Queen's Speech at the recent
meeting of Parliament.   Her Majesty does no more than express
the enthusiastic determination of the British people to prosecute
the war against Russia " with the utmost vigor & effect."   Every
indication of public opinion throughout the Country is in accordance with this sentiment.   It is emphatically a people's war;
& whether rightly or wrongly, they believe it to be a war against
the extension of despotism & in favor of progress & free institutions.   Viewing it in this light, they are much annoyed that
their " transatlantic Cousins " should seem to sympathise with
Russia rather than with themselves.   In fact, this circumstance
has rendered us less popular with them than we were six months
ago.   Their only apprehension appears to be that the dynastic
prepossessions which many of them attribute to leading members
of the Ministry have heretofore prevented & may hereafter
prevent the Government from prosecuting the war with proper
vigor.   In the present state of public feeling in this Country,
I cannot believe that the British Ministry could venture to offer
any terms of peace which the Emperor of Russia would be
willing to accept.

What may be the effect of the so called Austrian Alliance
I cannot venture to predict, as it has not yet been published.

Should this contain any guarantee to Austria of her Italian & Hungarian possessions, it will render the Ministry very obnoxious to the British people.

I have the honor to acknowledge the receipt of your Despatch No. 67, of the 20th Ultimo.

Yours very respectfully

JAMES BUCHANAN.

HON: WILLIAM L. MARCY,
    Secretary of State.

TO MR. MARCY.[1]

Private.   LEGATION OF THE UNITED STATES.
LONDON 15 December 1854.

MY DEAR SIR/

In appointing a Secretary to this Legation, in the place of Col: Sickles, I would ask it as a personal favor from the President & yourself *that you would select no person who cannot write a fair, plain, & legible recording hand. Without this qualification, no matter what other talents & acquirements he may possess, I care but little for the appointment of any person during the remainder of my time.*

The Secretary to this Legation ought, however, to be a man of steady application & industrious habits. Young gentlemen who desire to see the world & pass much of their time in social enjoyments may accomplish their purpose, in a great degree, as Secretaries of other Legations, without detriment to the public service. Not so in London. Here it is necessary for the Secretary to work hard & perform a great variety of heterogeneous services which must otherwise be performed by the Minister himself. In that event his time which ought to be occupied in more important duties must be devoted to all sorts of miscellaneous correspondence. The number of letters daily received at the Legation containing inquiries of different kinds has surprised me very much.

Should a suitable person be selected, he might, during my time, besides being highly useful to myself, acquire such knowledge & habits of business as would be nearly indispensable to

---

[1] Buchanan Papers, Historical Society of Pennsylvania.

my successor for the first few months. And if he should have
no experience in foreign affairs, his position here for a time
would be of the most awkward & embarrassing character. I beg
you "to lay these things to heart," in the choice of a successor
to Col: Sickles. I purposely refrain from recommending any
person. Indeed, I would not know whom to recommend.

I am anxiously looking for the President's message, which
we expect to receive on Monday morning next, the 18th Instant.
The British people know but little of the Mosquito question, &
literally nothing of the Bay Islands.

Yours very respectfully

JAMES BUCHANAN.

HON: WILLIAM L. MARCY.

TO MR. MASON.[1]

LEGATION OF THE UNITED STATES.

LONDON 18 December 1854.

MY DEAR SIR/

I had an intimation from a friend in Washington by the
steamer of Monday last that Mr. Sanders had circulated his
Swiss & French letters in envelopes stamped with the Stamp
of this Legation. To-day has brought me a Despatch from
Washington stating this fact & that one of these had been placed
in the hands of Mr. Jerome Bonaparte of Baltimore & is, also,
known to Mr. Sartiges. Never have I been more astonished in
my life than at this information; & I have instituted a rigid inquiry to ascertain in what manner the stamp of this Legation
could have been thus abused. I need scarcely say to you that it
was without my authority or consent. I trust that no person
who knows me could for a moment suppose that I could have
given my sanction to such an act. I now write you that you
may disavow it on my part in the most solemn & explicit terms,
should the occasion offer in conversation with Mr. Drouyn de
L'Huys. Indeed it may become necessary to do this, long before
my answer to the Despatch of Mr. Marcy can reach Washington.
It is a long time since any occurrence has given me so much
uneasiness.

---

[1] Buchanan Papers, Historical Society of Pennsylvania.

With my kindest regards to Mrs. Mason & the family, I remain, as ever, very respectfully

Your friend

JAMES BUCHANAN.

HON: JOHN Y. MASON.

TO MR. MARCY.[1]

Private.   LEGATION OF THE UNITED STATES.

LONDON 22 December 1854.

MY DEAR SIR/

I have received your favor of the 3rd Instant; & although, according to the proverb, "a fair exchange is no robbery," yet Heaven forbid that I should exchange even my present position for the State Department. This would truly be "out of the Frying Pan into the fire." To be serious, I should be very sorry, in the event of your coming to England, that I should be thought of as your successor; though I do not deem this probable. In that contingency, however, I should certainly decline the honor. I again repeat, if you have any such desire or intention, that it would be important, on Mrs. Marcy's account as well as your own, that you should be here a fortnight before my departure. This would be rendered less necessary, should you send me such a Secretary of Legation as I have described in my last week's letter. Indeed without such a person, I would advise no friend to accept the London mission & *I hope he will be sent immediately;* Col: Sickles was to resign as soon as he reached Washington. If it suits your own views & wishes, I shall be very glad to have you for my successor. The importance of this mission cannot be overestimated, & no second or third rate man ought ever to be thought of for it.

I was much disappointed that the President in his message did not enter into a brief explanation of the present position of the Central American questions. In England, the people know nothing about them. They have some vague idea of the Mosquito question; but no Englishman not in Executive office with whom I have ever conversed had even heard of the question of "the Bay Islands." The President's message was the only

---

[1] Buchanan Papers, Historical Society of Pennsylvania.

means of communicating this information to the British public; because no other of our public documents is republished in England. I am persuaded, had this been done, that public opinion in this Country would have been brought to bear upon the Ministry & might probably have induced them to reconsider the determination expressed in Lord Clarendon's last note. *The message would have arrived here in the very nick of time.*

I observe in a number of American Journals the statement made positively that the Conference at Ostend was *the voluntary action* of the American Ministers. Surely this ought to be corrected. *Never did I obey any instructions so reluctantly.* And yet I continue to be entirely satisfied with our report.

Both Miss Lane & myself desire to be most kindly remembered to Mrs. Marcy.

Yours very respectfully

JAMES BUCHANAN.

HON: WILLIAM L. MARCY.

P. S. I beg you without delay to send me such a Secretary as I have described. I much need him at the present moment.

I have partly prepared & could easily complete a Despatch in answer to your last; but I wait till the next Steamer for further information. I myself have been so prudent & cautious in regard to the revolutionists here as to have leaned back. I have strong sympathies for the Poles, Hungarians, & Italians; but none at all for the French. They have chosen Louis Napoleon, & let them have him. De gustibus non disputandum. I am not partial to him, neither to Ledru Rollin, Louis Blanc, or Victor Hugo, or any red Republicans & Socialists. The two latter named I never saw; the first I have met twice. On the last occasion, a mere accidental meeting, we differed toto cœlo on a point of some consequence.

Mr. Sanders, like his predecessors, had the privilege of the Despatch Bag to send his letters & papers to the U. S. He doubtless thus sent some of his French letters to his friends, one of whom has reached Jerome Bonaparte. In this there was nothing wrong *except the Stamp,* about which I am now enquiring. Even Mr. Sartiges will not, I presume, have the impudence to complain that a citizen of the U. S. has sent what he pleased to the U. S. I was absent at the Conference when the French letter appeared. From all I can learn, none of them were ever stamped. The package sent to Mr. Fay is a very serious affair,

& I am now endeavouring to fix the blame upon the proper person. You will be gratified to learn, however, that but two of these packages were ever sent, one to Fay & the other to Belmont. The rest were stopped; *& all this without my knowledge.* But I will write at length.

TO MR. SICKLES.[1]

LEGATION OF THE UNITED STATES.

LONDON 22 December 1854.

MY DEAR SIR/

I have just learned from Mr. Cates what induces me to address you this letter. He says you told his son you would return to London early in January & had requested him to say to the Landlady you would pay for your rooms after a given day in that month which I do not now recollect. Perfect frankness is necessary to friendship; & you know I would not have consented to your return to the United States, had you not informed me you would resign when you reached Washington. The idea of a visit in August & another in December would expose us to just censure. Besides, I have considered it an act of friendship to state to all inquirers that your professional & private interests at home absolutely required that you should leave the Legation. In fact I have already urged Marcy to appoint your successor speedily. You know what is the condition of the office & how much I need assistance to redeem it from the chaos in which it is placed. I would write thus to no person except yourself, & am very sorry for the intimations I gave to Forney. I must have a Secretary who can write a good hand & be pretty much of a drudge during the remainder of my time in England.

Now what Cates' son told him may be altogether false; but I write this from abundant caution, so that by no possibility can there be any difficulty between us. Indeed the Despatch which you took out is sufficiently explicit; & I yielded freely to your suggestion that you should postpone your actual resignation until you reached Washington. Your refusal to rise when the Queen's health was proposed is still mentioned in society, but I have always explained & defended you.

---

[1] Buchanan Papers, Historical Society of Pennsylvania.

We have no news here since your departure. Com. Perry called to see me yesterday & told me that Belmont was very tired of his position. The Commodore will return to the U. S. by the Baltic on the 30th.

The Foreign Enlistment Bill is manifestly very unpopular in England. It could not have passed unless the Ministry had declared their intention of resigning in case it failed. It has been a severe blow, to their popularity. I have heard nothing of the Peabody affair since you left.

Please to remember me, in the very kindest terms, to Mrs. Sickles & Mad. Bagioli, & believe me to be, very sincerely, your friend

JAMES BUCHANAN.

DANIEL E. SICKLES, ESQ.

TO MR. MARCY.[1]

No. 52.   LEGATION OF THE UNITED STATES.
LONDON, 27 December 1854.

SIR:

I have the honor to acknowledge the receipt of your Despatch No. 68, of the 4th Instant. In this you inform me " that much has been said, at home and abroad, in relation to the interference of some of our Diplomatic Agents in the internal affairs of foreign Governments," &c., &c. And you also state that " the President is confident I will adopt the conclusion he has, that the circumstances therein presented " touching the conduct of this Legation, " could not be permitted to pass unnoticed."

Before entering upon an explanation of these circumstances, I desire to make one or two preliminary remarks.

I confess that my sympathies have been strongly enlisted in favor of the Poles, Hungarians, and Italians. These people, almost to a man, detest the foreign despotisms which have blotted their Nationalities from the map of Europe, and every lover of freedom must ardently desire that they should succeed in recovering their independence, though the prospect at present is far from encouraging. In regard to France, similar reasons do not

---

[1] MSS. Department of State, 66 Despatches from England.

exist.   It has not been subjected to a foreign Power; and whatever may be thought of the usurpation of Louis Napoleon, this has been sanctioned by a vast majority of the French people. Should they become tired of his dominion, they are abundantly able to relieve themselves from it.

Conscious that such have been my feelings and sympathies, for this very reason, I have, on all occasions, maintained a double guard, as a public Minister of my Country, over my conversation and conduct respecting Revolutionary plans and movements in Europe.   In my very rare and accidental intercourse with the unfortunate exiles themselves who have found a secure asylum in this Country, I have never conversed with them on these subjects, nor uttered a word which could possibly compromit either my Government or myself, as its Representative.   Indeed, I have not yet happened to see some of the most distinguished among them.   I have thus acted for the purpose of placing the Government at Washington above all suspicion.

And yet, notwithstanding all my prudence and precaution, I am now called upon to explain " circumstances " which appear to the President to present a different aspect.   The first of these is the granting of a passport to a certain Victor Fronde.   I might enter into a detail of circumstances respecting this case; but the substance may be embraced in a brief compass, and has already been communicated to you in my private letter of the 8th Instant. I addressed you this letter immediately after I had learned from Mr. O'Sullivan that Victor Fronde was the person to whom you had referred, without naming, in your private letters.   And here permit me to remark that if Mr. O'Sullivan had informed me in August last, when he wrote to you, that Fronde was employing his passport for the purpose of implicating this Legation in his revolutionary movements at Lisbon and Madrid, or if you had not felt yourself restrained from furnishing me the name and the scene of action of this individual, until you could consult Mr. O'Sullivan, his power to do mischief would long since have terminated.   I should have immediately written to Mr. O'Sullivan, and he would have done then what he has now done,—have sent for Mr. Fronde and cancelled the passport.   I may add that Mr. O'Sullivan has explained the whole affair to the Spanish Chargé d'Affaires at Lisbon, who will doubtless communicate it to his Government.

The Courier's Passport was issued to Mr. Fronde, without my knowledge, by Mr. Welsh, the Clerk of this Legation, in the

regular course of business.   He was represented at the time, by
a gentleman of character, to be a respectable American citizen
who was about to set out for Lisbon and Madrid, and was willing
to carry Despatches to our Legations at these places.   The passport was willingly issued by Mr. Welsh; because opportunities
rarely occur of transmitting Despatches directly to Portugal and
Spain, and Mr. Miller had then Despatches on hand which he was
desirous to send; though, as I now learn, Mr. Fronde, after
receiving his Passport, never called for them at the Despatch
Agency.   You are aware that this is a sort of distributing office
for all the Legations in Europe; and we are obliged to find
Couriers willing to render their services to the Government, in
conveying your Despatches to their different destinations, without money and without price.

I have truly said that this Passport was issued *without my
knowledge,* and I ought to explain the reason.   From the great
number and pressure of the applications for passports, it would be
impossible for me to give my personal attention to this business,
without a sacrifice of the important Diplomatic duties of the
Legation.   I am, therefore, compelled to sign Passports in blank,
and leave it to Colonel Lawrence and Mr. Welsh to fill them up,
under strict injunctions that whenever a case of the least doubt
or difficulty may occur, they shall appeal to me.   I have reason
to be satisfied with the manner in which these gentlemen have
performed this duty.   Indeed I may congratulate myself that
notwithstanding the great number of Passports issued, and the
misrepresentations in order to obtain them against which we
must constantly be upon our guard, no Passport, except that to
Fronde, has been granted, which, to my knowledge, we have had
reason to regret.

The next "circumstance" alleged is one of a grave character.   It is certain that Mr. Fay received a package, directed to
him under the Seal of this Legation, containing a number of
printed copies of Mr. Sanders' letter to the President of the Swiss
Confederation in favor of the right of asylum; which copies were
addressed, as is alleged, "to the leading revolutionary or ultra
liberal persons, principally in the Canton of Tessino."

This letter of Mr. Sanders created at the time no little sensation in Europe.   It was republished in the London Times, and
in other English Journals.   The principle which it advocated was
well calculated to make a strong impression upon the people, and
especially the Democratic party of Switzerland.   The mainte-

nance of the right of asylum by the Sultan in refusing to surrender Hungarian and Polish Refugees to the Emperors of Austria and Russia had contributed more than any other cause to
elevate his character throughout the world.   That the Republic
of Switzerland would have followed the example of the Sultan
cannot be doubted, had it not been surrounded by powerful
Despotisms able and willing to enforce obedience to their demands.   In this peculiar position, the Swiss Government would
be extremely sensitive to any seeming attempt on the part of a
Legation of the United States to circulate throughout Switzerland a letter written by an American Consul, and so well calculated in its nature to produce dissatisfaction among their
constituents.   In fact, such an attempt on the part of this
Legation would be a direct " interference " in the internal affairs
of Switzerland, and would deserve the President's disapprobation.
Under such circumstances, it is fortunate, that none of these
letters, with the stamp of the Legation upon them, ever reached
the individuals to whom they were directed.

This package to Mr. Fay was undoubtedly stamped at the
office of the Legation,—but by whom or under whose authority
I have found it impossible to ascertain,—was taken from thence,
along with other packages of a similar character directed to
several of our Ministers in Europe, by young Mr. Sanders, the
son of the late Consul, to Mr. Miller, the Despatch Agent, who
placed upon it the Seal of the Legation, and then delivered it to
a Bearer of Despatches for Mr. Fay.   Thus far is certain.   The
responsibility for sending this package to Mr. Fay undoubtedly
rests between Mr. Miller and Mr. Welsh.   Mr. Miller alleges
that when young Sanders brought the different packages, to
which I have already referred, to the Despatch Agency, he delivered him a written authority and direction from Mr. Welsh
to send them to the places of their destination; but says this has
been lost.   Fortunately, none were actually sent, as Mr. Miller
asserts, except the one in question and that to Mr. Belmont, because
Col: Lawrence happening to visit the Agency a short time after
they had been received there, and these packages having been
brought to his notice, he told Mr. Miller, very properly, that he
felt confident the stamp was placed upon them without my knowledge or authority, (which was certainly true) and that by forwarding them not only myself and the members of the Legation
but our Government itself might be seriously compromised; and
therefore he directed him to permit no other copies to be for-

warded from his office.   The consequence is, the remaining packages continued in the Despatch Agency until yesterday, when they were brought to the Legation.

The question, and the important question, remains—did Mr. Welsh give this alleged written authority to Mr. Miller, as Despatch Agent, to send these packages to their destination? That Mr. Miller believed Mr. Welsh had done so, is evident as well from his positive statement, as from his declaration to this effect made to Col: Lawrence—during the conversation to which I have referred—a short time after he had received the packages. This is rebutted, however, by the positive and explicit declaration of Mr. Welsh to the contrary; and I have ever found him to be a man of strict integrity and veracity.   It is unfortunate that the alleged note of Mr. Welsh cannot be found; for it is quite possible that Mr. Miller may have misunderstood its purport, if it ever existed.   Had Col: Lawrence repeated his conversation with Mr. Miller soon after it took place, I should have immediately instituted an inquiry into the matter, and the truth could then have been ascertained; but the fact is, I remained in entire ignorance of the whole affair until after I had heard from Washington.   Upon the whole, as no harm has been actually done, and as neither Mr. Welsh nor Mr. Miller could have intended to do anything wrong, I deem it best to pass this affair over without further notice, unless you should be of a different opinion.   I do not transmit the written statements which I have received from Mr. Miller, Col: Sickles, Col: Lawrence, and Mr. Welsh, deeming it best simply to furnish you the result.   Mr. Sanders was not appealed to, because he and his family had left for the United States.

I must confess that the third " circumstance " stated by you does not seem to me to be of a very grave nature.   It is easy to account for the manner in which copies of Mr. Sanders' French letter have reached the United States under the Stamp of the Legation.   It has always been the practice of this Legation to afford to our Consul at London the use of the Despatch-bag to send his letters and communications to the United States; and the communications of Mr. Sanders, as well as every thing else which has been sent from the Legation to Mr. Miller for the United States, have been stamped.   This was considered by the gentlemen in the office as nothing more than a warrant to Mr. Miller to place them in the Bag.   The practice was not necessary for this purpose; and I have ordered it to be discontinued, except in regard to letters and papers of an official character. Mr. Sanders has thus, undoubtedly, sent his French letter to friends in the United States. I am convinced, however, that none of these could have been sent to France under the official stamp. Mr. Miller is positive that none were ever forwarded by him to France or any part of the continent; and Mr. Mason, in a recent letter to me, states that he had never heard of them. When this letter appeared, I was absent on the continent attending the conference of Ministers, under your instructions, and Mr. Welsh accompanied me.

But even if I myself had sent one or more of these letters to friends in the United States, (which I never did,) under the Stamp of the Legation, and Mr. Jerome Bonaparte and Mr. Sartiges had acquired possession of them, this most unquestionably could afford no just cause of complaint on the part of the French Government. Very different, indeed, would be the case if I had sent such letters to be circulated in France. Any attempt on the part of Louis Napoleon to institute his system of espionage in the United States, for the purpose of ascertaining what our Despatch Bags contain on their passage home, would certainly be a most extraordinary proceeding. But it would be still more extraordinary if his Government should make the printed copy of a letter which had been sent home through the Despatch-Bag of this Legation, and which has been extensively republished in our Country, " an item in its list of pretended grievances " against our Government. I cannot believe that this will ever be done. This would be a direct attempt to interfere in our Domestic concerns, and would, at the least, be quite as reprehensible as any attempt on the part of our Government to interfere with the Domestic concerns of France.

Yours very respectfully

JAMES BUCHANAN.

HON: WILLIAM L. MARCY
    Secretary of State.

TO MR. MARCY.[1]

No. 53.   LEGATION OF THE UNITED STATES.
                        LONDON, 29 December 1854.

SIR:

I have the honor to acknowledge the receipt of your Despatch No. 69, of the 5th Instant.

I had a long and interesting conversation with Lord Aberdeen yesterday, at his private residence, upon the Central American questions, including that of Greytown. The result was, upon the whole, more promising and satisfactory than I had reason to anticipate. As Premier he felt himself at liberty to speak more freely on these subjects than Lord Clarendon had ever done. I regret that I have not been able to find time to report this conversation to you for to-morrow's Steamer.

In reference to your Despatch No. 57, of the 24th August last, I regret to inform you that, after diligent inquiry, I have not been able to discover the place of residence of Mr. John Levett Yeats, if he be still alive. This is not very probable, as the date of his affidavit, a copy of which you communicated to me with the note of the Attorney General, is more than thirty years ago. I shall, however, pursue my inquiries.

In reference to your Despatch No. 61, of the 2d October last, it affords me satisfaction to state that I have received a note from Lord Clarendon, of the 16th Instant, informing me that the request contained in my letter to him of the 23d ultimo " for the discharge of Joseph Kilgore, a minor and a citizen of the United States, from Her Majesty's army into which he had enlisted, was communicated to the Secretary of War, who has notified to me that orders have been given accordingly for Mr. Kilgore's free discharge."

In reference to your Despatch No. 67, of the 20th November last, I have to inform you that I have not yet heard of, or received, " the box containing two copies of the first part of Volume 15 " of Captain Wilkes' Exploring Expedition.

I transmit two copies of a notification which appeared in the London Gazette on the 19th Instant, communicated to me by Lord Clarendon on the 21st Instant, announcing that the blockade of the several Russian Ports therein mentioned had been raised; with a request that I " will have the goodness to transmit

---

[1] MSS. Department of State, 66 Despatches from England.

copies of this notification to your [my] Government, in order that it may, through that channel, become known to the citizens of the United States."

I have deemed the subject of sufficient importance to transmit you a copy of my note to Lord Clarendon, dated on the 15th August last,[1] asking indemnity from the British Government for George W. Colson, Master of the American ship "Moses Kimball," for the fine, costs, and attorney's fees, amounting to £16"16"0, which he was compelled to pay, under the sentence of British Magistrates who had no rightful jurisdiction of the case, with a copy of His Lordship's answer dated on the 23d Instant, announcing a compliance with my request.

I look with much anxiety for the appointment of a Secretary to this Legation.

Yours very respectfully,
JAMES BUCHANAN.

Hon: WILLIAM L. MARCY
    Secretary of State.

FROM LORD CLARENDON.[2]

Private.   THE GROVE, Dec. 30/54.
MY DEAR MR. BUCHANAN

Your letter of yesterday reached the F. O. after I left it & followed me to this place, where I am come for one day's quiet work.

I wish I could ask you even by the telegraph to return to town, for I long to finish our business together, but tho' small in interest & importance to us, it is large in point of honor, & with respect to that no one better than yourself will appreciate our difficulty.

There are two other obstacles in the way of immediate settlement. 1st. The Republic of Nicaragua is in a complete state of dissolution & getting worse every day.

2nd. The adoption of Captn. Hollins' proceedings & the manner in which the Greytown affair has been vindicated in the President's speech complicate the matter very much.—Let me ask you not as a Minister but a Friend what would be said of us both here & in the U. S. if we beat a retreat before such a *shower of hard words*.

However, it does not abate my desire & intention to settle the question *somehow* amicably.

You expressed a wish to keep aloof from the Falkland Islands difficulty, & so I determined not to bother you about it, but Captn. Lynch has been sent there again & was going to batter down the Govr.'s house because an

---

[1] To Lord Clarendon, Aug. 15, 1854, supra.
[2] Buchanan Papers, Historical Society of Pennsylvania.

American Citizen had been imprisoned for a breach of the Island law, tho'
Captn. L. knew at the time that he had been released & had left the Island.

Such acts are not favorable to such negotiations as you & I would like
to carry on.

Believe me, my dear Mr. Buchanan

Very faithfully yours

CLARENDON.

TO MR. MARCY.[1]

No. 54.   LEGATION OF THE UNITED STATES.

LONDON, 30 December 1854.

SIR/

In pursuance of a previous understanding, I called upon
the Earl of Aberdeen, at his private residence, on Thursday
last, the 28th Instant, & was received with great kindness. After
conversing upon several subjects, & especially the Russian war,
which is at present a universal topic in this Country, I said
I had called to see him for the double purpose of cultivating
more intimate personal relations with his Lordship, to which
I had been so kindly invited, & of conversing with him on the
Central American questions between the two Governments. I
did not know whether it would be *comme il faut* for me to
address myself to any member of the Government except Lord
Clarendon upon these questions; & if it were not, I would feel
myself indebted to him to put me right. That it was natural
an American Minister should resort to his Lordship when difficulties occurred between the two Countries, as it was well known
& justly appreciated in the United States that he had been
mainly instrumental in adjusting such difficulties on former
occasions.

He replied that it was perfectly proper for me to converse
with him upon the subject & he would be happy to hold such
a conversation with me. Whilst Lord Clarendon was the appropriate official organ of the Government in regard to Foreign
Affairs, he exercised a general superintendence over the whole.
He then expressed the hope that Lord Clarendon & myself got
along well together; & in answer I spoke of Lord Clarendon
in the strong and friendly manner which his conduct towards
me has uniformly deserved, but added, I was sorry to say, we
had made but slow progress in the Central American Questions.

---

[1] MSS. Department of State, 66 Despatches from England.

The conversation then branched off upon the Ashburton Treaty & the Oregon Treaty, as well as the agency of his Lordship in concluding them; but this I need not repeat.

I then asked him if he had found time, amidst his other important engagements, to bestow any particular attention upon the Central American questions. He said he had read the correspondence between Lord Clarendon & myself, & that my reply was a masterly & powerful paper. With several portions of it he entirely agreed; but from others he dissented. The Greytown affair was an unpleasant circumstance, & rendered it difficult for them at the present moment to settle these questions; but he did not believe that the Government of the United States could have intended any insult to the British Government by that unfortunate expedition. He had no doubt there were many lawless people at Greytown, & our Government might truly allege that we had in this affair taken a leaf out of their book, for Great Britain had on some occasions proceeded in a like summary manner against such people; but in this instance he thought our Government had gone beyond what they had ever done. He proceeded, & said that in regard to the Mosquito question, it could produce no serious difficulty between the two Countries. He made several remarks in a conciliatory spirit on this question, with which I need not trouble you; because as I have intimated to you heretofore, I feel satisfied they are nearly as anxious to relieve themselves from the Mosquito Protectorate, as we are that they should withdraw from it. The Greytown affair may interpose a momentary difficulty; but that will soon pass away & be forgotten.

Finding his Lordship disposed to speak freely, & not willing to interrupt him, I then merely remarked that he had said nothing in regard to the Bay Islands, which my Government believed to be a question of great & pressing importance. He then proceeded:—As to the Bay Islands, their claim to them rested entirely upon the question whether they could be considered as legitimate dependencies of British Honduras. He thought it was doubtful whether they could be considered in that light. He was not prepared to express a decided opinion on the subject. Still, he thought this question could present no insurmountable difficulty. According to the Scotch proverb, " where there was a will, there would always be a way." He then asked what interest the Government of the United States could have in these Islands. I told him we did not claim any territorial interest in them. That when our Gov-

ernment entered into the Clayton & Bulwer Treaty, we had
agreed not to acquire any territory in Central America, & they
had as an equivalent bound themselves, as we firmly believed,
to withdraw from all their Central American possessions & thus
place the two Countries on an exact equality in that region.
We were anxious, therefore, that they should restore these
Islands to the State of Honduras, to which, in our opinion, they
rightfully belonged; & this was our only interest.   Ruatan
had been captured from Honduras in 1831, by Colonel M'Donald,
the Superintendent of Belize, whom I believed to be a very
troublesome man, but was afterwards restored by the British
Government. This same Colonel M'Donald, however, had again
captured Ruatan in 1841, under circumstances of such a character as to meet the unqualified condemnation of Crowe, a
respectable British author, in his Gospel History of Central
America.

His Lordship then said, he thought it would be difficult
for them to maintain that the Bay Islands were dependencies
of Belize. He rather believed that the Islands referred to in
their Treaties with Spain were certain small Islands in the immediate vicinity of that settlement, & did not extend to so large
an Island as Ruatan & one at such a distance. He remarked
the Belize was a sort of exceptional settlement under their old
Treaty with Spain,—that they had never appointed a regular
Governor over it, as they had done over their other Colonies,
but a Superintendent.

This led to a conversation on the subject of the notes exchanged between Mr. Clayton & Sir Henry Bulwer previous to
the exchange of ratifications of the Treaty, the communication
of these notes to the Senate afterwards by Mr. Everett, & the
consequent discussions in that Body. In the course of this conversation, I told him emphatically that if it had been believed
by the Senate that the Treaty did not require them to withdraw from their Central American possessions, there would not
have been a single vote in that Body in favor of its ratification.

After some further conversation, in which he manifested
a most amicable spirit, I then asked what remained to prevent
us from at once proceeding to settle these unfortunate Central
American difficulties. Why should they remain as obstacles to
that firm & sincere friendship between the two nations which,
for one, I was so anxious to promote by every honorable means?
The trade between the two Countries was immense. In 1853,

their exports to the United States had been within a million & a half of pounds of the whole amount of their exports to all the Continental nations of Europe, Turkey alone excepted. That the interests of constitutional freedom, as well as the progress of civilisation throughout the world, required that Great Britain & the United States should be the best of friends.

Besides, I observed that the internal affairs of the Central American States were now in an unhappy & distracted condition, from which they could not probably be relieved until the difficulties were settled between Great Britain & the United States, when both could employ their good offices for this purpose. In the mean time Capitalists would not invest their money in the construction of Rail Roads & Canals across the different routes on the Isthmus, which must prove so valuable to the commerce of both nations.

His Lordship answered, that as to thoroughfares across the Isthmus, he had never considered them of so much importance as other people had done. The value & importance, however, of a sincere & lasting friendship between Great Britain & the United States could scarcely be overrated. No man could be more anxious than himself to promote the best understanding between the two Countries. Whilst this had at all times been his desire, their existing war with Russia was a good reason why they should feel at the present time doubly anxious to cultivate the best relations with the United States.

After some conversation in regard to the existing & projected thoroughfares across the Isthmus, & the practicability of a thorough Cut Canal, I took my leave, his Lordship saying he would be most happy to see me at all times, & expressing the desire that I might speedily call again.

In this interview, he made a favorable impression upon me. He is believed, even by his political opponents, to be a frank, sincere, & honest man, & he has always professed to entertain friendly feelings for our Country. Should nothing occur on the other side of the Atlantic further to complicate the Greytown difficulty, on which they are extremely sensitive, there would seem to be a better prospect than heretofore of settling the Central American questions.

Yours very respectfully

JAMES BUCHANAN.

HON: WILLIAM L. MARCY,
    Secretary of State.

1855.

TO LORD CLARENDON.[1]

Private.   HORNBY CASTLE,
                                            2 January 1855.

MY DEAR LORD CLARENDON/

I have received your note of the 30th ultimo.

"The point of honor" involved in the settlement of the Central American questions is, I confess, too deep for my vision. Like truth it lies in the bottom of a well.

The fact that Nicaragua is at present in a sad condition appears to me to be a strong reason for the immediate settlement of these questions. The friendly offices of the two Governments acting in concert will be required to put things to rights in Central America.

There are surely no hard words in the President's message directed to England in regard to the Greytown affair, & he certainly never intended to say anything which could give just cause of offence to the British Government.

But what will Mrs. Grundy say to the settlement? I know not what on this side of the Atlantic; but I feel confident of what she will say on the other side. This will be that Buchanan has made a capitulation under which Great Britain is not removed from the usufruct of Belise which she still holds under the old Spanish Treaty, despite The Clayton & Bulwer Treaty. It is just like the capitulations by which The United States surrendered to Great Britain the one third of the State of Maine & nearly six degrees of latitude on the Pacific coast. So it is always in our negotiations with England.

As to the braggadocio of Captain Lynch, if he ever indulged in such a folly,—this I consider of no account.

Wishing your Lordship with all my heart many a happy New Year, I remain yours as ever

                                            JAMES BUCHANAN.

LORD CLARENDON.

P. S. We go to Mr. Brown's near Liverpool on Friday, & I hope to be in London on Monday or Tuesday. Have you forgotten the Consular Convention?

---

[1] Buchanan Papers, Historical Society of Pennsylvania.

TO MR. MARCY.[1]

No. 55.   LEGATION OF THE UNITED STATES.
LONDON, 12 January 1855.

SIR:

I have the honor to acknowledge the receipt of your "Strictly Confidential" Despatch, No. 70, of the 15th ultimo. Having recently written you at length on the subjects to which it refers, in my No. 52, I shall now confine myself to a few remarks.

Neither the letter of Mr. Sanders to the President of the Swiss Federal Council, as published in the London Times of the 21 August last, nor as it was published by Mr. Sanders himself in letter form in the English language, of which he furnished me a copy, had any note appended.

I am wholly ignorant who were the translators of this letter into French, German, Italian, and Spanish, or who were the authors of the notes to these translations referring to myself. These notes, as well as the letter itself, were published without my previous knowledge, sanction, or approbation. The translations were probably made by the unfortunate exiles now in London, who may have learned that I was in the habit of visiting the estimable and much esteemed family of Mr. Sanders, who were my near neighbors; and from this circumstance may have drawn unfounded conclusions.

Although this letter advocating the right of asylum was well received at the time by the British liberals, and contains nothing objectionable in the abstract had it been written by a private American citizen, except in such portions of it as manifestly go beyond the advocacy of this simple and sacred right, yet it was highly improper thus to implicate me as the public Minister of my Country, and indirectly my Government, with that of Switzerland; and at this conduct I strongly and emphatically expressed my disapprobation. In fact, the note annexed to the French letter was the only one which I understood; and it now appears, from the translations which you have sent me, to be the least exceptionable of the four.

It is but just to state that Mr. Sanders, although over-zealous in the cause of the exiles, was a good and obliging Consul who rendered me many services, the value and the loss of

---

[1] MSS. Department of State, 66 Despatches from England.

which the American Minister in London can alone properly appreciate.

You inform me that "the French Government pretends to know that the person mentioned in Mr. O'Sullivan's Despatch, [Victor Fronde] has returned to London with oral and written communications from Mr. Soulé to Ledru Rollin." This I believe to be but a mere pretence. My conviction to this effect is derived from the long, able, and most interesting narrative which Mr. Soulé gave to Judge Mason and myself of his proceedings at Madrid. After conversing with him freely and confidentially, we both arrived at the conclusion that his conduct had been greatly misrepresented. He certainly made a very favorable impression both on the Judge and myself; and in regard to myself, I may say, much more favorable than I had anticipated. I do not believe that, since his appointment to the Spanish Mission, he and Ledru Rollin have had any political connection or correspondence whatever. Besides, Mr. Soulé left Madrid for his estate in the French Pyrenees on the 1st September, and Fronde's passport is dated on the 16th August, so that I very much doubt whether the latter had arrived in Madrid before the departure of the former. Perhaps Mr. O'Sullivan's first Despatch would shew when Fronde left Lisbon for Madrid.

I have received your Despatches Nos. 71 and 72, of the 19th & 23d ultimo, respectively.

Yours very respectfully

JAMES BUCHANAN.

HON: WILLIAM L. MARCY,
    Secretary of State.

TO VISCOUNT CANNING.

(Enclosure in No. 59.[1])
Private.   U. S. LEGATION,
                    LONDON, 15 January, 1855.

MY LORD:

Pardon me for recalling your attention to the existing Postal difficulties between the two Governments, and suggesting that the Session of the American Congress, indeed the present

---

[1] Despatch to Mr. Marcy, No. 59, Feb. 2, 1855, infra. This enclosure is printed in S. Ex. Doc. 73, 33 Cong. 2 Sess. 64.

Congress itself, will expire on the 3d of March next. If, therefore, your Lordship should deem it proper to make any proposal
to me in relation to the rates of transit for the conveyance of
American Mails and letters through Great Britain to France,
according to the hope expressed in your note of the 20th November last, it is desirable that this should be done with no greater
delay than may be convenient.

Yours very respectfully,

(Signed)   JAMES BUCHANAN.

VISCOUNT CANNING.

TO MR. MARCY.[1]

No. 57.   LEGATION OF THE UNITED STATES.

LONDON, 19 January 1855.

SIR:

I again called upon Lord Clarendon on Wednesday last,
by appointment, on the subject of the proposed Consular Convention between the two Governments; but as we did not arrive
at a final conclusion, it is unnecessary to detail our conversation.
The law officers of the Crown are opposed to several of the
details in our Convention with France; but I have reason to
believe that we shall be able to agree upon all important
stipulations.

I embraced this occasion to speak strongly to Lord Clarendon in relation to the proceedings of James Finn, Esqr., Her
Majesty's Consul at Jerusalem, in regard to Mr. Murad, our
Vice-Consul there, and to other citizens of the United States in
that quarter of the world; and I deemed it proper to communicate to him not only the copy of Mr. J. Hosford Smith's letter,
but also a copy of your Despatch No. 62, on the subject. I told
him that I had read Mr. Smith's letter with care; and that the
terms in which you spoke of the conduct of Mr. Finn were,
in my opinion, fully justified by the statements in that letter
& the documents which accompanied it.

His Lordship promised to examine this case himself with
care and to demand explanations from Mr. Finn, of whom he
does not seem to entertain a high opinion. In the course of
our conversation on this matter, he pronounced a warm eulogium

---

[1] MSS. Department of State, 66 Despatches from England.

upon the character and conduct of the American Missionaries in that region.

We then branched off, as is our wont, upon the Central American questions and upon the opinions expressed by Lord Aberdeen to me, which I communicated to him and have reported to you in my No. 54. It is evident that Lord Clarendon differs from the Premier on these questions, though he expressed, as he had often done, a strong desire to settle them and an entire willingness to yield his opinions; and he promised to converse with Lord Aberdeen upon them without delay, and give me immediate notice of the result.

I have not been unmindful of your important Despatch, No. 52, of the 7th August last, instructing me to propose to conclude a Treaty with Great Britain establishing the principles that " Free ships shall make free goods," and that the property of a friend captured on board the vessel of an enemy shall not be confiscated, contraband in both cases excepted. The only reason why I have not hitherto formally presented this proposal is the moral certainty that it would be rejected; and this not because the present Ministry are opposed to it, but for the reason that they would not, in the midst of the existing war with Russia, be willing to encounter the opposition which such a Treaty would occasion. As I have before informed you, this war is emphatically a war of the masses of the people of England; and public opinion has been decidedly opposed and loudly expressed against the Government, even for having permitted any trade with Russia to be carried on by neutrals through Prussian Ports. This they could not have prohibited, without violating the law of nations.

The lawyers, a most powerful class in England, are strongly opposed to the principles of the proposed Treaty. Mr. John Phillimore, with whose high professional character and attainments you are well acquainted, although a strong and decided Liberal, in July last moved in the House of Commons, " That it is the opinion of this House, that however, from the peculiar circumstances of this war, a relaxation of the principle that the goods of an enemy in the ship of a friend are lawful prize, may be justifiable, to renounce or surrender a right so clearly incorporated with the law of nations, so firmly maintained by us in times of the greatest peril and distress, and so interwoven with our maritime renown, would be inconsistent with the security and honor of the Country."

The Ministry relieved themselves from this motion by proposing the Previous Question, which is widely different in its nature from our Previous Question. I mention these circumstances as the reason why I had not at an earlier period introduced the subject to the notice of Lord Clarendon.

I informed his Lordship, on this occasion, that I had received instructions from you to propose to consecrate by a Treaty the wise and just principle towards neutrals which they had established for their guidance during the continuance of the present war:—that the flag of a neutral shall protect the goods of an enemy; but that I did not intend at the present moment to enter upon the negotiation. He replied, in a significant manner:—" I presume this is the same Treaty you have already made with the Emperor of Russia." I said, " Yes, the very same. We trust that the British Government will now be willing to return to the practice which they had almost universally adopted in their Treaties with different nations, before the wars of the French Revolution,—of stipulating that ' free ships shall make free goods.' The rule which you have so properly adopted for the present war appears to justify this belief." He answered, " You were the first person I consulted about the adoption of this rule, and you are fully aware of the difficulties we had to encounter in adopting it. The lawyers, who are a very powerful class, were violently opposed to it, and talked as if they believed it would ruin the country. We think, however, it is a rule in accordance with modern civilization; but the conclusion of such a Treaty, under existing circumstances, is a different affair." I told him that my object at this time was merely to mention the subject to him; and that on a future occasion I would introduce it in a more formal manner.

I confess I am perplexed to know how to act in this matter, and should be glad to receive your advice. It is quite certain that a proposition to conclude this Treaty would now be rejected, for reasons of expediency, although the Ministry are not opposed to it and do not believe, as Lord Clarendon informed me on a former occasion, that the old rule will again be adopted in practice. It might, however, embarrass a future Ministry, desirous of pursuing the correct course, to have such a refusal placed on file in the Foreign Office. I have some time since collected the materials, partly from their own history, for a note on this subject, and to some extent have put them together, which, I think, ought to produce an effect; but was unwilling to meet a refusal. What I now propose is, with your assent, " to bide my time," but in any event to present this note before my departure from the Country; but if I should discover that the answer would be unfavorable, so to arrange that I shall not receive an answer. The note would then remain on record in the Foreign Office, and might be useful hereafter. In the mean time, I shall avail myself of every proper opportunity to mention the matter incidentally in my conversations with Lords Aberdeen and Clarendon. I shall feel much indebted to you for your advice as soon as may be convenient.

Under the French law of nations, " Free ships make free goods," and " Enemy's ships make enemy's goods." Under the British law, the rule is directly the reverse in both cases. One reason given by a member of the Ministry in the House of Commons for the rule of the present war was, that this is a compromise between the two nations,—the French having yielded their principle that " enemy's ships make enemy's goods," and the British theirs, that the goods of an enemy may be captured on board the vessels of a friend.

Their war with Russia then became a topic of conversation; and he expressed quite a decided opinion that the existing negotiations at Vienna would not lead to peace. In regard to the sympathy expressed in the United States for Russia, I told him that the causes for this were not those which had been assigned in the article in the Times of Tuesday last. The true cause was the belief that England and France were disposed to interfere with the rights of the United States on the other side of the Atlantic. He declared solemnly that there was not the least shadow of foundation for such a belief. On the contrary, it was their earnest desire to cultivate the most friendly relations with the United States. And he asked, " How can you believe otherwise, when you have just informed me that in the year 1853, the value of our exports to the United States was within less than a million and a half of being equal to that of our exports to all the nations on the Continent ? " I referred, in answer, to the recent conduct of the British and French Consuls acting in concert to prevent the United States from concluding a Treaty of Commerce with the Dominican Republic; and observed that on all occasions in which the United States were interested, the officials of the two Governments appeared " to hunt in couples," and to be ever ready to do us injury. He replied that there had been too much of this,—it was all wrong, and he would take care that for the future we should have no cause to complain on this account.

It is an astonishing fact that, according to the official Statistical tables of this Government, the value of British exports to the United States for the year 1853 amounted to £23,658,427, whilst that to all the nations of Europe, Turkey alone excepted, only amounted to £25,083,087. What has been the value of their exports during the year 1854, I have not yet been able to ascertain.

I transmit the Convention of Extradition with Hanover which was signed yesterday by Count Kielmansegge and myself; and trust that you will take care it shall be acted upon during the present Session of the Senate. The Count and his Government would both be greatly disappointed if this Convention should not be ratified at Washington before the 4th March. They appear to attach much importance to it.

Yours very respectfully

JAMES BUCHANAN.

HON: WILLIAM L. MARCY,
    Secretary of State.

TO MISS LANE.[1]

U. S. LEGATION,

LONDON 20 Jan. '55.

MY DEAR HARRIET/

I have rec'd yours of yesterday. In answer, I say, do just as you please & then you will please me best. I desire that whilst you remain in England you should enjoy yourself prudently & discreetly in the manner most agreeable to yourself. If you desire it, there can be no objection to a visit to Miss Hargreaves.

I send the letters received by the last steamer. I got one myself from Mr. Macalester, who says, " Please say to Miss Harriet that ' Job ' will be out in the spring, provided *the Boston gentleman* is disposed of (as *he* could wish) in the interim."

For my part, my impressions are favorable to "*Job;*" although I consider him rather a cold lover to wait for a whole year. He does not know that you will be home in the

---

[1] Buchanan Papers, private collection. Imperfectly printed in Curtis's Buchanan. II. 149.

spring, & that he may spare himself the voyage, nor did I so
inform Mr. Macalester.

I dine to-day "en famille" with General D'Oxholme.

With my kind regards to all, I remain yours affectionately

JAMES BUCHANAN.

TO MR. MARCY.[1]

No. 58.   LEGATION OF THE UNITED STATES.

LONDON, 26 January 1855.

SIR:

I have the honor to acknowledge the receipt of your Despatch No. 73, of the 6th Instant.

The Commission for the settlement of outstanding claims
between the United States and Great Britain has just terminated;
and Judge Upham, the Commissioner on our part, will return
home by to-morrow's steamer from Liverpool. The relation
which your instructions established between myself and the
American Commissioner and Agent renders it proper for me to
express an opinion of the manner in which these gentlemen have
respectively performed their duties. This is a pleasing office;
because it would scarcely be possible for any individuals to have
discharged these duties in a more satisfactory manner. The
business of the Commission was conducted by Judge Upham
and General Thomas, in their several spheres of action, with
much ability as well as indefatigable industry and perseverance;
and the result of their labors has proved to be quite as favorable
to our country as could have been reasonably anticipated. They
had many serious obstacles to overcome, arising chiefly from
the fact that the Convention had fixed the seat of the Commission at London instead of Washington.

The action of this Commission will be a great relief to
the two Governments. All the claims of the citizens and subjects of each on the Governments of the other, which had been
accumulating since the date of the Treaty of Ghent, (24 December, 1814) and had given rise to so much diplomatic correspondence, have happily now been decided and can no longer
become subjects of discussion. These claims in number exceeded
one hundred, and in amount involved millions of dollars. The
sum actually awarded was about $600,000,—of which the Ameri-

---

[1] MSS. Department of State, 66 Despatches from England.

can claimants will receive considerably more than one half. In this connection, I cannot forbear to observe that the sum of $3000 per annum, fixed by the Convention as the salary of the Commissioner, must have been wholly inadequate to defray the necessary expenses of himself and family in London; and I might make a similar remark in regard to the Agent and his family. Although it became the duty of these gentlemen to investigate and discuss the gravest questions of international law, involving large amounts, yet this salary falls far below even what is allowed as outfit and salary to a Chargé d'Affaires.

The decisions, in the main, of Mr. Joshua Bates, the Umpire, will prove that he was worthy of the highly responsible trust confided to him. No person has ever doubted his integrity; and his sound judgment and extensive and intimate knowledge of Commercial affairs were highly appreciated by the American Commissioner. His awards in the cases of the Enterprise, the Creole, and the Hermosa, although eminently just, in the face of prejudices so extensively prevailing in this country, as well as of decisions of the British Government, afford strong evidence of his independence.

Yours very respectfully

James Buchanan.

Hon: William L. Marcy
    Secretary of State

P. S. I have this moment received a note from Lord Clarendon, dated on the 24th Instant, relative to the complaint of J. Hosford Smith, our late consul at Beyrout, of which I transmit you a copy.

(Enclosure.)   Foreign Office, January 24, 1855.

Sir: I have duly considered the documents which you placed in my hands on the 17th Instant, on the subject of the complaints preferred by the American consul at Beyrout against Her Majesty's Consul at Jerusalem; and while I regret that any servant of Her Majesty should have given cause for such a representation being made against him, I am sensible that it is due no less to the United States Government than to the honor of Her Majesty's service that the matter should be most closely investigated.

Lord Napier, her Majesty's Secretary of Embassy at Constantinople, will accordingly be directed to proceed at once to Jerusalem to inquire into the charges brought against Mr. Consul Finn, and he will be desired on his passage through Beyrout to announce his arrival to the American Consul there, & invite him to accompany him to Jerusalem for the purpose of being present at the investigation, and he will request him to produce before him, for examination, such evidence as he may wish to offer in support of his complaints against Her Majesty's Consul.

I have accordingly the honor to suggest that you should apprise the United States Consul of the object for which Her Majesty's Secretary of Embassy has been sent to Syria, and request him to proceed in such manner as may best serve to elucidate the matters which are to form the subject of inquiry.

I have the honor to be, with the highest consideration, Sir,

Your most obedient humble servant,

(Signed) CLARENDON.

TO LORD CLARENDON.

(Enclosure in No. 59.[1])

LEGATION OF THE UNITED STATES,

LONDON 27 January 1855.

MY LORD:

I have received your note of the 24th Instant, & am gratified to learn that you have determined to investigate the complaints preferred by Mr. J. Hosford Smith, late Consul of the United States at Beyrout, against Mr. James Finn, Her Majesty's Consul at Jerusalem. I hasten, however, to remind you that in the copy of Mr. Marcy's Despatch which I had the honor of communicating to you, Mr. Smith is designated as "*late* United States Consul at Beyrout;" and I know not who may have been appointed his successor, nor where that gentleman is at present. I shall, however, immediately address a letter to the Consul of the United States at Beyrout, and request him, whoever he may be, to furnish all the aid in his power to Lord Napier in the prosecution of the investigation.

I have the honor to be, with the highest consideration,

Your most obedient servant,

(Signed) JAMES BUCHANAN.

THE EARL OF CLARENDON,

&c. &c. &c.

---

[1] Despatch to Mr. Marcy, No. 59, Feb. 2, 1855, infra.

TO MR. WOOD.

(Enclosure in No. 59.[1])

LEGATION OF THE UNITED STATES,

LONDON 27 January 1855.

SIR:

I some time since received a Despatch from the Hon: William L. Marcy, Secretary of State, dated on the 26th October last, from which the following is an extract:—" Mr. J. Hosford Smith, late United States Consul at Beyrout, in Syria, has addressed a letter to this Department under date the 5th June last, accompanied by a statement in detail relative to certain proceedings of James Finn, Esqr., Her Britannic Majesty's Consul at Jerusalem. From this statement it appears that Mr. Finn has behaved in a manner so improper in regard to Mr. Murad, the United States Vice Consul at Jerusalem, and in regard to certain citizens of the United States residing in that quarter, as to justify and require a representation upon the subject to be made to Her Majesty's Government. The report adverted to states, in its closing paragraph, that a copy would be transmitted to our Legation at London." The Despatch then proceeds to instruct me to bring this subject to the notice of Lord Clarendon, and " request that such explanations may be required of Mr. Finn as the report seems to call for,"—all of which I have accordingly done. I also, on the suggestion of Mr. Marcy, delivered to his Lordship the copy of the report in my possession. The original will, doubtless, be found on record in your Consulate.

In answer to my representations, I received, on yesterday, a note from Lord Clarendon, of which I transmit you a copy; and I have no doubt that in furnishing all the aid in your power to Lord Napier in the investigation of the very serious charges against Mr. Finn, you will be acting in conformity to the wishes of your Government. Indeed, I feel confident you would receive instructions to this effect, if they could be furnished in time.

Yours very respectfully

(Signed)   JAMES BUCHANAN.

HENRY WOOD, ESQUIRE,
    U. S. Consul, Beyrout.

---

[1] Despatch to Mr. Marcy, No. 59, Feb. 2, 1855, infra.

FROM VISCOUNT CANNING.

(Enclosure in No. 59.[1])

GENERAL POST OFFICE, January,[2] 1855.

MY DEAR SIR: My desire, if possible, to meet your wishes has prevented my replying earlier to your private note of the 15th instant. I regret to say, however, that, after again very carefully considering the subject, it is not in my power to make any proposal in regard to our transit rates on the correspondence between the United States and France.

The enclosed paper shows the modifications which have recently been introduced into our treaty with France; but the question of transit rates is still undecided, and although negotiations are in progress, I have little hope that they will be brought to a conclusion before the date mentioned in your note of the 3d of March.

Meanwhile, seeing that as yet no answer has been given to Lord Clarendon's letter to Mr. Ingersoll of May, 1853, I would suggest for your consideration whether it is not right that the full statement of the views of her majesty's government contained in that letter should receive a reply; and whether, if those views be objected to by your government, the grounds of objection should not be explained, and a distinct proposition made on the part of the United States.

On referring to the treaty of 1848, you will find that article 12 throws no peculiar obligations on England, though she alone of the three States concerned has as yet made any sacrifices. As stated by Lord Clarendon, the British government is willing, on certain conditions, to make a still further sacrifice, and I have reason to believe that France also is willing to reduce her charge on the correspondence in question; but she expects, and I think not unreasonably, that if France and England reduce their charges, the United States should do the same. As yet, however, the government of the United States, though pressing England for further reduction, has not, I believe, proposed any on their own part.

Believe me yours, very faithfully,

CANNING.

HON. JAMES BUCHANAN, &c., &c., &c.

TO VISCOUNT CANNING.

(Enclosure in No. 59.[3])

Private. LEGATION OF THE UNITED STATES.

LONDON, 1 February 1855.

MY LORD:

In acknowledging your Lordship's note dated " January,

---

[1] Despatch to Mr. Marcy, No. 59, Feb. 2, 1855, infra. This note from Viscount Canning is printed in S. Ex. Doc. 73, 33 Cong. 2 Sess. 65.

[2] So dated.

[3] Despatch to Mr. Marcy, No. 59, Feb. 2, 1855, infra. This note is printed in S. Ex. Doc. 73, 33 Cong. 2 Sess. 68.

1855," and received on Monday last, I must express my regret that you have not been able, as in November last you had hoped you would be, to make any proposal in regard to transit rates between Great Britain and the United States. Such a proposal might have proved the basis of a new Postal arrangement founded on principles of equal and just reciprocity between the parties; and rendered it unnecessary for the American Government to decide whether they will give the notice necessary to terminate the existing Convention.

Under this Convention, the United States pay Great Britain for transit service just double the sum they receive for a similar service; and their citizens in corresponding with France are taxed six cents more on each letter of a quarter of an ounce when sent by an American than if conveyed by a British steamer. Besides, the Convention is so defective as to have caused the British Postal authorities to believe that they have a right to charge and receive, as they actually did for a considerable period, the sea postage on all correspondence between the United States and France, via England, sent across the Atlantic in American Mail Packets, precisely as though the service had been rendered by British Packets, thus compelling those who corresponded by the American line to pay double sea postage.

At our interview in November last, I expressed what would be my sincere regret should the Government of the United States feel itself compelled, in self-defence, to resort to measures necessary, in its judgment, to produce a just and equal reciprocity in the postal relations between the two countries. These might give birth to a petty war of postal restrictions which could not fail to prove injurious to both, and especially to the British North American Provinces, whose trade with the United States has recently been placed on such a satisfactory footing by the Reciprocity Treaty. And all this, simply because Great Britain declines to relinquish 6d. per ounce for the purpose of equalizing her transit rates with those of a country to which her exports in 1853, (I have not seen a statement of those of 1854), were within a million and a half of being equal to those to all the nations on the Continent, Turkey alone excepted.

It is true, as your Lordship remarks, that no formal answer has been given to Lord Clarendon's letter to Mr. Ingersoll of May, 1853; and this solely because the subject had been exhausted, on our part, in the former correspondence, and this letter left no reason to hope that a continuance of it could be productive of a favorable result.

But the letter of Lord Clarendon, although not formally, has been substantially, and in my estimation satisfactorily answered in the letter of Postmaster General Campbell to Secretary Marcy of July 19th, 1853, which I left with your Lordship in November last, and of which I presume you have taken a copy. It would have been easy for me, as it would still be, to embody the facts and arguments so clearly presented in that letter in a formal note to Lord Clarendon; but your note of January shows, I regret to say, how unavailing this would have proved.

I return you my thanks for the copy of your Postal Convention with France, and I should feel still further obliged to you for a second copy, as well as two copies of the Convention of the 3d April, 1843.

Yours very respectfully,
(Signed)　JAMES BUCHANAN.

VISCOUNT CANNING.

TO MR. MARCY.[1]

No. 59.　　LEGATION OF THE UNITED STATES.

LONDON, 2 February 1855.

SIR:

In my last Despatch, No. 58, of the 26 ultimo, I sent a copy of Lord Clarendon's note to me of the 24th ultimo, relative to the complaint of J. Hosford Smith, our late Consul at Beyrout, against James Finn, Her Majesty's Consul at Jerusalem. I now transmit you a copy of my answer to Lord Clarendon's note, dated on the 27th January, and of my letter of the same date to Henry Wood, Esquire, our Consul at Beyrout. As the mail for the East will not leave London until Sunday, the 4th Instant, this delay has enabled me, by the arrival of the American Almanac in the mean time, to add the proper name of the Consul to the direction of the letter.

The Exequatur for F. B. Wells, Esqr., appointed Consul of the United States to Bermuda, was received on the 27th

----

[1] MSS. Department of State, 66 Despatches from London. The part of the despatch relating to postal matters is printed in S. Ex. Doc. 73, 33 Cong. 2 Sess. 63.

ultimo, and this, together with his Commission, has been forwarded to him at his post.

I have at length received "the Box containing two copies of the first part of Volume 15 of Captain Wilkes' Exploring Expedition," and shall immediately deliver these copies to Lord Clarendon, as I had already delivered to him, some time since, the two copies of the Second Part of volume 14 of the same work.

I transmit, in compliance with the request of the Council of "the Society of Arts, Manufactures, & Commerce," London, a copy of certain resolutions passed at their meeting on the 24th ultimo, in relation to the late reduction on international postage between Great Britain and France, together with the accompanying letter to myself from their Secretary, Mr. P. Le Neve Foster, of the 27th ultimo.

Having waited in vain for the "proposal" from Lord Canning (vide the Postscript to my Despatch No. 49, of 21 November last) in regard to the rates of Transit Postage between Great Britain and the United States, I deemed it proper, on the 15th ultimo, to address him a note reminding him of the subject. To this he answered by his note of "January, 1855," and I replied on the 1st Instant. I transmit copies of these three notes.

Although I think I understand our Postal difficulties with Great Britain tolerably well, yet the subject involves so much detail which can be perfectly understood only by those practically acquainted with it, that I do not feel great confidence in myself. *Should the Postmaster General,* after advising with the President and Cabinet, deem it expedient that the letter of Lord Clarendon to Mr. Ingersoll of May, 1853, shall receive a formal answer, according to the suggestion in the note of Lord Canning, I would respectfully suggest that this, or at least a precise statement of what it ought to contain, might be prepared by Judge Campbell. The Foreign Office here is, in fact, merely the organ of the Postmaster General of Great Britain in communicating with Foreign Governments on Postal affairs; and I should feel gratified if our Postmaster General would act upon the same principle. In this manner the Postmasters General of the two countries, who of all men are best acquainted with the subject, could conduct the correspondence using merely the signatures of the appropriate official organs for Foreign Affairs.

Although I entertain but little hope that our Postal difficulties with Great Britain will be brought to a satisfactory conclusion until after the United States shall have evinced a determination to act, yet to enable me to meet any contingency which may arise, I greatly desire to receive from our Post Office Department *such an Article or Articles supplementary to the existing Convention, drawn out at length,* as they would be willing to accept. This would render any mistake on my part impossible. It is true that the conclusion of such Articles would not be necessary to enable the British Government to do us justice in regard to the transit rates, yet they would prove a sure guide for my conduct.

Lord Clarendon informs me, by a note of yesterday, that my application of the 29th ultimo " for the discharge of Joseph Cassidy, alias Blanchard, from Her Majesty's Naval Service had been forwarded to the Admiralty, with a recommendation that it should be complied with."

Yours very respectfully,

JAMES BUCHANAN.

WILLIAM L. MARCY,
      Secretary of State.

ENCLOSURES.

Mr. Buchanan to Ld. Clarendon, 27 January, 1855. (Supra.)
Mr. Buchanan to Henry Wood, Esqr., Beyrout, same date. (Supra.)
Resolutions of Council of " Society of Arts, Manufactures & Commerce."
Mr. Foster's letter to Am. Minister, Jan. 27th, 1855.
Mr. Buchanan to Lord Canning, Jan. 15, 1855. (Supra.)
Lord Canning to Mr. Buchanan, with Postal Convention with France, " January, 1855," (Supra, after Jan. 27, 1855.)
Mr. Buchanan to Ld. Canning, 1 February, 1855. (Supra.)

TO MR. MARCY.[1]

No. 60.   LEGATION OF THE UNITED STATES.

LONDON, 9 February 1855.

SIR:

. . . You will perceive from the Public Journals that, after an interregnum of ten days, Lord Palmerston has succeeded in forming a Ministry. Judging from the antecedents of the

---

[1] MSS. Department of State, 67 Despatches from England.

new Premier, the change will not be for the better so far as our Country is concerned.

Yours very respectfully,

JAMES BUCHANAN.

HON: WILLIAM L. MARCY,
    Secretary of State.

P. S.   I send a copy of a note which I have this moment received from Lord Clarendon stating that the discharge of Joseph Cassidy, alias Blanchard, has been ordered by the Lords Commissioners of the Admiralty.

TO MR. MARCY.[1]

No. 61.   LEGATION OF THE UNITED STATES.
                    LONDON, 16 February, 1855.

SIR:

Since the Ministerial Crisis all public business has been suspended in this country, except such as relates to the existing war with Russia.   From a conversation which I casually had with Lord Aberdeen on the day before the vote against his Ministry in the House of Commons, I was confirmed in the belief that the Central American questions would have been settled, had he remained in power a few weeks longer.   The accession of Lord Palmerston, should he retain his often expressed opinions, will render this impossible.

You will be informed of the progress of the existing war against Russia, and the prospects of peace, by the London Times and other British Journals.   I may say, however, that I have just been told, by a high authority, that the Queen feels deeply mortified at the mismanagement of the war and the disasters which her brave troops have suffered in the Crimea.   The contrast presented there between the condition of the French and English forces is galling to the pride of every Englishman, and they loudly complain of Aristocratic incompetency.

But I sat down only to communicate to you a fact unknown to the public here, which was revealed to me by a Member of

---

[1] MSS. Department of State, 67 Despatches from England.   A part of the first paragraph of this despatch, relating to Central American questions, is printed in H. Ex. Doc. 1, 34 Cong. 1 Sess. I. 69.

the British Parliament who has recently returned from France, where he had several confidential interviews with the Emperor. He authorized me to inform you of it in confidence.

The Emperor read him a Despatch, which he had prepared himself with great care.   Of course it was signed by Drouyn de L'Huys.   A Copy had been delivered to Lord Cowley at Paris, and another sent to Count Walewski, in London.

This proposes that, in the future progress of the war, France shall furnish five soldiers for one furnished by England; *but that the command of the joint forces shall be entrusted to a French General,* both nations to pay an equal portion of the expense.   The Emperor, also, proposes, to place the combined fleet under the command of a British Admiral.

This proposition proves conclusively that Louis Napoleon is dissatisfied with the manner in which the war in the Crimea has been conducted by his ally.   In this view, I do not think the British Ministry will dare to assent to it.

The governing class in this country are doubtless anxious for peace.   The continuance of the war may still further demonstrate the incompetency of the existing system successfully to govern the country, and the necessity of a large infusion of the popular element in high places.   It is, also, the interest of the Czar to make peace, because it is now certain he will not be able to accomplish his object and annex Constantinople.   It would be wise then for him to bide his time.   But what of the Emperor of the French?   The conclusion of a peace unpopular in England could only change an administration; but peace without glory and without the capture of Sebastopol might in France change a dynasty.   In truth, the complications are so multifarious that no one can now venture to predict future events.   They expect much from the Mission of Lord John Russell to Vienna; but without detracting from his real merits, I think I may confidently venture to say that he never would have filled so large a space in the public eye had he not been a scion of the House of Bedford.

Yours very respectfully,

James Buchanan.

Hon: Wm. L. Marcy,
     Secretary of State.

TO LORD CLARENDON.

(Enclosure in No. 62.[1])

[March 1, 1855.]

The Undersigned, Envoy Extraordinary and Minister Plenipotentiary of the United States, has the honor to recall the attention of the Earl of Clarendon, Her Majesty's Principal Secretary of State for Foreign Affairs, to the subject of concluding a Consular Convention between the two Governments.

The correspondence of the Undersigned with American Consuls in different portions of the British Empire convinced him at an early period of his mission of the great value and importance of such a convention to the foreign commerce of both nations. Having brought this subject to the notice of the Earl of Clarendon in conversation, he was encouraged to believe that their opinions concerning it coincided. In consequence, he obtained from his Government instructions and a full Power to conclude such a Convention, and on the 23d of November last had the honor of submitting to the Earl of Clarendon a printed copy of the existing Consular Convention of the 23d February, 1853, between the United States and the Emperor of the French, with some amendments, as the basis of the negotiation.

The Undersigned was subsequently informed by the Earl of Clarendon that serious objections existed to several of the details of this Convention; whereupon, in order to obviate these difficulties, he proposed to confine the negotiation to three points, which he deemed the most essential. These were,—1. That seamen of the one party deserting from merchant vessels or ships of war whilst in the Ports of the other party should be restored. 2. That individuals who had been guilty of murder, mutiny, or other high crimes on board the merchant vessels of one party on the high seas, beyond the territorial jurisdiction of either, should not be permitted to escape on the arrival of such vessels in the Ports of the other party. And 3. That the merchant vessels of the one party, upon touching or arriving at the Ports of the other, should not have their voyages interrupted or destroyed by vexatious law suits arising out of trifling disputes between the masters and crews of such vessels, and relating exclusively to them, which could be much better adjusted upon their return to their own country.

---

[1] Despatch to Mr. Marcy, No. 62, March 9, 1855, infra.

The Undersigned, having since learned that the British Government are not yet entirely satisfied to accede to these three propositions, has deemed it proper to present them in the form of three distinct Articles, which he has now the honor of enclosing to the Earl of Clarendon. He will make a very few observations on each of them. And,

1. In regard to restoring deserters. The wonder is, that a stipulation for this purpose should have been so long delayed between two nations whose commercial intercourse is so vast. It is obviously the dictate of mutual justice, as well as policy, that seamen of the one arriving in the Ports of the other should not be permitted to desert their vessels and leave the master without the necessary crew. The United States have Treaties with all other commercial nations providing an appropriate remedy for this evil. From the information which the Undersigned has received he believes that in the Ports of the United States deserters from British merchant vessels have been generally restored in the same manner as those from the vessels of other nations. The same inconvenience and loss have not, therefore, been experienced by British as by American vessels. As soon, however, as it shall become extensively known that an unlimited license is reciprocally permitted by the two countries to desertion of the seamen of the one in the Ports of the other, the balance of injury will at least be equalised.

Surely it would be no hardship on the seamen of either nation to compel them to perform their contract according to its terms. Besides, a provision to this effect would prevent desertion, and render the application of the remedy, in most cases, unnecessary.

2. If it would be wrong to permit deserters from merchant vessels to escape, it would be much more so to suffer those who have committed murder, mutiny, or other high crimes on ship board, beyond the territorial jurisdiction of either of the parties, to go at large perfectly free from all danger of trial and punishment upon their arrival in the ports of the other party. A bare statement of this proposition would seem to be sufficient. The necessity for a Treaty stipulation on this subject can not be more forcibly illustrated than by the case, perfectly within the Earl of Clarendon's knowledge, of mutiny which occurred on board the American ship " Sovereign of the Seas," in the month of March last, on her voyage from Melbourne to London. On that occasion, ten persons proved to have been guilty of mutiny

were discharged from confinement, for the reason that no law exists in Great Britain authorising their detention. And indeed, Captain Warner, the master of the vessel, deemed himself quite fortunate in having escaped a suit for false imprisonment, with which he had been threatened by the mutineers. Thus, as the law stands at present, mutiny may be committed on the high seas on board any American vessel bound to a British Port, with perfect impunity. The lives of the passengers and the crew may thus be endangered or destroyed, and the property in freight, whether belonging to American Citizens or British subjects, be indiscriminately plundered.

At an early period of the history of the United States, instructions were issued to American Consuls abroad, prescribing the mode in which they should proceed by deposition to ascertain the guilt of individuals charged with having committed " piracy, mutiny, or any other offence against the laws of the United States " on board of American vessels arriving in their respective consular districts; and, after having performed this duty, they were then directed " to apply to the local authorities for means of securing the offenders while they remain in Port, and to provide the means of sending them without delay to the United States for trial." The Undersigned has never heard that such an appeal to the local authorities of any other country has been disregarded, though he is satisfied that no law exists in this country which would justify such British authorities in interfering. Hence has arisen, even with a view to self protection, the absolute necessity of a Treaty stipulation to prevent the greatest criminals from being turned loose to prey upon society.

3. The third Article, which is similar to that now in force between the United States and several commercial nations, will require a brief explanation. The principle on which it rests is, that the great interests of commerce should not be seriously injured by trifling differences and disputes which may have arisen during the previous voyage between the master and the crew of a British vessel arriving in an American Port, and so vice versa, in no manner affecting individuals of the country where the vessel temporarily remains. This Article, therefore, relates exclusively to such disputes, and prohibits the parties from commencing law suits against each other before a foreign tribunal, concerning wages, contracts, and the internal police of the vessel, which can be far more satisfactorily decided after their return home, by the tribunals of the country to which the vessel belongs.

But from abundant caution, and in order to prevent the possibility of injustice in cases requiring a speedy redress, the Article proposes to refer such disputes, for immediate but temporary adjustment, to the Consul of the proper country, acquainted with its laws and usages, leaving either party at perfect liberty, on the return home of the vessel, to pursue his remedy just as though there had been no such adjustment.

Great inconvenience and loss have resulted from these petty law suits in British Ports to American vessels. A single litigious or mischievous person on board, by instituting a suit against the master of a British or American vessel in a Port of the other party at which she happens to touch or arrive, may retard or break up the voyage altogether. The master may not be able to find the necessary security at a place where he is entirely unknown, and his imprisonment is the consequence. And even if he can obtain security, it is, in most instances, out of the question that he should be able to return and attend the trial. Surely neither Great Britain nor the United States have any reason to distrust the Judiciary of the other in deciding the differences among their own people, according to their own laws; and the master, officers, and crew cannot suffer injustice by merely postponing their law suits until the termination of the voyage and return home of the vessel.

The Government of the Undersigned is convinced that the embodiment of the three accompanying Articles, with such amendments as may be deemed advisable, in a Convention, would be highly advantageous to the commerce of both countries; and could do no possible injury to either. Other stipulations might be beneficial; but these are the most important.

The Undersigned has the honor to renew to the Earl of Clarendon the assurance of his distinguished consideration.

(Signed)   JAMES BUCHANAN.

LEGATION OF THE UNITED STATES,
    March 1st, 1855.
THE RIGHT HONBLE. THE EARL OF CLARENDON,
    &c., &c., &c.

ARTICLE I.—Deserters.

That Deserters from the Merchant vessels or ships of war of either of the high contracting parties, whilst in the Ports of the other, shall be restored. For this purpose the proper Consuls General, Consuls, Vice Consuls, and Commercial Agents of the one party may apply in writing to any Court, Judge, Justice, or other Magistrate of the other party, having competent power to issue warrants, stating that the person or persons therein named has or have deserted from a merchant vessel or ship of war whilst in any Port of the other party, and on proof by the exhibition of the Register of the vessel, ship's roll, or other official document, that such person or persons belonged at the time of desertion to the crew of any such vessel or ship of war, it shall be the duty of the said Court, Judge, Justice, or other Magistrate to issue his or their warrants to cause the said person or persons to be arrested for examination; and if on examination the facts stated are found to be true, then the person or persons so arrested shall be delivered up to the proper Consul General, Consul, Vice Consul, or Commercial Agent, to be sent back to the vessel or vessels from which they had deserted, or on the request and at the expense of the said Consuls General, Consuls, Vice Consuls, or Commercial Agents, they shall be detained in confinement until an opportunity shall be found to send them back to the Country to which the vessel from which they had deserted belongs. And the said Consuls General, Consuls, Vice Consuls, and Commercial Agents of the respective parties shall receive all necessary aid and assistance from the proper local authorities of the other party, for the search, arrest, detention, and sending back of such deserters. Provided, that no such person shall be detained in confinement more than three months after his arrest, but at the end of that period shall be set at liberty and shall not again be molested for the same cause: And provided, also, that if any such deserter shall have committed any crime or offence, his surrender may be delayed until the proper tribunal before which the case shall be depending or may be cognizable shall have pronounced its sentence and this sentence shall have been carried into effect.

Article 2.—Criminals.

When the crimes of Mutiny or Revolt, or the attempt to commit Mutiny or Revolt, Murder, or Assault with intent to commit Murder, Piracy, Robbery, &c., &c., &c., &c., have been committed on board the Merchant vessels of one of the contracting parties on the high seas and beyond the territorial jurisdiction of either, the accused persons shall not be suffered to escape on their arrival in such vessels in the Ports of the other party, but shall be sent to the country for trial against whose laws they have offended. For this purpose, it shall be the duty of the Consul General, Consul, Vice Consul, or Commercial Agent at the Port where such merchant vessel shall have arrived, to make application in writing to any Court, Judge, Justice, or other Magistrate having competent power to issue warrants, for a warrant to cause such accused person to be brought before him for examination, as well as process to compel the attendance of witnesses. And it shall be the duty of the said Consul General, Consul, Vice Consul, or Commercial Agent to cause to be brought before the said Court, Judge, Justice, or other Magistrate, the witnesses to prove the commission of such crime, whose testimony shall be taken by deposition signed by the said witnesses, and if it shall appear to such Court, Judge, Justice, or Magistrate, that the testimony thus given is sufficient in law to warrant the trial of the accused for the crime with which he is charged, then it shall be his or their duty to remand him to the custody of the master of the vessel from on board of which he had been brought for examination, to be sent therein for trial to the appropriate jurisdiction, or upon the request and at the proper cost and charge of the Consul General, Consul, Vice Consul, or Commercial Agent to cause him to be imprisoned & confined, until he can be sent for trial to the appropriate jurisdiction in some other merchant vessel belonging to the same party. And the said Consuls General, Consuls, Vice Consuls, and Commercial Agents of the one party shall receive all necessary aid and assistance from the proper local authorities of the. other party, to prevent the escape of such accused persons, and to cause them to be arrested in case they shall have escaped, and for securing them from the time of their arrival in Port until their departure. Provided this period shall in no case exceed three months: And provided, also, that all expenses incurred under this Article shall be borne by the proper Consul General, Consul, Vice Consul, or Commercial Agent.

ARTICLE 3.

Consular Jurisdiction in cases exclusively pertaining to the Masters and crews of vessels belonging to the country of the Consul.

In order to prevent the interruption or loss of the voyages of merchant vessels by vexatious law suits for trifling causes, in a foreign country, between the master, officers, and crew, which may be more appropriately referred for final decision to the tribunals of the country to which such vessels belong, it is agreed that the said Consuls General, Consuls, Vice Consuls, and Commercial Agents of the one party shall have the exclusive right to sit as Judges and Arbitrators in reference to disputes concerning wages, the execution of contracts, and the internal order and police of such vessels, whilst in the Ports of the other party, between the masters, officers, and crew of such vessels, without the interference of the local authorities, unless the conduct of the master, officers, or crew should disturb the order or tranquillity of the Country, or the said Consuls General, Consuls, Vice Consuls, or Commercial Agents should require their assistance, which shall not then be refused, in executing or supporting their own decisions. But this species of Judgment or decision shall only have a temporary effect, and shall not deprive the contending parties of their right to resort, on their return, to the judicial authority of the Country to which the vessel belongs.

TO MR. MARCY.[1]

No. 62.　　　LEGATION OF THE UNITED STATES.
LONDON, 9 March 1855.

SIR:

I have the honor to acknowledge the receipt of your Despatches No. 75 and 76 of the 6th and 12th Ultimos, respectively, and to inform you that in pursuance of the permission granted by the former, I have drawn upon the Department in favor of Col. A. H. Sibley for the sum of $284"46=£58"15"5.

---

[1] MSS. Department of State, 67 Despatches from England.

I transmit two copies of a notification of the blockade of Russian Ports in the Black Sea by the combined British and French Naval Forces, inserted in a Supplement to the London Gazette of the 2d Instant, together with a copy of the communication from the Foreign Office to myself which accompanied them.

I also transmit the copy of a note addressed by me to Lord Clarendon, on the 1st Instant,[1] proposing a Consular Convention between the two Governments, together with a copy of the three Articles referred to therein.

It would be tedious and useless to trouble you with a statement in detail of what passed at the different conferences between his Lordship and myself in relation to this Convention. Suffice it to say that an obstruction has been cast in the way of this measure, so necessary for the benefit of our commerce, by the Solicitor General, (Sir Richard Bethell.) His objections, which have been read to me, prove conclusively that he does not understand the subject. They did not appear to be satisfactory to Lord Clarendon; but yet he observed that, as it would be the official duty of the Solicitor General to carry the Bill necessary to give effect to such a Convention through the House of Commons, it would be vain to conclude it against his opposition or without the assurance of his support. I told him that, although it was not for me to judge, I should yet feel no apprehension whatever of the result in the House, notwithstanding the objections of the Solicitor General. As I should not have undertaken this business unless I had been previously satisfied that Lord Clarendon entirely coincided with myself, I deemed it proper, especially as he has never individually manifested any change of opinion, to bring the subject in a formal manner to his notice.

One incident I ought not to forget. In a conference some time since, he said there was no necessity for a Convention so far as Deserters from our Merchant Ships were concerned: that all the United States had to do, in order to secure their apprehension and return, was to accede to the terms of the Foreign Deserters Act of 1852; and then Her Majesty would issue an order in Council which, in this respect, would accomplish all we desired. I asked to see a copy of this Act; and found upon its perusal that it applied to " Seamen *not being slaves* who desert from Merchant Ships," &c., &c., of Foreign Powers. I then informed his Lord-

---

[1] Note to Lord Clarendon, March 1, 1855, supra.

ship, in emphatic terms, that the Congress of the United States
never would pass, and in my opinion never ought to pass, an
Act to give effect to this Act of Parliament. It was entirely
out of the question to imagine it possible that my Government
would consent to make the discrimination which this Act proposes, between slaves and freemen deserting from our vessels.
And that although I believed but few if any slaves were employed
as seamen, we could never sanction the principle which would
restore the freeman and grant permission to the slave to escape.
I have since heard nothing more of this Foreign Deserters Act.
It was passed on the 17th June, 1852, 15 Victoria, Cap. 26, and
is entitled " An Act to enable Her Majesty to carry into effect
Arrangements made with Foreign Powers for the apprehension
of Seamen who desert from their ships."

Count Kielmansegge, the Hanoverian Minister, called on
the 15th February last, and informed me he had just learned
from his Government that there was a mistake in the preamble
to the Convention recently concluded between him and myself,
in copying into it the following words from our Treaties with
Prussia and Bavaria: " The Constitution and Laws of Hanover, however, not allowing the Hanoverian Government to surrender their own subjects for trial before a Foreign Court of
Justice, a strict reciprocity requires, that the Government of the
United States shall be equally free from any obligation to
surrender citizens of the United States;" and he requested me
to write to Washington and have this mistake corrected. I told
him it was then too late, as the Senate would adjourn on the
3d of March. He asked if we could not correct this error in
form by a protocol on the exchange of ratifications, which I,
of course, answered in the negative.

He called again on Tuesday last and manifested much
anxiety upon the subject. After considerable conversation, it
was agreed that I should ascertain from you whether, after the
ratifications had been exchanged in due form, he might address
me a note expressing the intention of the Hanoverian Government not to publish, as a part of the Convention, these words
of the preamble inserted by mistake. I told him that as they
constituted no part of the Treaty and were merely an unfounded
recital, I did not think that you would object to the omission of
them from the copy published in Hanover; but that the whole
must be published in the United States. I do not perceive any
valid objection to this course; but I shall not, as I informed him,

proceed to the exchange of ratifications until you inform me that it will meet your approbation. Please to let me hear from you on this matter with as little delay as may be convenient. Should the Count agree to exchange the ratifications in the usual form, without afterwards addressing me any such note as I have mentioned, then I shall proceed to the exchange, leaving it to the Government of Hanover, on its own responsibility, to act in regard to publication as it may think proper.

General D'Oxholm, the Danish Minister at this Court, has often conversed with me on the subject of the Sound dues. A few days since he placed in my hands a letter addressed to myself, dated on the 26th ultimo, which I enclose to you in compliance with his request.

The death of the Emperor Nicholas and the accession of the Emperor Alexander 2d to the throne of Russia were at first generally considered as harbingers of a speedy peace. The funds in consequence immediately rose at London, Paris, and Vienna. Serious doubts have since arisen in the public mind on the subject, and the funds have fallen. One reason for this change is found in the general tone of the Manifesto of the new Emperor, especially in that part of it where he promises to accomplish the incessant wishes of Peter, Catharine, Alexander, and his father. I do not attribute much importance to this phraseology, unless indeed it has been dictated by the old fanatical Muscovite party, at the head of which is Constantine, the brother of the Emperor. This Prince and his party have undoubtedly had a fixed purpose of re-establishing the Byzantine empire and placing himself upon the throne of Constantinople. In my judgment, it is palpable that this object cannot be accomplished as a result of the present war, and therefore I believe that the Emperor Nicholas was sincere in desiring peace, and that his successor is equally sincere in this desire. Indeed, his prompt renewal of the powers of Prince Gortschakoff is strong evidence to this effect.

It is my impression that the great difficulty will proceed from France. Louis Napoleon is the soul as well as the strength of the Alliance. England plays but a secondary part; and anxious for peace as are her Governing Class, they must have united with the French Emperor in authorising the demand of such terms as he thought proper to exact; and these may be of a character to which the new Czar cannot accede.

Every effort has been made by the British Government to dissuade Louis Napoleon from his purpose of going to the

Crimea; and it is understood without effect.   It is certain that
he heard the appeals of Lord John Russell without manifesting
any symptom of change.   After sending such a magnificent army
to the Crimea, it may be dangerous for him to make peace without
achieving some great victory.   Besides, like his uncle, he is a
believer in his own destiny.   To join the army and win such a
victory would revive the glories of the great Emperor.   Sebastopol once taken, Louis Napoleon may then be willing to make
peace; but after this event, it is impossible to foresee what new
complications may arise.   These are not merely my own speculations, but those of well informed people here.

Yours very respectfully,
JAMES BUCHANAN.

HON: WILLIAM L. MARCY,
    Secretary of State.

————————

TO MR. MARCY.[1]

No. 63.   LEGATION OF THE UNITED STATES.
LONDON, 16 March, 1855.

SIR:

I have the honor to transmit to you two copies of a notification, received from Lord Clarendon, and inserted in a Supplement
to the London Gazette of the 9th Instant, announcing that the
Blockade instituted by the combined British and French Naval
Forces of the mouths of the Danube has been raised; and giving
notice that cruisers will be stationed off the mouths of that river
to capture any vessels laden with contraband of war destined for
the use of the enemy.

His Lordship requests, in his note to me of the 10th Instant,
that I " will have the goodness to transmit copies of this notification to your [my] Government, in order that it may through
that channel become known to the citizens of the United States."

Yours very respectfully
JAMES BUCHANAN.

HON: WILLIAM L. MARCY,
    Secretary of State.

————————

---

[1] MSS. Department of State, 67 Despatches from England.

FROM MR. SLIDELL.[1]

New Orleans, 3 April, 1855.

My dear Mr. Buchanan:

I wrote you a few hurried lines shortly after the adjournment of Congress. Since then I have read with great pleasure your Ostend manifesto. I say yours, for I think it carries with it internal evidence of its being the product of your sound judgment & practised pen. It has my unqualified approbation both as to form & substance. The only fault that can justly be found with the proceedings is one for which you are not responsible, the unnecessary formality of your meeting and the publicity given to its objects. You were right in your objections to the mode & place of meeting, & I deeply regret that you did not insist upon them. You might have met at Paris or London without any suspicion of your object, or what would have still been better, might have fully interchanged views by correspondence. One thing has struck me as perhaps giving a certain vantage ground to Marcy. It is this—that he seems, so far as I can judge from the published documents, only to invite you to confer about the best means of promoting the acquisition of Cuba by purchase, while you have reviewed the whole question of policy & suggested the possibility of recourse being had to measures of coercion. But as Marcy has not availed himself of this objection, it is probable that good reasons exist for his abstinence, in the papers that have not yet been given to the public. As to Marcy's course, I think that I can very readily account for it. His every thought is directed towards the Presidency, & he fancies that he sees in you the only obstacle to the realisation of his dreams. On this subject he is morbidly susceptible, & is constantly suspecting some deep laid scheme to supplant him. Poor man! if every one whose name has ever been mentioned in connection with the Presidency were translated to another world, I do not believe that he could obtain the vote of a solitary State for his nomination. Rumor is rife, probably without any foundation, that he will leave the Cabinet. On this score I am entirely indifferent, for I have no hope that any change can restore to the President the lost confidence of the party. Say what they will of Nebraska and Know-Nothingism, the personal unpopularity or rather the total want of consideration and influence of the administration has been the chief cause of our reverses. The mass of the party is as sound as ever, but no confidence is reposed in its nominal chief, & a party without a head is doomed to as certain destruction as an army without a general. I have written you a very gloomy letter. Perhaps a shocking cold under which I have been laboring since the adjournment of Congress may have its influence on the view I take of our political future, but I confess that I cannot see anything encouraging in the perspective. My family are all well. The climate of Louisiana seems to agree with them much better than that of Washington, but as I cannot make up my mind to be separated from them for many months at a time, we must run the risk of northern winters. Mrs. S. feels very sensibly the sacrifice of our comfortable home, which we cannot replace at Washington, but as a good wife submits with the best

---

[1] Buchanan Papers, Historical Society of Pennsylvania.

grace she can to what is unavoidable. She begs to be remembered to you. We will leave here in June, pass a few weeks in Washington, & then go to Newport. When do you intend returning home? Believe me ever faithfully
                              Your friend
Hon. James Buchanan,   John Slidell.
     London.

TO MR. MARCY.[1]

No. 64.   Legation of The United States.
                                      London, 5 April, 1855.

Sir:

I have the honor to acknowledge the receipt of your Despatches Nos. 77, 78, 79, and 80, of the 6th, 10th, 10th, and 20th ult. respectively.

There is one circumstance calculated to exercise an unfavorable influence on the relations between the two countries to which I desire to call your special attention; and this is, the profound ignorance which prevails among the mass of otherwise well informed people here concerning the Government, policy, and institutions of our country. All Americans who have travelled in England can testify to the fact. The cause is apparent. The London Journals never republish even a sketch of the debates or proceedings in Congress, and the same may be said, with rare exceptions, of which the President's Message is always an instance, in regard to our most important official documents.

A discussion in the Legislative Assemblies of Prussia, Sardinia, Belgium, or any other European State, on any important subject, is always noticed in these Journals, and the character of their leading statesmen and debaters is brought before the British people. American Statesmen and Parliamentarians who would do honor to any country are here entirely unknown even by name.

Articles from Continental Journals which are supposed to speak, whether officially or semi-officially, the sentiments of their Governments, are republished here with comments; whilst, according to my best recollection, no political article from the Washington Union, or any other Press of a similar character, has ever been republished in London since my arrival in this country.

When other nations are assailed or misrepresented for some reason or other, one or more London Journals are always ready

---

[1] MSS. Department of State, 67 Despatches from England.

and willing to defend them; but against such assaults the United States have no means of self protection. In this respect, no reciprocity exists between the two countries; because the British Government is always defended in our country, and British editorials, as well as news, constitute a principal staple of the whole American Press.

It follows from all this that the masses in this country have not the least idea of the existence of unsettled and dangerous questions between the two Governments. Even a distinguished member of Parliament with whom I am on terms of intimacy, and to whom but a few days ago I gave a copy of Mr. Mason's speech delineating the conduct of British and French officials in different portions of the world, was wholly taken by surprise at the statements which it contains. He had never heard of this speech. Such a speech proceeding from a gentleman deservedly occupying Mr. Mason's high official position in any European Legislative Body, would have attracted great public attention and been a subject of remark in all the leading Journals of this country. In no one of them, however, so far as I have observed, has it been republished or even noticed.

To the same Member of Parliament, I communicated some information concerning the Central American questions. He declared that for years he had supposed these questions had all been amicably and satisfactorily adjusted; and he ridiculed the Mosquito Protectorate. He said, however, that he apprehended no danger from this cause, and expressed his conviction that whenever the correspondence should be given to the world, public opinion in this country would soon compel their settlement. This I believed myself, and, therefore, regretted at the time, as you have reason to know, that the President had not in his last annual Message entered into a brief explanation of the position of the Central American questions. For a similar reason, I now regret that the correspondence on these questions had not been sent to Congress at its last Session. It might have been the means of reopening the negotiations, and this at an auspicious period, when it was peculiarly the interest of the British Government and the British people to have no dangerous outstanding questions with the United States. I should have had the document circulated generally among members of Parliament.

It might be inferred from what has been said that as the Public Press is generally a fair reflection of public opinion, the British people must necessarily be unfriendly or indifferent in their feelings towards the people of the United States. Judging both from my social intercourse in this country, which has been pretty extensive, and from manifestations which I have observed on public occasions, such an inference would not, in the main, be correct. All the numerous associations in this metropolis for literary, charitable, and scientific purposes have an anniversary dinner. To many of these I am invited, and I have attended on several occasions. At these dinners where I have been present, a toast in honor of the United States, or of the President, or of the American Minister, has never failed to call forth enthusiastic cheering; and is always preceded by the kindest remarks and congratulations upon the friendly relations which now so happily unite " the kindred nations."

Having a leisure hour this morning, before going to the Foreign Office by appointment at 4 o'clock I thought it might not be either uninteresting or useless to you to have your attention directed to the facts stated in this Despatch.

Yours very respectfully

JAMES BUCHANAN.

HON: WILLIAM L. MARCY,
    Secretary of State.

TO MR. MARCY.[1]

No. 65.   LEGATION OF THE UNITED STATES.

LONDON, 6 April, 1855.

SIR:

After my Despatch of yesterday's date, I called upon Lord Clarendon at the Foreign Office. The first topics were the existing war, the conference at Vienna, and the prospects of peace. From his Lordship's conversation, he evidently does not consider that these prospects are bright. Similar opinions had been expressed to me by Lord Palmerston a week ago. I ought, however, to observe that on my return home from the Foreign Office, I met Lord Aberdeen on his way there, who immediately asked me what I thought were the prospects of peace. I answered that I had just come from Lord Clarendon, who did not believe that they were favorable. He said that Lord Clarendon had never believed in peace; but it was his own impression that

---

[1] MSS. Department of State, 67 Despatches from England.

if peace should not be concluded at Vienna, Louis Napoleon would be the cause.

Lord Clarendon informed me that Louis Napoleon would visit England on Monday the 16th Instant, and return to Paris on Saturday the 21st; and expressed a strong conviction that he would then, after a brief period, proceed to the Crimea.

I now brought to his Lordship's notice the proposal contained in your Despatch (No. 77.) for the mutual payment of the awards under the claims Convention; with which he expressed himself entirely satisfied. He said he had suggested a similar proposal to Mr. Crampton. He regretted, however, that he could do nothing until after Parliament had appropriated the sum of $329,734.18, which had been awarded to American claimants; but promised to hasten this appropriation by all means in his power. He said the Chancellor of the Exchequer had not found himself able to present " the budget " to the House of Commons before the adjournment for the Easter Holidays; but he would do this immediately after the meeting of Parliament on the 16th Instant, and that I might assure you there should be no unnecessary delay.

In reference to your No. 78,—the Proclamation of the President giving effect to the Fishery and Reciprocity Treaty proves that before it was issued he had received the Act of Parliament to which you refer. We had some conversation on this subject; but not of the least importance.

He then informed me, as he had done on a former occasion, that he believed the three articles of the Consular Convention which I had last proposed, with some slight amendments, were entirely reasonable and would prove equally beneficial to both countries. That on this subject he had cut himself loose entirely from the Law Officers of the Crown, and had informed the Board of Trade, to which they had been referred, that it was a shame no such Treaty stipulations existed between our two great commercial nations; and the Board coincided with him in opinion. He would send the articles to me in the course of a few days, with the proposed trifling amendments, and they would carry a Bill through Parliament enabling them to give effect to the Treaty. I have encountered so many difficulties in this matter that I confess I still entertain some doubts, though not of his Lordship's sincerity, especially as he did not indicate the nature of the amendments.

I then mentioned that I had received a Despatch from you

(No. 78) covering the copy of a Despatch to you from Mr. Wheeler, our Minister in Central America, with copies of accompanying documents; of which I intended to leave him copies. These papers proved conclusively that the inhabitants of Greytown were of a most lawless and tumultuous character; indeed, that they were little better than banditti. That they had no responsible Government, and that life and property there were rendered wholly insecure. That whilst they were permitted to remain in their present lawless state, individuals would be unwilling to entrust their property and their lives over this great transit route; and that these evils could only be effectually remedied by restoring the possession of Greytown to Nicaragua.

For the first time in our intercourse, the placid temper of Lord Clarendon became much excited, and he criticised with some degree of severity the President's Message of December last, relative to the inhabitants of Greytown; he said they had a very good Government there—a Government which had been sanctioned by Mr. Webster himself, when Captain Hollins destroyed the Town. That to this wanton destruction their present condition must be attributed. The poor creatures had had their houses burnt about their ears and their property destroyed, and it was no wonder they should be driven to acts of desperation. He also observed that when the news first arrived, I had expressed the opinion to him that the act of Captain Hollins was not authorised by his Government and would not be justified by it.

In my turn I became excited, and spoke, also, with some degree of severity. I told him that his criticisms on the President's Message were altogether unjust. The character which it had attributed to the outlaws at Greytown was well and richly deserved. That the evidence before the world abundantly demonstrated this fact. It was true I had expressed the opinion to him that Captain Hollins was not justified in going so far as to burn Greytown, and had, in this respect, exceeded his instructions; but this not because its inhabitants did not deserve severe and exemplary punishment. That there never had been a Government in Greytown, deserving the name, since the British first captured it from Nicaragua, and it was a disgrace that such miscreants should occupy this important position on one of the great routes of transit between the two oceans. The property of British subjects as well as of American citizens, to a large amount, was thus constantly exposed to depredation and plunder.

I purposely omit some pretty sharp expressions used on both sides.

We then proceeded to converse in a calm manner in relation to Central American affairs; and I am sorry to say that from this conversation I have reason to believe that my anticipations will be realised in regard to the policy of Lord Palmerston's administration in Central America. I regret that I cannot report this conversation to you to-day in time to have it copied before the closing of the Despatch Bag; which I cannot delay for a later mail to Liverpool, as this is Good Friday, which is kept in England as strictly as though it were the Sabbath.

Not having in the least degree anticipated the feeling manifested by Lord Clarendon in regard to Greytown, and being unable to conjecture its meaning, I have deemed it my duty not to suffer a steamer to depart without communicating to you the fact; otherwise I should have waited and reported the entire conversation of the day by the steamer of next week.

I did not leave a copy of Mr. Wheeler's Despatch and the accompanying documents with Lord Clarendon, because I discovered in the former a paragraph which ought to be omitted. I shall send them to him to-morrow. His Lordship, in the course of the conversation, expressed a favorable opinion of Mr. Wheeler.

Yours very respectfully,

JAMES BUCHANAN.

HON: WILLIAM L. MARCY,
    Secretary of State.

TO MR. MARCY.[1]

No. 66.   LEGATION OF THE UNITED STATES.

LONDON, 7 April 1855.

SIR:

I now proceed to complete the Despatch of yesterday then left unfinished for the reason therein stated. In order, however, that you may justly appreciate the effect of the concluding portion of the conversation of Thursday evening last, between Lord Clarendon and myself, it will be necessary to bring to your notice some previous circumstances.

---

[1] MSS. Department of State, 67 Despatches from England.

In my Despatch (No. 54.) I reported a conversation held on the 28th December last with the Earl of Aberdeen, then Prime Minister, on the Central American questions. From this conversation, there was reason to hope that the British Government, notwithstanding the opinions expressed in Lord Clarendon's Statement of the 2d May, 1854, might eventually consent to settle these questions on terms conformable to the Clayton and Bulwer Treaty and satisfactory to the Government of the United States.

Within two or three days after this conversation, I intimated to Lord Clarendon, but in a purely private and unofficial manner, that should he have any important communication to make to me, it was desirable this should be done in time to reach Washington before the 4th March; because on that day Congress would adjourn. His Lordship, correctly understanding me to refer to the difficulties in Central America, expressed a strong desire to finish our business together; but observed that though small in interest and importance to them, it was large in point of honor. He added that the adoption of Captain Hollins' proceedings and the manner in which the Greytown affair had been vindicated in the President's Message had complicated the matter very much; but that this, however, did not abate his desire and intention to settle the question *somehow* amicably. I replied that there was nothing in the President's Message in regard to the Greytown affair which could give, or was intended to give, just cause of offence to the British Government.

I do not believe that at this time Lord Clarendon had been informed of my conversation with Lord Aberdeen on the 28th December, and I did not allude to it myself, deeming it better that this information should first proceed from the Premier to the Secretary for Foreign Affairs rather than from myself; and this, more especially on an informal occasion.

Having waited until the 17th January last, without hearing from Lord Clarendon, and presuming that ere this Lord Aberdeen must have conversed with him on the subject, I then stated to him at an official interview, as I informed you in my Despatch No. 57, the opinions which had been expressed to me by Lord Aberdeen on the Central American questions. His Lordship intimated, in answer, that Lord Aberdeen might not, or could not, have considered the peculiar position of the question in respect to Ruatan; and I told him that he had specially referred to this very question, and repeated what he had said upon the subject.

Although it was evident Lord Clarendon did not coincide in the opinion of Lord Aberdeen respecting Ruatan, yet he expressed a strong desire to settle the questions, and an entire willingness to yield to the judgment of the Premier. He added that he would converse with Lord Aberdeen upon the subject without delay, and immediately thereafter communicate to me the result.

I waited for some days without receiving any communication from Lord Clarendon, but did not deem this remarkable, because Mr. Roebuck, on Tuesday, the 23d January, the day on which Parliament met after its adjournment for the Christmas Holidays, had given the notice of the motion under which the Aberdeen Ministry fell; and Lord John Russell, on the same day, had resigned his office as President of the Council.

From this time until the final formation of Lord Palmerston's administration, all public business was suspended, except that which was absolutely necessary.

On Friday, January 26, Mr. Roebuck brought forward his motion in the House of Commons, and the debate upon it commenced.

On Sunday, 28th January, I called upon Lord Aberdeen merely to pay him a visit of respect and courtesy. The fate of his Ministry was to be decided the next day in the House of Commons, and the result was then considered doubtful. He was perfectly calm and tranquil. At such a time, and on such an occasion, I had not the least intention of introducing any topic of business. He himself, however, evidently adverting to our previous conversation, though not in express terms, observed I must wait patiently; there would be necessary delays in adjusting the matters in dispute between the two countries, but at last they would all be satisfactorily settled. He added, I might rest assured, whatever might be his fate, there would never be another Prime Minister of England entertaining unfriendly views towards the United States.

Of course, I expressed great satisfaction with what his Lordship had said.

From all this I inferred that Lords Aberdeen and Clarendon had conversed on the Central American questions, and was inclined to augur favorably of the result in case the Aberdeen administration should be sustained by the House of Commons.

The next day, Monday, January 29, Mr. Roebuck's resolution prevailed by a vote of 305 to 148, and Lord Aberdeen resigned his office.

After an interregnum of ten days, and after the Earl of Derby & Lord John Russell had successively failed in attempts to form a Ministry, Lord Palmerston succeeded in accomplishing the object; and on Thursday, 9 February, 1855, the list of the new Ministers was announced in the Public Journals.

From Lord Palmerston's antecedents I had nothing to hope; and, therefore, awaiting the course of events, I had not deemed it advisable again to call Lord Clarendon's attention to the Central American questions, until our conference on Thursday last.

After our conversation on that occasion, in direct reference to the Greytown affair, had ended, I then again adverted to the subject, and said that difficulties of this nature would never cease in Central America—the good understanding between the two Governments would be constantly endangered, and peace and harmony could never be restored among the Central American States themselves, until the questions relating to them should be finally settled between the two Governments. He said there seemed to be an insuperable difficulty in the way, in the opposite constructions placed by the two Governments on the Treaty. Whilst they, on their part, were firmly convinced it meant one thing, we, on our part, were equally convinced it meant another thing. They believed it to be wholly prospective in its character and that it did not interfere with any of their existing possessions in Central America, and they could not consent to surrender Ruatan. I observed that Lord Aberdeen entertained different opinions; and if he had remained in power for some time longer, I believed that these questions would have been satisfactorily adjusted. He told me he thought I was mistaken in regard to Lord Aberdeen's opinions respecting Ruatan. I told him I could not be mistaken in respect to them. I had written them down, with great care, immediately after the conversation took place, and but two days thereafter had reported them to my Government. His Lordship had distinctly stated that their claim to the Bay Islands rested entirely upon the question whether they could be considered as legitimate dependencies of British Honduras, and finally declared he thought it would be difficult for them to maintain that these Islands were such dependencies, at the same time giving his reasons for this opinion. In addition, on the very day before the vote in the House of Commons on Mr. Roebuck's resolution, Lord Aberdeen, in evident reference to our previous conversation, and without the most remote allu-

sion on my part to the subject, had stated to me there would be
necessary delays in adjusting these matters; but he had no doubt
they would all at last be satisfactorily settled.   I further stated
that he, (Lord Clarendon) also, differed from Lord John Russell
in the construction of the Treaty, and took from my pocket an
extract from the Despatch of Lord John to Mr. Crampton, dated
19th January, 1853, and read it to him as follows:—

"While Greytown was virtually a possession and Mosquito
a dependency of Great Britain, it was not unnatural that the
United States should have looked upon such a state of things with
jealousy and aversion, and should have thrown their weight into
the scale of Nicaragua, which contested with Great Britain the
right both to Greytown and Mosquito.   But those circumstances
exist no longer.   The Treaty of April, 1850, has entirely changed
the future,"—[After reading these last words, his Lordship interrupted me, and said emphatically, " Yes, the future; but did
not change the existing position of Great Britain."]—" if not
the present position of Great Britain with respect to Greytown
and Mosquito, and indeed to the whole of Central America; and
the great question now to be solved is how to turn the Mosquito
country to the best account, not merely for the benefit of Great
Britain or of the United States, but for the benefit of the whole
world."

When I had concluded the extract, I asked his Lordship if
it was his construction that the Treaty had produced no change
whatever in regard to their possessions in Central America.   He
declared that such was his construction of the Treaty.   Not even,
said I, in regard to the Mosquito Protectorate?   Yes, said he,
such is our construction of it in regard to the Mosquito Protectorate—the Treaty refers entirely to the future.   I informed
him, emphatically, I was greatly surprised to hear this from his
Lordship.   After a moment's pause, during which I thought he
appeared to be considerably embarrassed, I changed the subject
and called his attention to the case of James Welsh, referred to
in your Despatch No. 80.

From this conversation but faint hope can be entertained of
the adjustment of the Central American questions during the
administration of Lord Palmerston, in a manner which ought
to be satisfactory to the Government of the United States.   Indeed, it may be said with truth that his Lordship, as Minister
for Foreign Affairs, was the author of the modern Mosquito
Protectorate, and he held the same office in 1848, when Great

Britain expelled the Republic of Nicaragua from San Juan de Nicaragua and took possession of it in the name of the Mosquito King.

Lord Palmerston was, also, the Minister for Foreign Affairs in 1841, when the British forces under Col: M'Donald seized the Island of Ruatan from the Republic of Honduras and subjected it to British dominion.

I might refer to other acts and declarations of his Lordship at different periods indicating his aggressive policy in regard to Central America, but this would be wholly unnecessary. Suffice it to say that, from his antecedents and his well known character, we can have but little reason to expect that he will ever carry into execution the Clayton and Bulwer Treaty according to what we firmly believe to be its true construction.

It is yet too early to speculate upon the probable duration of Lord Palmerston's administration. I think I may truly say he has thus far disappointed public expectation; and by filling the offices with a larger proportion of the aristocratic or governing class than any of his predecessors, has given offence to the Liberals. A union between the two extremes, between the conservative and liberal members of the House of Commons, would, any day, place him in a minority. But what then? How could a Ministry be formed out of such heterogeneous materials? This is Lord Palmerston's present and probably his only security.

Yours very respectfully,

JAMES BUCHANAN.

HON: WILLIAM L. MARCY,
    Secretary of State.

P. S. I sent to Lord Clarendon to-day a copy of Mr. Wheeler's Despatch with the paragraph omitted beginning with the words,—"Since I have no other protection," &c., &c., together with copies of the accompanying documents.

TO MR. MARCY.[1]

No. 68.   LEGATION OF THE UNITED STATES.

LONDON, 20 April 1855.

SIR:

I have received your Despatch, No. 84, of the 31 ultimo.

---

[1] MSS. Department of State, 67 Despatches from England.

I have the honor to inform you that on Tuesday last, the 17th Instant, Count Kielmansegge and myself met and exchanged the ratifications of the Convention for the mutual extradition of Fugitives from justice in certain cases, which had been concluded at London on the eighteenth day of January, 1855, between the United States and the Kingdom of Hanover. I read to the Count that portion of your Despatch (No. 84) relating to this subject, with which he was entirely satisfied.

I now transmit, through the Despatch Bag, in obedience to your instructions, the copy of this convention ratified by the King of Hanover, which I received from the Count in exchange for the copy ratified by the President, together with a certificate of the Exchange of Ratifications.

I also send a translation from the German into English of His Hanoverian Majesty's Act of Ratification, furnished me by Count Kielmansegge.

Your Circular of the 29th ultimo, transmitting two copies of the Act of Congress passed at the last Session to regulate the carriage of passengers in steam ships and other vessels, has also been received.

The Emperor and Empress of the French arrived in this city on a visit to the Queen on Monday evening last, and will return to Paris on Saturday. Their reception by the British people has been all they could have desired. Indeed, their visit has been one continued triumph. It is needless for me to enter into particulars, as the public journals furnish these in detail.

The Diplomatic Corps attended yesterday at the French Ambassador's to be presented to the Emperor and Empress. The manner of my reception *by both was peculiarly cordial and kind*. Indeed, this was observed by those present. Considering the brief occasion, I had more than the usual amount of conversation with them. In that with the Emperor, among other things, he expressed a strong desire that peace and friendship might always be maintained between France and the United States and never be interrupted, which sentiment I cordially reciprocated. Perhaps this sentiment is not in exact accordance with a portion of the address read by him on Thursday last at Guildhall,—all of which was evidently prepared with great care & deliberation.

It would seem from your remarks that the three articles of a Consular Convention proposed by me to Lord Clarendon contained something new and unusual. This is not the case. The first and third of the three articles are of the same nature with those of the 9th and 8th articles of our existing Consular Convention with France; but were intended, after different conversations with Lord Clarendon, to be more precise and guarded, and to obviate objections which might be made to these latter articles, as well as to those of a similar character in several of our existing Treaties.

The Second of the three articles is intended simply to carry into effect the 35th Article of the old consular instructions, for the purpose of sending criminals home for trial who had committed offences against the laws of the United States on board of our merchant vessels.

I shall, however, pause in my proceedings and thoroughly re-examine the question.

The necessity for such a Convention with Great Britain on these subjects as we have with other Commercial Nations becomes more apparent every day.   For example, at the very time your Despatch arrived, I received a letter from William Winthrop, Esqr., our Consul at Malta, dated on the 6th Instant, informing me that since the arrival of the American ship, the " Queen of Clippers," in that Port, " more than 20 of her crew have deserted, leaving only fifteen men on board to take care of a ship of 2360 tons,—a number wholly insufficient for the purpose." He adds that these men are on shore threatening to sue the mates for ill treatment.

Mr. Winthrop appealed to the Governor, the Admiral, and the Police to induce them to arrest and restore the Deserters; but all in vain, each expressing regret that he had no authority to act in the premises.

The first Consular Convention with France to which you refer (that of the 14 Nov: 1788) certainly does confer very inconvenient powers upon consuls.   Its 12th article constitutes them judges, respectively, in " all differences and suits between the subjects of the Most Christian King in the United States, or between the citizens of the United States within the dominions of the Most Christian King."   It is not confined " to disputes concerning wages, the execution of contracts, and the internal order and police of such vessels, whilst in the ports of the other party, *between the masters, officers, and crew of such vessels.*" (Vide the proposed 3d article and the 8th article of our present Consular Convention with France, which is probably still too general in its terms.)

I have met General D'Oxholm casually since the receipt of

your Despatch and have made the inquiry of him which you request. He informs me that no Treaties exist between Denmark and the other Baltic Powers requiring that evidence must be produced of the payment of the Sound dues before vessels can enter their ports; but that municipal regulations to this effect exist in the Ports of Russia and Prussia.

Yours very respectfully
JAMES BUCHANAN.

HON: WILLIAM L. MARCY,
Secretary of State.

TO MR. MARCY.[1]

No. 69.   LEGATION OF THE UNITED STATES.

LONDON, 26 April 1855.

SIR:

You have already been privately informed of my intention to terminate my official duties as Minister to Great Britain on the 30th September next; but the time has now arrived when it has become proper that I should communicate this determination to the President in an official manner.

When I consented to accept this Mission, which had been so kindly tendered to me by the President, it was distinctly understood between us that I should be permitted to resign it, if I so desired, after a service of two years. This period will expire on the 23d of August next; but it is more convenient that I should remain until the end of the then current quarter. I have, therefore, to request that the President may be pleased to transmit me a letter of recall in sufficient time to enable me to terminate my Mission and take leave of the Queen on the 30th September next.

Yours very respectfully,
JAMES BUCHANAN.

HON. WILLIAM L. MARCY,
Secretary of State.

---

[1] MSS. Department of State, 67 Despatches from England.

TO MR. MARCY.[1]

No. 70.   LEGATION OF THE UNITED STATES.
                          LONDON, 4 May 1855.

SIR:

I have the honor to acknowledge the receipt of your Despatch No. 85, of the 11th ultimo, but not of the "Silver Trumpet which the President desires to present to Captain Bosdet of the British bark Ellen."

I transmit, herewith, two copies of a Notification received from Lord Clarendon and inserted in the London Gazette of the 27th ultimo, " announcing the establishment of the Blockade of certain Russian Ports in the Baltic by the united British and French Naval Forces."

His Lordship requests, in his note to me of the 28th ultimo, that I " will have the goodness to transmit copies of this Notification to your [my] Government, in order that it may through that channel become known to the citizens of the United States."

Yours very respectfully,

JAMES BUCHANAN.

HON: WILLIAM L. MARCY,
        Secretary of State.

FROM LORD CLARENDON.

(Enclosure in No. 71.[2])   [May 10, 1855.]

The Undersigned, Her Majesty's Principal Secretary of State for Foreign Affairs, has had the honor to receive the letter which Mr. Buchanan, Envoy Extraordinary and Minister Plenipotentiary for the United States, addressed to him on the 20th ultimo, enclosing copy of the Act of Congress for carrying into effect the Convention upon the subject of Claims between Great Britain and the United States of February the 8th, 1853, and also a copy of a Despatch from the Secretary of State of the United States, suggesting that, in order to avoid delay and the trouble of making remittances, Her Majesty's Government should give you a release to the United States for the amount, $277,102.88 = £57,252.13.4, awarded to British subjects, and pay to you the difference between that sum and the amount awarded to Citizens of the United States, $329,734.18 = £68,131.0.7½, being $52,631.30 = £10,878.7.3½, on which you will be authorized to give to Her Majesty's Government a release for the amount awarded to Citizens of the United States, $329,734.18 = £68,131.0.7½.

In reply, the Undersigned has the honor to inform Mr. Buchanan that

---

[1] MSS. Department of State, 67 Despatches from England.
[2] Despatch to Mr. Marcy, No. 71, May 11, 1855, infra.

Her Majesty's Government are quite willing to adopt the mode of settlement proposed by Mr. Marcy, instructions having been sent to Her Majesty's Minister at Washington to propose a similar arrangement, before Mr. Buchanan's letter was received by the Undersigned.

Mr. Crampton was at the same time instructed to ascertain from Mr. Marcy his opinion as to the manner in which certain points should be settled as to the expenses of the commission, which had been left by the Commissioners for the decision of the two Governments.

These points are:

1st. The time when the salaries of the Commissioners should commence and terminate: 2dly, what travelling expenses, if any, should be allowed to the appointed place of meeting and return from the same: and 3dly, the compensation to be allowed to the Umpire. It has since been ascertained that Mr. Bates does not wish for any compensation for his services as Umpire, and Mr. Crampton has been so informed; the two first points therefore only remain to be determined. But assuming that, as agreeably to the Second Clause of the 6th Article of the Convention each Government is to pay the stipulated rate of salary to its own Commissioner (each Government reimbursing itself out of the ratable deduction from the sums awarded,) so any further allowance to be made on the heads submitted by the Commissioners will in like manner be paid by each Government separately, it would only remain to apportion between the two sums charged in the account annexed to the Report of the Commissioners for Clerk's Salary and Contingent Expenses, amounting to £935.9.10, which sum has been paid by the British Government, and a ratable proportion of which is therefore to be repaid by the United States.

Total of the account at page 315	£2588.16.6
Strike out am't of salary of Commissioners	1653. 6.8
Rem'd	£935.9.10

The proportions in which that sum will have to be divided, being the same as that which the total amount of awards bears to the amount awarded to each party, are as follows:

$$\begin{array}{lll} & & \text{£ s.d.} \\ \text{Amount of awards to British Claimants} & 57252.13.4 & = 427.3.3 \\ \text{Do. to United States Claimants} & 68131.0.7\tfrac{1}{2} & = 508.6.7 \\ \hline & 125383.13.11\tfrac{1}{2} & = 935.9.10 \end{array}$$

Her Majesty's Government have therefore a claim upon the Government of the United States for the sum of £508.6.7, as their share of the expenses of the Commission, each party paying its own Commissioner at the stipulated rate; and that sum they propose to deduct from the balance of £10,878.7.3½ payable as explained, to the United States, on account of the awards.

If this plan meets with Mr. Buchanan's concurrence, the Undersigned will take steps for proceeding to a settlement with the least possible delay.

The Undersigned avails himself of this opportunity to renew to Mr. Buchanan, the assurance of his highest consideration,

(Signed)   CLARENDON.

FOREIGN OFFICE, May 10, 1855.
J. BUCHANAN, ESQR., &c. &c. &c.

TO MR. MARCY.[1]

No. 71.   LEGATION OF THE UNITED STATES.
                          LONDON, 11 May 1855.

SIR:

'I have the honor to acknowledge the receipt of your Despatch No. 86, of the 19th ultimo.

I enclose the copy of a note from Lord Clarendon of the 4th inst., stating that "the Commissioners for the Affairs of India have informed him that the usual instructions will be sent to the Governor General of India for the recognition" of Mr. Richard Lewis as Vice Consul of the United States at Calcutta.

I transmit the copy of a note of yesterday's date, just received from Lord Clarendon, on the subject of the final adjustment and payment of the amount of the awards under the Claims Convention of the 8th February, 1853.[2] This, as you will perceive, whilst it recognises the mode of settlement suggested in your Despatch No. 77, of the 6th March last, proposes, in addition, to settle the amount of the expenses of the Commission, and thus make an end of the whole business.

The terms appear to be in conformity with the Treaty; as it expressly provides that "Each Government shall pay its Commissioner," &c. &c. Deducting, therefore, the salary of the Commissioners from the amount of the expenses of the Commission, as is proposed, the balance would be £935.9.10, which, ratably, according to the amount of the sums awarded to British and American claimants respectively, would make our proportion of the expenses £508.6.7;—less than ¾ of one per cent. of the amount awarded to American Claimants.

It may, also, be observed that if the salaries of the Commissioners were not deducted from the expenses, but apportioned ratably between the two Governments, we would pay more than one half of these salaries.

I have not a copy of the report of the Commissioners in my possession, nor have I had time to verify the calculations in Lord Clarendon's note; but I shall go to the Foreign Office and examine the report, and if I find all to be correct, I shall make an end of the affair with Lord Clarendon, before the departure of the next steamer, in the manner he has proposed. In doing this and avoiding the great delay which would result from waiting

---

[1] MSS. Department of State, 67 Despatches from England.
[2] Note from Lord Clarendon, May 10, 1855, supra.

to hear from you, I believe I shall act in conformity to the spirit of your instructions.   When I receive the balance, £10,370.0.8½, I shall deposit it to the credit of the United States with Messrs. Baring Brothers & Co. in that form which, after consultation with them, shall be deemed most advisable.

I also send you the Blue Book, which I received last night from Lord Clarendon, containing " papers relating to the Negotiation at Vienna on the Eastern question."

The resignation of Drouyn de L'Huys, the very able French Minister for Foreign Affairs, and the appointment of Count Walewski to his place, are leading political topics of the day. It is generally, and I believe correctly, understood that this resignation was occasioned by the dissatisfaction of the Emperor with the Minister's conduct at Vienna, in having gone further than his instructions warranted in the interests of peace.   It is now believed that the Emperor, in view of the dilatory policy of Austria and since the attempt upon his life, has abandoned his purpose of going to the Crimea; his personal and political safety both rendering it expedient that he shall remain in France. Should he make peace without glory to his arms in the East, his throne might be in danger, and, therefore, it would seem to be his policy to continue the war in the hope of the capture of Sebastopol or some other brilliant victory.

Although the conduct of the Russian Plenipotentiaries is much censured in England, yet what would be thought by this Government if an attempt were made on the part of a Foreign Power to limit the number of British vessels of war in the English Channel, or by our own if a similar attempt were made to limit the number of American vessels of war in the Gulf of Mexico?   The limitation of the power of Russia in the Black Sea could only be effectually accomplished with honor to Russia by making it an open sea like the Baltic or the Mediterranean, free to the vessels of war of all nations; and this the Russian Plenipotentiaries have offered.

The Administration of Lord Palmerston does not gain ground in public opinion; and its speedy fall is predicted by many.   Its present safety, as I have observed in a former Despatch, rests entirely on the heterogeneous materials of which the opposition is composed.

Yours very respectfully

JAMES BUCHANAN.

HON: WILLIAM L. MARCY
    Secretary of State.

TO MR. MARCY.[1]

No. 72.   LEGATION OF THE UNITED STATES.
                    LONDON, 18 May 1855.

SIR:

I have the honor to inform you that I have received a note from Lord Clarendon dated on the 11th Instant, stating " that orders have been given by the proper authority for the discharge of *Patrick* Hourigan from Her Majesty's Service." Immediately upon the receipt of this, I addressed a note to his Lordship informing him that the Christian name of Hourigan was Michael and not Patrick, and requesting him to have the mistake corrected.

I have received the Exequatur of James Arrott, Esquire, appointed Consul of the United States for Dublin, and this, together with his Commission, has been forwarded to him at his post.

Since the date of my last Despatch, No. 71, I have been furnished by the Foreign Office with the Report of the Commissioners under the Claims Convention; and having examined it with care, I addressed a note to Lord Clarendon on the 14th Instant, of which I now transmit a copy, in answer to his of the 10th, a copy of which accompanied my last Despatch. He appointed this day, at four o'clock, to terminate the business; and I have no time before the closing of the Despatch Bag to do more than send you the receipt from Lord Clarendon to myself for the sum of £57,252.13.4, and the Statement signed by us, which fully and clearly explains the whole proceeding. I shall to-morrow morning deposit the amount of the draft, £10,370.0.8, referred to in the Statement, with Messrs. Baring, Brothers & Co., to the credit of the United States, and transmit you a certificate of the deposit by the next steamer.

Of course, I gave Lord Clarendon a receipt for the sum of £68,131.0.7½, in terms corresponding with those of his receipt to me.

In haste, yours very respectfully,

JAMES BUCHANAN.

HON: WILLIAM L. MARCY,
        Secretary of State.

---

[1] MSS. Department of State, 67 Despatches from England.

TO MR. MARCY.[1]

No. 73.   LEGATION OF THE UNITED STATES.
                                        LONDON, 19th May 1855.

SIR:

Referring to my Despatch of yesterday (No. 72) I now transmit a receipt from Messrs. Baring Brothers & Co., dated on this day, for the sum of £10,370.0.8—" ten thousand three hundred and seventy pounds and eight pence, which sum has been placed to the credit of the United States Treasury,—' Account, British Claims'—subject to the orders of the Secretary of State." This, together with a copy of my receipt to Lord Clarendon, of yesterday, for the sum of £68,131.0.7½—sixty-eight thousand one hundred and thirty-one pounds seven pence halfpenny,— which I now enclose, will place the Department in possession of all the papers relating to the final adjustment and settlement between the two Governments of the awards under the Claims Convention of the 8th February, 1853. I left to Messrs. Baring Brothers & Co., as Bankers of the United States, to decide under what head in their accounts, and in what form, the deposit to the credit of the United States should be made.

Yours very respectfully,

JAMES BUCHANAN.

HON: WILLIAM L. MARCY,
        Secretary of State.

TO MR. MARCY.[1]

No. 74.   LEGATION OF THE UNITED STATES.
                                        LONDON, 25 May, 1855.

SIR:

I have the honor to transmit herewith two copies of a Notification received from Lord Clarendon and inserted in a Supplement to the London Gazette of the 18th Instant, " announcing the establishment of the Blockade of certain Russian Ports in the Baltic by the combined British and French Naval forces," on the 28th day of April last.

I have received a letter from Colonel Seibels, our Minister at Brussels, dated on the 17th Instant, in relation to this Block-

---

[1] MSS. Department of State, 67 Despatches from England.

ade, which contains an extract from a note addressed by the
Russian Minister at Brussels to the Belgium Minister for Foreign
Affairs, a copy of which the Colonel informs me he has transmitted to you. In this note, the Russian Minister informs the
Belgium Government that an English official messenger, not
named, (Parlementaire) had been sent to Baltischport, it is presumed by Admiral Dundas, to give notice, among other things,
that neutral ships found in Russian ports at the commencement
of the blockade laden with goods the property of Russians would
not be permitted to depart, in the same manner as if their cargoes
belonged to neutrals. This would be in violation of the British
Declaration of the 28th March, 1854, " waiving the right of
seizing enemies' property laden on board a neutral vessel."

Soon after I received this letter from Col: Seibels, I met
the Danish Minister at this Court, who was then on his way to
the Foreign Office, and communicated its contents to him. He
said he would mention the subject to Lord Clarendon and let me
know the result. He yesterday informed me that his Lordship
had assured him he neither knew, nor approved of any such
reservation as that mentioned " against Russian property found
on board of neutral vessels."

If any such reservation had been authorized by this Government, it would surely have been mentioned in the Notification
of blockade which I now transmit. Still, it is not improbable,
from the irregularity and confusion of the administrative system
in this country, and from the want of explicit instructions, that
the British Admiral in the Baltic may have authorized the notification alleged to have been given at Baltischport.

I shall inquire further into this matter.

The Box containing the Silver Trumpet for Captain Bosdet
has at length been received, and I have sent it to the Foreign
Office, with a note to Lord Clarendon, of which I enclose a copy.

Yours very respectfully,

JAMES BUCHANAN.

HON: WILLIAM L. MARCY,
    Secretary of State.

FROM MR. MARCY.[1]

Private and confidential.

WASHINGTON, May 28, 1855.

MY DEAR SIR:

In looking over a file of the "London Times," I observe in one of them a complaint against the United States for want of sympathy for the allies. It might not be proper to notice such a topic in a despatch or in a note from you to the Minister of Foreign Relations, but an allusion to it would find a very proper place in a conversation with him. The allegation is, to some extent, true. It is a matter of some surprise that the British Ministry, and persons so well informed as the editors of the "Times," should not be aware of the cause of this phase of public sentiment in this country. Great Britain as well as France, since the "entente cordiale," has placed herself in our path, and attempted to obstruct us in whatever direction we have attempted to move. Many of the facts to prove this assertion—not all of them—were alluded to in the speech of Mr. Mason at the last session of Congress. You will readily call to mind many others not noticed by him.

In a letter published in the "Times," not many months ago, it was offensively stated that, when the allies had broken the power and humbled the pride of Russia, they would then show the United States the value of steam, and teach them a lesson of moderation. The want of good faith on the part of Great Britain in regard to the Clayton and Bulwer treaty, and the constant succession of offensive articles in the British press against the Government and people of this country, are well calculated to extinguish all sympathy in our people with England in her present cause—and probably would have the same effect, if it was a much better cause.

The allies may not be fully aware of the high tone of dictation which they assume towards other nations. They undoubtedly think that if all other Powers would suffer these self-constituted guardians to manage their affairs, all would be wisely done. England did not think, in the days of the elder Napoleon, that he or the French nation were fit to rule the whole world or even the Continent of Europe, and she ought not to be surprised that we think that the like task ought not to be committed to the joint labors of the allies.

The qualification made to you by Lord Clarendon of his declaration in Parliament, that the policy of the allies extended to both hemispheres, &c., is not very satisfactory. It is much less so since the reiteration of the same sentiment by Louis Napoleon, in his speech at the opening of the French Chambers last winter. This matter is somewhat worsened by his allusion to slavery in his recent speech in London.

It is now no longer a matter of doubt that British agents have been engaged, with the approval of their Government, in recruiting soldiers for its army in the Crimea within the limits of the United States.

While the British press is denouncing, in unmeasured and bitter terms, this Government for conniving at the organization of expeditions against other Powers, Great Britain has agents employed in violating our laws

---

[1] Buchanan Papers, Historical Society of Pennsylvania.

within our own borders. It is no longer a disputable fact that British agents are busy in all our principal cities in engaging men to go to the Provinces to enroll themselves in the British army, and the means for carrying on this operation are furnished by their Government. I do not believe there will be any difficulty in establishing the fact that not only the Canadian authorities, but the Home Government, have lent their direct sanction to this invasion of our sovereign rights and open violation of our neutrality laws. On this latter subject I shall send you a despatch, with the President's directions to present the subject to the attention of Her Majesty's Government.

Some time since, I promised to address you a communication on the subject of the interference of British agents with our negotiations with other Powers. There has been a longer delay than was expected in carrying out my intention, but it is not abandoned. If the people of Great Britain could see the conduct of her rulers towards the United States in its true light, I am quite sure they would not be surprised at our want of sympathy for them in their present cause.

Complaining is a business I very much dislike, either in nations or individuals, where it does not assume the character of a remonstrance against actual wrongs. As, between Great Britain and the United States, we have much better grounds for complaining than she has, her deportment towards us lays no foundation for our sympathy. Her cause has not the character in the eyes of others which she herself gives to it. In its true aspect, it appears to be a war against Russia, justified by a suspicion that the Emperor intended to do what she has been in the practice of doing for a century and a half—encroaching upon, absorbing, the territories of other nations.

The news has just reached us that Wise has been elected Governor of Virginia. It was an exciting and furious contest, and is justly regarded as a great triumph for the democratic party. Had the Know-nothings carried the Old Dominion—and they made a desperate fight for it—they would have considered themselves in the ascendant in the country, and felt quite sure of prevailing in the next Presidential election. Their defeat in Virginia, where they were very confident of success, will be very disheartening to them.

The condition of things in Kansas is very unpropitious. I confess I cannot see a favorable issue to the difficulties which have there arisen. If Governor Reeder goes back to the Territory, as I think he will, there is some reason to fear that he will be ill-treated, and his authority contemned. To supersede him I am quite sure would produce consequences as mischievous as the worst effects which would attend his return.

Yours truly,

W. L. MARCY.

HON. JAS. BUCHANAN.

TO MR. MARCY.[1]

LEGATION OF THE UNITED STATES.

LONDON 8 June 1855.

MY DEAR SIR:

Ere this I had expected to receive an acceptance of my resignation and to hear from you on some other points. I desire to make a suggestion to you on a matter which I deem important. The new law has forbidden the employment of a clerk for this Legation at the expense of the Government; and yet the services of a Clerk are indispensable. Benjamin Moran, the present Clerk, is all that can be desired. He is one of the most industrious men I have ever known and seems to take delight in labor. Besides, his politics are firmly Democratic. I shall retain him in his place at his present salary until the end of my time ($800=£165.5.9.) After this, he has an offer of £200 per annum from General Campbell; but he would prefer to remain in the Legation at his present lower salary; and I think, *here* he ought to remain. By the time this can reach you, you will doubtless know who is to be my successor; and I would request that you should inform me, as soon as you may be able, whether he would agree to retain Mr. Moran at his present salary. I repeat, that in all respects Mr. Moran is an agreeable and useful clerk.

Lord Palmerston has regained much of his lost ground by assuming a warlike position. His present attitude is in accordance with the prevailing sentiment of the British people. They seem to be determined to fight on until they can recover their ancient military character. How long this feeling may continue is another question. The war and the necessary taxes begin to press heavily upon certain classes, and particularly such mechanics and artisans as are employed in the fabrication of what may be called luxuries. It is very long since they have had so cold & backward a season as the present in England. The harvest will be very late, and serious apprehensions have been entertained respecting the crop. The last few days, however, have been seasonable.

I take it for granted that you do not intend to come here yourself. If I should be mistaken, however, I still cordially repeat my former offers. I have no doubt of the great advan-

---

[1] Buchanan Papers, Historical Society of Pennsylvania.

tage you might derive from being here a short time before my departure. My house is an excellent one, in a high and healthy part of the city, and is exceedingly well furnished,—a rare advantage. It is in a highly respectable, though not the most fashionable part of the city. I have the Austrian, the Spanish, the Belgian, and Brazilian Ministers for neighbours. If the room or rather rooms occupied as an office could be appropriated to domestic purposes, it would be all that could be desired. Still, my successor, on view, ought to decide for himself.

I am most anxious about the result of the Virginia election; and this both for the cause and the man who represents it. I trust we may receive the news of Wise's election by the next steamer. Although I can have no possible personal interest in the result, yet I almost feel as though I were a party in the contest. It would be truly disastrous, should Know-nothingism gain a footing in the South. I have long been expecting to hear from you as to my course on the " Free ships Free goods " Treaty, &c. &c. &c.

With my very kindest regards to Mrs. Marcy and my respectful compliments to the President, I remain,

Yours very respectfully

JAMES BUCHANAN.

HON: WILLIAM L. MARCY.

P. S. Ex-Presidents Van Buren and Fillmore are now both here.

TO MR. MARCY.[1]

Private & confidential.

LEGATION OF THE UNITED STATES.

LONDON 15 June 1855.

MY DEAR SIR/

I have received by the last Steamer your favor of the 28th ultimo containing several very proper suggestions in regard to what ought to be my private conversations on certain subjects with Lord Clarendon. I am happy to inform you that I had anticipated these suggestions & have often conversed with him as well as others concerning the attempts of French & English officials throughout the world to frustrate the policy of the

---

[1] Buchanan Papers, Historical Society of Pennsylvania.

United States.   I pressed this subject strongly upon him at an official interview reported in Despatch No. 57 of the 19th January last; & you will there find his declaration " that there had been too much of this,—it was all wrong, & he would take care that for the future we should have no cause to complain on this account."   I have since been waiting for your Despatch on this subject promised in your private letter of the 25th February last.

I have not said any thing formally to Lord Clarendon about British recruiting in the United States; & I shall be happy to receive & obey your promised instructions on this subject.

One thing is very certain, that I speak my mind very freely to these people in all that relates to the interest of our Country; though I trust I do this in such a manner as to afford no just cause of offence.

We have sufficient real causes of complaint against England without relying on those which are unfounded or equivocal; & of this character I am convinced is the construction placed in the United States on the remark of Lord Clarendon in the House of Lords, " that the policy of the allies extended to both hemispheres," &c. &c.   In two official conversations this construction was disclaimed by Lord Clarendon.   Vide my Despatch No. 25 of the 17 March, 1854, & No. 29 of the 14th April, 1854.   Can any thing be more clear & explicit than the disclaimer reported to you in the last of these Despatches?   I might add that on several other occasions in private conversation I have alluded informally & pleasantly to this subject; & he has always disclaimed the meaning imputed to him & spoken of General Cass's Anglophobia, &c. &c.   It is, also, but just to remark that from my conversations & previous knowledge of the course of England & France in conjunction, in regard to that portion of South America watered by the La Plata & its branches, & their fair & liberal conduct, in this matter, towards the United States, I had myself placed a similar construction on Lord Clarendon's remark to that which he afterwards declared to me was its true meaning. It did not occur to me he could have been guilty of the extreme folly, especially at that critical moment, of proclaiming the intended interference of France & England in our affairs on the other side of the Atlantic, even if such an intention existed; as he must have foreseen that such a declaration would give serious & just offence to the United States.

With the feelings & intentions of the Emperor of the French towards the United States, I am not sufficiently acquainted to speak positively.   I fear they are not very kind, notwithstanding his own declarations, & those of Lord Clarendon to myself, of a different character. The Empress when here gave me a strong, I might almost say a pressing invitation to visit Paris during the Grand Exhibition; & should I do so, which is my present purpose, I shall probably know more on this subject before my return.

The English are extremely sensitive in relation to the apparent sympathy in the United States for the cause of Russia. Inquiries are made of me respecting this wherever I go. There is a strange, jealous, inconsistent, & almost inexplicable feeling in this country towards their "transatlantic cousins." They like us & they don't like us. On Wednesday last, I was present at the "inauguration," as they call it, of the new cattle market in a remote part of the city to take the place of the ancient Smithfield Market. Prince Albert presided, & more than a thousand people sat down to lunch. In different portions of the apartment the flags of England, France, Turkey, & our stars & stripes were intertwined!!! A strange conjunction! This was pointed out to me & remarked upon with evident satisfaction by an Admiralty Lord who sat next me at the table.

The late signal successes of the allies over the Russians in the Crimea have considerably raised the spirits of the British people, as well as the price of stocks, which is a true barometer of public opinion.

I know not when I have been so much gratified as at the news of Wise's election. Both Appleton & myself awaited the result with the most anxious solicitude.

Messrs. Van Buren & Fillmore are both now here. Since my arrival in London I have talked pretty freely to Lord Clarendon & others in regard to the neglect with which our distinguished countrymen who occupy or have occupied high official stations were treated at Court & by the court circle, compared with the attentions lavished upon foreign continental princes, their relatives & titled officials. Whether this has produced any effect, I cannot pretend to say. Certain it is, however, that the civilities extended to Mr. Van Buren & Mr. Fillmore have been greater than past experience might have taught us to expect. Still they have not been what they ought to be, on the part of the Court. Mr. Fillmore was presented to the Queen at a private audience on the day before the Drawing Room, instead of in the crowd on that occasion; but this was on my suggestion in a note to the Master of Ceremonies. Miss Lane & myself dined with him at the Palace on Wednesday last; but he was not placed in that distinguished position at table which would have been assigned to the near relative of any petty German Prince; & I observe that in the Court Circular his name is placed near the end of the list of guests, that of Mr. Van Buren, who dined with Her Majesty on the day following, being the very last on the list. *The Queen ought to give a dinner to an ex-President as the principal guest, & assign him the post of honor at the table.* Still I do not complain, for they have done more than I had expected; & the Queen's character as well as her conduct towards myself is above all exception. She always asks me in the kindest manner after the health of the President.

I do hope you will inform me what are the "abuses" of which you complain & which you have visited with so severe a penalty in regard to our Despatch Bag from London. I venture to say no abuses exist, unless Mr. Miller, who so far as I know & believe is an industrious & faithful officer, has placed matter in the Despatch Bag other than that which he has received from the Legation.

With my kindest regards & those of Miss Lane to Mrs. Marcy, I remain yours very respectfully

JAMES BUCHANAN.

HON: WILLIAM L. MARCY.

TO MR. MARCY.[1]

No. 76.   LEGATION OF THE UNITED STATES.

LONDON, 15 June 1855.

SIR:

I have the honor to acknowledge the receipt of your Despatch No. 88, of the 28th ultimo, in which you state that you have "reason to believe that abuses have been committed in the conveyance of letters and other articles, not entitled to the privilege, by the Mail Bags between the Legation at London and this Department." I trust you will deem it due to this Legation to specify these "abuses." I know that since my attention has been directed to this subject by occurrences which took place some months ago, nothing has been sent from this Legation to Mr. Miller to be placed in the Despatch Bags, except what, at

---

[1] MSS. Department of State, 67 Despatches from England. The part relating to court dress is printed in S. Ex. Doc. 31, 36 Cong. 1 Sess. 23.

least in my estimation, has been entirely proper. Indeed, all that we have sent would occupy but little room.

Both Mr. Appleton and myself consider it a hard measure of justice, without having received any previous notice of the alleged "abuses," to be deprived of the use of the Bag almost altogether for our private correspondence; for such is the effect of your decision "that the Despatch Agents at Boston & New York have no right to open the Bags in their transit from London to Washington." The law requiring prepayment is an excellent law, and I had provided myself with U. S. Post Office Stamps to be attached to letters from members of the Legation and their families to persons in the United States. We had supposed that these letters prepaid would be deposited in the Post Offices at New York and Boston for transmission to their places of destination. The consequence now is, that we must send most of our letters by the ordinary foreign mail, and that twenty-four cents postage will be charged on each.

In my Despatch No. 24, of the 24th February, 1854, in speaking of Court Costume, I expressed the hope that I was done with this subject forever. It is proper, however, I should inform you that the dress worn by myself and the members of this Legation has recently been recognized as an appropriate Court dress for other American Citizens, and what is remarkable, also for British Subjects.

Some weeks since Mr. J. R. Tyson of Philadelphia arrived in London and expressed a desire to be presented at Court. Not wishing him to appear in the absurd and ridiculous Court Costume prescribed for civilians, I addressed a note to Sir Edward Cust, the Master of Ceremonies, inquiring whether Mr. T. might not be received by Her Majesty in a dress similar to my own. The response was brief and satisfactory. It is dated May 16th, 1855, and is as follows:

My DEAR SIR: I consider the dress adopted by you to be quite sufficient to fulfil Court Etiquette either for an American or an English gentleman, &c., &c., &c.

Mr. Tyson was accordingly presented in this dress at the Birthday Drawing Room on the 19th May; and Mr. Fillmore and Mr. Henry E. Davies, his companion, have appeared at Court in the same costume.

Yours very respectfully

JAMES BUCHANAN.

HON: WILLIAM L. MARCY
    Secretary of State.

TO MR. MARCY.[1]

No. 78.   LEGATION OF THE UNITED STATES.
LONDON, 29 June 1855.

SIR:

I have the honor to acknowledge the receipt of your Despatches, Nos. 90 & 91, of the 7th and 9th Instant, respectively.

Previous to their receipt, I had made an appointment for a meeting with Lord Clarendon on Wednesday last, without having any specific matters of importance to bring to his notice. The arrival of your 91 in the mean time, however, enabled me to refer to the subject of enlistments by British Officials and Agents for the British Army in the United States. I told him I had received instructions from you to bring this subject to His Lordship's notice, which I intended to do by a formal note; and now merely mentioned it for the purpose of apprising him that such was my intention. I then took occasion to observe that the Government of the United States was able proudly to declare that, from the days of Washington until the present moment, they had always faithfully performed their neutral duties. In confirmation of this, I might state that no Russian Privateers, about which they had expressed so much anxiety, had been fitted out in our Ports, and to refer to the unceasing vigilance with which unlawful expeditions to Cuba had been watched and prevented by the Government of the United States. I said I was sorry that the British Press had most unjustly denounced our Government for secretly encouraging filibustering expeditions, although they ought to know that such conduct was alike opposed to our uniform practice, our principles, and our interest.

His Lordship in reply assented to the correctness of my observations. He said they had learned that a number of British subjects and Germans in the United States were anxious, on account of the pressure of the times, to enter the British service, and they were not aware that our neutrality laws applied to such cases. He highly approved of these laws; and as soon as he had discovered that such a proceeding was likely to give offence to the authorities at Washington, he had addressed a Despatch to Mr. Crampton on the subject, with authority to make you acquainted with its contents. [According to diplomatic usage, you had a right to ask for a copy of this Despatch, and it could

---

[1] MSS. Department of State, 67 Despatches from England.

not have been refused.] He proceeded to state that a fortnight ago Lord Panmure had sent instructions to Halifax which
would effectually put an end to all such attempts, and that nothing was further from their intention than to violate our neutrality laws. He then asked if these laws really prevented individuals
in the United States from entering into engagements to go abroad
for the purpose of afterwards enlisting. I told him that most
certainly they did, and that without this it would be easy to
evade the provisions of our neutrality laws; and I then referred,
as an example of the manner in which this might be done, to the
notice of the Lieutenant Governor of Nova Scotia, but told him
I would soon address him more particularly on the subject.

In the course of the interview we had some conversation in
relation to the three articles of a Consular Convention proposed
by myself. This subject I have not pressed since the receipt of
your Despatch No. 84, of the 31st March last, though I confess
that after re-examination the difficulties you present do not strike
me with the same force they have done yourself; and I am constantly reminded by my correspondence with our consuls of
the necessity of some stipulation for restoring seamen deserting
from our Merchant vessels in different British Ports. In answer to this Despatch, I addressed you in mine of the 20th April
(No. 68); but not having since heard from you on the subject,
I infer that I have not succeeded in removing your difficulties.
But I do not suppose there is much prospect of concluding any
such convention, for which, however, His Lordship professes to
be extremely anxious. Indeed, he became quite excited in conversing about it,—spoke in very strong terms of the obstructions
cast in his way by the Solicitor General, and said he had told
him in a late conference it would be a shame for England to have
it published to the world that, on account of the opposition of
the Law Officers of the Crown, they could not conclude a consular convention with the United States similar to conventions
which the United States already had with so many other commercial nations. I told him I had said all I intended to say on
the matter, but should expect an answer to my proposition, and
he might, if he thought proper, place their refusal to conclude
the convention on the ground he had stated; and he replied that
he should certainly do this, and relieve himself from all personal
responsibility. (We shall see.)

I observed that as soon as it should become generally known
in the United States that they would enter into no stipulations

to restore Deserters from American vessels, and that we were not bound, on our part, to restore Deserters from British vessels, their seamen would probably leave their vessels in our Ports in much greater numbers than American seamen now left our vessels in British Ports. He said this would be a bad state of affairs; they already had a law upon this subject [the Foreign Deserters Act of 1852], and why could we not comply with that law? I told him this was impossible,—we could never recognise the distinction which that law made in favor of slaves over freemen; and he replied that, in the present state of public opinion in England, it would be in vain to attempt to pass an Act through Parliament which did not exempt slaves from being delivered up as deserters. I said I was sorry to hear this. The interference of the British people with Domestic slavery in the United States, —a subject which did not concern them, and in which they had no right to interfere,—had done much to alienate the two countries from each other.

I am much pleased with your reply to Mr. Crampton's verbal note proposing to constitute an independent Government at Greytown. I confess, however, I should have been more pleased with it had you referred, as you perhaps might have done not inappropriately, to their obligations under the Clayton and Bulwer Treaty. I doubt not that any English Administration, except perhaps the present, would cheerfully accede to the just and proper terms of arrangement respecting Greytown proposed by yourself, provided there was a silent acquiescence in their dominion over Ruatan, to which I know you would never consent. This Island is one of those commanding positions in the world which Great Britain has been ever ready to seize and appropriate. It enables her to control our commerce in the Caribbean Sea and on its transit to California and Oregon. She now possesses it in violation of a solemn Treaty with the United States; and we can never voluntarily yield to her dominion over it without a loss of character before the world and something like national disgrace. Deeply impressed as I am with the vast importance to both of preserving friendly relations between the two countries, and willing as I should be to make sacrifices on questions of mere policy to accomplish this object, yet we are too young and too proud a people to surrender any point of national honor. Perhaps I may feel too strongly upon the subject, arising out of my past connection with it, now however at an end.

There begins to be an uneasy feeling, especially in quarters having the deepest interest in trade with the United States, that all is not well in the relations between the two countries. Several members of the House of Commons have asked me for information in regard to the Central American questions; and but a few days ago a distinguished and influential member proposed to call upon the Government for the production of the papers, if this would meet my approbation; but I did not feel myself at liberty to give any encouragement to make the call. I told him this was a question for himself to decide on his own responsibility. He then asked what the President had said about these questions in his last Message; and I shewed him the paragraph. He said he thought, upon the strength of this paragraph, he would, without asking for the papers, propound a question to Lord Palmerston as to the present state of the relations between the two countries. I replied,—this was also a question he must decide entirely for himself; I could neither encourage nor discourage him. It is a week since I held this conversation, and I have since heard nothing more of the matter.

In this interview with Lord Clarendon, I informed him it was my intention, before I left the country, which it was my purpose to do early in October, to submit a formal proposition to him, in obedience to my instructions, for the conclusion of the Treaty respecting neutral rights to which I had referred in previous conversations. He intimated that he was himself favorable in principle to such a Treaty; but alluded to the difficulties in the way. I feel pretty confident they would be unwilling, at this time, to give such a proposition either an affirmative or a negative answer. I have been expecting a Despatch from you on this subject.

The truth is, that the whole policy of the governing class is to pursue the old and beaten track as long as possible. Year after year reports are made in Parliament in favor of the correction of known abuses. These recommendations are always resisted, until public opinion forces them to yield. They fear any change. It is quite notorious that the inefficient administration of the different and interfering branches of the War Department has been the cause of most of their disasters in the Crimea, and that the Civil Departments of the Government require great reform. Whether the present agitation in favor of administrative reform will do much practical good is extremely doubtful. In any event, no more reform will be granted than may be absolutely required by public opinion. In the event of the capture of Sebastopol, which they now expect with confidence, the cries for reform may be drowned in the shouts and self-gratulations for victory and the recovery of their military prestige. Count Persigny, the French Ambassador, told me the other day that the disasters of the allies in the Crimea were attributable to their two incompetent Generals (Canrobert and Lord Raglan.) They are now relieved from both.

I transmit herewith two copies, received from Lord Clarendon, with a note dated on the 23d Instant, of a " further notification inserted in the London Gazette of the 22d Instant, respecting the Blockade of Russian Ports in the Gulph of Finland by the combined British & French naval forces," with the request that I would have " the goodness to transmit copies of this notification to your [my] Government in order that they may through that channel become known to the citizens of the United States."

Yours very respectfully
JAMES BUCHANAN.

HON: WILLIAM L. MARCY,
    Secretary of State.

TO MR. MARCY.[1]

No. 79.   LEGATION OF THE UNITED STATES.
LONDON, 6 July 1855.

SIR:

I have the honor to acknowledge the receipt of your Despatches, Nos. 92 & 93, both of the 16th ultimo.

Mr. Alberdi has not yet arrived in London, at least to my knowledge. After conversing with him, I shall not fail to communicate to the British Government the course which the President intends to pursue as well towards the Argentine Confederation as the Republic of Buenos Ayres.

I transmit herewith the copy of a further notification received from Lord Clarendon, with a note dated on the 30th ultimo, inserted in the London Gazette of the 29th ultimo, " respecting a blockade of Russian Ports on the Coast of Fin-

---

[1] MSS. Department of State, 67 Despatches from England.

land by the combined British and French Naval forces," which his Lordship requests me to transmit to my Government, in order that it may through that channel become known to the Citizens of the United States.

Yours very respectfully

JAMES BUCHANAN.

HON: WILLIAM L. MARCY,
    Secretary of State.

TO LORD CLARENDON.

(Enclosure in No. 80.[1])

LEGATION OF THE UNITED STATES.

LONDON, 6 July, 1855.

The Undersigned, Envoy Extraordinary and Minister Plenipotentiary of the United States, has been instructed to call the attention of the Earl of Clarendon, Her Majesty's Principal Secretary of State for Foreign Affairs, to the fact that numerous attempts have been made, since the commencement of the existing war between Great Britain and Russia, to enlist soldiers for the British army within the limits of the United States; and that rendezvous for this purpose have been actually opened in some of their principal cities. When intimations were thrown out that British Consuls in the United States were encouraging and aiding such enlistments, Mr. Crampton, Her Britannic Majesty's Minister at Washington, exhibited to the Secretary of State the copy of a letter which he had addressed to one of these Consuls disapproving of the proceeding and discountenancing it as a violation of the Neutrality Laws of the United States. After this very proper conduct on the part of Mr. Crampton, it was confidently believed that these attempts to raise military forces within the territory of a neutral nation from whatever source they may have originated, would at once have been abandoned. This reasonable expectation has not been realized; and efforts to raise recruits within the United States for the British army are still prosecuted with energy, though chiefly in a somewhat different form. To arrest a course of proceeding which so seriously compromitted the neutrality of the nation, in the

---

[1] Despatch to Mr. Marcy, No. 80, July 13, 1855, infra. The note to Lord Clarendon is printed in S. Ex. Doc. 35, 34 Cong. 1 Sess. 10.

existing war, prosecutions were instituted by order of the American Government against the offenders. This led to developments establishing the fact that the Lieutenant Governor of Nova Scotia has had a direct agency in attempts to violate the Neutrality Laws of the United States. This will appear from the copy of a notification issued by that functionary, dated at Halifax on the 15th March last, and believed to be genuine, a copy of which the Undersigned has now the honor to communicate to the Earl of Clarendon. This notification has been published in the newspapers of the United States. In consequence, it is believed, of this document, purporting to be official, the practice of recruiting still proceeds with vigor, notwithstanding the legal measures adopted by the officers of the United States to suppress it. The American Government are constantly receiving information that persons are leaving, and have left, the United States, under engagements contracted within their limits, to enlist as soldiers in the British army on their arrival in the British Provinces. These persons are provided with ready means of transit to Nova Scotia, in consequence of the express promise of the Lieutenant Governor of that Province to pay " to Nova Scotian and other ship masters," the cost of a passage for each poor man *" willing to serve Her Majesty,"* " shipped from Philadelphia, New York, or Boston."

The disclosures made within the very last month, upon a judicial investigation at Boston, (a report of which is now before the Undersigned,) afford good reason to believe that an extensive plan has been organized by British functionaries and agents, and is now in successful operation in different parts of the Union, to furnish recruits for the British army.

All these acts have been performed in direct violation of the Second Section of the Act of Congress of the 20th April, 1818, which provides,—" That if any person shall, within the territory or jurisdiction of the United States, enlist or enter himself, or hire or retain another person to enlist or enter himself, or to go beyond the limits or jurisdiction of the United States with intent to be enlisted or entered in the service of any foreign prince, state, colony, district, or people, as a soldier, as a marine or seaman, on board of any vessel of war, letter of Marque, or Privateer, every person so offending shall be deemed guilty of a high misdemeanor, and shall be fined not exceeding one thousand dollars, and be imprisoned not exceeding three years," &c. &c.

The plain and imperative duties of neutrality, under the law of nations, require that a neutral nation shall not suffer its territory to become the theatre on which one of the belligerents might raise armies to wage war against the other. If such a permission were granted, the partiality which this would manifest in favor of one belligerent to the prejudice of the other could not fail to produce just complaints on the part of the injured belligerent, and might eventually involve the neutral as a party in the war.

The Government of the United States, however, did not leave the enforcement of its neutral obligations to rest alone on the law of nations. At an early period of its history, in June, 1794, under the Administration of General Washington, an Act of Congress was passed defining and enforcing its neutral duties; and this Act had been supplied, extended, and enlarged by the Act already referred to, and now in force, of the 20th April, 1818. Under both these Acts, the very same penalties are imposed upon all persons implicated, whether the actual enlistment takes place within the territory of the United States, or whether an engagement is entered into to go beyond the limits or jurisdiction of the United States, " with intent to be enlisted or entered in the service of any foreign prince," &c., &c. Without the latter provision the former might be easily evaded in the manner proposed by the Lieutenant Governor of Nova Scotia. If the law permitted any individual, whether official or unofficial, to engage persons in Philadelphia, New York, and Boston to serve in the British army, and to enter into contracts to transport them to Halifax, there to complete the formal act of enlistment, then it is manifest that this law, to a very great extent, would become a dead letter.

The Undersigned is happy to know that in this respect the policy of the British Government is identical with that of the United States. The Foreign Enlistment Act (59 Geo. 3, ch. 69), like the Act of Congress, inflicts the same penalties upon any individual who shall, within the British dominions, engage " any person or persons whatever " " to go or to agree to go or embark from any port of His Majesty's dominions, for the purpose or with intent to be so enlisted," as though the enlistment had actually taken place within the same.

And here it may be worthy of remark that neither the Foreign Enlistment Act nor the Act of Congress is confined to the enlistment or engagement of British subjects or American citizens, respectively, but rightfully extends to individuals of all nations:—" to any person whatever." The reason is manifest. The injury to the neutral principally consists in the violation of its territorial sovereignty by the belligerent for the purpose of raising armies; and this is the same, no matter what may be the national character of the persons who may agree to enter the service.

The Government of the United States can look back with satisfaction to the manner in which it has performed its neutral duties at every period of its history; and this often at the imminent risk of being involved in war.

In the early stage of the present war, the British Government very properly turned its attention towards the neutrality laws of the United States; and particularly to the provisions which forbid the fitting out and manning privateers for foreign service. Any remissness in enforcing such provisions would have been justly regarded by that Government as a violation of the neutral relations of the United States. It is not difficult to conjecture in what light the conduct of the American Government would have been viewed by the Allies, had it not denounced and resisted any attempt on the part of their enemy to send its agents into the ports of the United States to fit out privateers and engage sailors to man them. But would the Government of the United States be less censurably neglectful of the duties of neutrality, were it now to suffer one of the Allies to recruit armies within its borders, than it would have been, had it permitted the other belligerent to resort to American seaports for the purpose of organizing a privateer force to take a part in the present war?

In view of all these considerations, the President has instructed the Undersigned to ascertain from the Earl of Clarendon how far persons in official station under the British Government have acted, whether with or without its approbation, either in enlisting persons within the United States or engaging them to proceed from thence to the British Provinces for the purpose of being there enlisted; and what measures, if any, have been taken to restrain their unjustifiable conduct.

The President will be much gratified to learn that Her Majesty's Government has not authorised these proceedings, but has condemned the conduct of its officials engaged therein, and has visited them with its marked displeasure; as well as taken decisive measures to put a stop to conduct so contrary to the law of nations, the laws of the United States, and the comity which ought ever to prevail in the intercourse between the two friendly Powers.

The Undersigned has the honor to renew to the Earl of Clarendon the assurance of his distinguished consideration.

JAMES BUCHANAN.

THE RIGHT HONBLE. THE EARL OF CLARENDON,
    &c. &c. &c.

TO MR. MARCY.[1]

No. 80.   LEGATION OF THE UNITED STATES.

LONDON, 13 July 1855.

SIR:

I have the honor to acknowledge the receipt of your Despatches, Nos. 94, 95, 96, and 97, of the 21st, 21st, 25th, and 26th June, respectively.

I transmit the copy of a note which I yesterday addressed to Lord Clarendon, in obedience to your No. 94, communicating to the British Government the thanks of the President for the aid rendered by Commander Curtis, of Her Majesty's Steam Sloop "Brisk," to the American Merchant ship "North Carolina."

I herewith transmit the copy of a note addressed by me to Lord Clarendon, dated on the 6th Instant, and prepared in conformity with your instructions (No. 91) on the subject of the enlistment and employment of soldiers for the British army within the limits of the United States;—which I trust may receive your approbation. It was sent to the Foreign Office on the 7th, but its receipt has not yet been acknowledged.

Yours very respectfully,

JAMES BUCHANAN.

HON: WILLIAM L. MARCY,
    Secretary of State.

---

[1] MSS. Department of State, 67 Despatches from England. The last paragraph is printed in S. Ex. Doc. 35, 34 Cong. 1 Sess. 10, together with the note to Lord Clarendon of July 6, supra.

TO MR. FLINN.[1]

LEGATION OF THE UNITED STATES,

LONDON 13 July 1855.

MY DEAR SIR/

I have received your very acceptable letter of the 19th ultimo; & although very much pressed for time at the present moment, cannot deny myself the pleasure of answering it. I am truly sorry to learn that Mrs. Flinn is in poor health. I trust that ere this she may have entirely recovered.

No public event for many a day has afforded me such heart-felt satisfaction as the triumphant election of Mr. Wise; & this as well for the sake of the man as the cause. Democracy would not have been Democracy had it not made war upon Know-nothingism. A secret political society bound together by unlaw-ful oaths, whose objects were to persecute a religious denomina-tion & to deny civil rights to naturalised foreigners, was so totally at war with the principles & practice of the Democratic party that it necessarily encountered their determined opposition. I am glad to learn by every steamer that it cannot long endure. Our people must enjoy the liberty of going to Heaven their own road, & if they don't get there it is their own fault.

You are right in all your conversations in stating em-phatically that I am not a candidate for the Presidency. The office has no longer any charms for me, & I am now as anxious to pass into the shade of private life & enjoy peace & tranquillity during the remnant of my days, as I ever was to reach that high distinction. I have written in this spirit to every friend who has addressed me on the subject. The circumstance of my absence during the late exciting questions at home has turned for the moment some considerable degree of public attention towards me; but this will gradually vanish away as the friends of the aspirants who desire the office bring their claims more & more into public view.

My excellent friend Lynch, to whom I owe so much, is very chary about writing. He very rarely writes to me. I am re-joiced that he had determined to attend the Harrisburg Conven-tion, & trust that the next steamer will bring me the news of Mr. Plumer's nomination as Canal Commissioner.

I am truly sorry to hear of the removal of John H. Houston.

---

[1] Buchanan Papers, Historical Society of Pennsylvania.

I am warmly attached both to himself & his family, & cannot believe that he ever joined the Know-nothings.

Please to say to my good & valued friend Danl. I. Jenks that I have received his letter of the 15th ultimo, but have not time to answer it by this steamer.

Every thing goes well & smoothly with me so far as the business of the Legation is concerned. Appleton is all I can desire as a Secretary of Legation, & the Clerk, Mr. Benjamin Moran of Philadelphia, performs his duties to my entire satisfaction. Still I shall heartily rejoice when relieved from its labors.

Jenks informs me that Col: Forney is travelling through the South & West, & intimates that I may know all about his movements. In this respect I am a Know-nothing. He never informed me of his intention to make such a trip, though I occasionally hear from him & am always rejoiced when his letters arrive. His obligations to General Pierce are so strong, & he possesses such a warm & grateful heart, that he ought to be for the General's succession, especially as I am not a candidate.

From your friend, very respectfully,

JAMES BUCHANAN.

WILLIAM FLINN ESQUIRE.

FROM LORD CLARENDON.

(Enclosure in No. 81.[1])   [July 16, 1855.]

The Undersigned, Her Majesty's Principal Secretary of State for Foreign Affairs, has the honor to acknowledge the receipt of the note which Mr. Buchanan, Envoy Extraordinary and Minister Plenipotentiary of the United States, addressed to him on the 6th Instant, respecting attempts stated to have recently been made to enlist within the limits of the United States soldiers for the British army.

The Undersigned must in the first instance express the regret of Her Majesty's Government if the Law of the United States has been in any way infringed by persons acting with or without any authority from them; and it is hardly necessary for the Undersigned to assure Mr. Buchanan that any such infringement of the Law of the United States is entirely contrary to the wishes and to the positive instructions of Her Majesty's Government.

The Undersigned, however, thinks it right to state to Mr. Buchanan that some months ago Her Majesty's Government were informed from various sources that in the British North American Possessions, as well as in the United States, there were many subjects of the Queen who, from sentiments of loyalty, and many foreigners who, from political feeling, were anxious to enter Her Majesty's service and to take part in the war. Her Majesty's

---

[1] Despatch to Mr. Marcy, No. 81, July 20, 1855, infra.

Government, desirous of availing themselves of the offers of these volunteers, adopted the measures necessary for making generally known that Her Majesty's Government were ready to do so, and for receiving such persons as should present themselves at an appointed place in one of the British Possessions. The right of Her Majesty's Government to act in this way was incontestable; but at the same time they issued stringent instructions to guard against any violation of the United States Law of Neutrality, the importance and sound policy of which Law has been so well expounded by Mr. Buchanan, in whose remarks upon it, as well as upon the Foreign Enlistment Bill of this country, Her Majesty's Government entirely concur.

It can scarcely be matter of surprise that when it became known that Her Majesty's Government was prepared to accept these voluntary offers, many persons in various quarters should give themselves out as agents employed by the British Government, in the hope of earning reward by promoting, though on their own responsibility, an object which they were aware was favorably looked upon by the British Government. Her Majesty's Government do not deny that the acts and advertisements of these self-constituted and unauthorized agents were in many instances undoubted violations of the Law of the United States; but such persons had no authority whatever for their proceedings from any British Agents, by all of whom they were promptly and unequivocally disavowed.

With respect to the Proclamation by the Lieutenant Governor of Nova Scotia, inclosed in Mr. Buchanan's note, the Undersigned can assure Mr. Buchanan, with reference both to the character of Sir Gaspard Le Marchant and to the instructions he received, as well as to his correspondence on these instructions, that that officer is quite incapable of intentionally acting against the Law of the United States; and in proof that he did not in fact do so, the Undersigned begs leave to refer Mr. Buchanan to the legal decision given, on the particular point adverted to by Mr. Buchanan, by Judge Kane on the 22nd of May last, in the United States Circuit Court at Philadelphia. The Judge says: " I do not think that the payment of the passage from this country of a man who desires to enlist in a Foreign Port comes within the Act " [the Neutrality Act of 1818.] " In the terms of the printed Proclamation there is nothing conflicting with the Laws of the United States. A person may go abroad, provided the enlistment be in a foreign place, not having accepted and exercised a commission. There is some evidence in Hertz's case that he did hire and retain, and therefore his case would have to be submitted to a jury. In Perkins's case there was testimony upon which a jury might convict. In Bucknell's case it appears that there was a conversation at which he was present, but no enlistment, or hiring, or retaining. The conversation related as to the practicability of persons going to Nova Scotia to enlist. If the rule I have laid down be correct, then the evidence does not connect him with the misdemeanor."— " Mr. Bucknell is therefore discharged, and Messrs. Perkins and Hertz are remanded to take their trial."

As regards the proceedings of Her Majesty's Government, the Undersigned has the honor to inform Mr. Buchanan that Mr. Crampton was directed to issue strict orders to British Consuls in the United States to be careful not to violate the Law; and Mr. Crampton was enjoined, above all, to have no concealment from the Government of the United States. In the absence of Mr. Crampton from Washington, Her Majesty's Chargé d'Affaires placed in Mr. Marcy's hands a despatch from the Undersigned on this subject, expressly stating that "Her Majesty's Government would on no account run any risk of infringing this (the neutrality) law of the United States."

The Undersigned has, however, the honor, in conclusion, to state to Mr. Buchanan that Her Majesty's Government, having reason to think that no precautionary measures, with whatever honesty they might be carried out, could effectually guard against some real or apparent infringement of the Law which would give just cause for complaint to the Government of the United States, determined that all proceedings for enlistment should be put an end to, and instructions to that effect were sent out before the Undersigned had the honor to receive Mr. Buchanan's note; as the Undersigned need hardly say that the advantage which Her Majesty's service might derive from enlistment in North America would not be sought for by Her Majesty's Government, if it were supposed to be obtained in disregard of the respect due to the Law of the United States.

The Undersigned has the honor to renew to Mr. Buchanan the assurance of his consideration.

(signed)   CLARENDON.

FOREIGN OFFICE, July 16, 1855.
THE HONBLE. JAMES BUCHANAN.

TO LORD CLARENDON.

(Enclosure in No. 93.[1])

LEGATION OF THE UNITED STATES,
LONDON, 18 July, 1855.

The Undersigned, Envoy Extraordinary and Minister Plenipotentiary of the United States, has the honor to acknowledge the receipt of the note which the Earl of Clarendon, Her Majesty's Principal Secretary of State for Foreign Affairs, addressed to him on the 16th Instant, in answer to his note of the 6th Instant, on the subject of the enlistment and employment of soldiers for the British army within the United States; and the Undersigned will have much satisfaction in transmitting a copy of His Lordship's note to the Secretary of State by the next Steamer.

The Undersigned has the honor to renew to the Earl of Clarendon the assurance of his distinguished consideration.

(Signed)   JAMES BUCHANAN.

THE RIGHT HONBLE. THE EARL OF CLARENDON,
&c., &c., &c.

----

[1] Despatch to Mr. Marcy, No. 93, Sept. 28, 1855, infra. Printed in S. Ex. Doc. 35, 34 Cong. 1 Sess. 26.

FROM LORD CLARENDON.[1]

Private.   GROSVR. CRESCT. July 19/55.

MY DEAR MR. BUCHANAN:

I beg to enclose the copy of a letter from Major Butler to Lt. Colonel Bolton which you desired to have from the State Paper office.

I have caused enquiry to be made in several Departments respecting the Govt. property destroyed at Fort Ticonderoga, but without success. I also referred to the Colonial office and beg to enclose the answer which I received. I fear there is no chance of obtaining the information.

I have had several communications with the Solicitor General, verbal and written, about the Convention, which I am as anxious as yourself to conclude, for I feel as you do that the present state of things is an opprobrium to two great commercial and maritime Countries like the United States & England, but I have not been able to come to an understanding with him. I venture to trouble you with a memorandum which I have made from the last written opinion of the Solicitor General, in order that you may be aware of the difficulties which he sees in the proposed arrangement, & I shall be much obliged for any remarks upon it that you may favor me with.

If I remember rightly, you told me that Conventions similar to the one which you propose to us have been agreed to between the United States & several other Countries & that they have not given rise to any difficulty. If you would have the goodness to furnish me with a copy of one of these documents I might perhaps turn it to good account with our Lawyers. Believe me

Very faithfully yours

CLARENDON.

MEMORANDUM.

It is an essential principle of criminal justice that no man ought to be imprisoned on a criminal charge without the certainty of being at the earliest period put upon his Trial on that charge.

Nor ought any man to be taken into custody and sent to take his Trial on a criminal charge to a distant place or country, where there is no reasonable certainty of ensuring the attendance of those who have personal knowledge of the circumstances attending the commission of the alleged crime; and who are therefore the only competent Witnesses, as well for the defence as for the prosecution.

But these principles are wholly disregarded by the 2d of the draft articles inclosed in Mr. Buchanan's note of the 1st of March last, and it seems obvious that in many, if not the majority of cases, the provisions of that article would fail of securing the ordinary means for the administration of Justice.

This will be best illustrated by an example.

An American vessel leaves New York on a Whaling Voyage, or on a Voyage to India and China. She puts in at the Cape of Good Hope, and a

---

[1] Buchanan Papers, Historical Society of Pennsylvania.

charge of mutiny or robbery is brought before a British Magistrate by the American captain against an English seaman. The depositions are taken, and the evidence is sufficient to justify the man being committed to take his Trial. According to the Article, the accused person is either to be delivered as a Prisoner to the Captain, or to be sent by some other ship to New York for Trial. But the American ship, if she ever returns to New York, will probably not return there for 2 or 3 years, and what in the mean time is to be done with the Prisoner? This is not an extreme case, but one very likely to occur; and in fact the case is the same in principle, tho' not in extent, if we take an ordinary merchant vessel trading between Baltimore and Bristol. The seaman accused and committed at Bristol would be sent to Baltimore for Trial, but with no certainty that the persons whose evidence is essential to save his life may not (if Passengers) be left at Bristol, or (if Seamen) have quitted the ship before her return to Baltimore. Suppose the crime to be alleged to have been committed by a Seaman upon a Passenger in an American ship during a voyage from Boston to Liverpool. The seaman, having been arrested at Liverpool, is to be sent to Boston for Trial; are the Witnesses both for the prosecution and defence to be sent there too? Some of them may be persons who will have no intention of returning to Boston. It would be easy to multiply such instances, and to show that the proposed Article, instead of promoting the administration of criminal justice, would be calculated to produce a contrary effect.

If it be asked, "Have you no remedy for the present existing evil of the entire failure of Justice?" There seems no better remedy than that the Criminal Courts of England and America shall by mutual legislation be empowered to take cognizance of Crimes committed on the High Seas by persons on board the ships of either country.

With regard to the objects contemplated by the other draft articles proposed by Mr. Buchanan:—

1st. As to Article 1. There would be no difficulty in extending to American vessels all such facilities as the law permits for apprehending deserters from merchant vessels, and sending them on board their ships; those facilities being such as are described in the Act of Parliament 15 and 16 Victoria, c. 26. This might be done either by an Article of a Convention, or by an Order in council which might be issued under the Act above referred to, on Mr. Buchanan simply giving official assurance that equal facilities are or will be given to British vessels in the United States.

2ndly. Nor would there be any objection to conclude an Article on the subject treated of in the 3d of Mr. Buchanan's Articles; to the effect that no jurisdiction shall be exercised by the Courts of either country at any port or place at which a vessel of the other may touch in the course of her voyage, with respect to any cause of dispute or matter of litigation of a civil nature between the master and crew of such vessel, except at any port or place where the voyage and term of service of one of the litigating Parties may have terminated; and that in any such case, and in any other cases on the application of the Consul of the nation to which the vessel belongs, the Justices or other officers possessing summary jurisdiction shall exercise the same jurisdiction with regard to disputes between the Masters and Seamen of such vessels as they can exercise between the Masters & seamen of national vessels.

Such an Article would however require the authority of Parliament, and therefore Her Majesty's Government could conclude it only subject to obtaining such authority.

July 19, 1855.[1]

TO MR. MARCY.[2]

No. 81.   LEGATION OF THE UNITED STATES.

LONDON, 20 July 1855.

SIR:

I have the honor to acknowledge the receipt of your Despatches Nos. 98, 99, 100, and 101, of the 28th and 30th June and of the 2d and 3d July, respectively.

I transmit the copy of a note received from Lord Clarendon, dated on the 16th Instant, in answer to mine of the 6th Instant, on the subject of the enlistment and employment of soldiers for the British army within the limits of the United States. In acknowledging the receipt of this note, I have informed his Lordship that I shall have much satisfaction in transmitting a copy of it to the Secretary of State by the next Steamer.

I also transmit the copy of a note received from Lord Clarendon, dated on the 16th Instant, in answer to mine of the 12th, which communicated to the British Government the thanks of the President for the aid rendered by Commander Curtis, of Her Majesty's Steam Sloop " Brisk," to the American merchant ship " North Carolina."

I have received from the Department of State a copy of the new edition of Wheaton's Elements of International Law, for the use of the Legation.

I transmit herewith two copies of a notification received from Lord Clarendon, with a note dated on the 18th Instant, inserted in the London Gazette of the 17th, " announcing the establishment of a blockade of Russian Ports in the White Sea by the combined British and French naval forces;" which his Lord-

---

[1] This memorandum was enclosed to Mr. Marcy by Mr. Buchanan with his despatch No. 83, of August 3, 1855, infra. It was received by Mr. Buchanan on July 20.

[2] MSS. Department of State, 67 Despatches from England. The paragraph relating to recruitment is printed in S. Ex. Doc. 35, 34 Cong. 1 Sess. 15.

ship requests me to transmit to my Government, " in order that it may through that channel become known to the citizens of the United States."

In regard to your Despatch No. 99, concerning the use of the Despatch Bags, I shall make a few observations.

You appear throughout to have confounded this Legation with the Despatch Agency in London; although our connection with it, like that of other Legations, consists simply in sending our Despatches, private letters, &c., once per week to Mr. Miller to be placed in the bag. I repeat again emphatically that nothing has been sent from this Legation to him since the period mentioned in my Despatch No. 76, except what in my estimation has been entirely proper. In confirmation of this, and after carefully examining the Inventories of the Despatch Bags of the Atlantic and Baltic which you have forwarded here, I believe they contain not a single letter, or newspaper, or anything else, which was placed in the Bag on my request, by my direction, or with my knowledge, except the letter to the Chevalier de Cueto. I did send a very few private letters written by myself in the Bag by both of these steamers, of which I always keep a register; but, strange to say, not one of these is mentioned in either Inventory. Ever since the period to which I have alluded, I have made it a point to see personally that nothing should be sent from the Legation to the Despatch Agency, except what was clearly within the long established rules.

If you had acted upon the distinction between the Legation and the Agency, and instructed the Minister to inquire into the alleged abuses of the latter, I should have most cheerfully performed this duty. Even as it is, I have taken upon myself to advise Mr. Miller to place nothing in the Despatch Bag for any person in London, except the Consul, which he shall not receive from this Legation; and if you should think proper to add your instruction to my advice, I am persuaded there would be no cause for complaint hereafter. He is faithful, honest, industrious, and obliging, and is devoted to his duties; but is one of those persons who can with difficulty say No.

I am gratified that you have relaxed the rule prescribed in your Despatch of the 28th May last, & that my letters to persons, although not residing in Washington, and not relating to official business, if prepaid, can now go forward to their destination without being considered " as sea borne letters." Still, since you have deemed it unsafe to entrust your agents in New York and

Boston to open the bags, we shall use them but little for this purpose.

Whilst I shall obey your instructions implicitly, I still venture to express the opinion that some discretion ought to be allowed to a minister in London to use the bag in certain cases beyond these instructions.

It has always been the practice to send in the bag letters to gentlemen who have been Ministers in this country, from their English friends; and yet I do not believe I have sent a dozen, certainly not twenty, such letters since I have been in London.

So far as I am acquainted with the practice of different Legations, it has always been deemed an act of international comity to send Despatches and letters for each other in their respective bags; and as the United States rarely, if ever, employ paid messengers, we have certainly gained more than we have lost by this practice. When in St. Petersburg, I sent many of my Despatches & letters to London in the bag of the British Ambassador, and received many such Despatches and letters through the same channel.

I do not recollect whether "the four large bundles" directed to Mr. Figaniere, the Portuguese Minister, by his Government, were sent from this Legation to the Despatch Agency or not; but if not, they certainly would have been sent before the receipt of your instructions. And why? Because every thing that comes in the Despatch Bag from the State Department—all private letters, packages, &c., whatever they may be, from the United States, directed to our Minister at Lisbon, are regularly sent in the Despatch Bag of the Portuguese Minister in London. Under these circumstances, I could not have refused to send even "the four large bundles" to Mr. Figaniere. Besides, this was an exceptional case, and may never again occur. Nor would the Government have lost $66 postage had these bundles not been sent in the bag. They would surely not have been transmitted by mail. Besides, the British bag to Mr. Crampton would doubtless have been at the service of Count de Lavradio, the Portuguese Minister in London.

There are some matters of a public nature for which it is difficult to refuse the use of the Bag. For example, I was obliged, a few days ago, most reluctantly to refuse to send in this manner reports of the Royal British Agricultural Society to four of our State Agricultural Societies. At this very moment, whilst I am writing, I have received a letter from the Foreign

Correspondent of the " Royal Institute of British Architects," with three accompanying packages. I send the letter and the packages to you merely to shew the nature of the applications which are sometimes, though not often, made, and have been always heretofore granted, and promise not again to violate your instructions in this particular.

By the last steamer (the Atlantic) there came in the Despatch Bag, from a gentleman of high respectability in New York, a package of books (I know not what they are) for Sir John Packington. Should he desire to send something in return to his correspondent, it will sound strangely for me to say to him, although you have received your package by the Despatch Bag, I have been instructed that you shall not return your answer by the same channel.

In regard to the "cumbersome packages" to which you refer as found in the Despatch Bags, addressed to private individuals, with printed labels, &c., and with the seal of the Legation upon them,—not one of these ever saw, the Legation, and no man in London would, I think, even venture to request either Mr. Appleton or myself to send such packages in the Despatch Bag. You do not seem to be aware that Mr. Miller has always had a seal of the Legation in his possession, and must continue to have it unless he should be obliged to bring every Despatch Bag which he sends to the United States, or to the Continent, nearly two miles to this Legation for no other purpose than merely to have the seal affixed.

Instead of the plan which you propose, of identifying the letters from members of this Legation by requiring them to endorse their names upon these letters, I shall adopt another which will be equally efficacious for your purpose. The few letters which we may send to the Department by the Bags shall be placed in a single envelope and directed either by Mr. Appleton or myself to Mr. Hunter, who is well acquainted with the handwriting of both. I have sent but very few newspapers to the United States, either in or out of Bags,—and I shall send no more by the latter conveyance.

I have been informed by a note from Mr. Bates, of the firm of Baring Brothers, & Co., that they have received instructions from the State Department which will prevent them from paying the salary of the Minister and Secretary of Legation at the end of each month as heretofore. This will put me to no other inconvenience during the brief remnant of my term than to borrow the amount of my salary at the end of each month, to be repaid at the end of the quarter, which I can do readily. I speak, therefore, only in behalf of my unknown successor. He will have no outfit, and will be obliged, according to the uniform custom here, to pay his household expenses at the end of each month. Under these circumstances it may be very inconvenient for him to be in London three months before he can draw for any part of his salary.

Yours very respectfully
JAMES BUCHANAN.

HON: WILLIAM L. MARCY
    Secretary of State.

TO LORD CLARENDON.[1]

Private.   U. S. LEGATION, LONDON,
                                        21st July 1855.

MY DEAR LORD CLARENDON,

Many thanks to you for your kindness in procuring and sending the papers which I requested. But you thus always act.

In regard to the Consular treaty, I had given this up after our last conversation. The unfortunate subject of Slavery which has done & will continue to do so much injury in the relations between the two countries, I thought, from your remarks, would effectually prevent Great Britain from restoring deserting sailors to the United States, although [it is] notorious that slaves are never employed as sailors in foreign voyages by my countrymen. I had thought it was a very simple matter to apply the principles of our Extradition Treaties to high crimes committed on the ocean as well as on the land. At present, according to your established law and practice, a murder may be committed any day, of the most valuable person of either Country, on board a Collins Steamer, and on her arrival at Liverpool the murderer is set at liberty, and the Captain may consider himself fortunate if he should not be sued for false imprisonment. The law may be the same in the United States, and reciprocate this evil in regard to murders and other high crimes committed on board one of the Cunard Steamers on her way to New York; though I am persuaded the practice has been altogether different.

---

[1] Buchanan Papers, Historical Society of Pennsylvania.

The Solicitor General treats this great question involving the life and property of all people who "go down to the sea in Ships" in the spirit of his highly respectable profession. He imagines a case of hardship which may possibly occur, should the extradition of criminals on the ocean as well as on the land be provided for, and hence infers that no provision ought to be made. Such reasoning would bring the world to a "Stand Still" and arrest the progress of the most conservative human improvements. The truth is that from the high character of the Judiciary in both Countries, from the humanity of Juries, and for the very reasons stated by the Solicitor General, it would be very difficult to convict any person for a crime committed on the ocean, unless in very clear cases.

I believe that we now have Conventions with every commercial nation in the world except England, providing for the first and third points of my proposition. The necessity for a provision for the second point had never been rendered manifest until the recent occurrence of the discharge of the mutineers in London. In regard to other nations this has never been found necessary. The Consular instructions adopted at an early period of our history, to which I have referred specially in my note to you of the first of March last, have proved sufficient.— If you think there is any possibility of concluding a Convention, I shall be happy again to confer with you on the subject.

I cannot omit this occasion of expressing my high personal satisfaction at the able, firm, and consistent course pursued by your Lordship in conducting the late negotiations. Although I entertain my own opinions in regard to the present war, and sincerely wish England were fairly and honorably out of it, yet I heartily congratulate you for having presented so clear a record, free from ambiguity and doubt, & requiring no explanations, no apologies, no "doubling and twisting."

Yours very respectfully

James Buchanan.

TO MR. MARCY.[1]

No. 82.   LEGATION OF THE UNITED STATES.

LONDON, 27th July 1855.

SIR:

I have the honor to acknowledge the receipt of your Circular of the 10th Instant, relative to the use of the Despatch Bags.

I have received a note from Lord Clarendon, dated on the 19th Instant, in reply to mine of the 19th June, requesting Her Majesty's Exequatur for D. M. Huckins, Esquire, appointed Consul of the United States at Cape Town; in which he informs me " that the Governor of the Cape has been instructed to report whether he is aware of any objection to an Exequatur being issued to Mr. Huckins, and that if in his opinion no such objection exists, he is authorized to recognise Mr. Huckins as Acting Consul pending the transmission of his Exequatur."

I have received (on the 24th inst.) the Exequatur for Israel D. Andrews, appointed Consul General of the United States for the British North American Provinces, and this, together with his Commission, has been forwarded to him at his post, St. John, N. B.

In obedience to your instructions (No. 101) I have addressed a note to Lord Clarendon requesting the discharge of David L. Caldwell. I do not, however, find the slightest allegation, even in his own letter of the 19th May last, which accompanied your Despatch, that he had been impressed into the British service, and from this it is doubtful, to say the least, whether he had been actually deceived.

I have had two interviews with Mr. " Juan B. Alberdi, Chargé d'Affaires of the Argentine Confederation " to this Court, and have communicated to him the substance of your Despatch No. 93. It was agreed between us that when he thought the proper time had arrived, he would give me notice, and I should then call upon Lord Clarendon and inform him of the views of the President and the course which he intends to pursue in relation to the Argentine Confederation and the Republic of Buenos Ayres. Our last interview took place on Wednesday the 18th Instant, and since that time I have not seen him.

I have not yet been able to obtain the list of claims for return duties on woollens, to which you refer in your Despatch

_____

[1] MSS. Department of State, 67 Despatches from England.

No. 100; but I hope to do so in time to forward it to you by the steamer of August 4th.

Yours very respectfully

JAMES BUCHANAN.

HON: WILLIAM L. MARCY,
  Secretary of State.

TO MR. MARCY.[1]

No. 83.   LEGATION OF THE UNITED STATES.
LONDON, 3 August 1855.

SIR:

I have the honor to acknowledge the receipt of your Despatch No. 102, of the 15th ultimo.

Referring to that part of my Despatch No. 78, of the 29th June, relating to the proposed Consular Convention between Great Britain and the United States,—I received from Lord Clarendon, on the 20th ultimo, a " Memorandum," dated on the 19th, of which he thus speaks in a *private* note accompanying it:—" I have had several communications with the Solicitor General, verbal and written, about the Convention, which I am as anxious as yourself to conclude, for I feel as you do, that the present state of things is an opprobrium to two great commercial and maritime countries like the United States and England; but I have not been able to come to an understanding with him. I venture to trouble you with a ' Memorandum ' which I have made from the last written opinion of the Solicitor General, in order that you may be aware of the difficulties which he sees in the proposed arrangement, and I shall be much obliged for any remarks upon it that you may favor me with," &c. &c. &c.

I send a copy of this " Memorandum." [2]

I do not furnish you a copy of the whole of his Lordship's *private* note, though I feel myself quite at liberty to give you a copy of my entire answer, dated on the 21st ultimo, so far as it relates to this subject. It is as follows: . . .[3]

In reply to this, I received a *private* note from His Lordship,

---

[1] MSS. Department of State, 67 Despatches from England.

[2] See note from Lord Clarendon, July 19, 1855, supra.

[3] See the answer, supra, under date of July 21, 1855. In the despatch Mr. Buchanan quotes the whole, except the first and last paragraphs.

dated on the 24th ultimo, of a satisfactory character, so far as his own individual opinion was concerned, in which he says, among other things:—" I am sure that you and I could in an hour lay the ground for a better state of things."

In this condition of affairs, I received opportunely a letter from Nathaniel Hawthorne, Esquire, our Consul at Liverpool, dated on the 30th ultimo, of which, together with the enclosed affidavits I transmit you copies.

You will perceive that these raise the question clearly and distinctly whether an " assault with an intent to commit murder," *on board an American vessel on the high seas,* is embraced by the provisions of the 10th [Extradition] Article of the Treaty of Washington of the 9th August, 1842.

In my official note to Lord Clarendon of the 31st ultimo, of which I send a copy, requesting a warrant for the arrest of Henry Norris Johnson, charged with this crime, you will observe that the facts necessary to raise the question are distinctly stated.

I accompanied this with a *private* note from myself of the same date, of which the following is a copy:—

" I send, accompanying this, a requisition for the extradition of Henry Norris Johnson. The crime charged and clearly proven against him is ' assault with intent to commit murder.'

" The place:—On board an American ship on the high seas, whilst on her voyage from New York to Liverpool; and therefore, under the law of nations, ' within the jurisdiction ' of the United States, according to the terms of the Treaty. (Wheaton, 157.)

" The Treaty not only provides for the extradition of criminals who ' shall seek an asylum,' but also of those who ' shall be found ' within the territories of the other party; and throughout the subsequent part of the article, the language employed is ' the fugitive or person so charged,' in the alternative.

" It is manifest that the Article embraces not merely such criminals as have fled from justice, but all others who have committed the crimes mentioned, & ' shall be found ' within the jurisdiction of the other party.

" The crime and not the flight is, as it ought to be, the question.

" If this construction be correct, and I do not see how it can be contested, then the second of my propositions for a Consular Convention becomes, in a great degree, unnecessary. The crime of mutiny, or an attempt to commit mutiny, might simply be added to the list embraced by the Extradition Treaty.

" Please to give this subject a little of your own personal attention.

" The decision of the case of extradition now submitted will decide the whole matter, so far as the crimes enumerated in the treaty are concerned."

On the next day, August 1st, I received a note from Lord Clarendon, of which I send a copy, transmitting a warrant from Sir George Grey, the Secretary of State for the Home Department, for the apprehension of Henry Norris Johnson,—which I immediately forwarded to Mr. Hawthorne.

I also received a *private* note from Lord Clarendon of the same date, in which he says:—" I did as you desired in your letter of yesterday and took the matter in hand myself—no lawyer having been consulted, there was neither difficulty nor delay, as you will have seen by my official note."

I transmit, herewith, two " copies of a further notification inserted in the London Gazette of yesterday [27th July, received from Lord Clarendon on the 28th] respecting the blockade of Russian Ports in the Gulf of Bothnia by the combined British and French Naval Forces;" and his Lordship requests that I " will have the goodness to transmit copies of this notification to your [my] Government, in order that it may through that channel become known to the citizens of the United States."

Mr. Appleton has had in charge the subject of your Despatch No. 100, and has received a note from Mr. Russell Sturgis, one of the partners of the House of Baring Brothers & Co., dated on the 31th ultimo, in which he states that he has seen Mr. Barry, who says, " the list [of claimants for the return of woollen duties, under the Convention of 8 February, 1853] waits only for one or two names (Mr. W. Brown and Mr. Rathbone), and as soon as he gets them he will send it at once to Judge Upham."

You will observe by the London Times of this morning that Lord Palmerston last night in the House of Commons, in answer to an inquiry of Mr. Thomas Milnor Gibson, stated as follows:—" With regard to the question which arose in the United States [respecting the enlistment or engagement of soldiers for the Foreign Legion] I beg to inform the right honorable gentleman that a similar arrangement [to that at Heligoland] was made at Halifax, by which any persons going there from whatever quarter might be enrolled; but it appearing that that had led to questions within the territory of the United States as to whether or not the law of that country had been violated, Her Majesty's Government, being desirous that no such questions should by possibility arise, has put an end to the enlistment of forces which used to take place at Halifax." (" Hear, hear.")[1]

I need scarcely observe that the extracts which I have made in this Despatch from the *private* notes of Lord Clarendon are merely intended to present to you a full view of the matters to which they relate, and ought not, at least for the present, to be published.

Yours very respectfully,

JAMES BUCHANAN.

HON: WILLIAM L. MARCY,
 Secretary of State.

ENCLOSURES.

1.—" Memorandum " from Lord Clarendon, dated 19 July, 1855. (See supra, under July 19.)

2.—Letter from Nathaniel Hawthorne, Esq., to Mr. Buchanan, dated at Liverpool, 30 July, 1855. (See below.)

3.—Affidavits in the case of Henry Norris Johnson. (Not given here.)

4.—Mr. Buchanan to Lord Clarendon, dated July 31, 1855. (See below.)

5.—Lord Clarendon to Mr. Buchanan, dated August 1, 1855. (See below.)

6.—Two copies London Gazette, July 27, 1855, containing Notification of further blockade of Russian Ports in the Gulf of Bothnia. (Not given here.)

(Enclosure in No. 83.) CONSULATE OF THE UNITED STATES,
            LIVERPOOL, 30th July, 1855.

SIR:

 I beg to enclose herewith affidavits of the Master and three of the crew of the American ship " Cultivator," charging Henry Norris Johnson with the crime of assault with intent to commit murder, on board the said vessel, while within the jurisdiction of the United States, in order that you may make requisition for the surrender and extradition of the accused, under the tenth section of the treaty with Great Britain of 1842.

 Johnson is now in confinement on board the vessel in the Dock at this Port, and must be kept there until the Magistrate can issue a warrant for his apprehension, which he cannot do until he is notified by the Secretary of State of your having made the requisition.

 With high respect I have the honor to be

Your Obed. Servant,

(signed) NATHL. HAWTHORNE.

To HIS EXCELLENCY, JAMES BUCHANAN.

---

[1] The foregoing paragraph is printed in S. Ex. Doc. 35, 34 Cong. 1 Sess. 18.

(Enclosure in No. 83.)

LEGATION OF THE UNITED STATES,
LONDON, July 31st, 1855.

MY LORD,

I have the honor to furnish you a letter just received from Nathaniel Hawthorne, Esquire, United States Consul at Liverpool, bearing date on the 30th instant, together with the original depositions taken before him at Liverpool on the 28th & 30th instant, from which it seems clear that Henry Norris Johnson, a seaman belonging to the American Merchant Ship " Cultivator," was on the tenth instant guilty of the crime of " assault with intent to commit murder " on Charles Ryan, another seaman on board the said ship, when seven days out from Port on her voyage from New York to Liverpool, the said crime being committed " within the jurisdiction of the United States; and that the said Henry Norris Johnson is now ' to be found ' at Liverpool."

I have, therefore, to request that your Lordship would grant, or cause to be granted, the warrant required by the Act of Parliament to the proper Magistrate or Magistrates at Liverpool for the arrest of the said Henry Norris Johnson, to answer to the charge of " assault with intent to commit murder " on Charles Ryan, on board the said ship, and to be further dealt with, according to the provisions of the tenth article of the treaty of Washington of the 9th August, 1842.

Yours very respectfully

JAMES BUCHANAN.

THE RIGHT HONORABLE THE EARL OF CLARENDON,
&c. &c. &c.

(Enclosure in No. 83.)

FOREIGN OFFICE, August 1st, 1855.

SIR,

I did not fail to refer to Her Majesty's Secretary of State for the Home Department your letter of yesterday's date requesting the extradition, under the 10th article of the Treaty of Washington of the 9th of August, 1842, of Henry Norris Johnson, a seaman belonging to the American Merchant Ship " Cultivator," who is charged with the crime of assault with intent to commit murder, and who is stated to be at Liverpool; and I have the honour to transmit to you herewith a warrant which has been issued under the hand and seal of Secretary Sir George Grey for the apprehension of the above mentioned person.

I return herewith the Depositions enclosed in your letter.

I have the honor to be, with the highest consideration, Sir,

Your most obedient humble servant,

(Signed) CLARENDON.

THE HONORABLE JAMES BUCHANAN.
&c. &c. &c.

TO MR. MARCY.[1]

No. 84.   LEGATION OF THE UNITED STATES.

LONDON, 10 August 1855.

SIR:

I have the honor to acknowledge the receipt of your Despatch No. 103, of the 20th July last.

For want of something more important, I am induced, on account of an unpleasant incident which has recently occurred at the Liverpool Custom House, to make some observations on a subject with which the State Department ought to be acquainted.

In this, as I believe in all other countries, foreign Ministers import what they please for their own use, and also receive articles from their respective Governments, free of duty. I have exercised this right in a very limited manner, generally preferring to purchase from English dealers all articles for domestic purposes (with the single exception of wine,) rather than conform to the stringent regulations required in order to avail myself of it. In fact, the authorities here would seem to act upon the presumption that all foreign Ministers would be smugglers if they could. As an example of the process required, I transmit a copy of the application I was obliged to make to Lord Clarendon for the importation free of duty of the Eleven Packages containing copies of Wheaton's Elements of International Law, and Newspapers, sent by the Department for distribution among our Legations and Consulates in Europe.

From some mistake or omission at the Department, which has previously occurred on more than one occasion, I have never until this day received any advices concerning these Packages, nor did I know of their arrival, or even of their existence, until a notice arrived to this effect from the Liverpool Custom House. In order to ask for a Treasury Order for their admission duty free, it became necessary that I should ascertain what they contained; and for this purpose I directed them, through Mr. Miller, to be opened. It was then discovered that their contents consisted of the Volumes of Wheaton, a package of Newspapers, and *about six pounds of cigars, the duty on which is nine shillings per lb., with 5 per cent. additional duty.*

Believing that these cigars had been fraudulently inserted in the packages and not having the most remote idea whence or

---

[1] MSS. Department of State, 67 Despatches from England.

from whom they came, I did not deem it proper to ask that they should be covered by the Treasury Order. The inference which the Custom House officers at Liverpool seem to have drawn, strangely enough, from this refusal on my part to violate my duty (as will appear from Mr. Hawthorne's letter of the 9th Instant, a copy of which I send together with my answer,) is that the American Legation "has been detected in an attempt at petty smuggling." That is,—because we refused to ask for the admission of these cigars duty free, which we might readily have done had this been proper, that therefore we desired to smuggle them and evade the payment of duty which would have been remitted on our request.

The occurrence nevertheless is an unpleasant one, especially as these packages would appear to have come directly from the Department; and I therefore request that you would endeavor to ascertain how the cigars came to be inserted in the packages. That this was not done at the Department, I am thoroughly convinced; because, from my knowledge of the gentlemen employed in it, I do not, for a moment, harbour the suspicion that any of them would be concerned in such an act. They must have been fraudulently introduced by some person after the packages left the Department. If you could ascertain by whom or under whose care these packages were sent, this might lead to some discovery.

From what I have said, you will be convinced of the necessity of accompanying every package sent to the Legation by a letter of advice to Mr. Miller or myself, stating the contents.

I have several times spoken to Lord Clarendon concerning the stringency of the rules applied to Foreign Ministers at British Custom Houses, and stated my belief that the practice was altogether different in regard to articles sent from abroad to foreign Ministers at Washington; and that we acted on the presumption that no person occupying such a position would ever consent to receive any articles free of duty except those to which he was entitled. I would thank you to inform me whether I have been correct in this statement.

Yours very respectfully

JAMES BUCHANAN.

HON: WILLIAM L. MARCY
    Secretary of State.

TO MISS LANE.[1]

LEGATION OF THE UNITED STATES
LONDON, 18 August, 1855.

MY DEAR HARRIET/

I enclose a letter to you from Mr. H. Randall, which I opened, seeing that it came from Manchester & believing it was about the shawls. I have sent the two shawls mentioned in the letter as requested to Messrs. Stavert, Figomala, Miller & Co., Glasgow, & informed Mr. Randall where you are & that you would not be in London until Monday the 27th Instant.

There is no news of any consequence. I dined yesterday with Sir Richard Pakenham at the Traveller's Club & we had a pleasant time of it. I shall meet him again at dinner on Tuesday next at Count Lavradio's, to which you were also invited.

Sir Richard is a sensible man. He has absolutely resigned & has only been prevailed upon to attend the coronation of the young King of Portugal as British minister. He will be back from Lisbon in October. He says he is determined not to wear out his life from home; but pass the remnant of his days among his relatives & friends in Ireland. I am persuaded he has not the least idea of marrying a young wife, though younger than Sir F.—He was born in '97 & Sir F. in '96. I am in favor of a considerable disparity between the ages of husband & wife for many reasons & should be especially so in your case. Still, I do not think that your husband ought to be *more than double your own age.*

With my kindest regards to Mr. & Mrs. Shapter & Sissy, I remain

Yours affectionately

JAMES BUCHANAN.

MISS HARRIET LANE.

---

[1] Buchanan Papers, private collection. Imperfectly printed in Curtis's Buchanan, II. 150.

TO MISS LANE.[1]

LEGATION OF THE UNITED STATES,
LONDON, 20 August, 1855.

MY DEAR HARRIET/

I enclose you a number of letters including all received by the Atlantic.

There is one, I presume, from Lady Ouseley. I wrote to her & informed her of the circumstances of your visit to the Isle of Wight, & your intention to pass some time with me at the Star & Garter before proceeding to Lancashire & our intention then to visit them & Miss Gamble.

I learn by a letter from John H. Houston that poor Jessie is very ill of a typhoid fever & her recovery doubtful to say the least. Brother Edward had been sent for & was expected.

I have received instructions from Gov. Marcy on the Central American questions which render it almost morally certain that from their nature they cannot be executed before the 30th September, with declarations that I am the most proper person &c. &c. &c. to carry them into effect, & not a word about my successor. Indeed Mr. Hunter, the Chief Clerk, writes me as follows under date of 6th August: " I hear nothing as to who is to be your successor. It is no doubt a difficult question to decide."

With my kindest regards to Mr. & Mrs. Shapter & to my own Sissy, I remain

Yours affectionately

JAMES BUCHANAN.

MISS HARRIET LANE.

TO MISS LANE.[2]

LEGATION OF THE UNITED STATES,
LONDON, 23 August, 1855.

MY DEAR HARRIET/

I know nothing at present which will prevent me from accompanying Mr. Appleton to the Isle of Wight. Why should I not occasionally take " a spree " as well as Mr. Shapter? You

---

[1] Buchanan Papers, private collection. Imperfectly printed in Curtis's Buchanan, II. 150.

[2] Buchanan Papers, private collection. Partly printed in Curtis's Buchanan, II. 150.

may, therefore, secure me a room in the hotel should this be deemed necessary. I shall be there some time on Saturday. Till then, farewell!

Yrs. affectionately

JAMES BUCHANAN.

P. S. I have just rec'd yrs. of yesterday. Mr. Appleton will want a room. We shall dine at the hotel. Mark this.

TO MR. MARCY.[1]

No. 86.   LEGATION OF THE UNITED STATES.
LONDON, 24 August, 1855.

SIR:

I have had the honor to receive, on Monday last, your Despatch No. 104, of the 6th Instant.[2] In this I am instructed to bring the Central American questions, which have arisen under the Treaty of the 19th April, 1850, to an issue with the British Government and to obtain an explicit declaration of the position Great Britain is determined to maintain relative to these questions. This duty I shall cheerfully perform, according to my best ability; without, however, entertaining much hope that Lord Palmerston's administration will recede from the position which they have already so clearly indicated. Still, the gravity and responsibility of a final answer in the negative to our just demands under this Treaty may, possibly, cause them to reconsider and to change their avowed opinions in regard to its true construction. I should entertain better hopes of such a result, were it possible at the present moment to enlighten the British people on the nature of these questions, and thus, probably, to bring public opinion to bear in our favor upon the Ministry. This cannot now be done until after the next annual message of the President to Congress; and it may be then too late.

Your instructions will most probably delay my separation from the Mission until after the 30th September. Lord Clarendon is still absent with the Queen in France, and will not return to London until some time next week. After I shall have prepared and presented my note to him in obedience to them, there

---

[1] MSS. Department of State, 67 Despatches from England.
[2] H. Ex. Doc. 1, 34 Cong. 1 Sess. I. 69.

may be considerable delay in obtaining an answer; and even then, it may become necessary to transmit this answer to you and await your reply.

I had calculated with perfect confidence, and anticipated with great satisfaction, my return to the United States early in the month of October, and had made all my arrangements accordingly. Indeed, up till the receipt of your Despatch, I had inferred that the President deemed it advisable, before demanding a final and explicit answer on the Central American questions, to await a change in the British (Palmerston) Ministry, and in the mean time to bring these questions before the Public of both countries by his next annual Message. In this inference it appears I was mistaken; and it has now become my duty, whatever time this may require, to carry into effect your instructions, according to my best judgment and with all due deliberation. On the performance of this duty the President and yourself may confidently rely, whatever may be the personal inconvenience and disappointment to myself.

Yours very respectfully,

JAMES BUCHANAN.

HON: WILLIAM L. MARCY,
Secretary of State.

TO MISS LANE.[1]

U. S. LEGATION,
LONDON, 28 Aug: 1855.

MY DEAR HARRIET/

I opened a letter for you from Glasgow. It is dated on the 24th & announces the sending of the two shawls—" Grey centre with black & scarlet border." They have not yet been received, neither had those I returned been received.

There was no letter for you by the Asia. I send the three last Heralds. Poor Mr. Lawrence had been given up.[2] There were no longer any hopes of his recovery.

Col: L. is still in Paris. His brother & lady are, I understand, in London, & will leave for home by the Arago from Southampton to-morrow.

---

[1] Buchanan Papers, private collection; Curtis's Buchanan, II. 151.
[2] Abbott Lawrence, of Boston.

I had not a word from Washington,—*official or unofficial.*
Nothing about poor Jessie.

We had a very pleasant time on our return from Black Gang
Chine & indeed throughout our excursion.

The Shanklin Chine is much more picturesque than the
Black Gang affair. No news.

With my kindest regards to Mr. & Mrs. & Miss Shapter &
Mrs. Coleman, I remain, in haste,

Yrs. affectionately

JAMES BUCHANAN.

P. S.   No letters for me from Philadelphia or Lancaster.

P. S.   The shawls have arrived from Glasgow & Grey [1]
says they are all right according to yr. order.

TO LORD CLARENDON.

(Enclosure in No. 87.[2])

LEGATION OF THE UNITED STATES,

LONDON, 30 August, 1855.

The Undersigned, Envoy Extraordinary and Minister
Plenipotentiary of the United States, has been instructed to
propose to the Earl of Clarendon, Her Majesty's Principal Secretary of State for Foreign Affairs, the conclusion of a convention between the United States and Great Britain, recognizing
the principles in favor of neutral commerce:—that free ships
shall make free goods, contraband of war excepted; and that the
goods of a friend captured on board the vessels of an enemy, with
the like exception, shall not be subject to confiscation. And,
furthermore, that the parties shall " apply these principles to
the commerce and navigation of all such Powers and States as
shall consent to adopt them, on their part, as permanent and
immutable."

The Undersigned has, also, the honor of communicating
for the Earl of Clarendon's consideration, the Projet of a convention which has been transmitted to him by the Secretary of
State, for the purpose of giving effect to these principles.

---

[1] Miss Lane's English maid.

[2] Despatch to Mr. Marcy, No. 87, August 31, 1855, infra. This note is
printed in S. Ex. Doc. 85, 34 Cong. 1 Sess. 3.

The Government of the United States has, from its very origin, on all suitable occasions, exerted its influence to establish the principle that free ships shall make free goods. It has ever believed that the practice of violating the neutral flag for the purpose of seizing and confiscating enemies' property had its origin in a barbarous age and was wholly inconsistent with the spirit of advancing civilization. Acting on this conviction, it has concluded many successive treaties with different nations, the first that with France in 1778, adopting the principle that the flag shall protect the cargo. It therefore hailed with peculiar satisfaction the high authority of Her Britannic Majesty's Declaration announcing this principle as the guide of her Government during the existing war with Russia.

The President of the United States, believing that this declaration affords an auspicious occasion for obtaining the general consent of commercial nations to recognize the principles which it sanctions as a part of the public law, has, accordingly, invited France, as well as other Powers, to enter into arrangements for this purpose similar to that now proposed to Great Britain.

It is scarcely necessary to observe that the present proposal does not proceed from any apprehension that Great Britain will ever hereafter reverse the precedent she has so recently established. It has been solely dictated by a desire to give to the principles of Her Majesty's declaration the solemn sanction of both Governments; and thus, by their combined influence, to recommend the adoption of them to the other nations of the civilized world.

In issuing this declaration, Her Majesty has done no more than return to the just and liberal policy on which Great Britain had acted during a long period previous to the wars of the French Revolution. We have been recently informed by an eminent British statesman that during the century and a quarter which preceded these wars, the all but invariable rule of British friendly relations, as established by Treaty with the great Maritime Powers of Western Europe, was, " free ships, free goods." Indeed, it has been observed by a high authority on international law (Wheaton), that " there is a great preponderance of modern treaties in favor of the maxim, *free ships, free goods,* sometimes, but not always, connected with the correlative maxim, *enemy ships, enemy goods;* so that it may be said that for two centuries past there has been a constant tendency to establish by compact the principle that the neutrality of the ship should exempt the cargo, even if enemy's property, from capture and confiscation as prize of war."

A reference to the numerous treaties concluded within this period among the great maritime Powers of Europe, Great Britain included, will abundantly justify this statement.

The struggle which Great Britain triumphantly maintained against nearly all the other nations of Europe from 1793 till 1815 caused her during this period to fall back upon the ancient and rigorous rule of capturing and confiscating the goods of an enemy on the vessel of a friend. A favorable conjuncture of circumstances, however, has led her to resume the more liberal policy which she announced at the commencement of the present war with Russia. Great Britain, by surrendering her claim to capture the goods of an enemy on the vessels of a friend, in deference to the French rule, and France, on the other hand, by yielding her claim to confiscate the goods of a friend on the vessels of an enemy, in deference to the British rule, have, indeed, come to happy accord. The two great maritime Powers of Europe have thus united in recognising principles well calculated to advance the cause of civilisation, to secure the just rights of neutrals, and promote the best and lasting interests of all commercial nations.

It is unnecessary, at this day, to advance arguments in support of the general doctrine that the flag shall protect the cargo. Why should a neutral be compelled to abandon a fair and accustomed trade in lawful articles with its friend, simply because that friend has become the enemy of a third Power? The rights of war ought not, in the nature of things, to extend further than to exact from neutrals the interruption of all trade with a blockaded port, and to subject articles contraband of war to capture and confiscation.

There are some considerations, however, in favor of this principle which apply with peculiar force to Great Britain and the United States.

So various and so momentous are the interests involved in preserving and perpetuating peace and friendship between these countries, that it is the imperative duty of both, so far as may consist with their essential rights, carefully to abstain from any course of policy which might endanger their friendly relations.

The exercise of the belligerent right of search is, at best, a delicate proceeding, and must ever arouse watchful jealousy on the part of the people of both countries. According to the established public law, a vessel on the high seas is considered a portion of the territory of that nation to which she belongs. The search of such a vessel by either party when belligerent will never be submitted to with good will by the other being neutral, should this extend beyond the necessity of ascertaining whether there are articles on board contraband of war on their way to the enemy. When the search proceeds further and seeks to discover whether there is enemy's property on board, its character is altogether changed. The searching officer then becomes a judge in his own cause and decides a question of property in which his own pecuniary interests are directly involved. Under such circumstances the temptation is strong to feel might and forget right.

On the other hand, the British or American master of the vessel searched would naturally consider himself the injured party, and with that susceptibility to wrong which is both the characteristic and the pride of the people of both countries, would become indignant at what he might believe to be the unfair and arbitrary conduct of the searching officer. Hence bad blood could not fail to be the result, and constant and dangerous reclamations would thus arise between the two nations. Their past history fully justifies such apprehensions.

Should the searching officer decide that enemy's goods have been found on board, what is then the consequence? The voyage is broken up—the vessel is conveyed to the country of the captor, however distant it may be, to await the decree of a Court of Admiralty; and whether this results in the affirmance or reversal of the searching officer's preliminary decision, the loss, in many instances, is nearly the same to the owner of the vessel and cargo. Should the Court decide that the property seized does not belong to the enemy, the party injured is, notwithstanding, deprived of all redress for the wrong, provided it be their opinion that probable cause existed for the seizure. But if, in the judgment of the Court, no such probable cause had existed, even then the injured party is turned for redress to the prosecution of a tedious law suit in a foreign country against the captor, the delay, trouble, and expense of which would in many cases render the remedy of little or no value; and in the end, he might prove to be insolvent.

The undersigned cannot be mistaken in supposing that, if the United States should be engaged in war and Great Britain remain neutral, the search by American cruisers for the property of their enemy on board of British vessels would give rise to many serious complaints on the part of British subjects. On the other hand, the past history of the two countries unfortunately proves that the search of American vessels by British cruisers for enemy's property has already produced the most unhappy consequences. The truth is, that, from its very nature, great abuses are inseparable from the exercise of this right of search.

The establishment of the principle, " Free ships, free goods," will effectually remove all these dangers. Even if the sacrifices made by either party when belligerent, arising from the abandonment of the opposite rule, were far greater than they will ever prove to be, what comparison would they bear to the evils resulting to both nations from a state of hostilities brought about under its malign influence?

The Undersigned has the honor to renew to the Earl of Clarendon the assurance of his distinguished consideration.

JAMES BUCHANAN.

THE RIGHT HONBLE. THE EARL OF CLARENDON, &c. &c. &c.

TO MR. MARCY.[1]

No. 87.   LEGATION OF THE UNITED STATES.
LONDON, 31 August, 1855.

SIR:

I have the honor to transmit to you the copy of a note of yesterday's date[2] which I have sent to Lord Clarendon, proposing, on the part of the United States, to conclude a convention with Great Britain on the subject of neutral rights, in compliance with your instructions (No. 52) of the 7th August, 1854.

I should have delayed this some time longer, but the important issue which will most probably be made between the two Governments in the Central American questions, in obedience to your instructions No. 104, of the 6th August, might have precluded me altogether from proposing to the British Government to conclude a treaty on this or any other subject. After the con-

---

[1] MSS. Department of State, 67 Despatches from England. The first paragraph is printed in S. Ex. Doc. 85, 34 Cong. 1 Sess. 3.

[2] Note to Lord Clarendon, August 30, supra.

versation with Lord Clarendon reported in my Despatch (No. 66) of the 7th April, but little hope can be entertained that Lord Palmerston's administration will recede from the position which the former so distinctly took upon that occasion.

Yours very respectfully,

JAMES BUCHANAN.

HON: WILLIAM L. MARCY,
        Secretary of State.

TO MR. MARCY.[1]

No. 88.   LEGATION OF THE UNITED STATES.
                            LONDON, 4 September 1855.

SIR:

On Friday last, after having received a very long communication from Mr. Alberdi, I called upon Lord Clarendon at the Foreign Office, for the purpose of " explaining to the British Government the course which the President has determined to pursue towards Buenos Ayres and the Argentine Republic; and to ascertain what that of Great Britain now is or is likely to be." I took with me your Despatch No. 93, of the 16th June last, and read it over carefully to him, deeming this the most satisfactory method of communicating to him the President's intentions. When I had finished the reading, he said he concurred in every word the Despatch contained, and was gratified that the President had determined upon a course in accordance with that which the British Government had already adopted. They had paid no attention to the protest of Buenos Ayres against the treaty with the Argentine Confederation, and he had simply acknowledged its receipt. They had accredited no Minister to Buenos Ayres and had merely a Vice Consul at that port. They had, on the other hand, accredited a Minister (Captain Gore) to the Argentine Confederation, who had been received with great distinction at Rosario. Since his death another Chargé and Consul General had been appointed to that Republic, William Dougal Christie, Esquire, recently Secretary of Legation in Switzerland. He was yet in England on leave, but would soon depart for his post.

He said he had endeavored to persuade France to pursue the

---

[1] MSS. Department of State, 67 Despatches from England.
VOL. IX—26

same course, urging that the purpose of Buenos Ayres in standing out against the other thirteen States of the Confederation was to defeat the commercial objects of the treaties with France and England; but in this he had proved unsuccessful. The French Minister stated that there were so many Frenchmen in Buenos Ayres who had deep interests at stake, that the Government felt itself obliged to appoint a Minister to that State. Accordingly they had accredited the same Minister to both Governments. And what, said his Lordship, has been the consequence? The French Chargé has been coldly received both at Buenos Ayres and Rosario, as ought to have been anticipated from sending the same Minister to two hostile countries. He was scarcely treated with decent respect upon his arrival at Rosario from Buenos Ayres. His Lordship expressed the hope that you had sent the same instructions to our Minister at Paris which I had received. I stated this was highly probable, but I did not know.

He then asked if the President had determined to withdraw the Minister from Buenos Ayres. I told him that the best answer I could give to this question was again to read to him that portion of your despatch relating to this subject; which I accordingly did.

He said that Mr. Alberdi appeared to be a very gentlemanly man, but was a most voluminous writer; to both of which propositions I assented.

I have not seen Mr. Alberdi since my interview with Lord Clarendon.

I enclose, herewith, the copy of a note from the Hanoverian Legation in London, dated on the 23d ultimo, together with " the Number 21 of the official law publication of the Kingdom of Hanover, containing the Royal patent, dated 23d July, 1855, for the publication of the treaty concluded on the 18th January last between Hanover and the United States for the mutual extradition of certain criminals."

> Yours very respectfully,
>> JAMES BUCHANAN.

HON: WILLIAM L. MARCY,
    Secretary of State.

FROM PRESIDENT PIERCE.[1]

WASHINGTON, Sept. 10, 1855.

MY DEAR SIR

I cannot regard with indifference any circumstance calculated to interrupt your plans or occasion inconvenience in relation to your proposed return to the United States, still, in view of the pending Central American questions, your last despatch and your two letters to Gov. Marcy of the 17th and 24th of August afforded me great satisfaction. Whatever the result of negotiations may be, touching this embarrassing subject, I deem it very important that you "see it out." I have been reluctant to urge you to remain at London beyond Sept. 30th, but shall never fail to appreciate the high considerations which have prompted your determination. If detained until the rough weather of Autumn, will it not be agreeable to you to remain till Spring?

Ever & sincerely yr. friend,

FRANK. PIERCE.

HON. JAMES BUCHANAN,
Envoy &c. &c. &c. London.

TO LORD CLARENDON.

(Enclosure in No. 89.[2])

LEGATION OF THE UNITED STATES,
LONDON, 11 September, 1855.

The Undersigned, Envoy Extraordinary and Minister Plenipotentiary of the United States, has been instructed by the President again to call the attention of the Earl of Clarendon, Her Majesty's Principal Secretary of State for Foreign Affairs, to the Central American questions pending between the two Governments, under the convention of the 19th April, 1850.

The President has directed the Undersigned, before retiring from his Mission, to request from the British Government a statement of the positions which it has determined to maintain in regard to the Bay Islands, to the territory between the Sibun and the Sarstoon, as well as the Belize settlement, and to the Mosquito Protectorate. The long delay in asking for this information has proceeded from the President's reluctance to manifest any impatience on this important subject whilst the attention of Her Majesty's Government was engrossed by the war with

---

[1] Buchanan Papers, Historical Society of Pennsylvania.

[2] Despatch to Mr. Marcy, No. 89, Sept. 11, 1855, infra. This note is printed in H. Ex. Doc. 1, 34 Cong. 1 Sess. I. 73.

Russia. But as more than a year has already elapsed since the termination of the discussion on these questions, and as the first Session of a new Congress is rapidly approaching, the President does not feel that he would be justified in any longer delay.

Whilst it is far from the purpose of the Undersigned to reopen the general discussion, he has been instructed to communicate to the Earl of Clarendon the conclusions at which the President has arrived upon the whole case.

After having carefully reviewed and reconsidered all the questions involved, with the light cast upon them by the Earl of Clarendon's statement of the 2d May, 1854, the President has expressed his unwillingness to believe that the positions which he conceives to be rather indicated therein than finally adopted will be adhered to by the British Government.

It was, in his opinion, the manifest intention of the convention to exclude both the contracting parties from holding or occupying as well as from acquiring territorial possessions in Central America; and that this intention is not clothed in ambiguous language, but is set forth in explicit terms. The United States have bound themselves not to acquire any such possessions, and Great Britain has stipulated not to " assume or exercise any dominion over any part of Central America." Indeed, without such a reciprocal engagement no mutuality whatever would have existed between the covenants of the contracting parties. Whilst the United States are excluded from occupying, colonising, or exercising dominion over any part of Central America, it cannot be admitted that the same restriction, imposed in the very same language, is not equally applicable to Great Britain.

The President, therefore, confidently believes that Great Britain is bound by the first article of the convention of 1850 to withdraw from the possession she now holds of Ruatan and the other Central American Islands on the coast of the State of Honduras, as well as from the territory in Central America between the Sibun and the Sarstoon which has been encroached upon by Her Majesty's subjects. He is also of opinion that the possession of the British Government at the Belize should be restricted to the limits and objects specified in the treaties between Great Britain and Spain of 1783 and 1786.

In regard to the alleged Protectorate over the so-called Mosquito Kingdom:—the President has instructed the Undersigned to say it was his confident belief that this Protectorate had been finally disposed of by the convention. It is therefore much to his regret that he finds it is still continued as the basis of British dominion over an extensive region in Central America.

Even although Great Britain admits that the convention has imposed restrictions on the Protectorate claimed, yet she still continues to exercise the same dominion over the Mosquito Coast which she had done before its date. Indeed, at the present moment, no visible power, civil or military, exists in the Mosquito territory, except that which is exercised by British subjects, notwithstanding the convention expressly prohibits both parties from using any protection which either may afford to any State or people, for the purpose of occupying, fortifying, or colonising, the Mosquito Coast or any part of Central America, or for the purpose of assuming or exercising dominion over the same.

The declaration of the British Government that this Protectorate is only employed for the security of the rights of the Mosquito Indians, and that it is ready to abstain from further interference in that country whenever these rights can, in a proper manner, be guaranteed to them, cannot be recognized by the United States as having any foundation in the convention. The President considers this to be a question between Nicaragua and the Indians within its territory, with which neither Great Britain nor the United States has any right to interfere, except in friendly conference with the authorities of that State.

Having thus distinctly presented to the British Government the views of the Government of the United States in regard to the obligations imposed by the convention of 1850, the President feels assured that the Earl of Clarendon will, with characteristic frankness, be equally explicit in presenting the views of the British Government in regard to these obligations.

In conclusion, the Undersigned is instructed to state that the President does not doubt that the interest of the two countries and their mutual desire to maintain existing friendly relations will alike inspire each party with a conciliatory spirit, and enable them to overcome all obstacles to a satisfactory adjustment of the Central American questions.

The Undersigned has the honor to renew to the Earl of Clarendon the assurance of his distinguished consideration.

(Signed) JAMES BUCHANAN.

THE RIGHT HONBLE. THE EARL OF CLARENDON, &c. &c. &c.

TO MR. MARCY.[1]

No. 89.   LEGATION OF THE UNITED STATES,
LONDON, 11 September, 1855.

SIR:

I have the honor of transmitting to you the copy of a note which I this day addressed to Lord Clarendon on the Central American questions, in obedience to your instructions of the 6th ultimo, (No. 104). I shall, of course, be anxious to learn whether it has received the President's approbation. It has been prepared with much care, my purpose having been to employ conciliatory language so far as this might be done consistently with the President's instructions and the attainment of the objects which he had in view.

Yours very respectfully,
JAMES BUCHANAN.

HON: WILLIAM L. MARCY,
Secretary of State.

TO MR. MARCY.[2]

No. 90.   LEGATION OF THE UNITED STATES.
LONDON, 14 September 1855.

SIR:

I have the honor to acknowledge the receipt of your Despatches, Nos. 105 and 106, of the 25th & 27th of August, respectively.

In regard to your No. 105,—I think, from the information I have obtained, there can be no doubt but that the cigars attempted to be smuggled were placed in one of the bags containing copies of Wheaton's International Law, by the bearer of despatches. The name of this person I cannot ascertain; but am informed by a highly respectable gentleman, well known to me, who came out with him on " the Atlantic," which left New York on the 27th June last, that he was a German Jew. He appeared

---

[1] MSS. Department of State, 67 Despatches from England; H. Ex. Doc. I, 34 Cong. I Sess. I. 73.
[2] MSS. Department of State, 67 Despatches from England.

most anxious about the landing of the bags, and complained loudly that he was not permitted to go ashore with them in the Mail Boat. He had been boasting on the passage what privileges he would enjoy on landing at Liverpool; and it appeared to my informant that he was altogether unfit to be trusted with a Courier's passport. I am anxious to ascertain the name of this person, and request you to obtain it for me. I have in vain applied to Mr. Hawthorne and Mr. Miller for this purpose. Neither of them has been able to discover it.

Yours very respectfully,

James Buchanan.

Hon: William L. Marcy,
　　Secretary of State.

TO MR. MARCY.[1]

No. 92.　　　　　　Legation of The United States.

London, 21st September, 1855.

Sir:

An unpleasant incident has occurred here of which it has become my duty to give you information.

Tal. P. Shaffner, Esquire, who is connected with the different Telegraph lines in the United States, came to London last Autumn on business, as he informed me, connected with the establishment of a Telegraph between Europe and America. From my intercourse with him, he appears to be an intelligent and respectable man. He applied to the Gutta Percha Company of London, to sell him a quantity of Electric Telegraph wire, with Galvanic Batteries, and a parcel of a particular kind of Fusees intended for submarine exploding purposes, only manufactured at that establishment. This company, being in the employment of the British Government and suspecting that these articles might be intended for Russia, at first refused. Upon his representations, however, that they were intended only for use in the United States and for the benefit of our Government, and after having consulted an agent of the British Government, the company finally consented to make the sale. So jealous, however,

---

[1] MSS. Department of State, 68 Despatches from England.

were they that these articles might be sent to Russia, that they refused to deliver them unless directed to the War Department at Washington; and in regard to the Fusees, they made it a condition that these should be delivered into my hands to be sent by the Despatch Bag to the Secretary of War. The package of Fusees was accordingly brought to me by Mr. T. B. Smithies, the Confidential Clerk of the Company, in December last, and I ordered it to be placed in the Despatch Bag. This I cheerfully did, because Mr. Shaffner had repeatedly assured me that it was highly important that the Secretary of War should obtain these Fusees, as they were of a superior character and unknown in the United States. Indeed, he took much credit to himself for having obtained them for our Government. The result will appear from the deposition of Captain Field, herewith enclosed, and obtained upon the request of Mr. Smithies. The Captain placed in my hands a recommendation of himself from the Senators and Representatives of Tennessee in Congress, of which I transmit a copy.

Mr. Smithies informs me that the company feel bound to represent the whole transaction to the British Government. I assured him there was no living man who would more intensely scorn the idea of participating in any such fraud as that alleged than the Secretary of War. I observed to him, at the same time, that it was his own want of caution to have added to the simple direction to the " War Department, Washington," on these packages, that of " For Mr. Shaffner—Experiments." This addition would naturally cause the Secretary of War to deliver these packages to Mr. Shaffner without inquiry.

The British Government look with much apprehension to the infernal machines at Cronstadt intended to blow up their ships of war; and when they discover that their own wires, Galvanic Batteries, and fusees have been employed for this purpose, through the misrepresentations and agency of Mr. Shaffner and his employment of the name of the " War Department," they will be very much provoked. It is almost certain they will bring the subject to my notice, and I am willing that they should, because it is easy to explain the whole affair so far as the Secretary of War is concerned.

Of course the improper conduct of Mr. Shaffner depends entirely upon the veracity of Captain Field. He says he happened to be dining in company with Mr. Smithies, and in conversing about Mr. Shaffner, he had incautiously and unintentionally

proceeded so far that he "could not back out," but was obliged
to go on and tell the whole story.
  I send, also, the deposition of Mr. Smithies.
  Yours very respectfully,
  JAMES BUCHANAN.

HON : WILLIAM L. MARCY,
  Secretary of State.

(Enclosure in No. 92.)
  I, Captain Matthew Dickerson Field of Massachusetts, at present staying
at the Golden Cross Hotel in London, make oath and say that in the early
part of this present year three large packages of Electric Telegraph Wire and
Galvanic Batteries, which I understood had been shipped from England
addressed to the "War Department, Washington—For Mr. Shaffner's Experiments," were re-forwarded from Washington to New York, and were
warehoused in Cyrus W. Field's store, No. 11 Cliff St., New York, without
having, as I believe, been opened in Washington.
  The said packages were opened and re-packed at the request and under
the direction of Tal. P. Shaffner, President of the St. Louis & New Orleans
Telegraph Company, and with the utmost despatch were shipped on board
the "Herman" or the "Washington" on the 20th or 24th March, 1855, for
Bremen.
  The said Tal. P. Shaffner desired me to accompany him to Russia by
way of England, with which request I complied, and sailed in company with
him on the 4th April last from New York by the Atlantic.
  The said Tal. P. Shaffner had with him a parcel about the size of a
man's hat, which he on several occasions referred to as being of great value
to the Russian Government. Such parcel contained a number of Fusees for
Submarine Exploding purposes.
  The said Tal. P. Shaffner was the bearer of some official despatches to
Liverpool or London, and during the voyage from New York to Liverpool he
requested and prevailed upon the purser of the Atlantic to fill up a *blank*
despatch paper, which he, the said T. P. Shaffner, had by some means become
possessed of before leaving New York; and I declare that such blank despatch paper was filled up by the said purser to the effect that the said
T. P. Shaffner was the bearer of official despatches to Liverpool or London
and *St. Petersburg.*
  The said Tal. P. Shaffner also in my presence sealed, with a very
large seal, the parcel of Fusees, which gave the parcel an official appearance
similar to the official despatches. The Despatch Paper and the official-
looking seal secured a ready landing of the parcel in Liverpool.
  From Liverpool we proceeded to London, & from thence to Berlin by
way of Ostend. At Berlin the said Tal. P. Shaffner handed the bag containing the said parcel of Fusees to the Russian Minister for the purpose of
being forwarded by him to St. Petersburg, at which latter place I again saw
it when handed to the said T. P. Shaffner.
  I have reason to believe that the aforesaid Telegraph Wire which was
shipped to Bremen, and the said Fusees which the said Tal. P. Shaffner
handed to the Russian Government, and for which he received a large

consideration, are now submerged at Cronstadt for the purpose of blowing up the War Vessels of the Allies.

M. D. FIELD.

Sworn before me in the Consulate
of the United States at London this
twentieth day of September A. D. 1855.   (Seal)
ROBERT B. CAMPBELL
Consul U. S. A. London.

(Enclosure in No. 92.)

I, Thomas Bywater Smithies, confidential clerk to the Gutta Percha Company, 18, Wharf Road, City Road, London, make oath and say

That on the 24th of November last, Mr. Tal. P. Shaffner of the American Telegraph Confederation, New York, called at the Works of the said Company and ordered thirteen Miles of Telegraph Wire, together with twelve Galvanic Batteries and fittings; also one hundred fusees for Submarine Explosions. Mr. Shaffner stated that these goods were for Experiments at the American War Department at Washington, and he wrote on a sheet of paper the following address to which they were to be forwarded.

WAR DEPARTMENT, UNITED STATES,
Washington, D. C.
For Mr. Shaffner.   Experiments.

They were to be shipped through Brown, Shipley & Co., Liverpool.

These articles being contraband, owing to the present War, the Gutta Percha Company had to communicate with our Government Authorities before they could be shipped.

After the most solemn assurances from Mr. Shaffner to Mr. Scanlan, the Government Inspector, that the Wire and fusees were bona-fide for the American War Department, and the statement of Mr. Archibald of the Conservative Club and Rusland Hall, Lancashire, that Mr. Shaffner's word might be relied upon, it was finally agreed that the Exportation should take place, provided the small package of Fusees was placed in the hands of His Excellency the American Ambassador, Mr. Buchanan, to be forwarded in his private bag direct to Washington.

Accordingly on the 15th December, 1854, three large packages containing the Wire and Batteries were forwarded to Liverpool. I then waited upon His Excellency, the American Ambassador, who smilingly said, on my handing him the packet of Fusees, " You may make yourself perfectly easy that these will never find their way to Russia; the American Government has too much respect for England and Neutrality to allow them to be used against you;" or words to the same effect.

The next tidings I had of these Fusees, and Wire, were the circumstances as detailed in Captain Field's Affidavit made before the American Consulate in London on the 20th September, 1855.

T. B. SMITHIES.

Declared at the Guildhall London
this 21st day of September 1855 before   (Stamp)
me
JOHN HUMPHREY.

FROM LORD CLARENDON.

(Enclosure in No. 93.[1])

[Sept. 27, 1855.]

Mr. Buchanan, Envoy Extraordinary and Minister Plenipotentiary of the United States at this Court, will probably have received from his Government a copy of a letter which Mr. Marcy, Secretary of State of the United States, addressed to Mr. Crampton, Her Britannic Majesty's Envoy Extraordinary and Minister Plenipotentiary in the United States, on the 5th of this month, on the subject of the communication which the undersigned, Her Majesty's Principal Secretary of State for Foreign Affairs, had the honor to make to Mr. Buchanan on the 16th of July, in reply to his note of the 6th of that month, complaining of the proceedings of British Agents and British Colonial Authorities in raising within the States of the Union recruits for the British Military service, in violation (as was alleged) of the Act of Congress of the 20th of April, 1818.

The Undersigned had hoped from the answer which he received from Mr. Buchanan on the 18th of July that the explanations and assurances which he had given on this subject in his note of the 16th of that month would have proved as satisfactory to the Government of the United States as they appeared to be to Mr. Buchanan, and it was therefore with no less disappointment than regret that Her Majesty's Government perused the letter addressed by Mr. Marcy to Mr. Crampton on the 5th Instant, of which the Undersigned encloses a copy to Mr. Buchanan in case he should not have received it from Washington.

In his letter Mr. Marcy, laying less stress than Mr. Buchanan did upon the alleged infraction of the Municipal Laws of the United States, dwells chiefly upon the point, which was but slightly adverted to by Mr. Buchanan, of an assumed disregard of the Sovereign Rights of the United States on the part of the British Authorities or the Agents employed by them.

Her Majesty's Government have no reason to believe that such has been the conduct of any Persons in the employment of Her Majesty, and it is needless to say that any person so employed would have departed no less from the intentions of Her Majesty's Government by violating International Law, or by offering an affront to the Sovereignty of the United States, than by infringing the Municipal Laws of the Union, to which Mr. Buchanan more particularly called the attention of the Undersigned. Her Majesty's Government feel confident that even the extraordinary measures which have been adopted in various parts of the Union to obtain evidence against Her Majesty's servants or their agents, by practices sometimes resorted to under despotic institutions, but which are disdained by all free and enlightened Governments, will fail to establish any well founded charge against Her Majesty's servants.

The British Government is fully aware of the obligations of international duties, and is no less mindful of those obligations than is the Government of the United States. The observance of those obligations ought undoubtedly to be reciprocal, and Her Majesty's Government do not impute to the Govern-

---

[1] Despatch to Mr. Marcy, No. 93, Sept. 28, 1855, infra. This note is printed in S. Ex. Doc. 35, 34 Cong. 1 Sess. 23.

ment of the United States that, while claiming an observance of those obligations by Great Britain, they are lax in enforcing a respect for those obligations within the Union.

But as this subject has been mooted by Mr. Marcy, Her Majesty's Government cannot refrain from some few remarks respecting it.

The United States profess neutrality in the present war between the Western Powers and Russia; but have no acts been done within the United States, by citizens thereof, which accord little with the spirit of neutrality? Have not arms and ammunition and warlike stores of various kinds been sent in large quantities from the United States for the service of Russia? Have not plots been openly avowed and conspiracies entered into, without disguise or hindrance, in various parts of the Union, to take advantage of the war in which Great Britain is engaged, and to seize the opportunity for promoting insurrection in Her Majesty's Dominions and the invasion thereof by an armed Force proceeding from the United States?

Her Majesty's Government have been silent on these matters, which they did not consider indicative of the general feelings of the American People, for remembering the many ties and sympathies which connect the People of the United States with the two powerful Nations who are engaged in the present contest with Russia, they were convinced that a free, enlightened, and generous race, such as the citizens of the Great North American Union, must entertain on the important questions at issue sentiments in harmony with those which animate not only the British and French Nations, but the great mass of the Nations of Western Europe; and Her Majesty's Government would not have adverted to the exceptional course pursued by a certain number of individuals if it had not been for the above mentioned statements in Mr. Marcy's note.

But Her Majesty's Government think themselves entitled to claim the same credit for sincerity of purpose and uprightness of conduct which they readily allow to the Government of the United States, and to expect that their assurance should be received that as they have enjoined on all Her Majesty's servants a strict observance of the Laws of the United States, so they have no reason to believe that any of Her Majesty's servants or any agents duly authorised by those servants have disregarded those injunctions in respect to the matters which form the subject of this note.

The Undersigned requests Mr. Buchanan to accept the assurance of his highest consideration.

CLARENDON.

FOREIGN OFFICE,
    September 27, 1855.
THE HONORABLE JAMES BUCHANAN,
    &c. &c. &c.

TO LORD CLARENDON.

(Enclosure in No. 93.[1])
LEGATION OF THE UNITED STATES.
LONDON, 28th September, 1855.

The Undersigned, Envoy Extraordinary and Minister Plenipotentiary of the United States, has the honor to acknowledge the receipt of the note, dated on the 27th instant, from the Earl of Clarendon, Her Majesty's Principal Secretary of State for Foreign Affairs, in reference to the note of the 5th instant addressed by Mr. Marcy, the Secretary of State, to Mr. Crampton, Her Britannic Majesty's Minister at Washington, on the subject of the enlistment and engagement of soldiers for the British Army within the limits of the United States; and he will not fail to transmit to Washington a copy of His Lordship's note by to-morrow's Steamer.

The Undersigned forbears to make any observations on this note or to interfere in any manner with the correspondence commenced at Washington between the Secretary of State and Mr. Crampton, as he has received no instructions which would warrant him in so doing.

The Undersigned has the honor to renew to the Earl of Clarendon the assurance of his distinguished consideration.

(Signed)   JAMES BUCHANAN.

THE RIGHT HONBLE. THE EARL OF CLARENDON
&c., &c., &c.

TO MR. MARCY.[2]

No. 93.   LEGATION OF THE UNITED STATES.
LONDON, 28th September, 1855.

SIR:

I have the honor to acknowledge the receipt of your Despatch No. 107, of the 8th instant, with the accompanying documents.

I transmit to you the copy of a note of yesterday's date,

---

[1] MSS. Department of State, 68 Despatches from England; S. Ex. Doc. 35, 34 Cong. 1 Sess. 25.

[2] MSS. Department of State, 68 Despatches from England; S. Ex. Doc. 35, 34 Cong. 1 Sess. 22.

received this morning from Lord Clarendon,[1] in reference to your note to Mr. Crampton, of the 5th instant, on the subject of British recruitments in the United States, together with a copy of my note of this date,[2] acknowledging its receipt. I have been thus prompt in notifying His Lordship that I had no instructions which would warrant me in interfering with the correspondence commenced between Mr. Crampton and yourself at Washington, so that there might be no reason for any delay on the part of the British Government in sending their instructions to that gentleman. I doubt very much, however, whether the confident trust expressed by him in his note to you of the 7th instant will be realised,—that, after having been more fully put into possession of the views of his Government, he " shall be enabled altogether to remove the unfavorable impression which has been created as to the motives and conduct of Her Majesty's Government and their officers, including myself, [himself] in regard to this matter." Lord Clarendon's Note to me of yesterday renders it improbable that Mr. Crampton will receive any such instructions; and I doubt whether the expression of his confident trust to this effect has received the approbation of His Lordship.

I also transmit a copy of my note of the 18th July last [3] to Lord Clarendon, to which he refers in his note to me of yesterday. I communicated to you the substance of this note in my No. 81, of the 20th July,—though at that time I did not deem it necessary to send a full copy.

I have not time at present, before the closing of the bag, to make some observations which I had intended to do on the subject. I may resume it next week.

Yours very respectfully,

JAMES BUCHANAN.

HON: WILLIAM L. MARCY,
    Secretary of State.

---

[1] Note from Lord Clarendon, Sept. 27, 1855, supra.
[2] Note to Lord Clarendon, Sept. 28, 1855, supra.
[3] This is given under July 18, 1855, supra.

FROM LORD CLARENDON.

(Enclosure in No. 95.[1])

FOREIGN OFFICE, September 28, 1855.

The undersigned, her majesty's principal secretary of state for foreign affairs, has the honor to acknowledge the receipt of the note which Mr. Buchanan, envoy extraordinary and minister plenipotentiary of the United States, addressed to him on the 11th instant, stating that he had been directed by the President, before retiring from his mission, to request from the British government a statement of the positions which it has determined to maintain, in regard to the Bay Islands, to the territory between the Sibun and the Sarstoon, as well as the Belize settlement, and to the Mosquito protectorate, and setting forth the conclusions at which the President has arrived upon the whole case, namely, that it was the intention of the convention of the 19th of April, 1850, to exclude both the contracting parties from holding or occupying, as well as from acquiring territorial possessions in Central America, and that, consequently, Great Britain is bound to withdraw from the possession she now holds of Ruatan and other Central American islands on the coast of the state of Honduras, as well as from the territory in Central America between the Sibun and the Sarstoon; that the possession of the British government at Belize should be restricted to the limits and objects specified in the treaties between Great Britain and Spain of 1783 and 1786, and that the protectorate of the so-called Mosquito kingdom was finally disposed of by the convention.

The undersigned observes with satisfaction that, while thus expressing the opinion of the President of the United States on the several points thus enumerated, Mr. Buchanan announces that it is far from his purpose to re-open the general discussion upon them. Her majesty's government had, indeed, refrained from pursuing that discussion by replying to Mr. Buchanan's note of the 22d of July, 1854, because it appeared to them that the continuation of the correspondence was not likely to lead to any satisfactory conclusion; and, as her majesty's government are still of that opinion, the undersigned will confine his answer to Mr. Buchanan's present note within the same limits as those which Mr. Buchanan has prescribed to himself.

In answer, therefore, to the questions put by Mr. Buchanan, the undersigned has the honor to state to him, that her majesty's government adhere to the opinion which they have uniformly held, that the convention of April 19, 1850, was merely prospective in its operation, and did not in any way interfere with the state of things existing at the time of its conclusion. If it had been intended to do so, there can be no question but that, in conformity with what the undersigned believes to be the universal rule in regard to instruments of this nature, it would have contained, in specific terms, a renunciation, on the part of Great Britain, of the possessions and rights which, up to the conclusion of the convention, she had claimed to maintain, and such renunciation would not have been left as a mere matter of inference.

Neither can her majesty's government subscribe to the position that, if the convention did not bear the meaning attached to it by the United States, it would have imposed upon the government of the United States a self-denying

---

[1] Despatch to Mr. Marcy, No. 95, Oct. 4, 1855, infra. This note is printed in H. Ex. Doc. 1, 34 Cong. 1 Sess. I. 76.

obligation which was not equally contracted by Great Britain, and that such a state of things could not have been in the intention of the contracting parties, because, if the convention did bear the meaning attached to it by the United States, it would then have imposed upon Great Britain the obligation to renounce possessions and rights without any equivalent renunciation on the part of the United States. If the government of the United States can complain, in the one case, of the convention as presenting an unilateral character unfavorable to the United States, with much greater reason might the government of Great Britain, in the other case, if the assumption of the United States were to be acted upon in the construction of the convention, complain of it as prejudicial to England.

But looking to the object which the contracting parties had in view at the conclusion of the convention, namely, the security of the proposed ship canal, the British government consider that the design of the contracting parties was not to disturb any state of things then existing, but to guard against the future creation of a state of things which might by possibility interfere with the security of the proposed canal. That such was the true design of the convention is obvious from the provision in the sixth article, by which the contracting parties engaged to invite every State to enter into stipulations with them similar to those contained in the convention. But if the position of the United States government were sound, and the convention was intended to interfere with the state of things existing at the time of its conclusion, and to impose upon Great Britain to withdraw from portions of territory occupied by it, a similar obligation would be contracted by other States acceding to the convention, and the governments of the Central American States would, by the mere act of accession, sign away their rights to the territories in which they are situated.

The British government share the conviction of the President of the United States that the interest of the two countries, and their mutual desire to maintain existing friendly relations, will alike inspire each party with a conciliatory spirit, and enable them to overcome all obstacles to a satisfactory adjustment of Central American questions. The British government see no reason why it should be otherwise. The British government neither have the wish to extend the limits of their possessions or the sphere of their influence in that quarter, nor would any British interest be promoted by doing so; but the British government are not prepared to contract either the one or the other, in pursuance of the interpretation of a convention, to which interpretation they cannot subscribe.

The undersigned requests Mr. Buchanan to accept the assurance of his highest consideration.

CLARENDON.

Hon. James Buchanan, &c., &c., &c.

TO MR. MARCY.[1]

No. 94.   LEGATION OF THE UNITED STATES.
                            LONDON, 3d October, 1855.

SIR:

I have the honor to acknowledge the receipt of your Despatches Nos. 108, 109, and 111, of the 8th, 11th, & 13th September, respectively. Your 110 has not yet arrived.

In my last Despatch, No. 93, of the 28th ultimo, I stated that I had not then time, before the closing of the Bag, to make the observations I had intended on the subject to which it refers; but intimated that I might do so this week.

The alleged agency of Mr. Crampton in the recruitment of British soldiers within the limits of the United States presents a serious aspect. From the information contained in your Despatch (No. 91) of the 9th June, we had reason to expect a different course of conduct on his part. I need scarcely say that, had I been informed that Her Britannic Majesty's Representative at Washington had placed himself in the position attributed to him by Captain Strobel, I should not have expressed to Lord Clarendon my satisfaction in transmitting to you his note of the 16th July.

It is remarkable that Lord Clarendon, in his note to myself of the 27th ultimo, whilst commenting on your note of the 5th September to Mr. Crampton, should have been totally silent in regard to that gentleman, after what you had said respecting his conduct.

I cannot but regard as offensive the remark of his Lordship on "the extraordinary measures which," he alleges, "have been adopted in various parts of the Union to obtain evidence against Her Majesty's servants or their agents, by practices sometimes resorted to under despotic institutions, but which are disdained by all free and enlightened Governments," though he would doubtless say these were not intended to apply, in an offensive sense, to the American Government. He probably alludes to occurrences at Cincinnati and other places.

If arms and ammunition and warlike stores of various kinds have been sent in large quantities from the United States for the service of Russia, as his Lordship alleges, this is nothing more

---

[1] MSS. Department of State, 68 Despatches from England. The part of this despatch relating to recruitment is printed in S. Ex. Doc. 35, 34 Cong. 1 Sess. 27.

than our citizens had a right to do, subject to the risk under the law of contraband. Similar articles have been sent from the United States to Great Britain in large quantities. Besides, at the present moment, and ever since the commencement of the present war, many of our vessels have been engaged as transports by Great Britain and France to carry troops and munitions of war to the Crimea. When this business first commenced, I was applied to by masters and agents of American vessels for information as to what penalties they would incur by engaging in it, and I stated to them that their vessels would be lawful prize if captured by the Russians. For this reason, I advised them to obtain an indemnity from the Government employing them against this risk.

The "plots" to which his Lordship refers relate chiefly, I presume, (for I do not know), to the proceedings and "address of the Massachusetts Irish Emigrant Aid Society," at Boston, on the 14th August. These were republished in the London Times on the 11th September; and you will find an editorial on this subject on the following day.

In his bill of particulars, Lord Clarendon would doubtless have mentioned the alleged conduct of Mr. Shaffner (vide my Despatch No. 92), had this come to his knowledge. If it had not, this was perhaps caused by my remark to Mr. Smithies, that it was his own want of caution in adding to the direction to the "War Department" that of "Mr. Shaffner—Experiments," which, most probably, induced the delivery of the packages to Mr. Shaffner without examination. This consideration may have occasioned the Gutta Percha Company to withhold from the British Government a knowledge of the transaction. By the bye, I have written to Mr. Shaffner, who is now believed to be in St. Petersburg, on this subject, and await his answer.

The Foreign Enlistment Bill encountered strong opposition both in Parliament and throughout the country. It was contended that it would be degrading to the character of Great Britain as a Military Power to resort to Foreign nations for recruits for her armies. After its passage, the Ministry proceeded to carry it into execution in different countries, à la mode de Palmerston, without a proper regard to their sovereign rights as neutral nations. Against this several complaints proceeded from the Continent; but such are the power and dread of the Alliance, especially of France, that these did not become loud or serious.

The circumstances attending the failure of the British forces to capture the Redan, in the presence of the victorious French army at the Malakoff, have produced deep mortification among the British people. This was for some time suppressed, but is now manifesting itself extensively.

With reference to your No. 109—application has already been made for an Exequatur for Charles Huffnagle, Esqr., appointed Consul General for British India.

I transmit a copy of the note which I addressed to the Earl of Clarendon, on the 2d inst., in compliance with your instructions (No. 111), communicating through him the thanks of the President to Mr. Hay and Lieutenant Heath for the valuable assistance rendered by them to the American bark " Juniata."

Yours very respectfully,

JAMES BUCHANAN.

HON: WILLIAM L. MARCY,
    Secretary of State.

TO PRESIDENT PIERCE.[1]

LEGATION OF THE UNITED STATES.
LONDON 4 October 1855.

MY DEAR SIR:

I have received your kind favor of the 10th ultimo, and you will perceive from my Despatch of this date that I have now remained long enough to " see out " the Central American questions. The answer of Lord Clarendon is doubtless such as you had anticipated. You will at once perceive that under all the circumstances, both public & private, I ought not to linger here any longer than may be necessary; but I cannot take leave of the Queen until I shall have received my letter of recall. If it has not been already despatched, I hope it may be sent immediately.

The Legation may be most safely entrusted to Mr. Appleton during the period which may elapse before the arrival of a new minister. Indeed, there are few men in the United States of his age better calculated for the essentials of diplomatic duties. This I discovered when he was Chief Clerk in the State Department. I shall surrender my house on the last day of the present month, but have made an arrangement with the Landlady that the Lega-

[1] Buchanan Papers, Historical Society of Pennsylvania.

tion may continue here until the arrival of the new minister, at the rate of £10 per month. This could only have been effected in the hope she indulges that he may take her house, which she would consider an honor. He could not possibly do better for the same rent, as General Thomas will testify. She is in affluent circumstances, and has been quite liberal in all small matters. I shall accompany Miss Lane to Liverpool this evening, who will go home in the Atlantic on the 6th.

Mrs. Bigelow Lawrence called to see me yesterday in deep distress on account of the discharge of Midshipman Mercer, her sister's husband, from the Navy. She informs me that he was a good officer, as is testified by the fact that Commodore Macauley appointed him to do the duties of master on board the Princeton.

It appears that at the time of this appointment Midshipman Mercer had received assurances from the late Mr. Lawrence that he might obtain a place at Lowell, the emoluments of which would enable him much better to support his family; and he gave this as a reason to Commodore Macauley for declining to act as master, with which the latter appeared to be satisfied. Mrs. Lawrence believes this to have been the cause of his dismissal. When Mr. Mercer went on to Boston, Mr. Lawrence was no longer able to attend to business, and he did not get the place.

This is certainly a hard case, and I shall be personally very much gratified should you be able to do any thing for him. His father in Law, Judge Chapman of Bucks County, Pennsylvania, is a man of great respectability and influence. Col: Forney can tell you all about him. His wife is the daughter of the late Governor Shunk, of Pennsylvania.

I am sorry I have not time to write at greater length. Should any thing important occur to me, I shall write to Governor Marcy from Liverpool. This, however, will scarcely be necessary, as General Thomas, with whom I have conversed much, will be able to give you all the news.

Please to present me, in the kindest terms, to Mrs. Pierce.

With sentiments of the highest respect I remain

Your friend,

JAMES BUCHANAN.

His Excellency Franklin Pierce.

P. S. You seem to be at a loss for a successor to me. Why not appoint Mr. Glancy Jones? In my opinion, he is well qualified for the situation & would make a wise & prudent minister.

Besides, his appointment would gratify the Democracy of Pennsylvania. I make this suggestion without the knowledge of Mr. Jones & without having the least idea whether it would be agreeable to him or not.

I expected to have an interview with Lord Clarendon this morning; but the illness of his mother has prevented, & it is now postponed until Monday next.

TO LORD CLARENDON.

(Enclosure in No. 95.[1])

LEGATION OF THE UNITED STATES,
LONDON, 4th October, 1855.

The Undersigned, Envoy Extraordinary and Minister Plenipotentiary of the United States, has the honor to acknowledge the receipt of the note of the Earl of Clarendon, Her Majesty's Principal Secretary of State for Foreign Affairs, dated on the 28th ultimo, in reply to the note of the Undersigned of the 11th ultimo, in reference to the Central American questions between the two Governments; and he will not fail to transmit a copy of the same by the next Steamer to the Secretary of State at Washington.

Whilst far from intending to renew the general discussion of these questions, which has already been exhausted, the Undersigned, in passing, would make a single observation in regard to the Earl of Clarendon's remark that if the convention of the 19th April, 1850, had intended that Great Britain should withdraw from her possessions in Central America, " it would have contained in specific terms a renunciation " to that effect; " and such renunciation would not have been left as a mere matter of inference."

Now, it appears to the Undersigned that an engagement by a party not " to occupy " " or exercise any dominion over " territory of which that party is in actual possession at the date of the engagement, is equivalent in all respects to an agreement to withdraw from such territory. Under these circumstances, this is not " a mere matter of inference; " because the one proposition is necessarily & inseparably involved in the other, & they are merely

---

[1] Despatch to Mr. Marcy, No. 95, Oct. 4, 1855, infra. This note is printed in H. Ex. Doc. 1, 34 Cong. 1 Sess. I. 78.

alternative modes of expressing the same idea. In such a case, to withdraw is not to occupy—and not to occupy is necessarily to withdraw.

The Undersigned needs no apology for briefly adverting to another argument of the Earl of Clarendon, because it has now for the first time been advanced. He states that " if the position of the United States Government were sound, & the convention was intended to interfere with the state of things existing at the time of its conclusion and to impose upon Great Britain to withdraw from portions of territory occupied by it, a similar obligation would be contracted by other States acceding to the convention [under the 6th Article] and the Government of the Central American States would by the mere act of accession sign away their rights to the territories in which they are situated."

Confining himself strictly to this single view of the subject, the Undersigned would observe, that notwithstanding the general terms employed by the convention, an examination of its provisions, and especially of the Sixth Article itself, will prove it never intended that the Central American States should become joint parties to this Treaty with the United States, Great Britain and other Governments exterior to Central America. These States are the subjects on which the guarantees of the convention were to act, and the exclusion of all other Powers from the occupancy of Central America, with a view to the security not only of this canal but all other canals or railroads across the Isthmus, was one of the main objects to be accomplished by the Treaty.

The Earl of Clarendon has himself indicated how absurd it would be for the Central American Governments to become joint parties to this convention, according to the American construction. It would, however, be none the less absurd according to the British construction; because then, no Central American State could accede to the Treaty without confining itself forever within its existing boundaries and agreeing not to add to its territory and extend its occupation under any possible circumstances which might arise in the future.

Besides, were it possible for Nicaragua for example to become a party to this joint convention, she would then take upon herself the extraordinary obligation to use her own influence with herself, under the 4th Article, to induce herself to facilitate the construction of the canal, and to use her good offices to procure from herself " the establishment of two free ports, one at each end of the canal," both these ports being within her own limits.

Consequences almost equally extraordinary would result from other portions of the convention.

But although the contracting parties could not have intended that the Central American States should become joint parties to the convention, yet they foresaw that it would be necessary to obtain stipulations from one or more of them, individually, providing for the security of the proposed canal, adapted to their anomalous condition, and without interfering in any manner with their territorial possessions. Accordingly, in the 6th Article, and in the clause next following that commented upon by the Earl of Clarendon, the convention provides as follows:—" And the contracting parties likewise agree that each shall enter into Treaty stipulations with such of the Central American States as they may deem advisable, for the purposes of more effectually carrying out the great design of this convention, namely, that of constructing and maintaining the said canal as a ship communication between the two oceans, for the benefit of mankind, on equal terms to all, and of protecting the same," &c., &c.

In order to arrive at the conclusion that the Central American States are embraced in the general language of the first clause of the 6th Article, it would be necessary to overlook this second clause entirely, or at least to regard it as unnecessary & without meaning.

The Undersigned has the honor to renew to the Earl of Clarendon the assurance of his distinguished consideration.

JAMES BUCHANAN.

THE RIGHT HONBLE. THE EARL OF CLARENDON, &c., &c., &c.

TO MR. MARCY.[1]

No. 95.   LEGATION OF THE UNITED STATES.
                              LONDON, 4 October, 1855.

SIR:

I have now the honor of transmitting to you a copy of the note of Lord Clarendon of the 28th,[2] received by me on the 29th ultimo, in answer to my note of the 11th ultimo on the Central American questions; as well as a copy of my reply dated on the

---

[1] MSS. Department of State, 68 Despatches from England. The first paragraph of this despatch is printed in H. Ex. Doc. 1, 34 Cong. 1 Sess. I. 75.

[2] See note under Sept. 28, 1855, supra.

4th instant.[1]   Lord Clarendon's note is of such a character as might have been anticipated after the conversation between his Lordship and myself on the 5th April last, reported in my Despatch (No. 66) of the 7th of that month.   This note has been received so much sooner than I had anticipated, that if I were now in possession of my letter of recall, I might return home on the 6th of October, as I had originally determined.   It is impossible, however, that I should leave before this letter shall arrive, and it is certainly proper,—under all the circumstances,—that I should remain here no longer than may be necessary.   If, therefore, it shall not have been forwarded before the arrival of this Despatch, I trust it may be sent by the next succeeding steamer.

Should a period intervene between my departure and the arrival of a new minister, as would seem most probable, Mr. Appleton is entirely competent to discharge the duties of the Legation during the interim.   I would respectfully recommend that the President might confer upon him the appointment of Chargé d'Affaires; and this not only as due to his own merits, but necessary in a pecuniary view.   He cannot maintain himself here, as the responsible head of the Legation, on the salary of a Secretary of Legation, nor would it be convenient for him to advance his own money to the public and wait till Congress might grant him the salary of a Chargé.   Besides, he would have clerk hire to pay (a clerk being altogether indispensable), as well as office rent at the rate of £120 per annum.

Yours very respectfully
JAMES BUCHANAN.

HON: WILLIAM L. MARCY,
    Secretary of State.

TO MISS LANE.[2]

LEGATION OF THE UNITED STATES,
LONDON, 12 October, 1855.

MY DEAR HARRIET/
    I have been watching the weather since your departure & it has been as favorable as I could have desired.   If the winds & the waves have been as propitious as my wishes & my hopes

---

[1] See supra.

[2] Buchanan Papers, private collection.   Imperfectly printed in Curtis's Buchanan, II. 151.

induce me to believe, you will have had a delightful voyage. Good luck to you on your native soil! I miss you greatly; but know it was for your good that you should go home in this delightful weather, instead of encountering a winter passage.

Every person I meet has something kind to say of you. You have left a good name behind, & that is something; but not more than you deserve.

Poor Lady Ouseley has lost her son. I have not seen her since this sad event; but of course have called.

I have met Lady Chantrey, Mrs. Shapter, the D'Oxholmes, &c. &c., but need not repeat what they said.

Sir Henry Holland called on Wednesday immediately after his return & expressed both sorrow & disappointment that he had not seen you before your departure. He desired me to present you his kindest regards, & says, God willing, he will call upon you next summer in the United States.

Take good care not to display any foreign airs & graces in society at home nor descant upon your intercourse with titled people;—but your own good sense will teach you this lesson. I shall be happy on my return to learn that it has been truly said of you,—" she has not been a bit spoiled by her visit to England."

I forgot to tell you I had seen the good Duchess, who said many extravagant things about you.

I received a letter from Mrs. Plitt by the last steamer, directed to you, with instructions that if you had left I might open & read & then burn it; all which I have done.

I wrote to Miss Hetty by the Southampton steamer on Wednesday last & sent two of the Posts.

I shall give up the house towards the end of the month. Mr. Appleton now occupies your room & renders himself quite agreeable.

I have not seen Grey since you left; but she says she did put up your slippers in the black bag. I shall make it a point to see her & talk with her before she finally leaves the house. She has been absent; but is backwards and forwards.

I heard nothing from Washington by the last steamer respecting myself. I shall present my letter of recall & take leave of the Queen soon after it arrives. As you know, I am heartily tired of my position. But what then? I do not wish to arrive in the U. S. before the meeting of Congress. I am uncertain what I shall do; but will always keep you advised, having confidence that

you will not talk about my intended movements.   If you see
Van Dyke & Tyler, I wish you would inform me what you say.

Louis Napoleon at the present moment wields more real
power than ever his great uncle did.   All the potentates in Europe
dread him & are paying court to him.   He has England in leading strings nearly as much as Sardinia.   How have the mighty
fallen!

Mr. Piatt's resignation went to Washington by the Atlantic.
I presume this will be a relief to the Judge.[1]

Mr. Ward came to the Legation to take leave of you a few
moments after we left on Friday morning.   Consols have been
falling, falling continually for the past week, & this makes him
melancholy.

Mrs. Shapter promised to write by the steamer.   She has
arranged the account you left with her in a satisfactory manner.
She has not yet sent her letter, which I shall transmit by the
Bag.

Mrs. Lawrence called this morning to take leave of me.   She
appears to be much rejoiced at the prospect of getting home.

Please to remember me, in the kindest terms, to Mr. & Mrs.
Plitt, Mr. & Mrs. Van Dyke, & Mr. & Mrs. Tyler, & all other
friends.   Always

Yours affectionately,

JAMES BUCHANAN.

MISS HARRIET LANE.

TO MISS LANE.[2]

U. S. LEGATION,
LONDON, 19 October, 1855.

MY DEAR HARRIET/

Whilst I write I congratulate myself with the belief that,
under the blessing of Providence, you are again happily in your
native land & among kind friends.   The passage of the Baltic
from New York to Liverpool was one of the smoothest & most

---

[1] This refers to the resignation of Mr. Donn Piatt as secretary of legation
at Paris, John Y. Mason being then American minister there.

[2] Buchanan Papers, private collection.   Imperfectly printed in Curtis's
Buchanan, II. 152.

agreeable ever made. Hence we have every reason to believe that the Atlantic enjoyed the same favorable weather.

I had a very pretty note from Mrs. Sturgis[1] on the 15th Instant presenting me with a water-melon, in which she says: "I was sorry not to say 'Good bye' to Miss Lane in person; but we did not forget to drink her health and a prosperous voyage & we feel how very much we shall miss her & her praises another season." Of course, I answered this note in a proper manner.

The good but eccentric Duchess always speaks of you in terms of warm affection & regard & sends her kindest love.

Mr. & Mrs. Alston of South Carolina & Mr. Elliott, the Commissioner of that State at the Paris Exhibition, passed last Sunday evening with us. She is a superior woman & withal quite good looking & agreeable.

I received the enclosed letter from Mary to you on Monday last by the Baltic. Knowing from unmistakable signs that it came from Mary, I opened it merely to ascertain that she was well. I purposely know but little of its contents. I wrote to her yesterday & invited her to pay us a visit next spring, offering to pay the expenses of her journey. I suggested that it would scarcely be worth her while to pay us a visit for less than a year, & that, in the mean time, Mr. Baker's expenses would be much reduced & he would have an opportunity of arranging his affairs.

Doctor & Mrs. Le Vert, formerly Miss Octavia Walton, are now here. Strangely enough, I had never met her before. She is sprightly, talkative, & animated; but does not seem to understand the art of growing old gracefully. I shall make a favorable impression on her, I trust, by being a good listener. I have not seen her daughter; but they are all to be with me some evening before their departure, which will be in the Arago on the 24th Instant.

I have not received my letter of recall, & entertain but little hope that it will be sent before General Thomas shall reach Washington. I will keep you advised. I dine to-day with General D'Oxholme.

The repulse of the Russians at Kars astonishes me. The Turks & the French have acquired the glory of the present war. Our mother England is rather upon the background.

Sir William & Lady Ouseley are most deeply affected by the loss of their son. I saw her last night for the first time since the

---

[1] Mrs. Russell Sturgis.

428 THE WORKS OF JAMES BUCHANAN [1855

sad event & most sincerely sympathised with her. She became
calmer after the first burst of grief was over & talked about you.
On request of Sir William I write to-day to Mrs. Roosevelt giving her the sad information.

Lady Stafford requests me by letter to give you her warmest
regards & to tell you she hopes Heaven will bless you both in
time & eternity.

Mrs. Shapter looks delicate. I saw her yesterday. She said
she would write; but I have not yet received her letter. Should
it come, I shall send it by the despatch bag.

Remember me most kindly to Mr. & Mrs. Plitt, from the
latter of whom I have received a very kind letter.

Yours affectionately

Miss Lane.   James Buchanan.

TO MR. MARCY.[1]

No. 96.   Legation of The United States.
London, 25th October, 1855.

Sir:

I have the honor to acknowledge the receipt of your
Despatches Nos. 112, 114, and 115, of the 20th September and
the 3d and 5th October, respectively. *Your number 113 has not
yet been received.*

In reference to your No. 115,—I send a copy of the note,
dated on the 24th Instant, which I have addressed to Lord Clarendon when transmitting to him the chronometer and gold chain
from the President for Captain Gale of the barque " Rosina."

With reference to your No. 109,—I have received a note
from Lord Clarendon, dated on the 17th instant, of which I
transmit a copy, returning the commission of Mr. Charles Huffnagle, appointed Consul General of the United States in British
India, and informing me " that the Governor General of India
has been instructed to recognise Mr. Huffnagle in that capacity."

You will perceive from this note that " Her Majesty's
Exequatur is not required to enable the Consuls of foreign States
to enter upon their duties in Her Majesty's Possessions in the
East Indies."

A copy of Lord Clarendon's note, together with the Commission of Mr. Huffnagle, has been transmitted to him at
Calcutta.

---

[1] MSS. Department of State, 68 Despatches from England.

Referring to your No. 101 and my No. 82, I transmit copies
of two notes received from Lord Clarendon, dated respectively on
the 6th August and the 2d instant, in answer to my letter to him
of the 26th July, of which I also send a copy, requesting the discharge of David L. Caldwell, a citizen of the United States, from
the British Navy.

Justice to Tal. P. Shaffner, Esquire, requires that I should
transmit to you a copy of the correspondence between him and
myself in relation to the subject of my Despatch to you, No. 92,
of the 21st September. Accordingly I send a copy of my letter
to him of the 22d September, and of his two letters in answer,
dated at St. Petersburg on the 19 Sept./1st October and on the
20 Septr./2d October.

After the receipt of these letters, I addressed a note to Mr.
T. B. Smithies, stating to him briefly the purport of them and
offering to exhibit them to him at any time he might call at the
Legation; but I have not heard from him since. From this I
infer that the Gutta Percha Company have deemed it prudent not
to communicate a knowledge of the transaction to which they
relate to the British Government. If this had been done in their
present temper, we should doubtless have heard of it.

I also send a copy of the note from Lord Clarendon, dated
on the 4th Instant, in answer to mine of the 2d Instant, conveying the thanks of the President to Mr. Hay, British Chargé
d'Affaires at Tangier, and to Lieutenant Heath, of the British
steamer " Medusa," for the assistance which they afforded to the
American barque " Juniata."

Yours very respectfully,

JAMES BUCHANAN.

Hon : William L. Marcy,
    Secretary of State.

(Enclosure in No. 96.)
Official.   Legation of the United States,
                                    London, 22 September, 1855.
Tal. P. Shaffner, Esqr.
    St. Petersburg, Russia.
Dear Sir:
    I deem it to be my duty to enclose you copies of the affidavits of Captain
Matthew Dickerson Field and Mr. T. B. Smithies, Confidential Clerk to the
Gutta Percha Company, London, furnished to me by the latter. These affi-
davits, as you will perceive, seriously implicate your conduct, and refer to
the War Department, Mr. Archibald, and myself as your instruments, though
neither of us could have entertained the most remote suspicion that you

were capable of acting with bad faith. To Mr. Archibald this may do much injury, as he is a British subject and for reasons known to myself desires to stand well with the British Government.

I sincerely trust there is no foundation for the allegations of Captain Field; and I offer you, at the first moment, an opportunity to contradict them, if this can be done with truth, by your own affidavit, which may be taken before any American Consul. In writing to the Department of State upon the subject, I have spoken of the favorable impression you had made upon me, and stated that the charge against you " depends entirely upon the veracity of Captain Field."

You, of all others, best know what was done with the telegraph wire, the Galvanic batteries and fittings, and the fusees which you purchased from the Gutta Percha Company and which by your order were directed to the " War Department; " and, also, whether any of them have found their way to Russia, through your agency. Your explanation of the matter, under oath, would relieve the facts of the case from all embarrassment; and I shall look for it with much anxiety. It may arrive in London several weeks before I can hear from Washington.

Yours very respectfully,
(Signed)   JAMES BUCHANAN.

(Enclosure in No. 96.)

ST. PETERSBURG, Septr. 20/Oct. 2, 1855.

TO HIS EXCELLENCY JAMES BUCHANAN,
         Minister, &c. &c.
SIR:

My answer to Mr. Field's affidavit is not yet ready, and it may not be possible to send it by mail from Russia, but if it can be done with safety I will do so. It will embrace these points.

1st. That the blank passport was given me on the vessel just before sailing, together with the mail for the London Legation and a despatch for the St. Petersburg Legation. The person who was to take the despatches did not appear, and I was requested to accommodate the government by attending to it, and as there was not time then to write my name in the passport, I was requested to do so before arrival at Liverpool. The purser did write my name, Mr. Field telling me he was a good penman. It was not considered of any consequence at the time by Mr. Field.

2d. The package put under seal on the vessel was composed of my own papers, and my own seal was employed; besides there were no fuses whatever in it.

3d. In passing the Customs at Liverpool, the parcel was not noticed by the officers, as my baggage was soon seen to have been proper. So careful was I on this matter that I declined to carry one of Mr. Field's guns which he smuggled through England. Being bearer of despatches, I was very particular in not having anything improper.

4th. All the *wire* and *fuses* bought in England are owned by me and are partly in my possession, and the balance is with Prof. Morse on loan. The whole of the batteries, Gutta Percha jugs, are with Morse. I presume he has them all at Poughkeepsie, N. Y. They are not employed for the benefit of Russia as stated by Mr. Field, nor will they ever be to my knowledge and belief.

5th. The package given the Russian Legation in Berlin to be sent to St. Petersburg, was composed of Mr. Field's cannon ball, shells, and guns which he was, I suppose, intending to sell to the Russian Government. In the package were a number of my telegraph books. The reason I got the Russian Legation to send them was, that I was bearer of despatches. Field being my travelling associate, I might get into some trouble by being in such company.

6th. That I am not employed either directly or indirectly by the Russian Government in any manner whatever. That I have never received any pay nor a promise of pay for any services rendered or to be rendered, from the government, nor have I been requested to take part in the war affairs, but upon the contrary I have always in my negotiations guarded against a liability of such connections, confining myself to my own business.

7th. That I have declined to peddle new inventions of balls, shells, guns, &c., to the Russian government, and also that I objected to Mr. Field's doing so, while associated with me, and from which course upon my part I am now being the object of his malignity.

The above will embrace the points which will be in my answer, framed in detail so as to fully meet this malicious attack of Field. I am desirous of not retaliating upon him, as that will be left for the future if I deem it necessary to pursue the unfortunate man, who has proved himself to be a wicked man or a lunatic, & the latter I fear is the case.

Yours very respectfully,
(Signed)   TAL. P. SHAFFNER.

N. B. The interpretation of the aforegoing letter must not be applied in any manner to my Railroad and Telegraph negotiations for Russia.

T. P. S.

This letter can be used in such manner as Your Excellency may think proper.

The undersigned,[1] Taliaferro P. Shaffner, a citizen of the United States, in answer to the affidavit lately given by a certain Matthew D. Field of the United States in London, makes the following statement, viz.:

That about the 4th of April, 1855, the undersigned embarked on the steamer Atlantic for Liverpool. While on board and just before departure, the United States Despatch Agent in New York requested him to take charge of the despatches on board of the Steamer, as the gentleman who was to take them had not appeared. There were several bags of despatches for the Consul at Liverpool or for the Legation at London, and a small package of papers for the Legation at St. Petersburg. The said Agent gave the undersigned a blank passport, as bearer of despatches, (as he, the said Agent, had not time to fill it with the undersigned's name, on account of his having waited until the last moment for the proper person to appear) with the request that the undersigned fill it at sea with his name, which was done by the Purser of the ship, by the request of the undersigned and of the said Matthew D. Field, the said Purser being a good penman.

---

[1] This affidavit is given here, as completing the story; but it accompanied, not the present despatch, but Mr. Buchanan's No. 104, a month later.

The undersigned states that he was very particular in not compromising his country in passing any article not proper, and did refuse to carry articles ashore, or aid in any manner the said Field to deceive the custom officers at Liverpool in evading the custom regulations, in getting ashore guns, balls, shells, powder, &c., which he the said Field had with him for Russia, distinctly stating to the said Field that as he was Bearer of Despatches it was not possible for the undersigned to render him any aid whatever.

The undersigned further states that he does not remember of having stated to the said Field that he had anything of value to Russia, and if he did so speak, it must have been in jest, as there was nothing real to base such a remark upon.

Also, that the package sealed on the ship was private papers of the undersigned, pertaining to his own business, having no relation whatever to Russia or war affairs, and that the seal used was his own, and that at Liverpool it did not pass free of examination on account of being under seal. The seal was used as a substitute for twine.

The undersigned further states that the package sent from Berlin to Russia was composed of Field's balls, shells, guns, &c., which the undersigned requested to be sent, as he was fearful of trouble by being in company with Field as long as he had with him such war matters, and that there was nothing in said package belonging to the undersigned which has been given the Russian government except a telegraph book, published by the undersigned.

And further, that he has never received any pay from the Russian government in any manner whatever for services rendered or to be rendered, nor does the undersigned know of having done anything to merit from the Russian government any compensation whatever, excepting, however, that he may in the future receive pay on Rail Road or telegraph contracts, but in no manner pertaining to war matters.

And further, the undersigned has had nothing to do with submarine mines at Cronstadt or anywhere else in Russia, nor does he ever expect to.

And he states, further, that the wire, fuses, &c., purchased in London of Messrs. Slatham & Co., are to the best of his knowledge and belief still his property and not even taken out of the original sacking, and he believes that on his return to New York he can exhibit every fuse in their original state and in the original envelope, except some which were given Prof. Morse, with some of the wire, the batteries, canteens, &c., &c., and they also can doubtless be procured.

Finally, the undersigned states that he has had nothing to do with war matters in Russia, except some assistance given the said Field in the introduction of a cannon ball, which proved to be a failure and disgraceful to every body that had anything to do either with the ball or Field, and the undersigned states that he would not allow the said Field to further peddle war implements as long as he, the undersigned, was negotiating on the Rail Road and Telegraph affairs, and on this account Field became the enemy of the undersigned, and therefore the said Field has been impelled by a malicious feeling to give the affidavit mentioned in the caption of this, totally regardless of truth and honesty, but in consonance with a spirit of treachery to himself, his friends, and his country.

TAL. P. SHAFFNER.

BREMEN, November 5th, 1855.

U. S. Consulate, Bremen, Nov. 5th, 1855.
Sworn to and subscribed before me the fifth day of November, A. D. 1855. Witness my hand and seal of Office.
(Seal) · W. Hildebrand.

TO MR. MARCY.[1]

No. 97.   Legation of The United States.
London, 26 October 1855.

Sir:

I need scarcely direct your attention to the Leader in the London Times of yesterday morning, professing to state the reasons why so large a naval armament has been sent by the British Government to the North American and West Indian Naval stations. This speaks in such a tone of confidence that we might infer it had been written by authority, and yet this Journal has not been heretofore considered an organ of the present administration. Still, it has recently on more than one occasion manifested strong symptoms of good will towards Lord Palmerston. I would, also, refer you to Leaders on the same subject in the Globe of last evening and the Post of this morning. Both these Journals are friendly to the present administration; and the latter is believed to be a personal organ of Lord Palmerston, and is ever fulsome in his praise. But how far all or any of these articles speak his language I cannot positively assert.

When information was brought to my notice on Friday last, through the Daily Telegraph, (a copy of which I have already sent you) that a large additional Naval force had been despatched to our coasts, I could scarcely imagine, even if the statement should prove to be correct, that this could have been done with any menacing intention. Nothing had transpired which could lead to such a suspicion on my part. I nevertheless at once determined that I would ask Lord Clarendon for an explanation of the true state of the fact, and if the force had been sent, for what purpose this had been done. The Telegraph, however, having been but recently commenced and not being a Journal of much authority, I resolved to wait a few days for further developments. When the Times appeared on Thursday morning, I immediately addressed Lord Clarendon a

---

[1] MSS. Department of State, 68 Despatches from England.
Vol. IX—28

note requesting an interview; but up till the present moment (Friday, at 5 o'clock) I have not received an answer. In this I have been greatly disappointed, for I expected to be able to communicate to you the result of our interview by to-morrow's steamer.

I forbear, until after I shall have conversed with his Lordship, to make any comments on these insulting and unfounded articles so well calculated to excite hostile feelings between the people of the two countries. Meanwhile, from all I can learn, the statement contained in the Telegraph is strictly true; and it is reported that the vessels have sailed with sealed orders. They consist of the Pembroke, Cornwallis, Russell, Hawke, and Hastings, Screw ships of 60 guns each, all of which, it appears from the United Service Magazine, corrected to the 27th August last, had been recently employed on the Baltic station. The Captains of the four first whilst on that station were, and it is presumed still are, respectively, G. H. Seymour, G. G. Wellesley, F. Scott, and E. Ommaney. The name of the Captain of the Hastings is not given in the Magazine. These ships, familiarly called "Blocks," are seventy-fours cut down and with a screw applied. In addition to them there is the Powerful, 84, a sailing vessel, Captain T. L. Massie, which has been, I believe, recently employed as a transport for the Crimea; and the Rosamond, 6 gun paddle steamer, Commander S. S. L. Crofton, stated in the Magazine to be on "particular service." If you have not this number of the Magazine itself to refer to, you will find a copy of it in the London Times of the 5th of September last, furnishing a list of the "Stations of the Royal Navy in Commission."

Were Great Britain alone concerned, I should not apprehend any thing very serious from all this bluster; but in speculating upon its meaning we must take into consideration that the Emperor of the French is the soul, the guiding spirit, of the existing Alliance, and that Lord Palmerston may prove to be but too willing an instrument in his hands. That Louis Napoleon is unfriendly to our Country I do not doubt. He is not a hereditary despot feeling secure in his power, but in order to reach his present elevation has annihilated political liberty in France. His object, therefore, now is to convince the world that his Government better subserves the interests of mankind and of the French people than a Government of a freer form. As our institutions are in perfect contrast to his own, we present a standing reproach to his usurpation. The Press in France is under a strict censorship; and it is, therefore, a significant sign that nothing ever appears in it in relation to our country, as I am informed and believe, except what is unfavorable and unfriendly. This may have already produced its effect, at least to some extent; as I learn from intelligent Americans who have recently visited France, after an absence of some years, that the general conduct and tone of the French people towards our countrymen has become much less kind than formerly. Mr. Mason, however, can furnish you more reliable information on this point than myself.

The allies are fighting for " the balance of power," and the effect will most probably be to impair the power of Russia to such a degree as no longer to leave her a counterpoise to that of France, and to make Louis Napoleon the arbiter of the continent. And this, too, by the aid of England!

I enclose a letter to you from Dr. Parker, who has just come here from an interview with Lord Clarendon at the Foreign Office. The expressions of his Lordship to the Doctor were kind and conciliatory towards our country; *but he said nothing of the naval armament which had been despatched.* By the bye, I have been informed this moment by an American gentleman who has been on change to-day that it was reported there that only two Screw steamers had been actually sent, and no other vessel. This differs from all my previous information. We shall not learn the exact truth until after my interview with Lord Clarendon.

Yours very respectfully

JAMES BUCHANAN.

HON: WILLIAM L. MARCY,
  Secretary of State.

TO MISS LANE.[1]

LEGATION OF THE UNITED STATES,

LONDON, 26 October, 1855.

MY DEAR HARRIET/

I have but little time to write before the closing of the Mail, having been much & unexpectedly engaged to-day.

Almost every person I meet speaks kindly of you. I dined

---

[1] Buchanan Papers, private collection. Imperfectly printed in Curtis's Buchanan, II. 153.

with Lady Talbot de Malahide on Tuesday last & she desired me specially to send you her kindest love. Doctor, Madame & Miss Le Vert passed last Sunday evening with me. She is a most agreeable person. I think it right to say this of her, after what I wrote you in my last letter.

I dine to-day with Lady Chantrey, where I am to meet Dr. Twiss.

Grey left yesterday morning on a visit to her relatives in Devonshire. I made her a present of a sovereign to pay her expenses there besides paying her week's wages. I have enlisted Lady Chantrey warmly in her favor, & I hope she may procure a place.

I received by the last steamer a private letter from Governor Marcy in answer to mine requesting my letter of recall. He informs me it had been sent & was then on its way. There is something mysterious in the matter which I cannot explain. It has not yet arrived though it ought to have been here before your departure. Before that, I had received Despatches Nos. 109 & 111. Despatch No. 110, the intermediate one, has not yet come to hand. I presume my letter of recall was in the missing Despatch. I have my own suspicions; but these do not attach to Governor Marcy. His letter was frank & friendly & was evidently written in the full conviction that I would have received my recall before his letter could reach me. Some people are very anxious to delay my return home.

Now the aspect of things has changed. The British Government has recently sent a considerable fleet to our coasts & most inflammatory & abusive articles in reference to the object of this fleet have appeared in the Times, the Globe, & the Morning Post. I have no doubt they will be republished all over the United States. The aspect of affairs between the two countries has now become squally; & Mr. Appleton will not consent to remain here as chargé till the new minister arrives. In this he is right; & consistently with my honor & character, I could not desert my post under such circumstances. I may, therefore, be compelled to remain here until the end of December or even longer. This will depend on the time of the appointment of my successor, which may not be until the meeting of Congress. It is possible that Mr. A. may return home by the Pacific on the 3d November. He is very anxious I should consent to it, which however I have not yet done.

I trust I may hear of your arrival at home by the Pacific on

to-morrow.   The foggy & rainy weather has commenced & the
climate is now dreary.   Mr. & Mrs. John Wurts of New York
passed the evening with me yesterday.   He is an old friend &
she an agreeable lady.   They will return by the Pacific.

Please to remember me most kindly to Mr. and Mrs. Plitt,
& believe me always to be yours affectionately

JAMES BUCHANAN.

MISS LANE.

TO MR. MARCY.[1]

No. 98.   LEGATION OF THE UNITED STATES.

LONDON, 30 October 1855.

SIR:

On the evening of Friday last, several hours after the
Despatch Bag had left for Liverpool, I received a note from
Lord Clarendon appointing yesterday at one o'clock for our
interview.   Soon after my arrival he commenced the conversation by saying he was sorry that the feelings of the Cabinet at
Washington were so unfriendly to them.   That Mr. Cushing,
the Attorney General, had written a letter to Philadelphia about
the Hertz trial in which he commented harshly and unjustly on
his note to me about enlistments, and had gone so far as to call
British officers and agents in the United States " Malefactors."
I told him that I was confident he was mistaken in attributing
to the Cabinet at Washington any hostile feeling towards the
British Government; and that as to the letter of Mr. Cushing, of
which he complained, I could say nothing about it, as I had not
seen it; but I thought he must be laboring under some mistake;—
that the Despatch Bag from Washington, by the " Pacific," had
arrived at the Legation just before I left there to meet his
Lordship, and I had not had any time to examine its contents.
It would doubtless contain something on the subject.   That
when in acknowledging the receipt of his note to me on the
subject of enlistments I had expressed the satisfaction I should
feel in forwarding it to Washington, I had not the most remote
idea that Mr. Crampton was implicated in these enlistments; and
I felt quite sure such was the case in regard to yourself at the

---

[1] MSS. Department of State, 68 Despatches from England.   A part of this
despatch, relating to enlistments, is printed in S. Ex. Doc. 35, 34 Cong. 1
Sess. 28.

time you sent me your instructions; but that the trial of Hertz at Philadelphia, much to my surprise, had brought this fact to light. He said that Crampton was placed there in a very unpleasant and embarrassing situation; he had no means of defending himself before the American public, and if he had, it would not be proper for him to resort to them; but I would be astonished to learn that the witnesses against him had perjured themselves and were not worthy of the least credit. I told him I did not conceive how this could be, as the facts testified by them were sustained by written documents; but intimated my desire to waive the subject for the present and proceed to the business for which I had sought the interview.

I then said:—You have sent a large naval armament to your West India and North American stations, and I desire in the spirit of frankness and friendship to request you to inform me the reason why so many vessels of war have been despatched to the vicinity of our coasts. If this has not been done with a hostile or menacing intention, which I do not believe it has, then the sooner the truth is known the better. It was to prevent, if possible, the irritation among our people which the appearance of such a fleet would naturally produce, that I had on Thursday morning requested an interview with you, so that the explanation might arrive in the United States by the same steamer which would convey the intelligence that the fleet had been sent.

He replied:—The fleet has not been sent with the least unfriendly intention. We have learned from unquestionable authority, and from affidavits, that a large, fast, and powerful steamer has been built at New York under the direction of a Russian Naval officer, and that she is now altogether or nearly ready for sea. That this officer is to take her out from that port as a Russian privateer, and that the object is to intercept our ships from Australia conveying gold to this country. Besides, three or four other steamers are building in New York for the same purpose. We are also informed that it was intended to capture one of the Cunard steamers and make her a Russian privateer.

His Lordship then said he was extremely sorry he had not been able to give me an interview on Friday, in time for the steamer, on account of the dangerous illness of his mother.

I observed:—All this is perfectly new to me. I think your information must be wholly unfounded. I have never heard that a steamer was building in New York to be made a Russian privateer; and from my intercourse with my countrymen I do not think it possible this could have been the case without my having received intimation of it. Besides, the Government of the United States has justly prided itself upon the fidelity and success with which it has at all times preserved its neutrality; and no Government had ever deserved more credit for this than that of General Pierce. It had in every instance, without exception, succeeded in suppressing all lawless expeditions; and never at any period was there less reason than at the present to apprehend danger from this cause. Our neutrality law confers upon the Government ample power to prevent the sailing of any Russian privateer built and equipped in our ports; and surely you can have no reason to doubt, considering the strict neutrality we have hitherto observed, but that the President will prevent the sailing of any such privateer.

His Lordship here branched off upon the Irish question. He said that until very recently he had treated as mere idle rumors all that had been said about an expedition from the United States to Ireland. When he spoke of the expedition to Ireland I smiled incredulously, which his Lordship observing, said I might smile, but that Mr. Crampton who had previously treated these rumors in the same manner until recently, now thought them worthy of serious attention, and had felt it to be his duty to call upon Mr. Marcy and represent the case to him. He observed that two vessels had recently come from the United States to Ireland containing three hundred Irishmen, and the object seemed to be to return to their country piecemeal to create disturbances. I told him I supposed these were Irish Emigrants who had got tired of our country and were returning to their native land; and I went on to show the utter impossibility that there could be any reason for such an apprehension. Indeed, from all appearances, there has never been a period in the history of Ireland, since its connection with England, when any attempt to excite the people to insurrection against the British Government would be so perfectly Quixotic as at the present moment.

In justice to his Lordship, I must observe that he did not assign any apprehensions for Ireland as in any degree the cause for despatching the fleet.

He strongly condemned the article in the Times of Thursday last, and that in the Morning Post of the next day, which he said was still worse,—complained that the Press was constantly embarrassing them in their foreign relations, and protested in the strongest manner that the Government had no connection with any of these journals and they did not speak its language. He was thankful that the Presses and Governments of the two countries all united could not get up a war between them; the people of both would prevent such an unnatural war.

I told him I had written home by the last steamer that I had not understood the Times to be an Organ of the present Government; but I had always heard that the Globe and the Post were connected with it. I knew they were very friendly to it, and the Post was considered "Lord Palmerston's own." He denied this in an emphatic manner and spoke of the Post rather disparagingly. I told him that on my way to the Foreign Office I had called at the Athenæum Club to see an article in the Globe on Friday evening last, which I had understood was different in its tone from the article on Thursday evening; and there was a coincidence in Friday evening's article with what he had informed me were the causes for sending out the fleet. He hesitated for a moment, and said a gentleman who, he believed, was in some way connected with that journal had called at the Foreign Office and he had given him some such information; but he had not read the article itself since its appearance.

I observed that the President's forthcoming message would probably present the true state of the Central American questions to Congress, and as their fleet would arrive but a short time before, our people might connect this movement with these questions and view it as a menace. He declared that this movement had no connection with these questions, & made light of any such idea.

He then commenced to speak on the subject of Mr. Crampton, &c. &c. I told him we had better defer this until after I had read the Despatches and papers which I had received by the Pacific. He said he believed it was better, as he had not himself read the Despatches he had received that morning. We agreed upon Thursday next at half-past three for our meeting, so that we might be able to write to Washington by next Saturday's steamer.

In your confidential Despatch of the 12th Instant, you state as follows:—" I do not find by any of your communications to me an account of your action upon Despatch No. 102, and it is fair to infer from the tenor of Lord Clarendon's note and your acknowledgment of it that it had not been brought to his notice."

In making this remark, you could not have referred to dates.

It was not possible to have brought any thing contained in your No. 102, of the 15th July, to his Lordship's notice previous to the 16th July, the date of his note to me to which you refer. Your Despatch did not arrive here until the 30th July; and ten days previous thereto, I had transmitted a copy of this note to you with my Despatch No. 81, of the 20th July.

But I have not since taken any action upon your No. 102, for the plainest reason. I had, previously to its arrival, transmitted to you a copy of Lord Clarendon's note already referred to, of the 16th July, on the subject of the enlistment and employment of soldiers for the British army within our limits, and had informed his Lordship, in acknowledging the receipt of this note, that I should have much satisfaction in transmitting a copy of it to the Secretary of State. Of course, it would have been improper for me to take any new step in this matter until I should learn whether this note would prove satisfactory to yourself. Again:—Your No. 102 states that after many months had elapsed British officers were still proceeding to violate our laws and persist "in carrying on the obnoxious scheme without any open disapproval by the Home Government or any attempt to arrest it;" and one of the two express instructions which the President gives me in conclusion is "to say to Her Majesty's Government that he expects it will take prompt and effective measures to arrest their proceedings." Now, these measures had been already adopted; but could not possibly have been known to you. Lord Clarendon's note had entirely changed the aspect of the case from the view which you took of it, and must necessarily have taken of it, at the date of your No. 102. The general tenor of this note—its disavowals and its regrets—were certainly conciliatory, and the concluding paragraph declaring that all proceedings for enlistments in "North America" had been put an end to by Her Majesty's Government, for the avowed reason that the advantages which Her Majesty's Service might derive from such enlistments would not be sought for by Her Majesty's Government if it were supposed to be obtained in disregard of the respect due to the law of the United States, was highly satisfactory. It was for these reasons that I expressed the satisfaction I would have in communicating it to you. Then came the declaration of Lord Palmerston to the same effect in the House of Commons on the 2d August, in which he explicitly declared that, in order to avoid questions with the United States, the Government "had put an end to the enlistment of forces which used to take place at Halifax." This declaration was, to my knowledge, received with much satisfaction by Mr. Milner Gibson, who had made the inquiry of Lord Palmerston, as well as by many other liberal Members of Parliament. Very different indeed had been the conduct of the British Government in this respect towards certain continental States.

I can assure you that I did not entertain the most remote idea that this question had not been satisfactorily adjusted, until I learned the complicity of Mr. Crampton in the affair. This was officially communicated to me in your Despatch No. 107, of the 8th, received on the 24th September, with a copy of your letter to Mr. Crampton on the 5th, and his answer of the 7th of the same month. From these it appears you had thought it due to Mr. Crampton, no doubt properly, to take the affair in hand yourself, and this you have done in an able manner in your letter to that gentleman. Thus much I have deemed necessary to place myself *rectus in curia*.

Yours very respectfully,

JAMES BUCHANAN.

HON: WILLIAM L. MARCY,
    Secretary of State.

TO MR. MARCY.[1]

No. 99.   LEGATION OF THE UNITED STATES.

LONDON, 2 November, 1855.

SIR:

I have the honor to acknowledge the receipt of your Despatch No. 113, of 1st of October (the non-arrival of which is mentioned in my No. 96), and of Nos. 116 and 117, dated 13th & 15th October, respectively; of Duplicate of No. 118, October 13th; of "*Confidential*," of October 15th, and of No. 119 of October 16th.

According to the appointment mentioned in my last Despatch, I met Lord Clarendon yesterday afternoon at the Foreign Office. After some unimportant conversation, I told him that on my return to the Legation on Monday last I found a Despatch from yourself on the recruitment question which I

---

[1] MSS. Department of State, 68 Despatches from England. Extracts from this despatch are published in S. Ex. Doc. 35, 34 Cong. 1 Sess. 34, 246.

had been instructed to read to him and furnish him a copy if requested. He said he had, also, Despatches from Washington on the same subject. I then stated that, Mr. Crampton having promised in his note of the 7th September to address you again after hearing from his Lordship, I should be glad to know whether he had furnished instructions to Mr. Crampton for this purpose. He told me he had not—that he had pursued the usual diplomatic course in such cases, in addressing me a note in answer to the note addressed by you to Mr. Crampton. I said, Very well,—then your note to me of the 27th September is the answer to Mr. Marcy's note to Mr. Crampton of the 5th of that month; and the Despatch which I was about to read to him was your answer to his note to me of the 27th September. To this he assented.

I then read to him your Despatch to me of the 13th October; to which he listened throughout with great apparent attention. After the reading he requested a copy, & I delivered him the duplicate which you had forwarded. He then asked what was the nature of the satisfaction from the British Government to which you had referred in your Despatch just read. I said that the best mode of giving him the information was to read to him this Despatch of yours to me, which I accordingly did, except the last paragraph but one, of which he also desired a copy, and I promised to furnish it. I had prepared myself to state in conversation the substance of what this Despatch required from the British Government; but having the Despatch with me I thought it better at the moment, in order to prevent all misapprehension, to read it to him, as it had evidently been prepared with much care. I have sent him a copy of it to-day; except the paragraph to which I have already alluded.

I then stated, his Lordship would observe that the Government of the United States had two causes of complaint. The one was such violations of our neutrality laws as might be tried and punished in the Courts of the United States. The other, to which I especially desired to direct his attention, consisted in a violation of our neutrality under the general law of nations, by the attempts which had been made by British officers and agents, not punishable under our municipal law, to draw military forces from our territory to recruit their armies in the Crimea. As examples of this, I passed in review the conduct of Mr. Crampton, of the Lieutenant Governor of Nova Scotia, and the British Consuls at New York and Philadelphia.

I observed that in his note of the 16th July he had assured me that the individuals engaged in recruiting in the United States acted upon their individual responsibility and had no authority for their proceedings from any British officials, by whom their conduct was condemned. In addition, he had stated that instructions had been sent out to Sir Gaspard Le Marchant to stop all enlistments in North America. [Yes, his Lordship observed, they were sent out on the 22d June last.] I said I had expressed the satisfaction which I felt in transmitting this note to Mr. Marcy; and was, therefore, sorry to say satisfactory proof existed that Mr. Crampton and other British officers had before and since been engaged in aiding and countenancing these proceedings and recruitments. In fact, Wagner had been convicted at New York for a violation of our neutrality law committed at so late a period as the 3d of August.

Lord Clarendon sat silent and attentive whilst I was making these remarks, and then took from his drawer several sheets of paper containing extracts from a Despatch of Mr. Crampton (received, as I understood, by the last steamer) some of which he read to me. Mr. Crampton emphatically denies the truth of Strobel's testimony and Hertz's confession, as well as all complicity in the recruitments. I expressed my surprise at this; and said that Strobel's character was respectable, so far as I had ever learned, and that his testimony was confirmed by several documents implicating Mr. Crampton, which had been given in evidence on the trial of Hertz. I told him he would see this on a perusal of the trial itself, of which I gave him a copy.

I asked him whether he intended I should communicate to you my recollection of the particular extracts he had read to me from Mr. Crampton's despatch. He said he would prefer I should not,—that he would examine and sift the subject with great care, and preferred to present these to you in his own language.

In concluding this part of the conversation, Lord Clarendon declared, in a sincere and emphatic manner, that nothing had been further from the intention of the British Government than to violate the neutrality of the United States or to give them cause of offence. He could, also, declare in regard to himself, personally, that he would not act in such a manner towards one of the weakest Powers, not even towards Monaco, and certainly would not do so towards the great and powerful Republic of the United States, for which he ever entertained the warmest feelings of respect and friendship.

I presume you may expect ere long to hear from Lord Clarendon, through a note addressed to Mr. Crampton, according to what he says is diplomatic usage.

We afterwards had some conversation about the invasion of Ireland, which I have never treated seriously. In regard to the Russian privateer alleged to be fitting out at the port of New York, I told him that since our last conversation I had seen two gentlemen who had just arrived from New York, who assured me they would be likely to know or have heard of it, were any such steamer building, and they treated the report to that effect on this side of the Atlantic as idle and unfounded. In reply he informed me that the fact was substantiated and the steamer described in a particular manner, which he detailed, by three depositions which had been forwarded by the British consul at New York to Mr. Crampton, who had brought the subject to your notice, and you had promised to inquire into it.

In the course of the conversation I observed to him that the most serious difficulty between the Governments might arise out of the Central American questions. He said that when two Governments disagreed about the construction of a treaty, the best and most natural mode was to refer the question to a third Power. At an early period of the negotiation, he had made this suggestion; but I had jocularly replied that the Emperor of Russia was the only Power sufficiently independent to act as an impartial umpire in the case, and they had gone to war with him. That we had tried Louis Napoleon on one occasion and he had decided against us.[1] I then asked him to state to what Power, sufficiently free from British influence, we could refer this question, even if such a reference were possible; and he hesitated for a reply. I then said, I know of none unless it might be " King Bomba." He laughed, and the conversation on this point dropped.

I then referred to the most extraordinary leading article in the Times of yesterday morning, and said it would seem that the writer had had information from the Foreign Office. Indeed, from this it might almost be inferred that I had encouraged them to recruit in the United States; and I expressed my regret that they had not informed me of their intention, for if they had done so, I thought I could have given them such reasons against it as might have prevented it altogether. He declared, in the most

---

[1] The case of the brig General Armstrong. See Moore, International Arbitrations, II. 1092 et seq.

solemn manner, that the Times had received no information either from him or, he was convinced, from any other person in the office. I told him there might be some leaky vessel about the office. He said he was certain there was not; but could not account for the manner in which the Times had obtained the information.

There was other conversation; but not of much importance. Besides, I have not time to report it or make the general remarks which I could desire. Suffice it to say, that I believe the storm which has been raised here by the sending of the fleet and by the first article in the Times will be productive of good. The English public, and especially the manufacturing and mercantile classes, have become excited and alarmed, and are now eagerly intent upon acquiring a knowledge of the questions in dispute between the two Governments. The dead calm in which the public mind had rested concerning American affairs has been succeeded by a storm; and the symptoms indicate strongly that Lord Palmerston will not be sustained in raising difficulties with the United States. We have been already ably defended in the Press.

Yours very respectfully,

JAMES BUCHANAN.

HON: WILLIAM L. MARCY,
    Secretary of State.

TO MISS LANE.[1]

LEGATION OF THE UNITED STATES,

LONDON 2 November 1855.

MY DEAR HARRIET/

I have truly but a moment to write to you. We did not learn your arrival by the Pacific, which I had expected with much interest.

Lord Clarendon told me yesterday that the Queen had expressed her regret not to have seen you before your departure. He said she had heard you were to marry Sir Fitz Roy Kelly, & expressed how much she would have been gratified had you been detained in England. We had some talk about the disparity of your ages which I have not time to repeat, even if it were worth

---

[1] Buchanan Papers, private collection; Curtis's Buchanan, II. 157.

repeating. I said it was supposed Sir Fitz Roy was very rich. " Yes," he said, " *enormously.*"

There is a great muss here at present about the relations between the two countries; but I think it will all eventually blow over & may do good. Every body is now anxious to know something about American affairs, & both in the Press & the Public we have many powerful defenders against the measures adopted by Lord Palmerston's government.

With my kindest regards to Mr. & Mrs. Plitt, I remain ever yours

Affectionately,

JAMES BUCHANAN.

TO MR. MARCY.[1]

No. 100.   LEGATION OF THE UNITED STATES.

LONDON, 7 November, 1855.

SIR:

I have the honor to acknowledge the receipt of your Unofficial Despatch of the 22d ultimo, and also of your missing Despatch No. 110, of the 11th September last, containing my letter of recall. This was not received until Monday last, the 5th Instant. I shall always regret the mistake which prevented it from leaving the Department until so late a period as the 22d of October. It has arrived here at a time when the relations between the two countries have assumed so threatening an aspect on this side of the Atlantic, that I cannot at the present moment retire without violating my sense of duty. I have secured a passage in the " Arago " from Southampton on the 19th December; but I hope it may become proper for me to leave the Mission before that day, as I am anxious in the mean time to visit Paris. It was with difficulty that I prevailed upon Mr. Appleton not to return home by the steamer of the 3d Instant. He has now, much to my satisfaction, consented to remain until the 19th December. On that day, and I trust much earlier, I shall leave him in charge of the Legation with entire confidence that he is fully competent to discharge its duties.

In reference to your No. 115, I transmit a copy of the note of Lord Clarendon, dated on the 26th ultimo, acknowledging the receipt of my note to him of the 24th ultimo, and of the chro-

---

[1] MSS. Department of State, 68 Despatches from England.

nometer and gold chain for Captain Gale, of the bark " Rosina."

I have received the Exequatur for V. Holmes, Esquire (vide your No. 116) appointed Consul of the United States for Galway, and on the 3d Instant I transmitted the same to him, together with his commission, at his post.

According to the United Service Magazine for October, corrected up till 26th September, the following were the British vessels of war on the North American and West Indian Stations:

NAMES.	GUNS.
Arab,	12
Argus,	6
Buzzard,	6
Boscawen,	70
Columbia,	6
Daring,	12
Espiegle,	12
Eurydice,	26
Hermes,	6
Imaum, (receiving ship)	72
Mariner,	12
Medea,	6
Netley,	8
Scorpion,	6
Termagant,	24
Vestal,	26
	310

According to the same magazine for November, corrected up till 27th October, the following were the vessels of war on the same Stations:

NAMES.	GUNS.
Arab,	12
Argus,	6
Boscawen,	70
Buzzard,	6
Columbia,	6
Cornwallis,	60
Daring,	12
Espiegle,	12
Eurydice,	26
Express,	6
Imaum,	72

NAMES.	GUNS.
Mariner,	12
Medea,	6
Netley,	8
Pembroke,	60
Powerful,	84
Rifleman,	8
Rosamond,	6
Scorpion,	6
Termagant,	24
Vestal,	24
Hermes,	6
	532 Guns.

In addition to these, unless their destination should be changed, there will soon be on these Stations,

The Hastings, 60, Capt. E. G. Fanshawe.

Hawke, 60.

Russell, 60.

making in all a fleet of 25 vessels carrying seven hundred and twelve guns. The increase, therefore, since the 27th September, has been nine vessels and 402 guns. But I presume I need scarcely trouble you with these details, as the United Service Magazine is doubtless received at the Navy Department.

Yours very respectfully,

JAMES BUCHANAN.

HON: WILLIAM L. MARCY,
Secretary of State.

TO MR. MARCY.[1]

No. 101.   LEGATION OF THE UNITED STATES.

LONDON, 9 November, 1855.

SIR:

I had an interview with Lord Clarendon on yesterday by appointment, and shall now report to you, as nearly as I can recollect it, our conversation. After the usual salutations, I said to him:—" Your Lordship, when we last parted, asked me

---

[1] MSS. Department of State, 68 Despatches from England. Extracts from this despatch are printed in S. Ex. Doc. 35, 34 Cong. 1 Sess. 36.

to help you to keep the peace between the two countries, which I cordially promised to do; and I have come here to-day to make a suggestion to you with this intent.

"You have now learned the prompt and energetic action of the Government of the United States in causing the seizure and examination of the vessel at New York which you had learned was intended for a Russian privateer. Upon this examination, she has turned out to be the barque Maury, built for the China trade and bound to Shanghai. The ten iron cannon in the hold and four on deck, together with the other arms on board, were designed to furnish arms to the merchantmen in the Chinese seas, to enable them to defend themselves against the Pirates so numerous in that quarter. The time of her sailing had been announced for three weeks in five daily journals, and she was to take out four Christian Missionaries. So satisfactory did the examination prove to be, that Mr. Barclay, the British consul, had himself assented to her discharge.

"Your Lordship stated to me, at our last meeting, that the reason why the British fleet had been sent to the vicinity of the United States was the information you had received that a Russian privateer had been built in New York and was about to leave that port to prey upon your commerce with Australia. You have now received the clearest evidence not only that this was all a mistake, as I predicted at the time it would prove to be, but also that the Government of the United States has acted with energy and good faith in promptly causing the vessel to be seized and examined. Now, My Lord, the cause having proved to be without foundation, the effect ought to cease, and I earnestly suggest to you the propriety of issuing an order to withdraw the fleet.

"The Times accompanied the annunciation that this fleet had been sent with the most insulting and offensive exposition of the reasons for this act, and several journals friendly to the present Government followed in the same spirit. When we take into view the existing difference between the two Governments about enlistments, and the still more dangerous questions behind, concerning Central America, all of which are well known to the people of the United States, what will be the inference naturally drawn by them when the news shall first burst upon them? Will it not be that this fleet has reference to these questions and is intended as a menace? I need not say what will be the effect on my countrymen. They well know that no reason ever existed in point of fact for apprehension on account of Russian privateers, and still less, if that be possible, for an expedition to Ireland; and they will not attribute the sending of the fleet to these causes. The President in his Message to Congress early in December will doubtless present to that Body the present unsatisfactory condition of the Central American questions; and it will require the cool and clear heads of the public men of both countries to prevent serious consequences from these questions. Now, it so happens that the news of the sending of the British fleet will arrive in the United States but a short time before the date of the Message, and will almost necessarily be connected in public opinion with these dangerous questions, thus rendering them more complicated. If you will, at the present moment, and before we can hear from the United States, voluntarily withdraw your fleet, upon the principle that the danger from Russian privateers of which you had been informed did not, in point of fact, exist, and at the same time do justice to the Government of the United States for having so faithfully preserved its neutrality, this would be to pour oil upon the troubled waters and could not fail to produce the best results. You might address a note either to Mr. Crampton or myself stating that the fleet had been withdrawn; and I am persuaded that this act of justice would have a most happy effect."

His Lordship in reply said in substance, (for I will not undertake to repeat his very words), that he thanked me for my suggestion and would take it into serious consideration; but of course he could do nothing without consulting the Cabinet. Of this, however, he could assure me most positively, as he had done at our former interview, that nothing could be further from their intention than any, even the most remote, idea of a menace, in sending out the fleet. Immediately after our conversation on Thursday last, he had sent to the Admiralty and requested that orders might be issued that the vessels sent out should not go near the coasts of the United States. Sir Charles Wood and Admiral Berkeley had both informed him that it was never their intention that they should approach our coasts, and he could assure me that none of these vessels would ever go " poking " about our ports. Besides, he said, Sir Charles Wood had informed him that but three vessels had been sent out, one to Bermuda and the other two to Jamaica. [I observed this was a mistake, but I would not interrupt him.] He replied, this was the information he had received from Sir Charles.

They had received what they had supposed to be the most authentic information that the Russian privateer was nearly ready to leave New York.   That she was a fast and powerful vessel, well armed, and one that it would be difficult to overtake; and that she intended to capture one of the Cunard steamers and employ her also for the purpose of cutting up their commerce with Australia.   That they also had information of the projected expedition to Ireland.   In this state of affairs he had received Mr. Marcy's letter to Mr. Crampton, the tone and language of which he said were not usual in diplomatic correspondence between friendly Governments and evinced what they believed to be a hostile feeling on the part of the Cabinet at Washington towards Great Britain.   This was afterwards confirmed by Attorney General Cushing's letter, which was of a most insulting character to himself personally and did him the greatest injustice.   It attributes to him the employment of contrivances to shelter their agents in the United States from conviction as " malefactors."   Besides, the American steamer " Fulton " had been employed in going from port to port throughout their West India Islands, making surveys, taking soundings, and inquiring into the strength of their fortifications.   Under all these circumstances they would have been condemned by the British people if they had taken no precautions against the danger which seemed to threaten.

I told him I must again express my regret that they had adopted the course of sending out a fleet without giving me, or giving you through Mr. Crampton, any notice of their intention. Had this been done, it must have led to explanations which would most certainly have obviated all difficulties.   The news of the sending of the fleet, accompanied by the article in the Times, when it reached the United States, would most probably excite much public indignation.   We had experienced a blast here; but when the counter blast reached us from the other side of the Atlantic, it would equal, if not surpass, that on this side in intensity.   The people of both nations were proud and jealous of their rights, and neither could brook an insult.   The statesmen of the two countries ought, therefore, to be peculiarly careful how they acted.   Wars often arose from small beginnings. When the news reached the United States, it would find the people calm and tranquil in relation to their foreign affairs and wholly unprepared for it.   It would burst upon them suddenly, and they would doubtless manifest their feelings in strong and defying language. This would return to England and react upon the people here, thus further increasing the difficulties, until at last by degrees the two countries might find themselves involved in war, although, with the exception of the Central American questions, there was no question of very serious importance between them. And such a war! It would exasperate the people of the two countries against each other to such a degree that the intervals of peace hereafter would be but little better than mere truces. The despotisms of the continent would be highly gratified by such a war between the two freest nations of the world, whilst the cause of liberty and civilization would everywhere suffer. I would not have it on my conscience for any human consideration to be the author of any act which might lead to such consequences. His Lordship, with much enthusiasm of manner, declared he heartily agreed with me in every sentiment I had expressed; and I must know from his frank and free communications with me how anxious he had ever been to preserve the most friendly relations with the United States. He said it was very true that the Despotisms on the continent would be highly gratified with such an unnatural war.

I observed it was true that Governor Marcy had expressed himself in strong and decided but, I thought, not offensive language in his letter to Mr. Crampton, because he had felt strongly on the subject; but I could venture to assure him that no offence was intended. And I might add that he had returned a Rowland for the Governor's Oliver, and now they both stood upon the same footing. I thought his Lordship's letter was in some portions of it not of a very conciliatory or diplomatic character. And, as to Mr. Cushing's letter of which he complained, it was merely conditional and inferential, and in employing the term " malefactors " he could not have intended it in its worst sense, and must have meant nothing more than " wrongdoers." He said he differed from me entirely in regard to Mr. Cushing's letter, which has evidently nettled him very much.

I then told him there was a mistake in regard to the number of ships they had sent to the North American and West Indian Stations, and explained the matter fully to him as I have done to you in my last Despatch. He took notes of this explanation and said he would inquire into it immediately.

[I have just received at the present writing a note from Lord Clarendon, dated yesterday & marked " Private," in which he states that he had just seen Sir Charles Wood, who informed him " that the Powerful, Rosamond, Cornwallis, and Pembroke are gone out—three of them *stationed* at Bermuda and one at Jamaica—that another vessel (I think the Malacca) is going out to replace the Rosamond, which is recalled, and that no other ships are going or have been ordered to go."

The Malacca is a Screw Corvette of 17 guns. It is now evident they have changed their intention of ordering the Hastings, the Hawke, & the Russell to the West Indies.]

I asked him if he had yet sent to Mr. Crampton a reply to your letter addressed to him through myself. He said he was sorry he had not yet been able to do so,—he had not received the necessary reports from their agents in the United States, & would only be able to write a private letter to Mr. Crampton on the subject by Saturday's steamer. We then had some conversation in relation to your Despatch No. 102, and he told me I might inform you he was entirely willing to discharge every soldier who had been recruited in the United States and pay for his passage home. That if he could obtain a list of these soldiers, he would cheerfully have them immediately discharged. It was against his wishes and instructions that the laws of the United States had been violated; and he was sorry that this had ever been done, whether with or without the authority of their agents. Mr. Crampton had kept nothing back from Mr. Marcy. I expressed my satisfaction at his willingness to discharge these soldiers; but said that in reporting the conversation to you I desired to be perfectly correct. Did his Lordship mean only the soldiers who had completed their enlistment within the United States, or did he mean to embrace those who had been engaged to leave the United States and to go to Canada for the purpose of being enlisted? The latter class of cases was as much within the penalties of our law as the former. He said he meant all— the latter as well as the former—whoever had been enlisted or engaged contrary to the law of the United States should be discharged.

He then returned to the Newspaper Press, and complained bitterly of the annoyance it had given them in different portions of the world, as well as in the United States, and instanced Germany;—these Presses spoke without the authority of the Government. I replied that the article in the Times of the first of November had convinced me that the writer must have had information from some member of the Ministry. It contained some statements which could only be known to those acquainted with the documents in the Foreign Office, though I had not the most remote suspicion (*I have not*) that the information was communicated by himself or any person attached to his office. I told him that in that article the Times had attributed to me absurd expressions which I had never used, and that I had on the day of its appearance sent the Editors a respectful note for publication correcting the misstatement, which they had never published, or noticed in any other manner. He said that this was very bad treatment; but was just in character with them and might have been expected.

I informed him that I had received my letter of recall and was anxious to leave, but I should not present it until the present storm, raised in a considerable degree by the Press on this side of the water, should blow over; and he expressed much satisfaction at my determination, and said some flattering things concerning myself which I need not repeat.

I then brought to his notice and explained to him the case of the Masters of vessels at Liverpool who had taken saltpetre on board previous to the recent order to prohibit its exportation, and delivered him a note on the subject, to which he promised to give his immediate attention.

He asked me if I had received the note he had addressed to me yesterday, informing me that all the necessary steps had been taken in Ireland, according to my request, for the extradition of the criminals at Cork. I said I had not; but was glad to hear it because this second decision shewed they had finally determined that the treaty embraces crimes committed on board of American vessels on the high seas. In the course of this part of the conversation, he said he was ashamed to speak to me about the Consular Convention, and had determined to do so no more until he could inform me he was ready, which he hoped to be in a very short time. This had given him more trouble than almost any thing he had ever undertaken. I observed that it had now become quite common for seamen to desert from our vessels in different ports of the British Empire, because they knew they could do so with perfect impunity. Such cases were often brought to my notice, and were greatly annoying and detrimental to our commerce.

His Lordship then adverted to the Shaffner case. He said he was reminded of it by what he had recently heard from Washington. He had been informed of it at the time of its occurrence and would have mentioned it to me if he had seen me soon after;

but attaching to it no particular importance, it had slipped his memory. This afforded me an opportunity of explaining to him the nature of the transaction in extenso, as it is already known to you; with which he expressed himself to be perfectly satisfied. It is evident, however, that he has no very favorable opinion of Mr. Shaffner.

On rising to take my leave, I again impressed upon him the importance of the suggestion I had made relative to the withdrawal of the fleet; and he promised to give it his most serious attention.

He then said,—About these Central American questions,— the best mode of settling them is by arbitration. I replied there was nothing to arbitrate. He said the true construction of the treaty was a proper subject for arbitration. I told him I did not consider it a question for construction at all,—the language was plain and explicit, and I thought this would be the almost unanimous opinion of the American people; but in writing to you I should mention what he had now said, as I had done what he had said at our former interview.

I have thus given you a faithful report of our conversation according to my best recollection. Lord Clarendon's manner is at all times courteous and kind; but upon this occasion it was peculiarly so, and he seemed to be deeply impressed with the subject. Were the decision to depend upon him, I am persuaded the fleet would be withdrawn; but this would not be in character with Lord Palmerston. There are unmistakable indications, however, from different quarters of England, and especially from the Manufacturing Districts, of strong disapprobation at the course of the Ministry towards the United States. We are defended in the public journals, and able and judicious communications in our defence have even been inserted in the Times. There is now quite a lull here, which will most probably continue until the blast shall reach us from your side of the Atlantic.

The Times exerts a wonderful influence in this country. Its circulation is more than 60,000 per day. Every body reads it,—every body abuses it,—and every body is influenced by it. To give you an instance: The English public, and to my own certain knowledge, several highly respectable and intelligent persons, really believed in the danger from Russian privateers fitted out in our ports, and in the inability if not want of inclination on the part of the Government to prevent this violation of our Neutrality laws. Nay, more, many even swallowed the absurdity of the Irish invasion. The consequence was, that when by the last advices all appeared to be quiet and peaceful in the United States, consols rose immediately. The reason avowed for this was, that there did not appear to be any immediate danger from Russian privateers or from an expedition to Ireland.

I shall now close this interminable Despatch.

Yours very respectfully,

JAMES BUCHANAN.

HON: WILLIAM L. MARCY,
Secretary of State.

TO MISS LANE.[1]

LEGATION OF THE UNITED STATES,
LONDON, 9 November, 1855.

MY DEAR HARRIET/

I have received your favors of the 21st & 22d October. I thank Heaven that you have arrived at home in health & safety. The weather since your departure has been such as you know prevails at this season, & London has been even too dull for me, & this is saying much for it.

I received my letter of Recall dated on the 11th September last on Monday the 5th Instant! with an explanation from Gov: Marcy of the mistake which had occasioned its delay. Had this been sent on the 11th September, I might with all convenience have accompanied you home, either on the 6th or at latest on the 20th October.

The storm which has been raised in England in regard to the relations between the two countries renders it impossible that I should leave the Legation at the present moment. Mr. Appleton has at length reluctantly consented to remain until my departure; & this relieves me from much embarrassment. I now hope to be at home early in January; but this for the present you had better keep to yourself. I may, in the mean time, probably visit Paris.

I regret that such unfounded reports respecting Mr. Mason's health should reach the United States.

You speak to me concerning the Presidency. You of all other persons best know that even if there were no other cogent

---

[1] Buchanan Papers, private collection; Curtis's Buchanan, II. 154.

reasons, the state of my health is not such as would enable me to undergo the intense anxiety & fatigue incident to wearing that crown of thorns. Of course I wish nothing said about the state of my health.

My friends in Pennsylvania constitute the ablest & most honest portion of the Democratic party. They now have the power in their own hands, & they ought *for their own benefit, not mine,* to take care that Penna. shall be represented by proper persons in the National Convention. They can, if they will, exert such a powerful influence as to select the best man for the country from among the list of candidates & *thus take care of themselves.* This would be my advice to them, were I at home. I hope they may follow it. As far as I can learn, President Pierce is daily growing stronger for a renomination.

I enclose you a note which I have received from the Duchess of Somerset.

I know not whether Mrs. Shapter will write to you to-day. I communicated your kind messages to her, with which she appeared to be much gratified, & spoke of you most affectionately.

You will be gratified to learn that Sir Fitz Roy does not bear malice. Mr. Bedinger in writing to me from Copenhagen on the 4th Instant says " I saw them both several times. Sir Fitz Roy & his charming niece (for so I found her) told me much of yourself & your *charming* niece, who they said had recently left you for America."

I have a very long Despatch for to-day & must bid you adieu! May God be with you to protect & direct you. Be prudent & circumspect & cautious in your communications to others. There are very few people in the world who can keep a secret. They must tell or burst.

My kindest regards to Mr. & Mrs. Plitt. I have written to the latter by the Bag. Ever yours,

Affectionately,

JAMES BUCHANAN.

MISS LANE.

FROM LORD CLARENDON.[1]

F. O. Nov. 16/55.

My dear Mr. Buchanan

With reference to our conversation of yesterday, I must again express the great value that we attach to a continuance of friendly relations with the United States, & assure you that as those friendly relations will never be disturbed by any act of ours, so we hope & trust that they will not be put in danger by any act of the United States Govt.

We are convinced that the value of those relations & the duty of maintaining them are felt alike by the two Govts., & we are consequently under no apprehension that they will be disturbed.

I have informed you that three ships had been sent to Bermuda & one to Jamaica & that they will not quit those Stations. They were sent there because it is the duty of those who are charged with the conduct of affairs in this country to be on their guard against all dangers which may appear in any part of the Horizon & let them come from what quarter they may; but I assure you that we have taken no step prompted by any hostile feeling or menacing intention on our part towards the United States. Believe me

Very faithfully yrs.

Clarendon.

TO LORD CLARENDON.[1]

Private.   Legation of the United States,

London, 16 November 1855.

My dear Lord Clarendon/

I have received your note of to-day, & regret to say it is not all I might have expected from our conversation of yesterday. It will not, I fear, exert that happy influence in restoring cordial relations between the two governments which, in this conversation, I so confidently predicted, and which I shall always so earnestly desire.

Yours very respectfully,

(signed)   James Buchanan.

------

[1] Buchanan Papers, Historical Society of Pennsylvania.

TO MR. MARCY.[1]

No. 102.   LEGATION OF THE UNITED STATES.

LONDON, 16 November, 1855.

SIR:

To-morrow's steamer from Liverpool will carry home Mr. John Appleton, the Secretary of this Legation.   I am truly sorry to part from him.   In every respect, he has performed his duties to my entire satisfaction.   Indeed, in my opinion he is well qualified to perform the duties of any Diplomatic station under the Government.   Whilst I regret his loss, I am compelled to yield my assent to the domestic reasons which have induced his determination to go home.   He will be able to give you reliable information of the state of affairs and the relations between the two Governments on this side of the Atlantic.

I had anticipated with great pleasure my release from this Legation before the present time.   The moment, however, that I learned the departure of the fleet for the West Indian and North American stations, and the purpose for which this fleet had been despatched, with the comments of the Times, Globe, and Post, I could not hesitate a moment as to my line of duty.   I could not desert my post in the midst of a storm, however inconvenient and disagreeable to myself personally to remain in it any longer.

I shall say nothing for the present about a Secretary of Legation, as the new Minister, whoever he may be, will doubtless be consulted on this subject.   In the mean time, I have written to my nephew, James B. Henry at Philadelphia, who is now about to be admitted to the bar, to come out here immediately.   As he writes a good hand and understands and speaks the French language, he will be of great use to me and I shall be able to get along with his assistance during the remainder of my time.   Still, should the President desire to appoint and send out a Secretary of Legation, I shall be happy to give him all the instruction in my power.   I need scarcely suggest how important it is that a suitable and industrious person should be selected for this station.

Within the last fortnight I have observed that the popularity of the war in this country is not so great as it has been heretofore. There certainly has been considerable change in this respect.   But Mr. Appleton can inform you not only of this change but of its causes.

---

[1] MSS. Department of State, 68 Despatches from England.

A war with the United States, at the present time, would not be popular in this country.   Still, I believe the people might be brought up to it by the Press, if they could be convinced, however erroneously, that their national honor required the sacrifice.   In the mass they are ignorant; and feeling that they have, in a great degree, lost their prestige as a military nation, they are extremely sensitive.   It is my belief, however, that if the Central American questions, which are the dangerous questions, should be brought before them, in a firm, calm, and temperate manner, as I have no doubt they will be by the President in his message, Lord Palmerston will be compelled either to yield or retire.   Whilst for one I should not hesitate to go to war with England at the present moment (though I do not believe in any immediate danger of war) if the honor of the country demanded this course, yet without a railroad to the Pacific we might suffer much in such a contest.   Had there been a railroad from Moscow to Sebastopol, the Allies would never have been able to make good their footing in the Crimea.

Yours very respectfully,

JAMES BUCHANAN.

HON: WILLIAM L. MARCY,
     Secretary of State.

TO MR. MARCY.[1]

No. 103.   LEGATION OF THE UNITED STATES.
                                LONDON, 16 November 1855.

SIR:

I had an interview yesterday afternoon with Lord Clarendon at the Foreign Office.   In requesting it, I had informed him that Mr. Appleton would return home by Saturday's steamer and this would be the last opportunity of reaching Washington before the President's Message.

We had much desultory conversation, of which I shall not attempt to make a full report.   It is evident that his Lordship is kept well informed of every thing passing at Washington.   He spoke of unfairness which he had heard existed in the published report of the trial of Hertz,—its extensive circulation by the Russian Legation at Washington,—the knowledge in advance

---

[1] MSS. Department of State, 68 Despatches from England.

of the Russian Minister there, that you were about to address your letter to Mr. Crampton, and the terms in which he announced this fact to other Members of the Diplomatic Corps, &c. &c. &c., all evidently tending to convey his idea of the partiality of our Government for Russia.

By the arrival of the last steamer we had received in the public journals a syllabus of the Attorney General's opinion in regard to violations of neutrality. In reference to this, his Lordship expressed his deep regret that a member of the Cabinet had issued " such a manifesto," because it evinced the hostile animus of the Government towards England. It was unnecessary to publish such a warning, as the alleged recruitments had long previously thereto ceased to exist. He said if the Lord Chancellor had acted in the same manner towards the United States we would be justly offended. He went on to refer to the universal hostility of the American Press towards them, and especially of the Union, thus evincing the unfriendly feelings of the American people and their partiality for Russia. He declared in the most solemn manner that their feelings towards our country were directly the reverse and it was their anxious desire to do every thing they honorably could to live in peace and harmony with us, and to promote sincere and lasting friendship between the two countries.

I shall not pretend to repeat what I said in this conversation, which had been hitherto quite desultory; but I told him they were greatly mistaken in supposing that the feeling in the United States was universally favorable to the Russians and against the Allies. A considerable portion of the Press took their side. If I were to judge of the feelings of the British people by their Press, and thus adopt his own standard, I might infer that these were universally hostile to our country, and went into particulars to shew the gross injustice which had been done us by the Press ever since I had been in England until the commencement of the present difficulties, since which, I admitted, there had been a considerable change.

I assured him that in regard to the President and his Cabinet, he was mistaken in supposing that any feeling hostile to England had actuated their conduct; and they desired to live on the best terms with Great Britain.

I told him that the sympathies in favor of Russia which existed in the United States arose chiefly from the impression that France and England, after having finished the war with

Russia, intended to interfere with our affairs on the other side of the Atlantic. That among other reasons for this impression which I need not repeat, was his own speech in the House of Lords, and that of Louis Napoleon at Guildhall. Here he interrupted me & said that in the remarks which he had made in the House of Lords, he need not repeat to me, that he had not the most remote idea or intention of referring to the United States. Far, very far from it. He had repeatedly disavowed this in the most solemn manner. I told him that I had done him entire justice in this respect in my correspondence with the Department, and never had believed he intended to refer to the United States; but the speech of Louis Napoleon at Guildhall was most unfortunate. He asked me what Louis Napoleon had said, and declared he did not know. I replied I had not a distinct recollection of the words, but he had stated substantially it was the mission of the Allies to abolish Slavery, or something to that effect. He replied that he must have meant " political slavery," for Louis Napoleon did not care about any other kind of slavery. Not much about the former, I replied; at which he laughed heartily.

He then declared emphatically and in the most deliberate manner that neither England nor France had ever thought of interfering in any manner in the affairs of our country or doing any thing which could give us just cause of offence. It was the sincere desire of both, so far as he knew and believed, to cultivate the most friendly relations with our country.

I then came to the object of my visit, and asked him what good news he had to communicate to me to be sent to the President before the delivery of his message; and what they had decided as to the recall of the fleet. In answer he repeated in substance a part of what he had said on this subject in our last conversation, and went on to state that, in that conversation, he had disavowed any intention of menace in sending the fleet;—that they had found the information on which they had acted in regard to Russian privateers to be incorrect;—that he had informed me only four vessels had been sent out, and these they would recall or withdraw (I do not recollect which word,) as soon as this could be done conveniently, and that in the mean time, during the brief period they might be obliged to remain at Bermuda and Jamaica, they should confine themselves to these Islands & their immediate vicinity and not go near the coasts of the United States. I told him I was gratified to hear this statement from his Lordship—I had not understood him, at our last conversation, to say anything positive in regard to the recall of the fleet & the orders that had been issued to regulate its conduct in the interim. He repeated, he had told me this in our last conversation; but I again stated I did not recollect it, though I might possibly have inferred as much from what he had said. It was my practice in my reports to you, when I had any doubt, rather to understate than overstate his remarks.

I then observed that the information he had just communicated could not fail to have a beneficial effect on the relations between the two countries at the present moment of excitement. When Great Britain found herself mistaken, she was great enough to acknowledge and correct her mistake, and he said this was true. I remarked that if I could have an official note from him embodying the substance of what he had just stated, to send home to the President by the steamer, this would, for obvious reasons, have a much better effect than any report I might make of the conversation, and this would be very desirable. He said he had no objection in the world to give me such a note. After pausing for a moment, he remarked that a proper deference for Lord Palmerston required that he should see this note before it was sent. He would write it down immediately in the very terms he had employed to me and send a messenger with it to Lord Palmerston in the country, near Southampton, with a request that he should just say Yes, or No, at the foot of it. He could send it to me at the latest by 5 o'clock to-day. I desired him, if possible, to send it at an earlier hour, as this would give me more time.

I have waited till half past four, when the note arrived, marked " Private," of which I transmit a copy;[1] and I regret to say, that neither in substance nor in tone does it come up to what I had reason to expect: & I shall so inform his Lordship.

Yours very respectfully

JAMES BUCHANAN.

HON: WILLIAM L. MARCY,
    Secretary of State.

---

[1] See note from Lord Clarendon to Mr. Buchanan, dated Nov. 16, 1855, supra. A copy of this note accompanied the present despatch.

TO MISS LANE.[1]

LEGATION OF THE UNITED STATES,
LONDON, 16 November, 1855.

MY DEAR HARRIET/

I have received your favor of the 30th ultimo per the " Atlantic."

General Webb's advice is likely to be followed, very much against my own will. I am now in the midst of the storm, & my sense of duty leaves me no alternative but to remain at my post until the danger shall have passed away or until President Pierce shall think proper to appoint my successor. Mr. Appleton goes home by this steamer. The President had sent him a commission as Chargé ad interim, to continue from my departure until the arrival of my successor. I resisted his importunities to go home as long as I could; but the last letter from his wife was of such a character that I could no longer resist. He is a *perfect* secretary as well as an excellent friend. He has been in the house with me since your departure; & I shall now give the house up for the present. The little cook has done very well.

I presume that ere this you know that Col: Forney has come out openly in favor of the renomination of Gen: Pierce. You know that I considered this almost unavoidable. General P. placed him in the Union & has maintained him there & afforded him the means of making a fortune. Besides, he is the Editor of the President's official journal. Under these circumstances, he could not well have acted otherwise, & I do not blame him for it. Still he will be severely attacked, & in self defence will be obliged to come out & say that he has acted thus because I had determined not to become a candidate for nomination before the National Convention; & this defence will be nothing more than the truth. This will possibly place Mr. Dallas and General Pierce as rival candidates before the Democracy of Penna., which might prove unfortunate. *But still be quiet & discreet & say nothing.*

If I had any views to the Presidency, which I have not, I would advise you not to remain longer in Philadelphia than you can well avoid. A large portion of my friends in that city are bitterly hostile to those whom you must necessarily meet there. I presume, without knowing, that Gov: Bigler will be the candidate of the administration for the Senate.

---

[1] Buchanan Papers, private collection. Imperfectly printed in Curtis's Buchanan, II. 155.

Lady Ouseley desires me to send you her kindest love; & I believe she entertains for you a warm affection. I have not seen her to deliver your message, since the receipt of your letter. —Lady Alice Peel, Lady Chantrey & others send their kindest regards. I dine with Mrs. Shapter to-morrow.

I shall write by the present steamer to James Henry to come out here immediately, as I may be detained until January or February, & I shall want some person to be in the house with me. Could I have foreseen what has come to pass, I might have been selfish enough to retain you here. I can scarcely see the paper for a "yellow fog." I wish you could call to see John G. Brenner & his wife.

Give my love to Mrs. Plitt & my kindest regards to Mr. Plitt.

Yours affectionately,

JAMES BUCHANAN.

MISS LANE.

Give my love to brother Edward and his family.

TO MR. MARCY.[1]

No. 105.   LEGATION OF THE UNITED STATES.
LONDON, 23 November 1855.

SIR:

I stated at the conclusion of my Despatch No. 103, of the 16th Instant, that the note of Lord Clarendon to me of that date neither in substance nor in tone came up to what I had reason to expect; and that I should so inform his Lordship. Accordingly, I transmit the copy of a note which I addressed to him on the same evening.[2] Its language is purposely as mild as possible, consistently with the expression of disappointment and dissatisfaction. To this note I have received no response.

I forgot to mention in my No. 103 that in our conversation on the 15th Instant Lord Clarendon had informed me he would send his answer to your last letter to Mr. Crampton by the then next steamer, (Saturday the 17th). I expressed the hope that it was of such a character as might prove satisfactory. He said it was conciliatory in its character; but their understanding of

---

[1] MSS. Department of State, 68 Despatches from England.
[2] See note of Mr. Buchanan to Lord Clarendon, Nov. 16, 1855, supra.

the law of nations differed from yours in regard to what acts violated national sovereignty. He did not offer to show it to me, nor did I ask to see it.

I have not called upon his Lordship this week, deeming it advisable to wait until Monday next, when I shall doubtless hear from you as well as learn the impression produced on the American people by the recent conduct of the British Government.

In the mean time, everything here has become comparatively calm and tranquil on the surface, although I know that considerable uneasiness is felt in regard to the present relations between the two Governments, especially among the commercial and manufacturing classes. I have also learned, in the strictest confidence however, that consultations have been held by distinguished and influential personages as to the best means of removing the danger of any interruption in the friendly relations between the two countries; and that strong representations have been privately made to members of the British Cabinet in regard to their conduct towards the United States.

The present unsatisfactory financial condition of Great Britain;—the dependence of their manufactories on the markets of the United States;—the strikes at Manchester for higher wages;—the dreadful condition to which the laboring poor will be reduced during the present winter from the high price of bread, and the pressure of the existing war, would all seem to point out the madness of provoking hostilities with the United States. And yet, notwithstanding all these, I am convinced that the masses of the British people are so much under the influence of the governing classes, and of the Press, and are withal so ignorant of our country and so arrogantly confident in their own power, that they may be brought up even to this extremity.

Yours very respectfully,

JAMES BUCHANAN.

HON: WILLIAM L. MARCY,
    Secretary of State.

TO MISS LANE.[1]

56, HARLEY STREET,
23 November, 1855.

MY DEAR HARRIET/

I have received your favors of the 5th & 6th Instants, & immediately posted your letters to the Duchess, Lady Ouseley, & Miss Hargreaves.

The weather here has been even more disagreeable than usual for the season & I have had a cough & clearing of the throat exactly similar to your own last winter. I have not used any remedies for it; & it is now, thank Heaven! passing away. Since Mr. Appleton left, I have got Mr. Moran to sleep in the house with me.

Lady Ouseley has been quite unwell; but she was able to ride out in my carriage yesterday. In requesting this, which I had offered, she says, " when you write to Miss Lane pray give her my best love, with many thanks for her kind note, which I will answer as soon as I am better."

In a letter from Mrs. Roosevelt dated on the 13th ultimo, after mentioning that she had learned your intention to return home, she invites you to make her house your home while in New York, &c. &c. &c. I have written to her to-day, thanking her for her kind invitation & expressing the desire that you should know each other better.

I agree with you in opinion that Mr. Tyson is not the man to succeed in public life or in captivating such fastidious ladies as yourself; but yet I have no doubt he is a good & amiable man, as he is certainly well informed. Much allowance ought to be made for wounded vanity. But I admit I am no judge in these matters, since you inform me that Mr. Welsh has been the admiration of Philadelphia ladies.

Mr. Van Dyke does not properly appreciate Mr. Tyler. I like them both very much, as well as their wives.

Van Dyke is able, grateful, energetic & influential; & should he take care of himself will yet win his way to a high position.

Do not forget to present my love to Lily Macalester & my kind regards to her father & Mrs. Lathrop.

I know of no news here which would interest you much. A

---

[1] Buchanan Papers, private collection; Curtis's Buchanan, II. 156.

few dinner parties are now given to which I have been invited. I dine to-day with Monckton Milnes & on Tuesday next with Sir Henry & Lady Holland.

Many kind inquiries are still made about you. I wish you would inform Eskridge without delay that I attach great importance to the immediate transfer of the Michigan Central R. R. stock about which I wrote to him by the last steamer. I hope, however, that ere this can reach you he will have attended to this business.

In one respect, at least, I am now deemed a man of great importance. In the present uneasy condition of the Stock Exchange, an incautious word from me would either raise or sink the price of consols.

I see much of Mr. Ward, & he, strange to say, is *thoroughly American* in our present difficulties. This has raised him much in my estimation.

With my kindest regards to Mr. & Mrs. Plitt, I remain always

Yours affectionately,

Miss Lane. James Buchanan.

TO MR. MARCY.[1]

No. 106. Legation of The United States.
London, 30 November, 1855.

Sir:

I have had the honor to receive your Despatch No. 122, of the 12th Instant, together with its enclosure.

Although I deemed it best not to solicit an interview with Lord Clarendon for the purpose of conversing with him about the important existing relations between the two Governments until after the arrival of the President's Message, yet having several small matters of business with him, I requested an interview *when it might suit his convenience,* in the hope that more important affairs might be incidentally introduced. His Lordship, however. was obliged to go to Windsor and remain there during the visit of the King of Sardinia to Her Majesty; and for this reason expressed his regret that he could not see me until after his return next week.

---

[1] MSS. Department of State, 68 Despatches from England.

Meanwhile, the news brought by the Baltic is considered "much more pacific" by the British people, to employ their own phrase, than they had anticipated. Partly in consequence of this and partly because of the vague rumors of approaching peace, the funds have risen a little and are much more firm than they were a week ago. The discussion of the questions between the two Governments still continues in the public Press, although with very little exact information of their true nature; but with a manifest change in our favor. They all deprecate a war with the United States, and several of the journals are quite severe on the conduct of the Ministry. Among these I may mention the Morning Herald, which is the principal organ of the Conservative or Tory party. This is significant.

It is certain that the impression prevails, and I am inclined to believe with good reason, that the Emperor of the French is quite willing to make peace upon reasonable terms. Not so the British people, judging from external appearances. Indeed, there would seem to be an emulation among public men, in their addresses to the people on different occasions, which shall insist most strongly upon the vigorous prosecution of the war; and this sentiment is always hailed with acclamations by the assembled masses. Lord Palmerston has done everything in his power to bring them up to this point, and on this his popularity mainly depends. It is, therefore, more than probable if he should now conclude a peace upon any terms to which the Emperor of Russia would submit, that public opinion would drive him from power. His opponents, hoping and believing that he may be forced to such a measure by Louis Napoleon and by the pressure of the war, stand prepared, should this occur, to denounce him as recreant to his pledges, and to the honor of England. This, in my opinion, is the present political game.

Notwithstanding appearances to the contrary, the sentiment in favor of peace is gaining ground, and there is a strong under current in that direction, especially among the Manufacturing & Commercial classes. Many shout for the continuance of the war who in their hearts are friendly to peace upon any reasonable terms.

Yours very respectfully

JAMES BUCHANAN.

HON: WILLIAM L. MARCY,
    Secretary of State.

TO MISS LANE.[1]

U. S. Legation,
London, 30 Nov: 55.

My dear Harriet/

I have received your favor of the 12th Instant from Lancaster. Ere this can reach you Mr. Appleton will have seen you & told you all about my affairs. I have but little to say to you of any consequence.

I saw the Duchess two or three days ago, & she spoke in raptures, as is her wont, about your " beautiful letter " & yourself. She begged me to say to you she would soon answer it.

I shall deliver your message to Mrs. Sturgis. . . .[2]

Van Dyke's message is like himself. He is a kind and true hearted fellow. I am persuaded, however, he does Tyler injustice. His being for Wise was but another name for being for myself. He had written me several letters of a desponding character. He thought the State was going all wrong,—great danger of Dallas, &c., &c., & attributed all to my refusal to be a candidate & not returning home at the time I had appointed. By the last steamer, however, I received a letter from him of a character altogether different. *Do not suffer your associations in Philadelphia to prevent you from treating Mr. & Mrs. Van Dyke & Mr. & Mrs. Tyler with kindness & attention.* I wish very much that Tyler & Van Dyke would become friends. This, I fear, will not be the case until after my return.

I shall be anxious to learn what plans you have adopted for the winter.

The enclosed letter from Lady Chantrey was handed to me by Charles. In a hurry I opened it. Why, said he, that is to Miss Lane, & was brought here from Lady Chantrey. I now take the cover off & enclose it to you, *assuring you that I have not read a single word of it.*

With my kindest regards to Mr. & Mrs. Plitt, I remain, in haste,

Yours affectionately,

James Buchanan.

Miss Lane.

---

[1] Buchanan Papers, private collection. Imperfectly printed in Curtis's Buchanan, II. 158.

[2] The passage here omitted is now illegible.

TO MR. MARCY.[1]

No. 107.   LEGATION OF THE UNITED STATES.

LONDON, 6 December, 1855.

SIR:

I have the honor to acknowledge the receipt of your Despatch No. 123, of the 16th ultimo, with its enclosure.

I herewith transmit a copy of a notification received from Lord Clarendon, and inserted in the London Gazette of the 29th ultimo, announcing the raising by the allied squadrons, on and from the 9th October last, of the blockade of the Russian Ports in the White Sea; with the request that I would transmit the same to my Government, that it may through that channel become known to the citizens of the United States.

I also transmit a Despatch from John L. O'Sullivan, Esqr., Minister Resident of the United States at Lisbon, to yourself, dated on the 13th ultimo, with its three enclosures.

You will observe that Mr. O'Sullivan states that he sends "this Despatch open through Mr. Buchanan, in order that if he should have anything worth while to add, which he may derive from Lord Clarendon or from Count Lavradio (the Portuguese Minister in London), he may be able to do so if he thinks proper."

I have little to add of any consequence, though I have conversed with Lord Clarendon on the subject. He is by no means prepared to recognise the Portuguese title to Ambriz or to any other portion of the territory on the African Coast between $5° 12'$ and $8°$ South latitude; though I think he might be brought to this, without much difficulty, provided Portugal would make a positive Treaty stipulation that the coast between these latitudes should be open to free trade with the Natives as it has been heretofore. He said he was to have a conference with Count Lavradio upon the subject, and would immediately inform me of the result. I saw the Count afterwards, who told me he was very soon coming to see me on the same subject. I told him, in civility which he well deserves, that I should be happy to see him, though the question is beyond my province and I have scarcely time to discharge my appropriate duties.

Yours very respectfully,

· JAMES BUCHANAN.

HON: WILLIAM L. MARCY,
    Secretary of State.

---

[1] MSS. Department of State, 68 Despatches from England.

TO MR. MASON.

(Enclosure in No. 125.[1])

LEGATION OF THE UNITED STATES,

LONDON, 6 December, 1855.

MY DEAR SIR:

I address you upon the request of Mr. Juan B. Alberdi, Chargé d'Affaires of the Argentine Confederation to England and France, who is now in Paris.

You are aware that a Treaty of Commerce was concluded between this Confederation and the United States, on the 27th July, 1853. This Treaty is similar to those concluded with England and France. The Province of Buenos Ayres has refused to join the other thirteen Provinces embraced by the Confederation, has protested against these Treaties, and has established and maintained an independent Government. To repeat the language of Governor Marcy in his Despatch to me of the 16th June last, "It is represented that the object of Buenos Ayres in taking and holding such a position is to secure to herself at the Port of Buenos Ayres the monopoly of foreign commerce to that country. She fears that by joining the Union of the other States foreign trade will be opened on the La Plata at Ports above that of Buenos Ayres. For this selfish purpose, she is naturally anxious to be recognised by foreign Powers, if not as a separate State, as one entitled to control the policy of the present Confederation."

Mr. Alberdi visited Washington before his arrival in England and held conferences with the Secretary of State, which resulted in the Despatch to which I have already referred. You, most probably, have received a Despatch of a similar character.

I was directed by this Despatch, which I read to Lord Clarendon, to explain to him " the course which the President has determined to pursue towards Buenos Ayres and the Argentine Republic and to ascertain what that of Great Britain is or is likely to be."

This duty I have performed, and I find that the two Governments are agreed not to recognise Buenos Ayres by accrediting a Minister to that country. France has pursued a different policy; and the object of Mr. Alberdi at Paris is to induce the French Government to adopt a policy similar to that of Great

---

[1] Despatch to Mr. Marcy, No. 125, Feb. 29, 1856, infra.

Britain and the United States.   How far you may be willing to aid him in accomplishing this object, if you have received no instructions on the subject, will be for yourself to decide.

Meanwhile, I have sent Mr. Alberdi a letter of introduction to you.   He was commended to me by Governor Marcy as a gentleman deserving my favorable notice, and " well acquainted with the state of things on the La Plata," " who will desire to explain fully to me the relations between the Argentine Republic and Buenos Ayres," and this he has certainly done in the most ample manner.   " The President, (concludes the Despatch) is satisfied that his Government is entitled, in a political and commercial point of view, to our friendly regards."

Yours very respectfully

JAMES BUCHANAN.

HON: JOHN Y. MASON,
    United States Envoy Extraordinary, &c. &c. Paris.

TO MR. MARCY.[1]

No. 108.   LEGATION OF THE UNITED STATES.

LONDON, 7 December, 1855.

SIR:

I had the interview with Lord Clarendon on Monday last, to which I referred in my Despatch No. 106, of the 30th ultimo. This was earlier than I had reason to anticipate, and the Despatch bag by the Asia had not reached the Legation.   After transacting satisfactorily some ordinary business, with which I need not trouble you, I told his Lordship that I had not then received my Despatches by the steamer; but after they should come to hand I might probably request him to grant me another interview during the week.   He said he should be most happy to do so, and I might appoint my own time either on Thursday or Friday, giving him previous notice.   I have not done this; because the Despatch bag contained no response to my Despatches Nos. 98 and 99, of the 30th October and 2d of November.   Not knowing in what light my conduct and conversations, as detailed in these Despatches, might be viewed by the President, I deemed it most prudent to wait until after I should hear from you.

---

[1] MSS. Department of State, 68 Despatches from England.

I need not repeat to you the news, which you will find detailed in the public journals, respecting the present tone of feeling in this country towards the United States. There is one incident, however, of sufficient significance to justify a passing notice as indicating the feelings of the most respectable classes of the population of London in regard to our country. At the reception of the King of Sardinia in Guildhall, on Tuesday last, when the entrance of the American Minister was announced, he was received with spontaneous, loud, and reiterated cheers. This was so marked as to attract the attention of every person present in that large assembly. It was impossible even for the Morning Post to deny this fact; but it is passed over by that journal in the following remark, which, without any such intention, adds to its significance.—" When Mr. Buchanan, the American Minister, appeared, some interest was evinced, as if people thought they could judge from the countenance of the diplomat either what he himself felt or what were the intentions of his nation towards our own."

I think I may now venture to predict, upon what I deem sufficient authority, that the war with Russia will end before the commencement of the next campaign. It is certain, I believe, that Austria has submitted propositions to the French and English Governments for its termination, with the assurance that if accepted by them and afterwards rejected by the Czar, she would at once break off all Diplomatic relations with him preparatory to a rupture. Louis Napoleon, as is confidently asserted, promptly expressed his willingness to accede to these propositions; and the British Government, as is believed, have since tardily and reluctantly followed his example, Lord Palmerston holding out until the last.

These propositions substitute for the third of the Vienna four points the conversion of the Euxine into a mere commercial sea, excluding from it vessels of war of all nations, as well those of Russia and Turkey as of other Powers.

The whole course and the mouths of the Danube, are, also, to be relieved from Russian dominion; and to render this purpose effectual, a small strip of territory on the North of this river, between the Euxine and the Pruth, is to be ceded to Moldavia.

Will the Czar accept these propositions? I do not doubt it. Russia is exhausted both in men and money, and her people have suffered dreadfully from the war. Her honor will be saved; because all the world will admit that it would be folly for her to continue the contest against the allies with the vast military Power of Austria superadded to their forces. Besides, I shrewdly suspect that Russia had been consulted by Austria before she submitted these propositions, which are not unreasonable in themselves, to France and England.

I shall not, at this time, attempt to speculate upon what will be the effect of such a peace upon Lord Palmerston's Government.

Yours very respectfully,

JAMES BUCHANAN.

HON: WILLIAM L. MARCY,
    Secretary of State.

———

TO MR. MARCY.[1]

No. 109.   LEGATION OF THE UNITED STATES.

LONDON, 14 December, 1855.

SIR:

I have not asked an interview with Lord Clarendon since the date of my last week's Despatch, not having yet heard from you in answer to any of my Despatches since the sending of the British Fleet to Bermuda and Jamaica. Under these circumstances, I have deemed it most prudent to await the arrival of the President's Message, before any renewal of my conferences with his Lordship. Meanwhile, every thing is quiet here, and all congratulate themselves that " the storm has blown over." I hear this sentiment everywhere I go and from every person who visits me. There is certainly no disposition at present on the part of the British people to have serious difficulties with the United States. The discussions in the public journals since the storm commenced have furnished them much better information in relation to our country than they had previously possessed.

Doubts begin to be expressed, especially since the fall of Kars, as to whether the Czar will accept the terms proposed by Austria and acceded to by France and England. Lord Palmerston would, it is believed, be gratified should they be refused by Russia. Never at any period have such vast preparations been made in this country for any campaign as for that of the next spring and summer, and never have they had such a navy afloat. They seem determined to recover the military prestige which

———

[1] MSS. Department of State, 68 Despatches from England.

they have lost during the last two campaigns. I have no doubt it will go hard with Russia, should not peace be concluded during the present winter.

The winter has set in here with unusual severity, and from the high price of provisions, and the inadequate demand for labor, the poor must suffer dreadfully before the Spring.

Referring to Despatch No. 2, from General Thomas to Mr. Appleton, of the 2d ultimo,—I have received a note from Lord Clarendon, dated on the 10th Instant, in which he states that he has " been informed by Mr. Secretary Labouchere that, as he is not aware whether Mr. Fairfield is or is not a resident in the Colony of Mauritius, the Governor has been instructed to ascertain whether this is the case, and, if he is so resident, to report whether he is aware of any objection to his appointment as United States Consul at Port Louis; but if he is not aware of any such objection, he has been instructed to recognise Mr. Fairfield provisionally in that capacity, until the arrival of the Exequatur."

Yours very respectfully,

JAMES BUCHANAN.

HON: WILLIAM L. MARCY,
　　Secretary of State.

TO MISS LANE.[1]

LEGATION OF THE UNITED STATES,

LONDON, 14 December, 1855.

MY DEAR HARRIET/

I have nothing of interest to communicate by this steamer. The past week has been dull, gloomy, & cold for the season. The walks in the park are covered with snow & I find them very slippery. The winter has set in with unusual severity, whilst the price of provisions is very high. God help the poor in this vast Babel! Their sufferings will be dreadful.

Although I have not suffered, either from ennui or despondency, yet I shall hail the arrival of James Henry with pleasure. I think it may be of service to him to be with me for a month or six weeks.

I am extremely sorry to learn that " Mrs. Plitt's health is

---

[1] Buchanan Papers, private collection; Curtis's Buchanan, II. 158.

very bad." She is a woman among a thousand. Most sincerely & deeply do I sympathise with her. Give her my kindest love.

I have heard nothing of the six shawls since your departure; but I have already written to Mr. Randall & requested him to send me the Bill, which I shall pay as soon as received. I am now getting rich very fast, though I still retain the house.

I have received your furs from Mrs. Shapter & shall send them to New York by the " Arago," which will leave Southampton on the 19th Instant. They are packed in a nice little box, directed to the care of George Plitt, Esquire. I shall, through Mr. Croskey, get Captain Lines himself to take charge of them & to pay the duty. Please to so arrange it that some friend at New York may be ready to receive them & refund him the duty which he may have paid.

I have again inadvertently opened a letter addressed to you which I enclose, & assure that I did not read a single word in it except " My dearest Hattie." I can, therefore, only guess who is the writer.

I started out yesterday & paid three very agreeable visits,— to the Countess Bernsdorff, Lady Palmerston, & the Duchess of Somerset. I found them all at home & had a nice little chat with each. The Duchess told me Lord Panmure had been with her & had been quite extravagant in his praises of what he termed my able, friendly, & discreet conduct in the late difficulties between the two countries. But for me, he said, these might have produced serious consequences. The Duchess, as usual, spoke extravagantly in your praise & desired her love to you.

I presume that Mrs. Lane & yourself have had a fine time of it hearing Rachel. She is quite competent to understand & appreciate the beauties of French tragedy. However this may be, she possesses as much knowledge in this line as thousands of others who will be quite enraptured with Rachel's acting. I am glad you are on good & friendly terms with her. From present appearances the war will end before the spring. This will be the case should the Czar accept the terms suggested by Austria & consented to by the allies.

With my kindest regards to Mr. Plitt, I remain
Yours affectionately
JAMES BUCHANAN.

MISS LANE.

TO MR. MARCY.[1]

No. 110.   LEGATION OF THE UNITED STATES.
                        LONDON, 18 December, 1855.
SIR:

I have had the honor to receive your Despatch No. 124, of the 30th ultimo, with the accompanying papers.

There was a trifling omission in the first sentence in my last Despatch, of the 14th Instant, which I would thank you to have corrected. Please to cause to be inserted in it the words, " *detailing conversations with his Lordship,*" so as to make the latter part of the sentence read, "in answer to any of my Despatches ' *detailing conversations with his Lordship,*' since the sending of the British fleet to Bermuda and Jamaica."

Referring to your No. 117, of the 15th of October,—I received on yesterday from Lord Clarendon the Queen's Exequatur for Albert Pillsbury, Esquire, appointed Consul at Halifax, Nova Scotia, and this, together with his Commission, has already been delivered to the Despatch Agent to be forwarded to him at his post on Saturday next by the Cunard steamer.

Referring to your No. 123, of the 16th November, I have received a note from Lord Clarendon, dated on the 15th Instant, in which he states that he has " been informed by Mr. Secretary Labouchere that as he is not aware whether Mr. Winter is or is not a resident in the Colony of Turk's Islands, the Governor has been instructed to ascertain whether this is the case, and, if he is so resident, to report whether he is aware of any objection to his appointment as United States Consul in Turk's Islands; but if he is not aware of any such objection, he has been instructed to recognise Mr. Winter provisionally in that capacity until the arrival of the Exequatur."

A copy of this note will be immediately forwarded to Mr. Winter at his post.

I regret that the difficulties in the organisation of the House have prevented me from receiving a copy of the President's Message by the " Canada." The British public expect a pretty strong expression of opinion in that document on the Central American questions; and I am persuaded this will do good. The rejection of your *ultimatum* by the Palmerstonian administration, and the consequent termination and failure of the negotia-

---

[1] MSS. Department of State, 68 Despatches from England.

tion, place the Governments in such an attitude towards each other as will excite serious apprehensions among the British people as to what may be the final result. This will, most probably, produce an external pressure upon the British Government which may result in causing it to reconsider its answer to your ultimatum, and to retrace its steps. Every thing remains quiet here so far as relates to the relations between the two countries; but much anxiety is expressed to see the Message. I have been often asked what would be its character; and I could only answer that I had no information whatever on the subject; but that when it arrived I had no doubt it would speak for itself in a proper and becoming manner.

The Senate having now assembled, I shall expect by every steamer to hear of the appointment of my successor.

Yours very respectfully,

JAMES BUCHANAN.

HON: WILLIAM L. MARCY,
Secretary of State.

TO MISS LANE.[1]

LEGATION OF THE UNITED STATES,
LONDON, 21 December, 1855.

MY DEAR HARRIET/

Since the date of my last letter, I have received the sad news of the death of poor Mary.[2] I need not inform you of my devoted attachment to her, & she deserved it all. Poor girl! she had her own troubles & she bore them all with cheerful patience. She is now at rest, I trust, in that heavenly home where there is no more pain & sorrow. Her loss will make the remainder of my residence here, which I trust may be brief, dreary & disconsolate.

How happy I am to know that you are now with Mrs. Plitt! She has a warm heart & a fine intellect & will better than any other person know how to comfort & soothe you in your sorrow. I am thankful that you are now at home.

With Mrs. Plitt's kind letter to me came that from Mrs. Speer to you & one from Lieutenant Beale to myself. I shall

---

[1] Buchanan Papers, private collection; Curtis's Buchanan, II. 159.
[2] Mrs. Baker.

always gratefully remember his kindness & that of his wife. His letter was just what it ought to have been. I wrote to Mrs. Plitt by the " Arago " from Southampton, which left on Wednesday last.

The death of poor Mary has been your first serious sorrow; because you were too young to feel deeply that of your parents. Ere this can reach you, a sufficient time will have elapsed for the first natural overflowings of sorrow. I would not have restrained them if I could. It is now time that they should moderate & that you should not mourn the dead at the expense of your duties to the living. This sad event ought to teach you the vanity of all things human & transitory & cause you to fix your thoughts, desires, & affections on that Being with whom " there is no variableness or shadow of turning." This will not render you gloomy; but will enable you the better to perform all the duties of life. In all calamitous events, we ought to say emphatically: " Thy will be done." At the last, all the proceedings of a mysterious Providence will be justified in another & a better world; & it is our duty here to submit with humble resignation. Although my course of life has been marked by temporal prosperity, thanks be to Heaven, yet I have experienced heart rending afflictions; & you must not expect to be exempt from the common lot of humanity. I have not seen Mrs. Shapter; but I sent her Mr. Beale's letter, which she returned with a most feeling note. She, also, wrote to you by the " Arago."

You will know sooner in the United States than I can at what time I shall be relieved. I shall now expect to hear by the arrival of every steamer that my successor has been appointed. Should he arrive here within a month or six weeks I still have an idea of running over to the Continent; but I have yet determined upon nothing. I have a great desire to be at home.

With my kindest love to Mrs. Plitt & my warm regards for Mr. Plitt, I remain

Ever yours affectionately
JAMES BUCHANAN.

MISS LANE.

TO MR. MARCY.[1]

No. 111.   Legation of The United States.

London, 28 December, 1855.

Sir:

I have the honor to acknowledge the receipt of your Despatch No. 125, of the 10th Instant, with the copy of the letter to you from the Secretary of the Treasury, which shall receive my immediate attention.

Awaiting the arrival of the President's Message, I have not asked for an interview with Lord Clarendon, since the date of my last Despatch.

The revelations made by Col: Tal. P. Shaffner to the New York Herald concerning Russia, which have been extensively republished and ridiculed by the British Press, have brought that gentleman before the public in this country. He has stated in his deposition, (now in your possession,[2]) before the United States Consul at Hamburg, on the 5th November last, doubtless with truth, " that the wire, fusees, &c., purchased in London of Messrs. Slatham & Co., are, to the best of his knowledge and belief, still his property and not even taken out of the original sacking, and he believes that on his return to New York he can exhibit every fusee in their original state in the original envelope, except some which were given Professor Morse, with some of the wire, the batteries, canteens, &c., &c., and they also can doubtless be procured."

For the sake of Col: Shaffner himself, as well as because of my representations to Lord Clarendon upon this subject, I shall be gratified to learn that his statements have been verified in the manner he has himself suggested. I intended to impress upon him the propriety of doing this immediately on his return to New York; but he did not call at the Legation when he last passed through England, nor did I know he had been here, until I saw his arrival by the Atlantic announced in the New York journals.

With reference to your No. 85, of the 11th April, 1855, and my No. 75 of the 8th June,—I now transmit copies of notes from Lord Clarendon and Captain Bosdet of the British bark " Ellen," in regard to the receipt by the latter of the Silver Trumpet presented to him by the President.

[1] MSS. Department of State, 68 Despatches from England.
[2] See despatch to Mr. Marcy, No. 96, Oct. 25, 1855, supra.

Referring to your No. 124, of November 30th, I have received a note from Lord Clarendon stating that he had referred to the War Department my note requesting the discharge of John R. Sweet from the British Army.

Yours very respectfully,

JAMES BUCHANAN.

HON: WILLIAM L. MARCY,
    Secretary of State.

TO MR. MARCY.[1]

LEGATION OF THE UNITED STATES,
LONDON, 28 December, 1855.

MY DEAR SIR:

I have received your favor of the 9th Instant. I expect the President's Message with much anxiety on Monday, as well as news of the appointment of my successor. I shall not present my letter of recall before Tuesday the 12th February next. I purpose to pass February on the continent, and shall, God willing! be home before the 1st of April, on which day my private affairs imperatively require that I should be in Lancaster. If by any accident neither Minister nor Secretary should in the mean time arrive, I shall leave the Legation in charge of General Campbell. It is always to be understood that I shall be most happy should my successor arrive at an earlier day, and the sooner the better. I do not write this in a public Despatch, simply because I think it ought not to appear on the face of the record. Now for my sake and the sake of all concerned, I hope you will attend to this matter. [P. S. Please to consider this portion of my letter to be *strictly confidential between us,* if an appointment has been made, or you know it will be made, in time to relieve me on or before the 12th February next.]

I have not the least doubt that your answer to Lord Clarendon's last will be all that it ought to be, and I shall be most happy to do every thing in my power informally (or officially, if so instructed) to bring the Crampton affair to a satisfactory conclusion. I have often presented you to His Lordship in the terms you so well deserve, to which he has ever freely responded, except in reference to your last letter to Mr. Crampton; and about this

---

[1] Buchanan Papers, Historical Society of Pennsylvania.

all has been communicated to you in my Despatches. Indeed, it is mainly in reference to this affair that I have determined so long to delay the presentation of my letter of recall.

In regard to the Central American questions,—I cannot perceive how it is possible that my presence here any longer can prove beneficial. Further negotiations on these questions, during the continuance of Lord Palmerston's administration, could lead to no favorable result. This administration is too far committed in their answer to the President's *ultimatum* to do us justice. Even if the President should desire to open new negotiations, these, for obvious reasons, had better be entrusted to a new Minister. The presentation of these questions, which I have no doubt has been made in the message in a manner to bring them home to the grave and serious consideration of the British people, will, I think, bear fruit in due season, but not whilst Lord P. remains at the helm.

The question of peace now rests with the Czar, and various are the speculations upon what will be his decision. The stock jobbers are sadly perplexed. My impression still continues that there will be peace before the time for opening another campaign. " Where there is a will there is a way; " and that such a will strongly exists in the mind of Louis Napoleon I entertain not a doubt. The revelations of the French Press, under a strict censorship as it is, would seem to be conclusive of this fact. It is quite in contrast with the British Press. It is possible that the old Russian Party, under the leadership of Constantine, may influence the Czar to return such an answer to the propositions before him as to forbid further negotiation; but this would be so manifestly against the interest of Russia, that I cannot indulge in such a supposition. In fact it is the interest of all parties to make peace, although the English would like to have the chance in another campaign of recovering their prestige as a military nation.

I rejoice that Mrs. Marcy is again with you. Her mild and salutary influence will do you much good. With my kindest regards to her, I remain,

Yours very respectfully,

JAMES BUCHANAN.

HON: WILLIAM L. MARCY.

TO MR. SLIDELL.[1]

LEGATION OF THE UNITED STATES,
LONDON, 28 December, 1855.

MY DEAR SIR:

I have received your favor of the 9th Instant, and now in compliance with your request return the statement of Mr. Duponte.

I have no reserves to yourself either on the subject of the Presidency or any other subject, and yet I cannot make up my mind to write, *even to you,* " acknowledging the obligation under which every public man should be of obedience to the popular will." This would be an avowal that I am a candidate, to which I feel an irresistible disinclination. My purposes are formed with much deliberation and are not easily changed. I shall be 65 on the 23d April next, and I had determined upon my line of life for the remnant of days with which a kind Providence might bless me, discarding every idea of the Presidency. It is perfectly true, as you say, that I had written to many friends that I would not be a candidate for this high office; and especially to every friend in Pennsylvania who addressed me on the subject. I had hoped that this would prevent any movement in my own State in my favor. But not so,—they paid no attention to my wishes, and after having commenced operations informed me that this was necessary to unite and consolidate the party and to give the honest, faithful, and true Democracy of the State their just influence. All they asked of me was that for the present I should write no more letters declaring I was not a candidate. I could not resist such an appeal proceeding from such friends. To this I assented. Nothing more. To the question which has been repeatedly asked me:—What will you decide should the Cincinnati Convention, without your agency, offer you the nomination?—to this I have uniformly answered that it would evince an extravagant degree of vanity for me to assume the possibility of an event so improbable; but if it should occur, then " sufficient unto the day is the evil thereof." This is the precise ground upon which I stand, and for the present, at least, I cannot depart from it.

No desire lurks in my bosom to become President.[2] This

---

[1] Buchanan Papers, Historical Society of Pennsylvania.

[2] The sincerity of Mr. Buchanan's reiterated expressions of a disinclination to seek the presidential nomination in 1856 is strongly borne out by the

you may think strange, knowing that I was anxious to be nominated by the last Baltimore Convention, if this could have been accomplished upon honorable principles. I can now leave public life, I trust, with credit. Should I become President, the case may be very different, after I shall have worn myself out with the toil and anxiety of the office. Still, I do not believe that the next President, should he really be the man for the place, would encounter insuperable difficulties. Unchangeable firmness tempered by prudent discretion would, I think, in a great degree, put down the slavery agitation. *The question has been settled by Congress, and this settlement should be inflexibly maintained.* The Missouri Compromise is gone, and gone forever; but no assault should be made upon those Democrats who maintained it, *provided they are now willing in good faith to maintain the settlement as it exists.* Such an understanding is wise and just in itself, and is necessary to reunite and strengthen

---

statement of Mr. S. L. M. Barlow, which is printed in Curtis's Buchanan, II. 170. Mr. Barlow, who had seen much of Mr. Buchanan early in 1856 in Europe, found, on his return to the United States, that Mr. Buchanan's friends were unorganized, and that unless earnest efforts were made by them Mr. Buchanan's nomination was impossible. Mr. Barlow narrates how the nomination was effected " almost wholly by the efforts of the friends of Mr. Buchanan, who were induced at the last moment to come to Cincinnati." The leader of the friends of Mr. Buchanan at Cincinnati was Mr. Slidell, who, after the nomination was made, declared that it had been effected without promises or commitments to any section or to any individual. This declaration Mr. Slidell afterwards repeated to Mr. Buchanan, just before his inauguration, in Mr. Barlow's presence. " Mr. Buchanan's opposition to the repeal of the Missouri Compromise left him," says Mr. Barlow, " without support from the ultra Southern leaders, many of whom believed that Mr. Douglas would be less difficult to manage than Mr. Buchanan. Louisiana was controlled through the personal influence of Messrs. Slidell and Benjamin, and Virginia was from the beginning in favor of Mr. Buchanan's nomination. Apart from these States, the South was for Pierce or Douglas. Mr. Buchanan's strength was from the North, but it was unorganized.

" To that time, no one had undertaken to speak for him. There were no headquarters where his friends could meet even for consultation. There was no leader—no one whose opinions upon questions of policy were controlling, and but for this almost accidental combination of his friends in Cincinnati, it was apparent that Mr. Buchanan could not have been nominated, simply because of this utter lack of that ordinary preliminary organization necessary to success, which was by his opponents alleged to be the foundation of his strength, but which in fact was wholly without existence.

" Mr. Slidell undertook this task, and before the meeting of the convention Mr. Buchanan's success was assured."

the Democratic party in the Northern States & to bring into the party the honest & independent Anti Free Soil Whigs. If I should be asked to denounce the Missouri Compromise, this would be asking me to eat my own words. It is well known how I labored in company with Southern men to have this line extended to the Pacific Ocean. But it has departed—the time for it has passed away, and I verily believe that the best, nay, the only mode now left of putting down the fanatical and reckless spirit of Abolition at the North is to adhere to the existing settlement, without the slightest thought or appearance of wavering, and without regarding any storm which may be raised against it. " Nolumus leges Angliæ mutare."

But what if the Cincinnati Convention should denounce the Missouri Compromise as unconstitutional, unjust, and violative of Southern rights, and ask me to mount upon this platform? I know well what answer you would give, were you placed in my position. Still, notwithstanding my very high respect for your judgment, I believe your personal friendship for myself, which I am proud to possess, has led you astray upon this occasion, and I do not believe I shall ever have to decide this question.

I have now written to you more freely than to any other friend the real sentiments of my heart.

With my kind regards to Mrs. Slidell, I remain always
Your friend,
JAMES BUCHANAN.

HON: JOHN SLIDELL.

TO MISS LANE.[1]

LEGATION OF THE UNITED STATES,
LONDON, 28 December, 1855.

MY DEAR HARRIET/

I have received your favor of the 11th Instant with the copy of Mr. Baker's letter, which I have read with deep interest. I wrote to you last week on the subject of poor Mary's death, which I deeply deplore. I hope that ere this can reach you your mind will have been tranquillized on that sad event. It would have been wrong,—it would have been unnatural had you

---

[1] Buchanan Papers, private collection. Imperfectly printed in Curtis's Buchanan, II. 160.

not experienced anguish for the loss of so good, kind hearted & excellent a sister. Still the loss is irreparable, grief is unavailing, & you have duties to perform towards yourself as well as your friends. To mourn for the dead at the expense of these duties would be sinful. We shall never forget poor Mary,— her memory will always be dear to us; but it is our duty to bow with submission to the will of that Being in whose hands are the issues of life & death. You know what a low estimate I have ever placed upon a woman, without religious principles. I know that in your conduct you are guided by these principles more than is common in the fashionable world; but yet if this melancholy dispensation of Providence should cause you to pay more attention than you have done to " the things which pertain to your everlasting peace," this would be a happy result. I have lost many much loved relatives & friends; but though age becomes comparatively callous, I have felt & feel deeply the loss of Mary & Jessie. Poor Jessie! She died breathing my name with her devotions. What can I do—what shall I do for her children?

I send by the Bag to the Department a letter from the Duchess, to whom, I believe, I have not mentioned our loss.

Sir William & Lady Ouseley dined with me a few days ago. There were no persons present except ourselves. She sincerely sympathizes with you. Time begins to produce its healing influence on her grief, though both she & poor Sir William have been sadly cast down by their calamity.

James Henry arrived here on Christmas evening after a passage of three weeks which he evidently enjoyed. He talks to Mr. Ward knowingly about every part of a sailing vessel. His plan of travel is quite extensive; far too much so for the sum he intends to expend. I shall gradually cut it down to more reasonable limits. . . .

Mr. Dallas has just returned from the Crimea & has made friendly inquiries about you.

No news yet of the appointment of my successor, notwithstanding the efforts of Mr. Appleton. I have not received the President's message, but expect it on Monday with much anxiety. Should I, then, hear nothing of a successor or secretary of legation, I shall give them formal notice that I will present my letter of recall on a particular day, & should no person arrive in the mean time, that I will leave the legation in charge of General Campbell.

I have just learned that Dr. Brown will leave in the Atlantic to-morrow. I shall send this & other letters by him to New York.

With my love to Mrs. Plitt & my kindest regards to Mr. Plitt, I remain always

Yours affectionately

JAMES BUCHANAN.

MISS LANE.

TO LORD CLARENDON.[1]

Private.   LEGATION OF THE UNITED STATES.

LONDON 31 December 1855.

MY DEAR LORD CLARENDON :

I desire to have the honor of an interview with you some day this week when it may best suit your convenience.

I have recently been provoked at seeing extracts from the New York Herald republished in the Times and other London journals, purporting to give the substance of my Despatches to Washington. These are sheer fabrications made to produce a sensation. The Herald is the very last journal in the whole country to whom any such communications would be made.

I observe an extract from the Herald in the Times of this afternoon, on a subject about which I did not write a line by the Baltic.

These reports, uncontradicted as they must be so far as I am concerned, are calculated to place me in an unfavorable light before the British public, and what is far worse, to give a false and erroneous impression of the relations between the two Countries.

Yours very respectfully

JAMES BUCHANAN.

---

[1] Buchanan Papers, Historical Society of Pennsylvania.

A-68-50

SP2/CLOSED
3
.B9
1905
v. 9